S0-BBY-317

THE OFFICIAL®

2012 BLACKBOOK PRICE GUIDE TO UNITED STATES PAPER MONEY

Livonia Public Library
ALFRED NOBLE BRANCH
32901 PLYMOUTH ROAD
Livonia, Michigan 48150-1793
421-6600
LIVN # 19

769.5
O

Livonia Public Library
ALFRED NOBLE BRANCH
32901 PLYMOUTH ROAD
Livonia, Michigan 48150-1793
421-6600
LIVN # 19
JUN 20 2012

THE OFFICIAL®

2012 BLACKBOOK PRICE GUIDE TO UNITED STATES PAPER MONEY

FORTY-FOURTH EDITION

BY MARC HUDGEONS, N.L.G.
& TOM HUDGEONS, Jr.
& TOM HUDGEONS, Sr.

HOUSE OF COLLECTIBLES

Random House Reference • New York

JUN 20 2011

Important notice: All the information, including valuations, in this book has been compiled from reliable sources, and efforts have been made to eliminate errors and questionable data. Nevertheless, the possibility of error, in a work of such immense scope, always exists. The publisher will not be responsible for any losses that may occur in the purchase, sale, or other transaction of items because of information contained herein. Readers who feel they have discovered errors are invited to write and inform us, so they may be corrected in subsequent editions.

Copyright © 2011 by Random House, Inc.

All rights reserved. Published in the United States by House of Collectibles, an imprint of The Random House Audio Publishing Group, a division of Random House, Inc., New York, and in Canada by Random House of Canada Limited, Toronto.

House of Collectibles and colophon are registered trademarks of Random House, Inc.

RANDOM HOUSE is a registered trademark of Random House, Inc.

Please address inquiries about electronic licensing of any products for use on a network, in software, or on CD-ROM to the Subsidiary Rights Department, Random House Audio Publishing Group, fax 212-572-6003.

This book is available for special discounts for bulk purchases for sales promotions or premiums. Special editions, including personalized covers, excerpts of existing books, and corporate imprints, can be created in large quantities for special needs. For more information, write to Random House, Inc., Special Markets/Premium Sales, 1745 Broadway, MD 3–1, New York, NY 10019 or e-mail specialmarkets@randomhouse.com

Visit the Random House Web site:
www.randomhouse.com

ISBN: 978-0-375-72323-0

ISSN: 0195-3540

Printed in the United States of America

10 9 8 7 6 5 4 3 2 1

Forty-Fourth Edition: June 2011

3 9082 11751 3906

CONTENTS

OFFICIAL BOARD OF CONTRIBUTORS

The authors would like to express a special thank you to:

W. R. "Bill" Rindoné, Bank Notes North West, PO Box 790, Aurora, OR 97002, for his collaboration and Market Review,

and **Regina Banks and Larry Felix at the Department of the Treasury,** Bureau of Engraving and Printing, Washington, D.C., for the articles on the BEP, and David Koble of Mid-American Currency.

PUBLISHER'S NOTE

The Official® Blackbook Price Guide to United States Paper Money is designed as a reference aid for collectors, dealers, and the general public. Its purpose is to provide historical and collecting data, as well as current values. Prices are as accurate as possible at the time of going to press, but no guarantee is made. We are not dealers; persons wishing to buy or sell paper money, or have it appraised, are advised to consult collector magazines or the telephone directory for addresses of dealers. We are not responsible for typographical errors.

NOTE TO READERS

All advertisements appearing in this book have been accepted in good faith, but the publisher assumes no responsibility in any transactions that occur between readers and advertisers.

SHARE YOUR KNOWLEDGE

We would be interested in your questions and comments regarding buying and selling one piece or an entire collection.

OR

You may have information that would be of interest to your fellow collector. In either case please write to:

Marc Hudgeons, PO Box 11,
Gwynedd Valley, PA 19437

Please send a SASE for a reply.

are you interested in becoming a. . . .

CONTRIBUTOR

If you would like to join our Board of Contributors and have your name printed in the next edition, please let us hear from you.

Please send a SASE for more information to:
Marc Hudgeons, PO Box 11,
Gwynedd Valley, PA 19437

THE OFFICIAL®

2012 BLACKBOOK PRICE GUIDE TO UNITED STATES PAPER MONEY

Market Review

By Bill Rindone

It's been a year of surprises. For those looking for a one-line description of the current market: Demand is relatively strong, prices are rising, and it appears that COLLECTORS are willing to go to the wall for items they cherish while investors, intent on protecting their assets, have decided that investing in rare currency is safe.

The economic downturn raised several questions regarding the field of collectible paper money and first we need to take a look at the timeline of the last several months. The economic downturn had a decided effect on our market by mid-2009. It was most seen in the field of auctions where most auction houses placed reserves on the lots that they were offering. This was done largely because of the uncertainty of where the actual market was and the fear that items might sell at extremely low prices due to a lack of buyers. Times were, at best, uncertain. One of the major auction houses decided to test new price highs which turned out to be a major disaster. The first shock was that only 20-25% of the items offered were sold at what we considered to be very stiff prices. Those sales appeared to be from collectors who had waited years for a particularly rare item to come to the marketplace and did not wish to wait another five to ten years before seeing another example. Other auction houses had similar results and, as we went into Fall, some bargains were to be found. These were particularly in lower priced items where buyers were on the sidelines watching and not sure whether to add to their collections or portfolios. By December everything changed and not only were bargains scarce, but prices firmed and collector demand retuned to previous levels. By Spring 2010 new price highs had been attained in several areas of interest. These advances were major in view of the current economic indicators.

Historically, we've not seen a major price downturn in the forty plus years we've been active. The greatest threat came in 1980 after the high inflationary years of 1978 and 79. In January of 1980, demand for collectible currency shut off. It was there one day and gone the next. Not too surprising as during 1978 and 1979's inflationary period we had seen prices rise 100-1000%. Interest levels were at all-time highs and the cost of living was rising at 21% a year. During 1980, 81, and 82 prices did not decline. There were just no buyers! By 1983 those that had been standing aside watching came back in and it was again business as usual. It is interesting to note that during other times of recent recession there has been no change in the strength of the market—aside from a thirty day hiatus after 9/11 when we all wondered what was happening.

Despite the recent economic downturn, the collectible currency market remains strong. Areas of softness seem to be restricted to the most common, inexpensive notes. This is most likely due to the hardships being endured by those just making ends meet. Currency runs a poor third to food and shelter. Other collectors have decided that, rather than spend $20 a week on smaller items, they would build up their dollars and purchase an eighty or hundred dollar item once a month. If a collector is inclined to investing while enjoying a collection this is a much better strategy.

Whenever inflation threatens, there is always a major flight into tangibles. Parties with funds always need a way to invest and protect their capitol which, in turn, drives the currency market. The value of tangibles, unlike the dollar, also rises in times of inflation. It is an accepted policy to invest in things that will rise with inflationary prices in order to preserve equity. Ironically, we see positive action at both ends of the spectrum. When the economy is good, we also see people with disposable income enter into this field. All in all, it's a great place to be!

This past year the hottest market continued to be Obsolete Notes. If you're thinking of investing in paper money, the trick is to purchase ahead of the curve. There are still excellent areas of investing available and we like the potential in Depression Scrip. This covers two primary time periods: 1907 was a banking "panic" and the banks issued their own notes in the form of Clearing House Certificates and Cashiers Checks with printed denominations. They are now more than one hundred years old, but still available at reasonable prices. At the time of the "Bank Holidays" in 1933, the government gave tacit approval to cities, counties, and merchants to issue their own currency. Although the laws, both then and now, held that it was illegal to issue such notes, the government was faced with bank closures and the lack of enough currency in circulation to allow normal commerce to continue. In order to stabilize commerce, they decided to take a blind eye to private issues of currency. When directly approached on the subject, they applauded the efforts of the issuers who had come to the aid of the country during this crisis.

The average buyer drops into one of three age brackets: 10-20 year-olds whose relatives help with their chosen hobby; 35-50, the age when the average person has achieved enough financial stability to seek those things he has dreamed about; and the retirement age, when he or she can find the time to pursue their dreams and have the capital to do so.

Large Size Notes: (1861–1923 series) Scarce and rare notes are volatile and very difficult to find. Purchase prices for nice notes grading Very Fine to About Uncirculated are usually well in advance of whatever is thought to be the current market. It is not unusual for dealers to attend a major auction on behalf of clients and leave without being able to purchase a single note at the prices that their clients authorized prior to the auction. MS-67 prices are dropping closer to MS-65 as the price range narrows for Gems in this range. Dealers are deep in stock of

Choice Uncirculated notes and find little collector/investor interest in this grade while all other grades between VF and Gem MS-67 are in strong demand.

Small Size Notes: (1928–present) Small size notes have recently awoken, and nice uncirculated Star notes are eagerly sought by collectors. High quality examples of the better small size notes are also in heavy demand and definitely scarce. This includes items such as better Legal Tender Red Seals, Silver Certs, Hawaii overprints, North African issues, Experimentals, Specialty Serial numbers, and Star notes, just to mention a few. New collectors are entering this area of collecting, and it is becoming extremely popular partially due to its relatively lower cost compared to other interests. It is still relatively easy to start a nice collection.

National Bank Notes: (1865–1929) Interest in this area is off from the pace of a few years ago. Rare notes from states that have a large collecting base are still doing well; however, even scarce notes are very soft in the marketplace. Rare notes issued in lesser states often go begging. An example of that is the recent auction featuring Don Kelly's collection of Ohio nationals. Don assembled this over decades and it contained some very rare and unique notes. The problem is that Ohio has never been a popular state for national collectors and that was evident in the prices the notes brought. A comparable note on California will bring 200% more than an Ohio note of the same stature. Nationals are usually collected by parties interested in a particular city, county, state, or area.

Fractionals: (1862–1876) These fractional and postal currency notes remain at the same levels they were five years ago. Steady interest has remained among long-time enthusiasts, but few new buyers have entered the market. The notes appear in 3c, 5c, 10c, 15c, 25c, and 50c denominations. Fractionals are generally suspended halfway between currency collectors and stamp enthusiasts.

Error Notes: (1862–present) This is another area that is hot. The interest and demand for unusual error notes is driving prices higher. New collectors are entering the field, which in turn, continues to create scarcity. There are only so many notes that fall prey to the Bureau of Engravings standards, and increased activity among collectors means more competition and fewer available error notes. Most of the collecting is confined to small-size U.S. currency due to the relatively few large-size errors and their staggering cost. This area had been somewhat overlooked in recent years and past prices had been static. This is no longer true!

Obsolete Notes: (1800–1877) This is where today's greatest pressure exists and issues continue to spiral upward in price. The last few years have seen prices advance, but recently there has been an upward explosion. No census exists for most issues, and, once again, doing your homework will pay dividends. A few years ago, I wrote that highly desirable notes were still available in the $15–$25 range. Now I would call it the $100–$500 range. Bargains are still plentiful, even at major auctions, if you know what you're looking for. The Web also provides access to a multitude of obsolete notes. I feel this is one of two areas that the newcomer should look at closely when starting a collection.

Obsoletes & Scrip from WESTERN STATES and TERRITORIES (1854–1924) has seen a dramatic increase in interest in the past few years. Actually, the interest has been present for a long time; however, before the advent of the World Wide Web, it was a great deal more difficult to find material. Now, with countless millions of buyers and sellers congregating on computer auction sites, we have the ability to find new and different notes for even the most specialized collectors.

Over the last three years, we've seen major auctions feature such outstanding collections as Schingoethe and the John J. Ford holdings that contained a lot of excessively rare western material. In 1967, when I entered this field, I would have never expected to see an obsolete hammered at over $100,000. Bargains still exist and, as example of that, we recently purchased a rare Arizona on a Web auction. Only two five cent examples were known to exist. The nicer of the two brought a solid four figure amount. The new member to the census was a discovery note as the first 10c to see daylight. Following the auction, the seller asked us if we would like the other two he had which were consecutively numbered to the one we purchased. As mentioned, there are still notes out there!

These western notes represent the settling of the U.S. frontier whether territorial enterprises, Mormon, frontier towns, bankers, early California merchants, Nevada silver mines, Indian tribes, or military fort sutlers. These were issued during the western movement of this great nation. Paper money was generally not trusted in the west from the mid- to late-1800s, and, with the major banks two or three thousand miles away, it became what one banker called "a necessary evil." A comprehensive section on Western Scrip appears later in this publication.

Depression Scrip (1893, 1907 & 1933) During the 1907 Panic, the majority of these notes were issued by banks or groups of banks. Most were done as Clearing House Certificates, Cashier's Checks, or Payroll Checks and were intended to circulate as money. The Panic and closure of banks started in late-October of 1907 and lasted until mid-January of 1908. Bank "Holidays" lasted up to 50 days and the crash of the stock market also occurred during this time. These notes are very collectible and a census is available through the hard work of Doug Corrigan. His census continues to prove that the '07s are substantially rarer than first thought.

In 1933 local governments and businesses once again found the commercial marketplace without adequate currency. The bank closures severely hampered everyone's ability to conduct business in a normal manner. Interest in 1933 Depression scrip continues to rise in price, but it is still a bargain in relation to other areas. Common notes sell for under $10 and extremely rare notes go for between $500 and $1200. We still see $500 notes sold for $20 or $30. In order to cash in on these bargains you need a modest price guide and to be willing to research unlisted notes. In this field, unlisted notes are almost always rare. This is an area where you can still be "ahead of the curve" and purchase notes that have great potential for the future. I highly recommend Depression scrip to the new collector.

Warrants, Bounties, and Bills of Exchange: (1845–1920) This is a fascinating area of collectibility, and one which has now come into its own due to availability of material through the Internet. Bills of Exchange were issued in the mid- to late-1800s—primarily in the West. Comparable to a modern Traveler's check, they were a means of safely forwarding money. Companies such as Wells Fargo, D.O. Mills and Page, and Bacon & Co. issued them in triplicate. They were called First, Second & Third Bills of Exchange. This was necessary due to conditions in the West. Indians, stage robberies, fires, or countless other events could easily cause the loss of cash or a single check. The three copies of these Bills were sent separately and at least one would survive the journey. These items can still be found at prices less than 5% of their auction value. Not only is it interesting to collect, but it can be financially rewarding.

Colonial Notes: (1690–1799) These remain stable in price. The lack of pretty vignettes and precision engravings has left these as little more than an outlet for those interested in early United States history. They've never been a highly popular item and have seen only marginal financial gains over the years. It continues to be an area of collecting which can best be described as slow but steady. Most are quite common and contemporarily lost most of their face value. This left a profusion of notes in the public sector to be handed down from one generation to another. Of those redeemed, most were cancelled and later found their way back into the public sector. Non-collectors assume that they are valuable due to their age and are usually disappointed in their value.

Military Payment Certificates: (1947–1973) MPC's were issued for the use of U.S. military personnel in foreign countries to thwart the black market sale of regular U.S. notes. They were redeemable only on military reservations, and were therefore very difficult for the local black market profiteers to handle. The notes are very colorful. Collecting a complete set of all notes issued is not beyond the financial means of the average collector. This is a specialty area that has good future potential and surprising current interest.

Related Areas: Early Checks (1800–1899) are popular and can be readily found in the market place at very moderate prices. Their popularity has been increasing and prices for Rare or Unusual are on the rise. Checks are usually collected for their outstanding vignettes or because of geographical area. There is also a strong interest in checks signed by famous people or for the U.S. Revenue stamps imprinted on the check paper. Vignettes of cowboys, Indians, steamships, and the like are common. Financial documents relating to various periods of our history are of great interest to collectors and easily find a home. Memorabilia or exonoumia of events such as world expositions are of great interest. Paper items from the American West are also widely sought after and many outstanding collections exist. Presidential, political, or historical items are also in the spotlight.

In closing I would like, once again, to refer to our commentary from past years: The entire spectrum of currency-related material is extremely healthy. Will it stay that way? Past history says it will, and what better way to be involved in the history of a nation than with its money. Money still represents the affluence that attracts worldwide interest to this most prosperous of all nations. This statement is still very accurate!

U.S. Paper Money
Bought and Sold

Specializing in: ~U.S. LARGE & SMALL SIZE Type, Fractionals, ***Error* Notes**, COLONIALS, *Nat'l Currency,* Obsoletes, ENCASED POSTAGE, MPC, Early Checks, Confederate, WESTERN EXONUMIA, Scrip, *Autographs* & Documents.

BANK NOTES NORTH WEST

P.O. Box 790, Aurora, OR 97002
1-(503) 694-1122
EMAIL: BNNW@bnnw.net
WEB SITE: http://www.bnnw.net/grading.htm

PUBLICATIONS

Get a global perspective on paper money collecting from ***The Bank Note Reporter***. This monthly tabloid is devoted entirely to U.S. and world paper money, notes, checks, and all related fiscal paper. Find current prices for national and international bank notes, plus an active buy/sell marketplace. *12 monthly issues are $24.98.*

The ***Numismatic News*** delivers weekly news and information on coin and paper money collecting with exclusive reports from the hobby's only full-time Washington Bureau. Accurate retail/wholesale value guide, current events, and up-to-date calendar make this the most comprehensive numismatic forum available. *52 weekly issues are $29.99.*

For more information, please contact:

Krause Publications
700 East State Street
Iola, WI 54990-0001
Phone 715-445-2214
Subscription Services
1-800-258-0929

NEW TRENDS IN TECHNOLOGY AND THEIR IMPACT ON COIN AND PAPER MONEY COLLECTORS

By Tom Bilotta
Carlisle Development Corporation

Over the past year, technology has continued to advance at a strong pace, and there have been many developments of interest to numismatic collectors. In this article we will discuss some of these developments with a focus on their relevance to collectors.

PORTABLE DEVICES

There has been an explosion in the use of portable devices over the past year. Use of these devices is growing rapidly and they come in many different forms. Included in this category are smartphones, tablet computers, iPad, netbook computers, and e-readers (such as the Amazon Kindle and the Barnes & Noble Nook). All of these devices provide potential function of value to collectors.

E-readers

Electronic readers have been substantially enhanced to provide much higher viewing quality. These devices now come in color and black and white and offer stunningly high image quality. They incorporate advanced user interface features as well as very smart touchscreen control.

Touchscreen technology, which has been in existence for decades, is now becoming a very significant intuitive user interface technology. For example, turning a page is accomplished by flicking your finger across the screen in the same motion used when reading from a book.

LCD monitor technology now provides very high quality color images good enough to view magazines which employ high quality 4-color printing.

These devices are not only for reading books, but also can be used to browse the internet, read and respond to e-mail, buy and sell items, participate in auctions, and search for information of interest.

E-readers offer several advantages with respect to netbook or laptop computers. These devices are very light, and typically have long battery life. One major advantage is that they turn on instantly, so if you have a wireless internet in your home, you may take an e-reader into your living room and access an online coin auction instantly while you are watching a movie.

Another use of e-readers is in conjunction with coin and currency collecting software such as the Collector's Assistant from Carlisle Development. The Collector's Assistant can generate reports consisting of listings of your collections including pictures. These reports can be output to a PDF format which can be viewed in high quality on an e-reader.

E-readers are very economical and advanced color units. They can be purchased for around $250.

Tablet Computers and the iPad

Tablet computing has been given a strong impetus with the release of the iPad by Apple. The iPad offers many of the advantages of an E-Reader, but is also capable of running software applications. Thus an iPad may be used to perform many functions that previously required a computer. The iPad, though larger than an e-reader, is very portable and very convenient for internet browsing. Other manufacturers have released tablet computers with similar capabilities and are expanding the marketplace for these devices. These devices are typically $500–$800.

Netbook Computers

Netbook computers are essentially small laptop computers. There are two advantages to these devices when compared to a traditional laptop. First, they are typically about 50% of the cost of a full laptop. Second, they are significantly lighter weight and more portable. These devices, however, have small viewing screens and often long startup times and don't offer much of an advantage over tablet computers.

Smartphones

Smartphones are used widely for internet browsing and viewing and responding to e-mail. Their strongest advantage is their dual function (also serving as a phone) and very small form factor. The disadvantage is the inconvenience of internet activity on a small screen.

Choosing the Right Portable Device for You

The choice of a portable device is a personal one and is driven by your typical usage, physical limitations, and other considerations. Many users will employ multiple portable devices for different purposes. Many coin collectors are older and would have difficulty with the small screen size and keys on an e-reader or smartphone and would be better served by a traditional laptop or tablet computer. If you find an affordable e-reader or tablet computer which provides adequate viewing quality for you, it will likely be a very convenient choice for all sorts of internet activity associated with your collecting pursuits.

THE INTERNET

As in recent years, internet activity by collectors continues to grow. One of the new terms associated with the Internet is Cloud computing.

Cloud Computing

Cloud computing is one of the latest terms to gain widespread use. Cloud computing is actually a simple concept. Instead of applications running on a personal computer, applications are run on a remote computer shared by users of a public or private community. In some instances the applications are free and in others there are monthly connect charges. Advantages of this paradigm include elimination of the need to install and update software on your own computer and ability to interact with your applications wherever you happen to be and with a wide variety of devices.

The disadvantages of cloud computing are the same as those that have traditionally affected shared solutions. If the servers go down or your internet service is interrupsted, you cannot access your application. There is also the problem of internet security and ensuring your sensitive data is not accessible to others.

Practically speaking, it is likely that cloud computing will offer value to collectors by allowing access to information provided by central sources. It is also likely, however, that considerations of security and availability will leave collectors wanting to manage their own collection data on their own computers.

COIN COLLECTING SOFTWARE

Coin collecting software that runs on your own computer bypasses the problems of internet catalogs and provides you with rich functionality to work with your collection.

Collectors who adopt computer inventory programs increase their enjoyment of collecting, provide the needed documentation to protect their collection, gain insight into the value of their collection, and better prepare their families to deal with their collection if the need arises.

In order to exploit the power that computers bring to collecting, the collector must acquire a base level of knowledge sufficient to harness this capability in a safe and productive manner. The remainder of this article will focus on some of the more important points of using numismatic inventory software.

Coin & Paper Money Inventory Software

One of the first applications of a computer is to organize a collection. This activity requires cataloguing what you have, deciding how it will be grouped and determining what kind of reports you will need. Reports will assist you defining your collecting objectives, tracking value, and assuring your collection is adequately protected and insured.

Organizing your collection with coin & paper money inventory software

Collectors of coins and currency fall into several categories. There is the serious collector who enjoys the hobby and pursues personally defined collecting objectives. Accumulators retain many of the coins that they receive in normal commerce and build up large quantities of unsorted coins. Investors use coin collecting to build portfolios intended to produce profits. Inheritors receive a coin collection or accumulation from their families and must decide how they will handle a potentially valuable asset.

All of these collectors have a common need to catalog their items and understand their value. Most collectors have many items with a very wide range of values. A modern inventory program can adapt to meet the needs of all types of users from novice collectors to experienced experts. It will incorporate a comprehensive database of coin and or paper money to assist the user in identifying and defining their collections as well as a flexible set of functionality to enable them to organize their collection in a manner consistent with their collection methodology.

Most collectors will want to create electronic organization that mirrors their physical collection. For example, someone with coin albums of common series such as mercury dimes, statehood quarters, or buffalo nickels will want to have software albums organized in similar fashion. Other coins might be grouped into coins for sale, duplicates, partial collections for other family members, or any other categorization which suits the collector.

Using your time wisely

When using computer software to catalog a coin or paper money collection it is important to use it in a manner consistent with your purposes and which will enhance your enjoyment. You should spend your time, therefore, working with the portions of your collection in which you have the most interest or where the primary financial value exists. For example, if you are collecting a complete set of Mercury dimes, you may wish to scan an image of each individual piece so that you can print picture catalogs of your collection. For these coins, you might choose to enter in complete information including purchase price, source, certification information, origin, etc. For this type of grouping you will also likely want to include coins that you don't have that are required to complete your collection, enabling you to generate want lists. This will also assist you in identifying the cost to complete your collection and planning your approach.

For large quantities of relatively inexpensive items or coins worth only bullion content and where you have no particular collecting interest, you might choose to only enter a single line item and not bother to take the time to list each coin individually. For example, if you have several hundred silver Washington quarters in circulated condition from the 1950's and 1960's you might enter a single line item 225 Washington Quarters with a date range and average value. In this way, large accumulations can be tracked with minimum effort and your attention can be focused on your real collecting interests. Your coin inventory program should adapt to all of these possible approaches to organizing your collection.

Evaluating coin and paper money inventory software

The quality of the software that you purchase will greatly impact the success of your efforts. One of the most important parts of a coin inventory program is the database. The database contains standard information about coins and paper money and saves the user from having to type this information manually. The greater the amount of information in the standard database, the easier the task of data entry. A modern coin collecting program, at a minimum, should include coin type, date, mint mark, denomination, and variety. Comprehensive programs, such as those made by Carlisle Development Corporation, also include such information as designer/engraver, coinage metal, size, weight, edge, and mintage. The organization of the database should reflect commonly used groupings and thereby provide user with guidance in organizing their collection.

Some inventory programs include current market values. It is important that these are updated frequently and produced by reliable sources. Coin values should evolve to include areas of high market interest. For example, over the past year, the market interest in high grade recent coin issues has become very high. It is also important to allow the user the ability to extend the database to include items that are not listed. These may be specialized varieties, private mint products, or other coin related collectibles.

Ability to share data with other programs and people is also very important. Most computerized collectors are connected to the Internet and will want to share some information with other collectors and dealers. The ability to export listings in common text readable formats for transmission over the Internet or for input into a word processor or spreadsheet is of great value in buying and selling coins and paper money.

Carlisle Development's inventory software, Collector's Assistant, provides a comprehensive database of all coins ever minted by the United States Mint. This includes all type coins by date and mint mark, bullion coins, sets, old and new commemoratives. Recent additions to the database are the fifty states circulating quarters and the new Sacagawea dollar. Coin values are licensed from Coin World, Inc., an industry leader in providing coin valuations. Quarterly updates are available by subscription allowing collectors to maintain trends of their values. Carlisle Development's Currency Collector's Assistant has a complete database based on Friedberg's Paper Money of the United States, 19th Edition. This database includes all U.S. paper money, including Confederate notes and encased postage stamps. A relationship with CDN, publisher of the Greensheet, makes value information available to the paper money collector in electronic format.

For collectors of ancient coins, Carlisle offers an add-on database containing color images of several hundred ancient coins and a specialized interface containing data entry fields appropriate for ancient coins. For example, the date field can handle and sort mixed AD/BC dates and has long fields for obverse and reverse inscriptions. The most recent additions to Carlisle Development's databases include the Euro Coin Database and World Currency Database.

Report Generation

Once you have entered your coin collection into an inventory program, the most important function will become its ability to generate a wide array of reports and/or exports for informational purposes.

For insurance purposes, you will probably want to have a detailed listing to identify items, their value, and where they are stored. You will want to generate partial lists of your collections for sales and trading. You may want to generate labels to aide in identifying your coins. You may want to look at your collection in many different ways, such as, sorted by value or metal content or collection completeness.

One common need of coin collectors is the printing of inserts for 2" flips. Once catalogued, computer software can allow you to produce customized flip inserts in a standard format of your own design.

Report generation is the subset of an inventory program which produces the listings that you view on the screen, print on paper, or export to other computer applications. Its flexibility will greatly impact its utility. For example, you may want to generate two listings of coins that you have for sale, one which includes your cost and target price (your copy) and one which does not include this information for general distribution to prospective buyers.

At various times, you will probably want to be able to list any subset of the information fields, filter based on a wide array of parameters and sort using different criteria.

As mentioned at the beginning of this article, report generation may be used to output PDF files which may be viewed using a portable device such as an e-reader.

Other functionality you should expect from your inventory software

Inventory software should be able to store all of the information in which a collector is interested. Specific fields will vary based on collector interest and purpose. Some will require detailed certification and descriptive information, others comprehensive purchase and sales history. Some collectors will want to have comprehensive recording of storage location and insurance information. Modern programs provide sufficient information fields to meet all of these needs.

Backup and restore functions should allow the user to easily protect the data they have meticulously entered. History charting enables the user to track the value changes of a part of their collection over time.

Good software must be easy to use and supported by context sensitive help which provides the user with detailed instructions in a "how to" format on all of the basic functions that they will wish to perform.

Availability of timely updates

Once you have taken the time to catalog your collection in a computer program, you will want to preserve your investment by having access to database updates incorporating information on new coin releases as well as changes in value. Your supplier of inventory software should have a timely program for availability of annual database and value updates.

Educational software for collectors

Adding significantly to your enjoyment of collections are electronic information sources that exploit the power of the computer to present you with high quality information in an easily accessible format. These programs can provide comprehensive knowledge of all aspects of coin collecting, detailed information on grading coins, and specialized information such as collecting coin varieties.

COIN GRADING

Most coin collectors will want to be able to grade their coins, at least to an approximate grade. This enables them to have an understanding of value as well as identify coins that might be appropriate for certification. Coin grading skill is built up through time and experience.

The Grading Assistant, offered by Carlisle Development is based on the official Grading Guide of the American Numismatic Association, now published by Whitman Publishing. It enables the user to view side-by-side images of their own coins along with various grades from the ANA grading set. These images are supported by detailed descriptions of the wear points for each grade. Using software such as the Grading Assistant, allows a user to develop their skill in grading coins and establish approximate grades for their collection.

VARIETY COLLECTING

The collecting of coin varieties is an exciting area of the hobby currently experiencing some growth. Varieties are the result of differences in the minting process or dies which produce design differences and or errors. These include such effects as doubling some features or letters, extra pieces of metal on the coin surface and die breaks. Variety collecting requires the collector to identify subtle differences in coin designs.

The Morgan dollar series is one of the most commonly collected and is categorized by many varieties. Carlisle Development offers a Top 100 Morgan Dollar CD, based on the book written by Michael Fey and Jeff Oxman. This CD provides pictures, identification information, and values for the most sought after and valuable Morgan dollar varieties. It provides a spectacular set of high quality pictures to assist you in identifying these coins and also the full text and information present in the book.

GENERAL EDUCATIONAL WORKS ON COLLECTING

There is much to learn about coin collecting, whether it is technical knowledge such as grading and authentication or practical knowledge such as buying and selling coins, attending trade shows, or participating in auctions. Educational computer software offers advantages over printed works in that the contents may be searched and indexed allowing the user to rapidly retrieve valuable information.

Carlisle Development offers the *Coin Collector's Survival Manual, Sixth Edition,* an interactive edition of the work by Scott Travers. This work provides information that every coin collector should have. The entire content of this book is provided in a searchable, interactive format. This allows the user to easily locate information based on word searching, topics, illustrations, bookmarks, a table of contents, or index. The most recent edition of this work contains the contents of *How to Make Money in Coins Right Now,* covering such topics as cracking-out coins for upgrade and premium coins. In addition to the contents of the book, a set of high quality grading images have been included for such topics as identifying MS-63, MS-65, MS-67 coins and toning. An interactive grading calculator brings to life the grading methods described in the book.

WELL DESIGNED COMPUTER SOFTWARE WILL ADD TO YOUR ENJOYMENT OF COLLECTING

Carlisle Development Corporation publishes the most comprehensive line of collector software available, especially regarding coins and paper money.

Central to Carlisle's product line is the Collector's Assistant, the most advanced and comprehensive collection software available. It is sold in a variety of configurations to serve collectors of over thirty collectible types from autographs to toys. Most extensive is support for coins and paper money. The Collector's Assistant family includes:

- United States Coin Database—complete listings of all U.S. coinage from 1793 to the present. 50 State quarter program and the Presidents dollar program are recent additions. This also includes Colonial and Hawaiian coinage.
- World Coin Database—A listing of over 5000 coin types from over forty-five countries, which may be extended by the user. Also in-

cludes comprehensive listings of Canada, Australia, Euro coinage and world bullion gold and silver coins.

- Ancient Coin Database—includes several thousand listings of Byzantine, Judaic, Roman, and Greek coinage along with several hundred images. Data entry screens are optimized for ancient-coin collectors including long fields for inscriptions and preloaded choice lists of rulers, ancient denominations, towns, mints and others.
- United States Currency Database—A complete listing of all United States currency based on Friedberg's 18th Edition, Paper Money of the United States. This also includes 120 high quality color images of early US currency.

To learn more about Carlisle Development's product line, visit our website at www.carlisledevelopment.com. You will find current product information and may also place orders. You can reach us by e-mail at support@carlisledevelopment.com or by phone at 800-219-0257.

COLLECTING ORGANIZATIONS

PROFESSIONAL CURRENCY DEALERS ASSOCIATION (PCDA)

Looking for a reliable paper money dealer? . . . Collecting rare paper money can be an enjoyable hobby. Imagine being able to own an example of fractional currency printed during the Civil War era, or a National Bank Note issued by a financial institution in your own state.

Whatever your collecting interests, the members of the Professional Currency Dealers Association (PCDA) will be pleased to assist and guide you. The members of this prestigious trade association specialize in virtually all the areas of paper money collecting.

Once you've started to collect, it can sometimes be a challenge to locate a dealer with a significant inventory. Members of the PCDA are the market makers for currency collectors. Whatever your interest, a PCDA member is certain to be able to supply you. Whether you are a beginner on a limited budget or an advanced collector of many years' experience, you can be certain that you'll find fair, courteous, and reliable treatment with a member of the Professional Currency Dealers Association.

CONTACT INFORMATION

General Information and Correspondence

James A. Simek
PCDA Secretary
P.O. Box 7157
Westchester, IL 60154
(630) 889-8207
e-mail: nge3@comcast.net

PCDA Publication

David A. Berg
PCDA
P.O. Box 348
Portersville, PA 16051

THE SOCIETY OF PAPER MONEY COLLECTORS (SPMC)

The Society of Paper Money Collectors (SPMC) invites you to become a member of our organization. SPMC was founded in 1961 with the following objectives: (1) Encourage the collecting and study of all paper money and financial documents; (2) Provide collectors the opportunity to meet and enjoy fraternal relations with their fellow collectors; (3) Furnish information and knowledge about paper money; (4) Encourage research about paper money and financial documents and publish the resulting information; (5) Promote legislation favorable to collectors; (6) Advance the prestige of the hobby of numismatics; (7) Promote rational and consistent classification of exhibits, and ENCOURAGE participation by our members; (8) Encourage realistic and consistent market valuations.

Paper Money, SPMC's bimonthly journal now in its 36th year, has repeatedly been selected by the ANA as the Best Specialty Publication in numismatics; the Numismatic Literary Guild has also selected *Paper Money* for first-place recognition. Virtually every article in every issue is written by an SPMC member, who receives no monetary compensation. SPMC coordinates and judges the exhibits at the largest all-paper show every year. SPMC co-sponsors many large all-paper shows held in the U.S. each year.

Information about membership may be obtained by writing to:

Frank Clark
P.O. Box 117060
Carrollton, TX 75011
e-mail: frankclark@spmc.org

PCDA MEMBERSHIP DIRECTORY

Michael Accavallo
Centurial Collectibles
P.O. Box 669
Coram, NY 11727
(516) 457-6573
Web site: www.centurial collectibles.com
e-mail: centurycoll@aol.com

All U.S. Paper Money
United States Large Size Type Notes
United States Small Size Type Notes
United States National Bank Notes
Unted States Fractional Currency
Obsolete Notes
Fancy and Low Serial Numbers Notes
Star Notes
PCGS and PMG Top Population Notes

Rick Allard
Cashmans Currency
P.O. Box 941840
Simi Valley, CA 93094
(805) 579-0339
Cellular: (805) 279-1641
Fax: (805) 579-0339
Web site: www.buyoldmoney.com
e-mail: cashmanscurrency@aol.com

United States Large Size Type Notes
United States Small Size Type Notes
Fancy and Low Serial Numbers Notes
Error Notes

Robert Azpiazu
First City Currency & Collectibles, Inc.
P.O. Drawer 1629
St. Augustine, FL 32085
(904) 794-0784
Fax: (904) 824-1018
Web site: www.fstctycurr.com
e-mail: fstctycu@bellsouth.net

United States Small Size Type Notes
Star Notes
Error Notes
Fancy and Low Serial Number Notes
FRN Blocks
Auction Representation
Estate Appraisals

Stephen Barber
S & P Colelctibles
P.O. Box 51416
Colorado Springs, CO 80949-1416
(719) 460-2054
e-mail: barbersp77@msn.com

United States Large Size Type Notes
United States Small Size Type Notes
United States Fractional Currency
World Banknotes
U.S. Coins

Doris Bart
Bart, Inc.
P.O. Box 2
Roseville, MI 48066
(586) 979-3400
Fax: (586) 979-7976
Web site: www.ExecutiveCurrency .com
e-mail: doris@ExecutiveCurrency .com

Auction Representation
Rare United States Small Size Notes
United States Large Size Type Notes
Error Notes
Autographed Notes

Frederick J. Bart
Bart, Inc.
P.O. Box 2
Roseville, MI 48066
(586) 979-3400

Fax: (586) 979-7976
Web site:
www.ExecutiveCurrency.com
e-mail: bart@ExecutiveCurrency.com

Error Notes
Serial #1 National Bank Notes
Uncut Sheets
Rare Small Size Notes
Large Size Type Notes

Keith S. Bauman
TNA Associates
P.O. Box 250027
Franklin, MI 48025-0027
(248) 647-8938
e-mail: TNAksbauman@earthlink.net

United States Large Size Type Notes
United States Small Size Type Notes
United States Fractional Currency
United States Military Payment Certificates
Confederate
World Paper Money
Numismatic Related Art Work

David A. Berg
Dave Berg, Ltd.
P.O. Box 348
Portersville, PA 16051
(724) 452-4586
Fax: (724) 452-0276
e-mail: davbergltd@aol.com
Web site: www.daveberglimited.com

Error Notes
Mail Order Price Lists
United States Fractional Currency
United States Large Size Type Notes
United States National Bank Notes
United States Small Size Type Notes

Phil Boerstler
Paradise Antique Currency
P.O. Box 20251
Wichita, KS 67208-1251
(316) 681-2157
Fax: (316) 681-2157
Web site:
www.ParadiseAntiqueCurrency.com
e-mail: paradise@southwind.com

Confederate
Obsolete Notes
United States Fractional Currency

Carl Bombara
P.O. Box 524
New York, NY 10116
(212) 989-9108
e-mail: CBcurrency@aol.com

United States Large Size Type Notes
United States Small Size Type Notes
United States National Bank Notes
Error Notes
Mail Order Sales
Auction Representation
Want Lists Serviced

C. "Bo" Borich
Pacific Numismatics
P.O. Box 268
Santa Cruz, CA 95061
(831) 475-9198
Fax: (831) 475-9128
e-mail: pacnumis@live.com

United States National Bank Notes—Especially Western States and Territories
United States Type Notes

Q. David Bowers
Stacks, LLC
P.O. Box 1804
Wolfeboro, NH 03894
(603) 569-0823
Toll Free: (866) 811-1804
Fax: (603) 569-3875
Web site: www.stacks.com
e-mail: qdbarchive@metrocast.net

Auction Services for American Colonial, Obsolete, Confederate, Federal Related Paper Money of all Eras
Celebrating 50 years in professional numismatics 1953-2003
Past president Professional Numismatists Guild (1977-1979)
Past president American Numismatic Association (1983-1995)

Jason W. Bradford
PCGS Currency
P.O. Box 10470
Peoria, IL 61612
(309) 222-8200
Toll Free: (800) 691-PCGS (691-7247)
Web site: www.pcgscurrency.com
e-mail: jbradford@pcgscurrency.com

Jennifer Cangeme
Denly's of Boston
P.O. Box 51010
Boston, MA 02205
(617) 482-8477
(800) HI DENLY (Orders Only)
Fax: (617) 357-8163
Web site: www.denlys.com
e-mail: jen@denlys.com

Colonial and Continental
United States Fractional Currency

United States Large Size Type Notes
United States Small Size Type Notes
Confederate
Obsolete Notes
United States National Bank Notes
Error Notes
Books and Supplies
Military Payment Certificates
World Paper Money
Auction Sales - Bidder Representative
Mail Order Price Lists
Encased Postage
Mylar D† Currency Holders
United States & Foreign Coins

I. Nelson Clark
I. Nelson Clark Banknotes
P.O. Box 883
Los Alamitos, CA 90720
(714) 761-3683
Cell: (714) 809-5120
Fax: (714) 761-3683
e-mail: inellclark@ca.rr.net

United States Currency
United States National Bank Notes

Arthur D. Cohen
Penfield Note Exchange
P.O. Box 311
Penfield, NY 14526-0311
(585) 377-4677
e-mail: adcohen@frontiernet.net

World Paper Money
Mail Order Price Lists
Custom Labels For Currency Holders, Flips and Slabs

Mary Counts
Whitman Publishing, LLC
3101 Clairmont Road
Atlanta, GA 30329
(404) 235-5317
Toll Free: (800) 852-2626
Fax: (404) 214-4398
Web site: www.whitmanbooks.com
e-mail: mary.counts@whitman books.com

Numismatic Publications and Supplies

Terry Coyle
Alex Perakis Coins & Currency
P.O. Box 246
Lima, PA 19037
(610) 627-1212
Fax: (610) 891-1466
e-mail: apcc1@msn.com (work)
Web site: www.perakiscurrency.com
e-mail: Terrycole13@yahoo.com

(PCDA Business)
United States National Bank Notes
United States Large Size Type Notes
United States Small Size Type Notes

Paul Cuccia
Belvidere Coins & Collectibles, LLC
2-B Market Street
Belvidere, NJ 07823
(908) 475-1088
Cell: (908) 319-1602
e-mail: holzcuccia@comcast.net

United States Large Size Type Notes
United States Small Size Type Notes
Obsolete Notes
United States National Bank Notes
Error Notes
Small Size Stars
World Paper Money

Jhon E. Cybuski, Jr.
Jhon E. Cash Currency, Coins, & Collectibles
2804 Woodlake Court
Highland Village, TX 75077
(214) 769-9936
Web site: www.jhoncash.com
e-mail: jhon@jhonecash.com

United States Large Size Type Notes
United States Small Size Type Notes
Error Notes
$5,000 & $10,000 Bills
United States Rare Coins & Collectibles

Edward A. Dauer
4850 West Oakland Park Blvd.
Suite 145
Fort Lauderdale, FL 33313
(954) 739-0978
Fax: (954) 739-2587
Web site:
www.amhistoryuscurrency.com
e-mail: EasyDog5@aol.com

All United States Currency
British Commonwealth Banknotes, especially Canada, Australia, New Zealand, and Great Britain

Steve Deeds
Bowers & Merena Auctions
18061 Fitch
Irvine, CA 92614
(949) 253-0916
Toll Free: (800) 458-4646
Fax: (949) 253-4091
Web site: www.bowersandmerena.com
e-mail: steved@bowersandmerena .com

United States Large Size Type Notes
United States Small Size Type Notes
United States Fractional Currency
Auction Sales

Alex Delatola
APD Currency Corp.
P.O. Box 677
Pittstown, NJ 08867
(908) 479-1899
Cellular: (212) 665-2112
Fax: (908) 479-1661
Web site: www.apdcurrency.com
e-mail: alex@apdcurrency.com

United States Small Size Type Notes
Specialist: Silver Certificates, United States Notes, Federal Reserve Notes, Gold Notes, Uncut Sheets and "Blocks of 4," Web Notes, Engraving Errors, Packs of Star and Block Notes
Canadian Paper Money

Phil Delia
Delia Coins & Paper Money
P.O. Box 530774
Livonia, MI 48153
(248) 991-9599
e-mail: phildelia@yahoo.com

World Banknotes
Stock Certificates and Bonds
Check and Fiscal Paper
United States Proof Claims

John DeMaris
P.O. Box 72
Boys Town, NE 68010
(402) 334-2756
e-mail: siramed@aol.com

Colonial and Continental
United States Fractional Currency
United States Large Size Type Notes
United States Small Size Type Notes
Confederate
Obsolete Notes
United States National Bank Notes

Thomas M. Denly
Denly's of Boston
P.O. Box 51010
Boston, MA 02205
(617) 482-8477
(800) HI DENLY (Orders Only)
Fax: (617) 357-8163
Web site: www.denlys.com
e-mail: tom@denlys.com

Colonial and Continental
United States Fractional Currency
United States Large Size Type Notes
United States Small Size Type Notes
Confederate
Obsolete Notes
United States National Bank Notes
Error Notes
Books and Supplies
Military Payment Certificates
World Paper Money
Auction Sales - Bidder Representative
Mail Order Price Lists
Encased Postage
Mylar D† Currency Holders
United States & Foreign Coins

Michael Findlay
Certified Coins of Canada
P.O. Box 2043
Augus, Ontario L0M 1B0
CANADA
(705) 423-1140
Toll Free: (888) 649-7777
Fax: (705) 423-1069
e-mail: ccdn@bconnex.net

Canadian Banknotes
World Banknotes
Canadian Merchants Scrip
Publisher: ***Canadian Coin Dealer Newsletter***

Don Fisher
Currency Unlimited
P.O. Box 481
Decatur, IL 62525
(217) 692-2825
Cell: (217) 433-2242
Fax: (217) 692-2825

Obsolete Notes
United States National Bank Notes
World Paper Money

Jim Fitzgerald—Spink Smythe
3100 Monticello Avenue, Ste. 925
Dallas, TX 75205
Toll Free: (800) 622-1880 ext. 1026
Web site: www.spinksmythe.com
e-mail: jfitzgerald@spink.com

United States National Bank Notes
United States Large Size Type Notes
United States Small Size Type Notes
United States Fractional Currency
Colonial and Continental
Confederate Notes
Obsolete Notes
Fiscal Documents—Focusing Mainly on Texas

Dennis Forgue
Harlan J. Berk, Ltd.
31 North Clark Street
Chicago, IL 60602
(312) 609-0016
Fax: (312) 609-1305
Web site: www.hjbltd.com
e-mail: dennis@hjbltd.com

United States Large Size Type Notes
United States Small Size Type Notes
Confederate
Obsolete Notes
United States National Bank Notes
Error Notes
Autographs

Jim Futrell
Tickle Your Fancy Currency
1908 Bladensburg Road, NE
Washington, DC 20002
(202) 306-9410
Web site:
www.tickleyourfancycurrency.com
e-mail: tyfcurrency@aol.com

Fancy & Low Serial Numbers
Star Notes
United States Small Size Type Notes
Want Lists Serviced

Steve Garvin
Honor Coin & Stamp
4001 U.S. 31 South, Suite D
Traverse City, MI 49684
(231) 943-9991
Web site: www.honor-coin-stamp.com

Michigan National Bank Notes
MPCs
Error Notes

Bill Geigner
C.P.G. Currency Connection
26210 Cherryhill Road
Manhattan, IL 60442
(815) 478-3320
e-mail: billgeigner@aol.com

United States Large Size Type Notes
United States Small Size Type Notes

Stephen L. Goldsmith
American Paper Money & Coin, LLC
P.O. Box 369
Woodmere, NY 11598
(917) 604-8823
e-mail: goldsmiths@optonline.net

Auction Sales
Autographs
Colonial and Continental
Confederate
Financial Documents
Mail Order Sales
Mail Order Price Lists
Obsolete Notes
Stocks, Bonds and Fiscal Documents
United States Fractional Currency
United States Large Size Type Notes
United States Small Size Type Notes
United States National Bank Notes
World Paper Money

Bill Grubb
Olde Mill Currency
P.O. Box 101
Telford, PA 18969
(215) 257-4380
e-mail: grubbwf@msn.com
Web site: www.oldemillcurrency.com

United States National Bank Notes
United States Large Size Type Notes
United States Small Size Type
Notes
Financial Stock Certificates
Savings Bonds

Bruce R. Hagen
Stack's Rarities, LLC
123 West 57th Street
New York, NY 10019
(212) 582-2580
(212) 582-5955
Fax: (212) 582-1946
Web site: www.stacks.com
e-mail: info@stacks.com

Auction Sales of United States
and World Coins, Medals, and
Paper Currency Appraisals
Colonial and Continental
Obsolete Notes and Proofs
United States Large Size Type Notes
United States Small Size Type Notes
United States Fractional Currency
United States National Bank Notes

Bruce R. Hagen
Pedigree Research Services
P.O. Box 431
Planetarium Station
New York, NY 10024
(212) 721-2028

Auction Representation
Obsolete Notes and Proofs
United States Federal Proofs, Essays
& Vignettes
Security Printing Archives, Histories &
Artifacts
American Financial Documents and
History

Specialized Pedigree Research Services
United States National Bank Notes
Services to the Trade Only

Larry Hanks
Hanks & Associates
P.O. Box 913
Indian Rocks Beach, FL 33785
(727) 593-1303
Toll Free: (800) 598-8188
e-mail: whanks3700@aol.com

United States Large Size Type Notes
United States Small Size Type Notes
United States National Bank Notes

Chad Hawk
Paper Money Guaranty
5501 Communications Parkway
Sarasota, FL 34240
(941) 309-1001
Toll Free: 1-877-764-5570
Fax: (941) 309-1002
Web site: www.pmgnotes.com
e-mail: chawk@pmgnotes.com

Grading & Authentication of:
United States Large & Small Size Currency
Fractional Currency, National Bank Notes, Confederate Currency, Military Payment Certificates, World Paper Money and Uncut Sheets of Currency

Ronald F. Hedglin
Sailboat Coins & Currency
P.O. Box 580
Streator, IL 61364-0580
(815) 672-2548
Cellular: (815) 674-2506
Fax: (815) 672-2906 Attn: Ron
e-mail: hedglin@thegreves.com

United States National Currency

Edward W. Henley
Unlimited Currency
P.O. Box 514
Greenville, IN 47124
Toll Free: (888) 923-7743
Web site: www.unlimitedcurrency.net
e-mail:
unlimited_currency@yahoo.com

United States Small Size Type Notes
Third Party Graded High Quality Notes

Roland Hill
Rare Choice Currency
P.O. Box 3737
Fort Myers, FL 33918-3737
(239) 731-5885
e-mail: trots@mindspring.com

United States Large Size Type Notes
United States Small Size Type Notes
United States National Bank Notes
United States Fractional Currency
Obsolete Notes
Colonial and Continental
Confederate
Civil War Photos
Rare Autographs
Canadian
Western Americana
Early Railroad
Star Notes
F.R.N. Red Seals

Meredith J. Hilton
Kagin's, Inc.
1550 Tiburon Blvd., #G-201
Tiburon, CA 94920
(415) 435-2601
Toll Free: (888) 852-4467
Fax: (415) 435-2601
Web site: www.kagins.com
e-mail: mjhilton@kagins.com

United States Large Size Type Notes
United States Small Size Type Notes
United States National Bank Notes
United Stateds Fractional Currency
Colonial and Continental
Mormon Currency
Hawaiian Currency
Confederate

Gregg Hoffman
Premier Precious Metals Coins & Currency
P.O. Box 28100
Santa Fe, NM 87592-8100
(505) 989-7680
(800) 557-9958
Fax: (505) 989-7685
Web site: www.premierprecious metals.com
e-mail: gahoffman2004@yahoo.com

United States Large Size Type Notes
United States Small Size Type Notes
Silver Dollars
Bust Type Silver Dollars
Older Type Coin

Richard L. Horst
P.O. Box 49485
Colorado Springs, CO 80949-9485
(719) 593-0761
e-mail: arelaitcho9@yahoo.com

Obsolete Notes
Confederate
United States Large Size Type Notes
Western Checks and Drafts
World Paper Money
World and Ancient Coins

Honorary Life Member
Ronald Horstman
P.O. Box 2999
Leslie, MO 63056
(573) 764-4139

St. Louis National Bank Notes
St. Louis Obsolete Notes
St. Louis Checks
St. Louis Merchants and Bank Tokens

Lowell C. Horwedel
P.O. Box 2395
West Lafayette, IN 47996
(765) 583-2748
Fax: (765 583-4584
Web site: www.horwedelscurrency.com
e-mail: lhorwedel@comcast.net

United States National Bank Notes
Colonial and Continental
United States Large Size Type Notes
United States Small Size Type Notes
Confederate
Obsolete Notes
Error Notes
Checks
Books and Supplies
World Paper Money
Mail Order Price Lists

Steve Ivy
Heritage Auction Galleries
3500 Maple Avenue, 17th Floor
Dallas, TX 75219-3938
(214) 528-3500
(800) 872-6467
Web site: www.ha.com
e-mail: steve@ha.com

Auction Sales of:
United States Large Size Type Notes
United States Small Size Type Notes
United States National Bank Notes
United States Fractional Currency
Error Notes
Colonial and Continental
Confederate
Obsolete Notes

Dustin Johnston
Heritage Auction Galleries
3500 Maple Avenue, 17th Floor
Dallas, TX 75219
(214) 409-1302
Toll Free: (800) 872-6467
Web site: www.heritagecurrency.com
e-mail: dustin@ha.com

United States Large Size Type Notes
United States Small Size Type Notes
United States National Bank Notes
United States Fractional Currency
Colonial and Continental
Confederate Notes
Obsolete Notes

Harry E. Jones
Harry E. Jones Rare Currency
7379 Pearl Road
Cleveland, OH 44130
(440) 234-3330
Fax: (440) 234-3332
e-mail: hjones6671@aol.com
Cell: (440) 263-4544

Error Notes
United States Large Size Type Notes
United States Small Size Type Notes
United States National Bank Notes
Obsolete Notes
Serial #1 Notes
Uncut Sheets

Jeffrey S. Jones
The Small Size Shop
P.O. Box 2007
Westerville, OH 43086
(614) 899-1803
Fax: (614) 899-1557
e-mail: jonesjeffrey@aol.com

United States Small Size Type Notes
Especially High Grade and Rare
Ohio National Bank Notes
Ohio Obsolete Notes

Glen I. Jorde
Paper Money Guaranty
P.O. Box 4755
Sarasota, FL 34230
(941) 309-1001
Toll Free: (877) 764-5570
Fax: (941) 309-1002
Web site: www.pmgnotes.com
e-mail: gjorde@pmgnotes.com

United States Large Size Type Notes
United States Small Size Type Notes
United States National Bank Notes
Confederate
Obsolete Notes
Checks
Mail Order Price Lists

Donald H. Kagin
Kagin's, Inc.
1550 Tiburon
Tiburon, CA 94920
(415) 435-2601
Fax: (415) 435-1627
e-mail: info@kagins.com

Gem United States Type Notes
United States Fractional Currency

Judith Kagin
X-tremely Fine, Ltd.
P.O. Box 25117
West Des Moines, IA 50265
(515) 243-7363
e-mail: kagins70@aol.com

High Quality and Rare United States Paper Money
Mail Order Sales

Christine Karstedt
Stack's, LLC
P.O. Box 1804
Wolfeboro, NH 03894
(603) 569-0823
Toll Free: (866) 811-1804
Fax: (603) 569-3875
Web site: www.stacks.com
e-mail: chrisk@stacks.com

United States Large Size Type Notes
United States Small Size Type Notes
United States National Bank Notes
Auction Sales

Don C. Kelly
Paper Money Institute
P.O. Box 85
Oxford, OH 45056
(513) 312-4760
Web site: www.donckelly.com
e-mail: don@donckelly.com

United States Paper Money
Colonial and Continental
Obsolete Notes
United States National Bank Notes

Laura A. Kessler
PCGS Currency
P.O. Box 10470
Peoria, IL 61612
(309) 222-8200
Toll Free: (800) 691-PCGS (691-7247)
Fax: (949) 833-7955
Web site: www.pcgscurrrency.com
e-mail: lkessler@pcgscurrency.com

Grading & Authentication of: United States Large & Small Size Type Notes, Fractional Currency, National Bank Notes and Confederate, Obsolete and MPC

Don Ketterling
DH Ketterling Consulting
3835-R E. Thousand Oaks Blvd., #136
Westlake Village, CA 91362
(818) 632-2352
Fax: (805) 418-7455
Web site: www.dhkrcc,com
e-mail: dketterling@roadrunner.com

United States Large Size Type Notes
United State Small Size Type Notes
United States National Bank Notes
Obsolete Notes
General Paper Ephemera

Lyn F. Knight
Lyn Knight Currency Auctions
P.O. Box 7364
Overland Park, KS 66207-0364
(913) 338-3779
(800) 243-5211
Fax: (913) 338-4754
Web site: www.lynknight.com
e-mail: lyn@lynknight.com

Auction Sales for National Conventions
United States Large Size Type Notes
United States National Bank Notes
United States Small Size Type Notes
United States Fractional Currency
Mail Bid Sales

David R. Koble
Mid America Currency
P.O. Box 1282
Bartlesville, OK 74005
(918) 335-0847
Cellular: (918) 914-1496
Fax: (918) 335-3110
e-mail: dkoble@cableone.net

United States Large Size Type Notes
United States Small Size Type Notes
United States National Bank Notes
United States Fractional Currency
Error Notes
Auction Representation

Paul L. Koppenhaver
Thalpa, Inc. / The Coin Haven
P.O. Box 34056
Granada Hills, CA 91394
(818) 832-8068
Fax: (818) 832-8987
e-mail: plkopp@as.net

United States Large Size Type Notes
United States Small Size Type Notes
United States National Currency
Sutler Scrip
Western Americana
Autographs
Exonumia

Robert J. Kravitz
Rob's Coins & Currency
P.O. Box 6099
J Chesterfield, MO 63006
(314) 878-3564
e-mail: RobsFractional@gmail.com

Specialist: United States Fractional Currency
All United States Currency
United States Large and Small Size Gold Certificates
Error Notes
Colonial and Continental Currency

Tim Kyzivat
P.O. Box 451
Western Springs, IL 60558
(708) 784-0974
Web site: www.kyzivatcurrency.com
e-mail: tkyzivat@kyzivatcurrency.com

Chicago Area National Bank Notes
Illinois National Bank Notes
United States Large Size Type Notes
United States National Bank Notes
United States Small Size Type Notes
Confederate Currency
Obsolete Notes
Error Notes

George H. LaBarre
George H. LaBarre Galleries, Inc.
P.O. Box 746
Hollis, NH 03049
(603) 882-2411
Toll Free: (800) 717-9529
Fax: (603) 882-4797
Web site: www.glabarre.com
e-mail: collect@glabarre.com

Obsolete Notes
Colonial and Continental
Military Payment Certificates
Error Notes
Confederate
World Paper Money
Autographs
General Americana

Dr. Frank G. Laiacona
P.O. Box 1512
Mt. Shasta, CA 96067
(530) 859-2814
Fax: (530) 926-9306
Web site: www.franksdollars.com
Web site: www.peacedollars.net
e-mail: cyncadom@juno.com

United States Large Size Type Notes
Series odf 1928 Small Size Notes
Peace Type Silver Dollars

Jay Laws
Scotsman Coins
11262 Olive Blvd.
St. Louis, MO 63141
(314) 692-2646
Fax: (314) 692-0410
e-mail: JLaws@scoins.com
Cell: (314) 210-4443

United States National Bank Notes
United States Large Size Type Notes
United States Small Size Type Notes
Confederate Currency
Military Payment Certificates

David Leong
Paper M, LLC
P.O. Box 1388
Seabrook, NH 03874
(216) 338-7723
Web site: www.paperm.com
e-mail: david@paperm.com

World Paper Money

Stuart Levine
P.O. Box 806
Marblehead, MA 01945
(781) 447-0552
Fax: (781) 477-0827
e-mail: stuartlevine@comcast.net

Colonial and Continental Currency

Scott Lindquist
P.O. Box 2175
Minot, ND 58702
Cellular: (602) 741-3385
e-mail: slindquist1963@gmail.com

United States and Canadian Currency - Large and Small
Canadian Charter Bank Notes
World Paper Money
Colonial and Continental
United States Fractional Currency
Confederate
Obsolete Notes
United States National Bank Notes
Error Notes
Books and Supplies
Military Payment Certificates
Auction Sales - Bidder Representative

Dana Linett
Early American Numismatics
P.O. Box 675390
Rancho Santa Fe, CA 92067
Early American History Auctions, Inc.
P.O. Box 3507
Rancho Santa Fe, CA 92067
(858) 759-3290
Fax: (858) 759-1439
Web site: www.earlyamerican.com
e-mail: dana@earlyamerican.com

Colonial and Continental
United States Fractional Currency
United States Large Size Type Notes
United States Small Size Type Notes
Confederate
Stocks, Bonds and fiscal Documents
Checks
Books and Supplies
Auction Sales
Mail Order Price Lists
Mail Bid Sales
Encased Postage Stamps
Historic Maps
Rare Autographs

Jess Lipka
Numismania
P.O. Box 847
Flemington, NJ 08822
(908) 782-1635
Cellular: (908) 500-1885
Fax: (908) 782-6235
e-mail: jesslipka@hotmail.com

United States National Bank Notes
United States Large Size Type Notes
United States Small Size Type Notes
Rare Coins

William Litt
William Litt Rare Coins & Currency
P.O. Box 221148
Carmel, CA 93922
(650) 430-2024
Fax: (650) 839-1038
Web site: www.williamlittcurrency.com
e-mail: billlitt@aol.com

United States National Bank Notes
United States Large Size Type Notes
National Bank Memorabilia

Claire Lobel
Coincraft
44 & 45 Great Russell Street
London WC1B 3LU
ENGLAND
(44) 20 7636 1188
Fax: (44) 20 7323 2860
e-mail: clairlob@aol.com

England, Scotland, Ireland, Channel Islands, Isle of Man
General World

John Markis
Trusted Traditions
275 Commercial Blvd, Suite 275
Lauderdale-by-the-sea, FL 33308
(954) 938-9700
Fax: (954) 938-9876
Web site: www.trustedtraditions.com
e-mail: sales@trustedtraditions.com

Certified Paper Money

Ray Marrello
Antique Currency LLC
10170 W. Tropicana Ave.
Suite 156-386
Las Vegas, NV 89147
(702) 202-0140
Toll Free: (877) 396-5322
Web site: www.rmcurrency.com
e-mail: rmcurrency@aol.com

United States Large Size Type Notes
United States Small Size Type Notes
United States National Bank Notes

David V. Messner
Constellation Numismatics
P.O. Box 209
Akron, PA 17501-0209
(717) 721-9504
Web site: www.errorcurrency.com

Error Notes
Colonial and Continental
United States Error and Die Variety Coins

James W. Miller
Miller's Coins & Currency, LLC
1218 East Hwy 80, Suite 700
P.O. Box 2452
Pooler, GA 31322
(912) 330-9919
Cellular: (912) 536-6222
Fax: (912) 536-6222
e-mail: jwmiller11@aol.com

Obsolete Notes
Confederate
Colonial and Continental
United States National Currency
United States Large Size Type Notes
United States Small Size Type Notes

Internet Auction Sales
Auction Bidder Representation

Michael G. Moczalla
Heritage Auction Galleries
3500 Maple Avenue, 17th Floor
Dallas, TX 75219
(214) 409-1481
Toll Free: (800) 872-6467
Web site: www.ha.com
e-mail: michealm@ha.com

United States Large Size Type Notes
United States Small Size Type Notes
United States National Bank Notes
United States Fractional Currency
Colonial and Continental
Confederate Notes
Obsolete Notes

Charles D. Moore
Charles D. Moore, Inc.
P.O. Box 5233
Walnut Creek, CA 94596
(925) 946-0150
Fax: (925) 930-7710

Auction Sales
Mail Bid Sales
Canadian and Related Paper Money
Canadian Cheques
Canadian Fiscal Documents

Richard Nachbar
Richard Nachbar Rare Coins
5820 Main Street, Suite 601
Williamsville, NY 14221
(716) 635-9700
Toll Free: (877) 622-4227
Fax: (716) 635-9762
Web site: www.coinexpert.com
e-mail: nachbar@coinexpert.com

United States Large Size Type Notes
United States National Bank Notes
United States Small Size Type Notes
United States Rare Coins

V.H. "Ossie" Oswald, Sr.
Ossie's Coin Shop
June to December
4560 Hamilton Blvd.
Allentown, PA 18103
(610) 965-9485
(610) 530-1588
Fax: (610) 965-9485
January 1 to May 31st
P.O. Box 810423
Boca Raton, FL 33497
(561) 483-9626
Fax: (561) 483-9626

United States Large Size Type Notes
United States Small Size Type Notes
United States National Bank Notes
Error Notes
Confederate
Better Broken Bank Notes
Mail Order Price Lists
Please Send Want Lists

John Pack
Stack's, LLC
P.O. Box 1804
Wolfeboro, NH 03894
(603) 569-0823
Toll Free: (866) 811-1804
Fax: (603) 569-3875
Web site: www.stacks.com
e-mail: melissak@stacks.com

Auction Consultation for All Types of Paper Money

Thomas N. Panichella
T&J Collectibles
P.O. Box 37
Colonia, NJ 07067
(732) 754-9671

Auction Sales
Appraisals
United States Currency of All Types
United States Coins of All Type
World Coins and Paper Money

Gary Parietti
L.I. Numismatics
P.O. Box 42
Bedford Hills, NY 10507-0042
(914) 242-6090
Fax: (914) 242-6091
Web site: www.linumis.com
e-mail: garyparietti@aol.com

United States National Bank Notes
Rare Coins
Autographs

Charles C. Parrish
P.O. Box 481
Rosemount. MN 55068
(651) 423-1039
e-mail: chuckparrish@frontiernet.net

United States Large Size Type Notes
United States Small Size Type Notes
United States National Bank Notes
Obsolete Notes
All Minnesota Nationals

Huston Pearson, Jr.
P.O. Box 1398
Ennis, TX 75120-1398
(817) 999-4713

United States Large Size Type Notes
United States Small Size Type Notes
Republic of Texas Notes
Texas National Bank Notes
United States Fractional Currency
Colonial and Continental Currency
Confederate
Military Payment Certificates
Obsolete Notes
Books and Supplies

Alex G. Perakis
Alex Perakis Coins & Currency
P.O. Box 246
Lima, PA 19037
(610) 627-1212
(610) 565-1110
Fax: (610) 891-1466
and
12941 North Pioneer Way
Tucson, AZ 85755
(520) 544-7778
Fax: (520) 544-7779
e-mail: aperakis@dakotacom.net
e-mail: apccl@msn.com
Web site: www.perakiscurrency.com

United States Fractional Currency
United States Large Size Type Notes
United States Small Size Type Notes
United States National Bank Notes
United States Obsolete Notes

Stephen Perakis
Alex Perakis Coins & Currency
P.O. Box 246
Lima, PA 19037
(610) 627-1212
(610) 565-1110
Fax: (610) 891-1466
e-mail: apcc1@msn.com
Web site: www.perakiscurrency.com

United States Fractional Currency
United States Large Size Type Notes
United States Small Size Type Notes
United States National Bank Notes

James Polis
4501 Connecticut Avenue, N.W.
Suite 306
Washington, DC 20008
(202) 363-6650
Fax: (202) 363-4712
e-mail: jpolis7935@aol.com

Colonial and Continental
United States Fractional Currency
United States Large Size Type Notes
United States Small Size Type Notes
Confederate and Southern States Currency
Confederate Bonds
Mail Order Price List

Richard H. Ponterio
Ponterio & Associates, Inc.
18061 Fitch Avenue
Irvine, CA 92614
(949) 253-0916
(800) 458-4646
Fax: (949) 253-4091

World Paper Money
Mexican Paper Money
Auction Sales
Mail Bid Sales

Vern Potter
Vern Potter Rare Fiscal Documents
P.O. Box 10040
Torrance, CA 90505-0740
(310) 326-0406
Fax: (310) 326-0406
Web site: www.vernpotter.com
e-mail: vern@vernpotter.com

United States Large Size Type Notes
Obsoletes Notes
Confederate Currency
Gold Rush and Civil War Documents
Historic Maps
Western Americana and Paper Ephemera
Stocks, Bonds, Checks and Fiscal Documents
Western Express and Postal History
Mining and Railroad Certificates and Documents

Matthew W. Quinn
Spectrum Currency
P.O. Box 18523
Irvine, CA 92623
(949) 955-1250
Web site: www.spectrumcurrency.com
e-mail: mattq@coins.com

United States Large Size Type Notes
United States Small Size Type Notes
World Paper Money

Lou Rasera
Southland Coins & Currency
P.O. Box 403
Woodland Hills, CA 91365
(818) 348-5275
Fax: (818) 348-5275
e-mail: ljrasera@aol.com
United States Large Size Type Notes
United States Small Size Type Notes
United States National Bank Notes
Confederate
Error Notes
Professional Auction Representation

Kent Robertson
U.S. Currency
P.O. Box 779
Charlestown, RI 02813
(404) 229-7184
e-mail: usckr26@yahoo.com

United States Large Size Type Notes
United States Small Size Type Notes
Obsolete Notes
Confederate Notes
Confederate Bonds
Political Memorabilia
Auction Representation

Edward M. Rothberg
Emporium Coin & Currency
P.O. Box 606
Moorhead, MN 56561
(800) 248-9751 or (800) 342-1994

United States National Bank Notes
United States Fractional Currency
Colonial and Continental
Errors
Obsoletes Notes
Canadian Currency
United States Coins

John N. Rowe III
Southwest Numismatic Corp.
6116 N. Central Expy., Suite 921
Dallas, TX 75206
(214) 826-3036
Fax: (214) 823-1923

United States Large Size Type Notes
United States Small Size Type Notes
Confederate
Obsolete Notes
United States National Bank Notes
Republic of Texas

O. E. "Dusty" Royer
Notes of Note
34 Lake Charles
St. Peters, MO 63376
(636) 922-4058 or (636) 441-0481
e-mail: dustyIB@netscape.net
World Currency
German Notgeld
Military Items

Gaylen Rust
Rust Rare Coin Co.
252 East 300 South
Salt Lake City, UT 84111
(801) 363-4014
(800) 343-7878
Fax: (801) 364-0929
Web site: www.rustcoin.com
e-mail: grust@rustcoin.com

Mormon and Related Items
Utah and Intermountain Area Notes

Sergio Sanchez, Jr.
Sergio Sanchez, Jr. Currency
P.O. Box 44-2809
Miami, FL 33144-2809
(305) 567-1515
Fax: (305) 567-1898
Web site: www.sanchezcurrency.com
e-mail: sergio@sanchezcurrency
.com

United States Large Size Type Notes
United States Small Size Type
Notes

Joe Sande
Joe Sande - Professional
Numismatist
P.O. Box 318
Nichols, FL 33863-0318
(863) 607-6337
Fax: (863) 607-6337

United States Large Size Type Notes
United States Small Size Type Notes
United States National Bank Notes
United States Fractional Currency
Mail Bid Sales

Jim Sazama
Jim Sazama, Inc.
P.O. Box 1235
Southern Pines, NC 28388
(910) 692-9357
Fax: (910) 692-9357
e-mail: csazama@nc.rr.com

United States Large Size Type Notes
United States Small Size Type Notes
United States National Bank Notes
Obsolete Notes
Confederate

Paul James Schupp
(Associate Member)
Legal Tender Currency
602 Menominee Drive
Lake in the Hills, IL 60156
(847) 946-1982
e-mail: schuppa@comcast.net

Currency for the Mid-Range Collector

George Schweighofer
Currency Quest
P.O. Box 384
Reynoldsberg, OH 43068
(614) 864-8875
Web site: currencyquest.com
e-mail: currencyquest@aol.com

e-mail (2): george@currencyquest
.com

All United States Currency

David E. Seelye
thempcman.net
P.O. Box 356
North Chili, NY 14514-0356
(716) 630-0481
e-mail: thempcman@verizon.net

Military Payment Certificates
Allied Military Currency

Donald Severance
Spectrum Currency North East
P.O. Box 140
Pembroke, NH 03275
(603) 485-2605
Web site: www.spectrumcurrency
.com
e-mail: dons@spectrumcurrency.com

United States Large Size Type Notes
United States Small Size Type Notes
United States Fractional Currency
New England National Bank Notes
Obsolete Notes

Joel Shafer
P.O. Box 170985
Milwaukee, WI 53217
(414) 350-6980
e-mail: grbaypa@aol.com

World Paper Money

Amanda Sheheen
A & O Auctions
P.O. Box 1711
Camden, SC 29020
(803) 432-2435
Web site: www.AOcurrency.com
e-mail: nooniebubba@truvista.net

Confederate Notes
Obsolete Notes and Scrip
South Carolina National Bank
Notes
Colonial and Continentals Notes
United States Fractional Currency
Military Payment Certificates
Books and Supplies
Auction Representative

Austin M. Sheheen, Jr.
P.O. Box 428
Camden, SC 29020
(803) 432-1424
Fax: (803) 432-1831
e-mail: ams@shgcpa.com

South Carolina Colonial Notes
South Carolina Obsolete Notes
South Carolina National Bank Notes
Eastman College Scrip

Micky Shipley
Micky's Currency
P.O. Box 114
Devils Lake, ND 58301
(701) 203-0036
e-mail: micky@qndtc.com

United States National Bank Notes
United States Large Size Type Notes
United States Small Size Type Notes

Randy Shipley
Shipley's Currency
709 Jim Town Road
Mooresburg, TN 37811
(423) 335-6811
Fax: (423) 921-0586
Web site: www.shipleyscurrency.com
e-mail: randy@shipleyscurrency.com

Confederate Notes
Southern States Currency
Obsolete Notes and Scrip
Confederate Fiscal Documents

Hugh Shull
P.O. Box 2522
Lexington, SC 29071
(803) 996-3660
Fax: (803) 996-4885

Confederate Notes
Obsolete Notes and Scrip
South Carolina National Bank Notes
Colonial and Continentals Notes
United States Fractional Currency
Stocks, Bonds and Fiscal Documents
Mail Order Catalogs
Books and Supplies
Auction Sales - Bidder Representative

James A. Simek
Numisgraphic Enterprises
P.O. Box 7157
Westchester, IL 60154
(630) 889-8207
e-mail: nge3@comcast.net

United States Large Size Type
Notes
United States Small Size Type
Notes
United States National Bank Notes
Error Notes
Hawaiian Related Material
Autographs and Documents
Numismatic Photography

James Sorn
Family Coins, Ltd.
P.O. Box 606
Oak Lawn, IL 60454
e-mail: jsorn@comcast.net

United States Large Size Type Notes
United States Small Size Type Notes
United States National Bank Notes
Colonial and Continental
Confederate
Obsolete Notes

David Steckling
Gold-N-Silver Rarities
1615 First Street South
St. Cloud, MN 56301
(302) 259-0233

Minnesota National Bank Notes
Minnesota Obsolete Notes
Obsolete Notes
United States Large Size Type Notes
United States Small Size Type Notes

Richard Stelzer
Paper Money Guaranty
5501 Communications Parkway
Sarasota, FL 34240
(605) 321-1449
Web site: www.pmgnotes.com
e-mail: rstelzer@pmgnotes.com

Grading & Authentication of:
United States Large & Small Currency, Fractional Currency, National Bank Notes, Confererate Currency, Miitary Payment Certificates, World Paper Money and Uncut Sheets of Currency

Mike Storeim
3092 Evergreen Parkway, Suite 201
Evergreen, CO 80439
(303) 670-3212
Cellular: (303) 903-9932
Fax: (303) 670-3216
e-mail: mike@numispro.com

United States Large Size Type Notes
United States Small Size Type Notes
United States National Bank Notes

David M. Sundman
Litttleton Coin Company, LLC
1309 Mt. Eustis Road
Littleton, NH 03561-3735
(603) 444-5386
Fax: (603) 444-3512
Web site: www.littletoncoin.com

United States Large Size Type Notes
United States Small Size Type Notes
United States National Bank Notes
United States Fractional Currency
United States Coins
Fixed Price Lists and Catalogs

Anthony J. Swiatek
Minerva Coins & Jewelry, Ltd.
P.O. Box 218
Manhasset, NY 11030
(516) 365-4120
Fax: (516) 365-4120
and
P.O. Box 684
Saratoga Springs, NY 12866
(518) 587-9451
Cell: (516) 375-3560
Web site: www.anthonyjswiatek.com
e-mail: uscoinguru@aol.com

United States Currency
United States Commemorative Coins
United States Gold & Silver Coinage

Allan L. Teal
P.O. Box 429
Chester Heights, PA 19017
(610) 459-5265
Fax: (610) 459-8821
Sunday at Store 7:30 AM - 4 PM

Anthony Terranova
Anthony Terranova, Inc.
P.O. Box 985, FDR Station
New York, NY 10150
(212) 787-5682
Fax: (212) 787-9323

Early American Paper Money
Colonial and State Coinage Issues
Early U.S. Mint Issues of Rare Gold
Historical American Medals
Services to the trade only

Greg Ton
P.O. Box 2861
Oxford, MS 38655
(901) 487-5944
e-mail: gton@aol.com
Web site: www.gregtoncurrency.com

Confederate Notes
Obsolete Notes and Scrip

Peter A. Treglia
Spectrum Currency
P.O. Box 18523
Irvine, CA 92623
(949) 955-1250
Fax: (949) 955-1824
Cellular: (617) 462-7267
Web site: www. spectrumcurrency.com
Email: petert@spectrum currency.com

United States Large Size Type Notes
United States Small Size Type Notes
Error Notes
Fancy Serial Numbers
United States National Bank Notes

Robert L. Vandevender II
American Paper Connection, Inc.
P.O. Box 1505
Jupiter, FL 33468
(815) 355-0233
Web site: www.americanpaper connection.com
e-mail: rvpaperman@aol.com

United States Large Size Type Notes
United States Small Size Type Notes
United States Fractional Currency
United States National Bank Notes

George K. Warner
P.O. Box 842
Sheridan, WY 82801
(307) 751-3230

United States Small Size Type Notes
Military Payment Certificates
United States Fractional Currency

Harry Warren
Mid-South Coin Co., Inc.
3894 Park Avenue
Memphis, TN 38111
(901) 324-2244
Fax: (901) 324-2249
Cell: (901) 494-2244
e-mail: midsouthcoin@aol.com

United States Large Size Type Notes
United States National Bank Notes

David Westerman
Bonita Rare Coins & Currency
P.O. Box 605
Lehigh Acres, FL 33970
(239) 369-2905
e-mail: mpdcoin@aol.com

United States Large Size Type Notes
United States Small Size Type Notes
Star Notes
United States National Bank Notes
United States Fractional Currency

Michael J. Westerman
Bonita Rare Coins & Currency
P.O. Box 605
Lehigh Acres, FL 33970
(239) 369-2905
e-mail: mpdcoin@aol.com

United States Large Size Type Notes
United States Small Size Type Notes
Star Notes
United States National Bank Notes
United States Fractional Currency

Barry Wexler
Numisvalu
P.O. Box 185
Jamison, NY 18929
(215) 444-0550
e-mail: nimisval@verizon.net

United States Large Size Type Notes
United States Small Size Type Notes
United States National Bank Notes
Colonial
Confederate
Obsolete Notes
Stocks, Bonds and fiscal Documents
Checks

Gene Wheeler
Gene Wheeler Rare Coins & Currency
P.O. Box 747
Seymour, TX 76380
(940) 888-3832
Fax: (940) 888-3807
Web site: www.gwcoins.com
e-mail: gwcoins@classicnet.net

All United States Notes

Louis Whitaker
River Hollow Coins
6700 Woodland Pkwy., Suite 230 #311
The Woodlands, TX 77382
(281) 516-1685
Web site: www.houstoncoins.com
e-mail: rhcoins@earthlink.net

All United States Notes

Harlan White
2425 El Cajon Blvd.
San Diego, CA 92104
(619) 298-0137
Fax: (619) 298-7966

United States High Denomination Notes
United States Paper Money

Gary Whitelock
Whitelock Rare Currency
P.O. Box 370392
Reseda, CA 91337-0392
(818) 739-9485

Cellular: (562) 673-0794
e-mail: whiteloc@ktb.net

All United States Notes

William Crutchfield Williams II
Crutchfield's Currency
P.O. Box 3221
Quinlan, TX 75474
(903) 560-0458
Web site: www.crutchwilliams.com
Web site: www.csatrainmen.com
e-mail: crutchtmoi@hughes.net

Republic of Texas
Confederate States of America
Southern States Currency
Mexican Bancos & Revolutionary Paper Money

Scott Winslow
P.O. Box 10240
Bedford, NH 03110
(603) 641-8292
(800) 225-6233
Fax: (603) 641-5583
Web site: www.scottwinslow.com

Autographs
Stock, Bonds and Fiscal Documents

John Yasuk
Florida Calls
Caribbean Sun Gold
JSG Boggs Market Place
P.O. Box 571084
Miami, FL 33257-1084
(305) 256-7201
Web site: www.floridacalls.com
Web site:
www.jsgboggsmarketplace.com
e-mail: john@floridacalls.com

Florida Obsolete Currency
Florida State Notes
Artist JSG Boggs Material
United States Large Size Type Notes
United States Small Size Type Notes
United States Small Size Packs
United States Small Size Star Notes
Radars, Repeaters, and Fancy Serial Numbers
Military Payment Certificates
World Paper Money

William Youngerman
William Youngerman, Inc.
Bank of America Bldg.
150 E. Palmetto Park Rd. #101
Boca Raton, FL 33432
(561) 368- 7707
(800) 327-5010 (Outside Florida)
(800) 826-9713 (Within Florida)
Fax: (561) 394-6084
Web site: www.williamyoungerman.com
e-mail: bill@youngermans.com

Specialist: United States National Bank Notes
Florida National Bank Notes
Florida Obsolete Notes
United States Large Size Type Notes
United States Small Size Type Notes
United States Fractional Currency
Confederate
Mail Order Price Lists

BUYING PAPER MONEY

Browsing in coin shops is the usual way in which beginners start buying paper money. Just about every coin dealer—and many stamp dealers—stock paper money to one degree or another, from a single display album with elementary material to vaults filled with literally millions of dollars worth of specimens. Be observant of condition when shopping from dealers' stocks. Get to know the dealer and become familiar with his grading practices. Some dealers will grade a specimen higher than another dealer, but this may be offset by the fact that they charge a lower price.

Bargains. Is it possible to get bargains in buying paper money? To the extent that prices vary somewhat from dealer to dealer, yes. But if you're talking about finding a note worth $100 selling at $50, this is unlikely to happen. The dealers are well aware of market values, and the slight price differences that do occur are merely the result of some dealers being overstocked on certain notes or, possibly, having made a very good "buy" from the public. What may appear to be a bargain will generally prove, on closer examination, to be a specimen in undesirable condition, such as a washed bill on which the color has faded.

Auction sales. Many coin auctions feature selections of paper money, and there are occasional sales (mostly of the postal-bid variety) devoted exclusively to it. There is much to be said for auction buying if you have some experience and know how to read an auction catalog.

Shows and conventions. Paper money is offered for sale at every coin show and exposition. These present excellent opportunities to buy, as the dealers exhibiting at such shows are generally out-of-towners whose stock you would not otherwise have a chance to examine. As many sellers are likely to be offering the same type of material, you have the opportunity to make price and condition comparisons before buying.

COLLECTING DO'S AND DON'TS

Paper money is not at all difficult to care for, store, and display attractively.

There is not much question that albums are the favorite storage method of nearly all paper money enthusiasts. Many ills to which paper money falls prey result from not being housed in a suitable album, or any album at all. Framing and mounting present some risk, as the item may then be exposed to long periods of direct sunlight, almost sure to cause fading or "bleaching" of its color.

Faded color. There is no known restorative for faded color.

Holes. It is suggested that no effort be undertaken to repair holes, as this will almost certainly result in a further reduction in value.

Missing corners. Missing corners can seldom be restored in a manner that is totally satisfactory. The best that can be done is to secure some paper of approximately the same color and texture, trim a small piece to the proper size, and glue it in place as described below. If a portion of printed matter is missing, this can be hand-drawn, in ink, after restoration. Obviously, this kind of repair is not carried out to "fool" anybody, but simply to give a damaged specimen a less objectionable appearance.

Repairs to paper money. Repair work on damaged or defaced paper money is carried out strictly for cosmetic purposes; to improve its physical appearance. Repairs, even if skillfully executed, will not enhance the value of a specimen, as it will still be classified as defective. Amateurish repair efforts can very possibly make matters worse.

Tears. Tears can be closed by brushing a very small quantity of clear-drying glue to both sides of the tear, placing the note between sheets of waxed kitchen paper, and setting it under a weight to dry. A dictionary of moderate size serves this function well. Allow plenty of drying time and handle gently thereafter.

Wrinkles. Wrinkles, creases, and the like can sometimes be improved by wetting the note (in plain water) and drying it between sheets of waxed paper beneath a reasonably heavy weight—five pounds or more. This should not be done with a modern or recent specimen if there is danger of losing crispness.

SELLING YOUR COLLECTION

Selling to a dealer. All dealers in paper money buy from the public, but not all buy every collection offered to them. Some are specialists and are interested only in collections within their fields of specialization. Some will not purchase (or even examine) collections worth under $100, or $500, or whatever their line of demarcation happens to be. Obviously, a valuable collection containing many hard-to-get notes in VF or UNC condition is easier to interest a dealer in than a beginner-type collection. If a dealer is interested enough to make an offer, this is no guarantee that another dealer would not offer more. In the case of a collection worth $50,000, offers from several dealers might vary by as much as $5,000. This is not an indication that the dealer making the lowest offer is unscrupulous. Dealers will pay as much as the material is worth to them, and one dealer may be overstocked on items that another badly needs. Or one dealer may have customers for certain material that another doesn't. For this reason it makes good sense, if you choose to sell to a dealer, to obtain several offers before accepting any. But should you sell to a dealer at all? The chief advantage is quick payment and reduced risk. The price may not be as high as would be obtained at auction, however, depending on the property's nature and pure luck.

Selling by auction. Auction selling presents uncertainties but at the same time offers the possibility of gaining a much better return than could be had by selling to a dealer. It is no easy matter deciding which route to follow. If your collection is better than average, you may be better advised to sell by auction. This will involve a waiting period of, generally, four to six months between consigning the collection and receiving settlement; over the summer months it may be longer. However, some auctioneers will give a cash advance, usually about 25 percent of the sum they believe the material is worth. In special circumstances a larger advance may be made, or the usual terms and conditions altered. One auctioneer paid $100,000 under a special contract, stipulating that the money was not to be returned regardless of the sale's outcome or even if no sale took place. But this was on a million-dollar collection. Auctioneers' commissions vary. The normal is 20 percent, but some houses take 10 percent from the buyer and 10 percent from the seller. This would appear to work to the seller's advantage, but such a practice may discourage bidding and result in lower sales prices.

Selling to other collectors. Unless the owner is personally acquainted with a large circle of collectors, this will likely involve running ads in periodicals and "playing dealer," which runs into some expense. Unless you offer material at very favorable prices, you are not apt to be as successful with your ads as are the established dealers, who have a reputation and an established clientele.

GLOSSARY

BROKEN BANK NOTE (a.k.a. obsolete note)

Literally, a Broken Bank Note is a note issued by a "broken" bank—a bank that failed and whose obligations could therefore not be redeemed. It may be presumed, by those who recall passing of legislation establishing the Federal Deposit Insurance Corporation, that banks failed only in the financial panic of 1929. During the 19th century, bank failures were common, especially in western and southwestern states. These were generally small organizations set up in frontier towns which suffered either from mismanagement or a sudden decline in the town's fortunes. Some collectors make a specialty of Broken Bank Notes.

DEMAND NOTES

Demand Notes have the distinction of being the first official circulating paper currency of this country, issued in 1861. There are three denominations: $5, $10, and $20, each bearing its own design on front and back. Demand Notes arose out of the coinage shortage brought about by the Civil War. A total of $60,000,000 in Demand Notes was authorized to be printed, amounting to several million individual specimens. Though this was an extraordinary number for the time, it was small compared to modern output, and only a fraction of the total survived. These notes were signed not by any specially designated Treasury Department officers, but a battery of employees, each of whom was given authority to sign and affix his name by hand in a slow assembly-line process, two signatures to each note. Originally the spaces left blank for signatures were marked "Register of the Treasury" and "Treasurer of the United States." As the persons actually signing occupied neither of these offices, they were obliged to perpetually add "for the . . ." to their signatures. In an effort to relieve their tedium, fresh plates were prepared reading "For the Register of the Treasury" and "For the Treasurer of the United States," which required nothing but a signature. This created a rarity status for the earlier specimens, which are now very desirable collectors' items.

ENGRAVING

Engraving is the process by which designs are printed on U.S. paper money. Bank note engraving involves the use of a metal plate, traditionally steel, into which the design is cut with sharp instruments called "burins" or "gravers." Ink is smeared over the surface and allowed to work into the grooves or lines comprising the design. The ink is then cleaned away from raised portions (intended to show blank in the printing). The engraving is pressed against a sheet of moistened paper, and the ink left in these grooves transfers to the paper, resulting in a printed image. When done by modern rotary press, it's a fast-moving process.

FEDERAL RESERVE BANK NOTES

Federal Reserve Bank Notes were issued briefly in 1915 and 1918. Like National Bank Notes, they were secured by bonds or securities placed on deposit by each Federal Reserve Bank with the U.S. government. While issued and redeemable by the member banks of the Federal Reserve system, these notes are secured by—and are obligations of—the government.

FEDERAL RESERVE NOTES

Federal Reserve Notes, the notes in current circulation, were authorized by the Federal Reserve Act of December 23, 1913. Issued under control of the Federal Reserve Board, these notes are released through twelve Federal Reserve Banks in various parts of the country. Originally they were redeemable in gold at the U.S. Treasury or "lawful money" (coins) at a Federal Reserve Bank. In 1934 the option of redemption for gold was removed.

FREAK AND ERROR NOTES

These are bills which, by virtue of error or accident, are in some respect different from normal specimens. See the chapter on Error or Freak Notes.

GOLD CERTIFICATES

When gold coinage became a significant medium of exchange, the government decided to hold aside quantities of it and issue paper notes redeemable by the Treasury Department. The first Gold Certificates for public circulation were released in 1882. The series lasted until the era of small-size currency, ending in 1928. In 1933 all were ordered returned to the Treasury Department for redemption, including those in possession of collectors. A new law in 1964 permitted their ownership by collectors, though they can no longer be redeemed for gold.

LARGE SIZE CURRENCY

Large Size currency is the term generally used to refer to U.S. notes issued up to 1929, which were somewhat larger in size than those printed subsequently. The increased size permitted more elaborate design, which seldom fails to endear Large Size currency to beginners. Some of the earlier examples (especially of the 1870s, 1880s, and 1890s) are works of art. Though economic considerations were mainly responsible for the switch to a reduced size, there is no doubt that today's notes are far more convenient to handle and carry. Large Size notes are sometimes referred to as "bedsheet notes."

NATIONAL BANK NOTES

This is the largest group of notes available to the collector. They were issued from 1863 to 1929 and present collecting potential that can only be termed vast. More than 14,000 banks issued notes, in all parts of the country. While the approach to collecting them is usually regional, sets and series can also be built up, virtually without end. The National Banking Act was instituted in 1863, during the Civil War, to permit chartered banks to issue and circulate their own currency. Printing was done at the U.S. Government Printing Office and the designs were all alike, differing only in names of the banks, state seals, bank signatures, and the bank's charter number. Each charter bank was limited to issuing currency up to 90 percent of the value of bonds that it kept on deposit with the government. Charters remained in force for twenty years and could be renewed for an additional twenty years. National Bank Notes circulated in the same fashion as conventional currency and, thanks to the bond-deposit system, gained public confidence. The financial panic of 1929, which brought ruin or near-ruin to many banks, put an end to National Bank Notes.

NATIONAL GOLD BANK NOTES

These notes were issued exclusively by California banks during the 1870s under the same terms as ordinary National Bank Notes, their values backed by bonds deposited with the government. Events surrounding their origins form a unique chapter in the history of American economy. Following the discoveries of substantial quantities of gold in California in the late 1840s, that metal soon became the chief medium of local exchange, largely because it was more readily available in that remote region than coinage. Later, when gold coins and tokens began to circulate heavily in California, banks became so swamped with them that they petitioned Washington for authority to issue Gold Notes that could be substituted for the actual coinage. On July 12, 1870, Congress voted favorably on this measure, giving the right to issue such notes to nine banks in California and one in Boston. The Boston bank, Kidder National Gold Bank, appears not to have exercised its right, as no Gold Notes of this institution have been recorded.

The California banks wasted no time in exercising their authority, the result being a series of notes ranging from $5–$500. All were printed on yellow-toned paper so as to be instantly identifiable. The banks issuing these notes were permitted to redeem them in gold coins.

REFUNDING CERTIFICATES

Refunding Certificates, a sort of hybrid between currency and bonds or securities, were issued under a Congressional Act of February 26, 1879. These were notes with a $10 face value which could be spent and exchanged in the fashion of ordinary money but drew interest at the rate of 4 percent per year. The purposes behind Refunding Certificates were several. They were chiefly designed to encourage saving and thereby curb inflation, which even at that time was becoming a problem. Also, they provided a safe means of saving for persons who distrusted banks (safe so long as the certificates were not lost or stolen), and, probably more important, were readily obtainable in areas of the country not well served by banks. In 1907 the interest was halted. Their redemption value today, with interest, is $21.30.

SERIAL NUMBER

The serial number is the control number placed on all U.S. paper bills, appearing below left-center and above right-center. No two bills in the same series bear repetitive serial numbers. The use of serial numbers is not only an aid in counting and sorting bills as printed, but a deterrent to counterfeiting.

SIGNATURES

The inclusion of signatures of Treasury Department officials on our paper bills, a practice as old as our currency (1861), began as a mark of authorization and as a foil to counterfeiters. The belief was that the handwriting would be more difficult to copy than an engraved design. Persons whose signatures appear on notes did not always occupy the same office. From 1862 to 1923, the two signers were the Treasurer and the Register (or Registrar as it appears in old writings) of the Treasury. Subsequently, the Treasurer and the Secretary of the Treasury were represented. These signatures are of great importance to collectors, as some notes are relatively common with certain combinations of signa-tures and others are rare. A "series" collection is not considered complete until one obtains every existingcombination, even though the specimens may be in other respects identical.

SILVER CERTIFICATES

Silver Certificates were authorized in 1878. America's economy was booming at that time, and the demand for silver coinage in day-to-day business transactions outdistanced the supply. Silver Certificates were not intended to replace coinage but to create a convenient medium of exchange, whereby the government held specific quantities of Silver Dollars (later bullion) and agreed to redeem the notes or certificates against them. In 1934 the Treasury Department ceased redemption of these notes in Silver Dollars, and on June 24, 1968, redemption in all forms was ended. The notes are still, however, legal tender at their face value. When printing of Silver Certificates was discontinued, a flurry of speculation arose and many persons began hoarding them. This was done not only in hope of eventual redemption for bullion but in the belief that such notes would become valuable to collectors. Though Silver Certificates are popular with hobbyists, they have not increased sufficiently in price to yield speculators any great profits—especially since many collectors saved specimens in circulated condition.

STAR NOTES

United States Notes, Silver Certificates, and Gold Certificates sometimes have a star or asterisk in place of the letter in front of the serial number. Federal Reserve Notes and Federal Reserve Bank Notes have it at the end of the serial number. These notes are known as "Star Notes."

When a note is mutilated or otherwise unfit for issue, it must be replaced. To replace it with a note of the same serial numbers would be impractical, and Star Notes are therefore substituted. Other than having their own special serial number and a star, these notes are the same as the others. On United States Notes and Silver Certificates, the star is substituted for the prefix letter; on Federal Reserve Notes, for the suffix letter. All defective notes are accounted for and destroyed by burning them in an incinerator.

Large stars after the serial number on the 1869 Series of United States Notes, and 1890 and 1891 Treasury Notes, do not signify replacement notes as are known in later and present-day Star Notes.

Serial numbers on early Large Size Notes were preceded by a letter and were ended by various odd characters or symbols. These characters are not known to have any significance, except to show that the number was terminated, and prevented any elimination or addition of digits. The suffix characters were replaced by alphabet letters on later issues of notes.

TREASURY OR COIN NOTES

Treasury Notes were authorized by Congress in 1890. Their official title was Coin Notes, as they could be redeemed for silver or gold coins. The series did not prove popular and was discontinued after the issue of 1891.

TREASURY SEAL

The Treasury Seal is the official emblem of the U.S. Treasury Department, which has appeared on all our currency since 1862. It is missing only from the early Demand Notes, issued in 1861, and some Fractional Currency. Two versions have been employed, distinguished readily by the fact that one (the original) bears a Latin inscription, while the current Treasury Seal is in English. The basic motif is the same, a badge displaying scales and a key. The original Seal, somewhat more decorative, was in use until 1968.

UNITED STATES NOTES

Also known as Legal Tender Notes, this substantial and ambitious series followed Demand Notes and constitutes the second earliest variety of U.S. paper currency. There are five distinct issues, running from 1862 to 1923. Though United States Notes are all "Large Size" and their designs not very similar to those in present use, they show in their successive stages the evolutionary advance from this nation's first efforts at paper money to its currency of today. The first issue is dated March 10, 1862. Denominations are $1, $2, $5, $10, $20, $50, $100, $500, $1,000, $5,000, and $10,000. Individuals portrayed included not only presidents but other government officials: Salmon P. Chase (Lincoln's Secretary of the Treasury), Daniel Webster, and Lewis and Clark. Some of the reverse designs are masterpieces of geometrical linework. A number of rarities are to be found among Legal Tender Notes, but in general the lower denominations can be collected without great expense.

WILDCAT NOTES

Wildcat Notes are the notes that were issued by so-called "wildcat banks" in the era of State Bank Notes before the Civil War. Numerous banks sprang up around the middle part of the 19th century, mostly in the west and southwest, operated by persons of questionable integrity. Some never had capital backing and were instituted purely as a front for confidence swindles. After issuing notes, the bank shut down, its directors disappeared, and owners of the notes were left with worthless paper. As news traveled slowly in those days, the same persons could move from town to town and work the scheme repeatedly. Notes issued by these banks, or any banks that became insolvent, are also called Broken Bank Notes. Apparently the origin of the term "wildcat" derives from public sentiment of the time, which held that owners of such banks had no greater trustworthiness than a wild animal. "Wildcat" may also refer to the rapid movement of swindling bank officials from one locality to another.

DEPARTMENT OF THE TREASURY, BUREAU OF ENGRAVING AND PRINTING

Reprinted with permission of the Department of the Treasury, Bureau of Printing and Engraving, Washington, D.C.

BUREAU FACTS

- Since October 1, 1877, all U.S. paper currency has been printed by the Bureau of Engraving and Printing, which began as a six-person operation using steam-powered presses in the Department of the Treasury's basement.
- Now 1,900 Bureau employees occupy 25 acres of floor space in two Washington, D.C. buildings flanking 14th Street. Currency and stamps are designed, engraved, and printed 24 hours a day, 5 days a week on 23 high-speed presses. An additional 600 Bureau employees are at the Western Currency Facility in Fort Worth, Texas, where currency is printed 24 hours a day, 5 days a week on 12 high-speed presses.
- In Fiscal Year 1999, at a cost of 4.5 cents each, the Bureau of Engraving and Printing produced for the Federal Reserve System a record 11.3 billion notes worth approximately $142 billion. Ninety-five percent will replace unfit notes, and five percent will support economic growth. At any one time, $200 million in notes may be in production.
- Of total production, notes currently produced are the $1 (48% of production time), $2 (1%), $5 (9%), $10 (11%), $20 (19%), $50 (5%), and $100 (7%).
- The Bureau also prints White House invitations and some 500 engraved items, such as visa counterfoils, naturalization documents, commissions, and certificates for almost 75 federal departments and agencies.

TOURS

BEP Public Tour Contact Information
Bureau of Engraving and Printing
14th and C Streets, S.W.
Washington, DC 20228
Telephone: *1.866.874.2330 (toll-free), 202.874.2330 (local)*
School Group Tours Fax: *202.874.6331*
Congressional Tours Fax: *202.874.0968*

VISITORS' CENTER

- At the Visitors' Center, history, production, and counterfeit exhibits showcase interesting information about U.S. currency.
- Many unique items can be purchased at the sales counter. Items include uncut currency sheets of 32, 16, 8, or 4 $1, $2, and $5 notes; a premium portfolio containing a new series 1996 $20 note with a low serial number and one of the last previous series $20 notes; a deluxe single note in the series 1996 with a low serial number; $150 worth of shredded currency in plastic bags that are sold for $1.50; engraved collectors' prints; souvenir cards; and Department of the Interior Duck Stamps.
- If you are planning a trip to Washington, please call our information number at 1.866.874.2330 (toll-free) for updated information or program changes.

MAIL ORDER SALES

The Bureau of Engraving and Printing (BEP) is experiencing extended delays in the delivery of incoming mail. At this moment, it is unknown when timely mail deliveries will resume. In order to get timely delivery of numismatic products, it is recommended that customers order by telephone, fax, or Internet.

- For telephone orders, call toll free at 1-800-456-3408.
- For fax orders, call toll free at 1-888-891-7585.
- For Internet orders, the BEP Web site is bep.treas.gov

INTERNET

The Bureau's **Internet address** is *www.bep.treas.gov/.* We also offer an **interactive website** at www.moneyfactory.gov/.

THE FEDERAL RESERVE BANKS

Reprinted with permission of the Department of the Treasury, Bureau of Printing and Engraving, Washington, D.C.

The Federal Reserve System is divided into twelve Federal Reserve districts, in each of which is a Federal Reserve Bank. There are also twenty-four branches. Each district is designated by a number and the corresponding letter of the alphabet. The district numbers, the cities in which the twelve banks are located, and the letter symbols are:

1-A—Boston
2-B—New York
3-C—Philadelphia
4-D—Cleveland
5-E—Richmond
6-F—Atlanta
7-G—Chicago
8-H—St. Louis
9-I—Minneapolis
10-J—Kansas City
11-K—Dallas
12-L—San Francisco

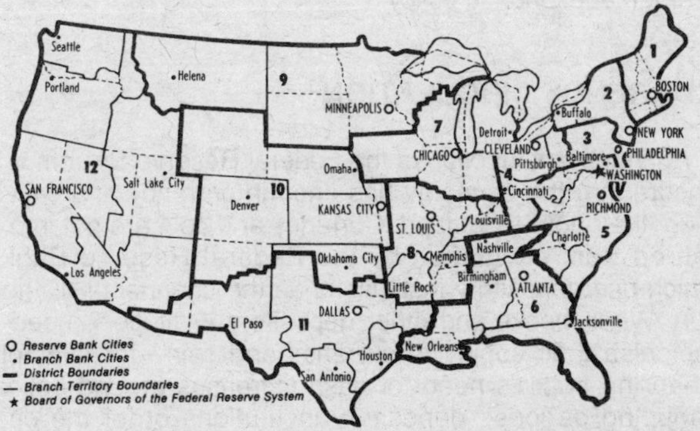

FEDERAL RESERVE SYSTEM

The Federal Reserve System was created by the Federal Reserve Act, which was passed by Congress in 1913, in order to provide a safer and more flexible banking and monetary system. For approximately 100 years before the creation of the Federal Reserve, periodic financial panics had led to failures of a large number of banks, with associated business bankruptcies and general economic contractions. Following the studies of the National Monetary Commission, established by Congress a year after the particularly severe panic of 1907, several proposals were put forward for the creation of an institution designed to counter such financial disruptions. Following considerable debate, the Federal Reserve System was established. Its original purposes were to give the country an elastic currency, provide facilities for discounting commercial credits, and improve the supervision of the banking system.

ECONOMIC STABILITY AND GROWTH

From the inception of the Federal Reserve System, it was clear that these original purposes were aspects of broader national economic and financial objectives. Over the years, stability and growth of the economy, a high level of employment, stability in the purchasing power of the dollar, and a reasonable balance in transactions with foreign countries have come to be recognized as primary objectives of governmental economic policy.

CURRENCY CIRCULATION

An important function of the Federal Reserve System is to ensure that the economy has enough currency and coin to meet the public's demand. Currency and coin are put into or retired from circulation by the Federal Reserve Banks, which use depository institutions as the channel of distribution. When banks and other depository institutions need to replenish their supply of currency and coin—for example, when the public's need for cash increases around holiday shopping periods—depository institutions order the cash from the Federal Reserve Bank or Branch in their area, and the face value of that cash is charged to their accounts at the Federal Reserve. When the public's need for currency and coin declines, depository institutions return excess cash to the Federal Reserve Bank, which in turn credits their accounts.

UNFIT AND COUNTERFEIT NOTES

The Federal Reserve Banks and the U.S. Department of the Treasury share responsibility for maintaining the physical quality of U.S. paper currency in circulation. Each day, millions of dollars of deposits to Reserve Banks by depository institutions are carefully scrutinized. The Reserve Banks are responsible for receiving, verifying, authenticating, and storing currency and shipping it as needed. Currency in good condition is stored for later distribution. Worn or mutilated notes are removed from circulation and destroyed. Counterfeit notes are forwarded to the U.S. Secret Service, an agency of the Treasury Department.

FEDERAL RESERVE NOTES

Virtually all currency in circulation is in the form of Federal Reserve Notes, which are printed by the Bureau of Engraving and Printing of the U.S. Treasury. The Reserve Banks are currently authorized to issue notes in denominations of $1, $2, $5, $10, $20, $50, and $100. Coins are produced by the Treasury's U.S. Mint.

CASH TRANSFERS

Currency and coin are used primarily for small transactions. In the aggregate, such transactions probably account for only a small proportion of the value of all transfers of funds.

32-SUBJECT SHEET LAYOUT

All U.S. currency is now printed with 32 subjects (notes) to a large sheet. The first printing is the greenback. The second printing is the face of the note, in black. This includes the portrait and border, the series year, the check letter and quadrant number, two signatures, and the face plate number. The sheet is then cut in half vertically for the third printing. This includes the black Federal Reserve seal, the four Federal Reserve district numbers, the green Treasury seal, and two green serial numbers.

The 32-subject sheet is divided into four quarters called quadrants for numbering and other controls. Each quadrant has its own numbering sequence for the eight notes, with serial numbers advancing by 20,000 to the next note. The quadrant number and check letter in the upper left section indicate the first, second, third, or fourth quadrant and the position of the note in the quadrant. In the lower right corner the position letter is shown again with a plate number. On the back of the note the same small number in the lower right is the back plate number.

FIRST QUADRANT		THIRD QUADRANT	
A1 A00000001A A100	E1 A00080001A E100	A3 A00320001A A100	E3 A00400001A E100
B1 A00020001A B100	F1 A00100001A F100	B3 A00340001A B100	F3 A00420001A F100
C1 A00040001A C100	G1 A00120001A G100	C3 A00360001A C100	G3 A00440001A G100
D1 A00060001A D100	H1 A00140001A H100	D3 A00380001A D100	H3 A004600001A H100
A2 A00160001A A100	E2 A00240001A E100	A4 A00480001A A100	E4 A005600001A E100
B2 A00180001A B100	F2 A00260001A F100	B4 A00500001A B100	F4 A00580001A F100
C2 A00200001A C100	G2 A00280001A G100	C4 A0050001A C100	G4 A00600001A G100
D2 A00220001A D100	H2 A00300001A H100	D4 A00540001A D100	H4 A00620001A H100
SECOND QUADRANT		FOURTH QUADRANT	

NUMBERING SYSTEM

The system of numbering paper money must be adequate to accommodate a large volume of notes. For security and accountability purposes, no two notes of any one class, denomination, and series may have the same serial number. The two serial numbers on each note have a full complement of eight digits and an alphabetical prefix and suffix letter. When necessary, ciphers are used at the left of the number to make a total of eight digits.

Whenever a numbering sequence is initiated for United States Notes or Silver Certificates, the first note is numbered A 00 000 001 A; the second A 00 000 002 A; the hundredth A 00 000 100 A; the thousandth A 00 001 000 A; and so on through A 99 999 999 A. The suffix letter A will remain the same until a total of twenty-five groups, or "blocks," of 99 999 999 notes are numbered, each group having a different prefix letter of the alphabet from A to Z. The letter "O" is omitted, either as a prefix or as a suffix, because of its similarity to zero. The 100 000 000th note in each group will be a Star Note, since eight digits are the maximum in the mechanical operation of numbering machines.

At this point, the suffix letter changes to B for the next twenty-five groups of 99 999 999 notes, and proceeds in the same manner as the suffix letter A. A total of 62,500,000,000 notes could be numbered before a duplication of serial numbers would occur. However, it has never been required to number that many notes of any one class, denomination, and series.

The Federal Reserve Notes printed for the twelve districts are numbered in the same progression as United States Notes and Silver Certificates, except that a specific alphabetical letter identifies a specific Federal Reserve district. The letter identifying each district is used as a prefix letter at the beginning of the serial numbers on all Federal Reserve Notes and does not change. Only the suffix letter changes in the serial numbers on Federal Reserve currency.

PORTRAITS AND BACK DESIGN ON SMALL SIZE NOTES

DENOMINATION	PORTRAIT	BACK DESIGN
$1	Washington	Great Seal of the United States
$2	Jefferson	Monticello
$5	Lincoln	Lincoln Memorial
$10	Hamilton	United States Treasury
$20	Jackson	The White House
$50	Grant	United States Capitol
$100	Franklin	Independence Hall
$500	McKinley	Five Hundred
$1000	Cleveland	One Thousand
$5000	Madison	Five Thousand
$10,000	Chase	Ten Thousand
$100,000	Wilson	One Hundred Thousand

DATING U.S. CURRENCY

Unlike coins, the date is not changed each year on U.S. currency.

The date appearing on all notes, large or small, is that of the year in which the design was first approved or issued. For instance, Large Size $1 United States Notes of the Series 1880 were issued with the same date until the new Series 1917 was issued. There was no further date change until the Series 1923.

The same rule applies to Small Size Notes. However, in this case a letter is added after the date to designate or indicate a minor change in the main design or probably a change in one or both of the signatures. For example: the $1 Silver Certificate of 1935 was changed to 1935-A because of a change in the size of the tiny plate numbers appearing in the lower right corners of the face and back of the note. It was changed again from 1935-A to 1935-B in 1945 when the signatures of Julian/Morganthau were changed to Julian/Vinson. Subsequent changes in signatures continued in the 1935 Series to the year 1963 when the signatures of Smith/Dillon terminated the issue with the Series 1935-H. Therefore, these notes were issued for twenty-eight years bearing the date 1935.

THE TREASURY SEAL

FORMER DESIGN:

The former design had the Latin inscription *Thesaur. Amer. Septent. Sigil.*, which has several translations. It was the Seal of the North American Treasury.

NEW DESIGN:

This new design drops the Latin and states THE DEPARTMENT OF THE TREASURY, 1789. First used on the $100 Note of the Series 1966.

GRADES AND CONDITIONS OF PAPER MONEY

CONDITION

The physical condition of a note or bill plays an important role in determining its value. There are many notes that have no premium value beyond face value in ordinary condition but are valuable or moderately valuable when uncirculated. Even in the case of scarce early specimens, the price given for an Average example is generally much less than that commanded by Fine or Very Fine condition.

Defects encountered in paper money include:

Creases, folds, wrinkles. Generally the characteristic that distinguishes uncirculated notes from those that almost—but not quite—qualify for such designation is a barely noticeable crease running approximately down the center vertically, resulting from the note being folded for insertion into a wallet or billfold. It may be possible, through manipulation or storage beneath a heavy weight, to remove evidence of the crease; but the knowledge that it once existed cannot be obliterated.

Discoloration. Discoloration is not as easy to recognize as most defects, but it must be classed as one. A distinction should be made between notes printed from underinked rollers and those which originally were normally colored but became "washed out." Sometimes washing is indeed the cause; a well-intentioned collector will bathe a note, attempting to clean it, with the result that its color is no longer strong. This should not happen if warm water is used, without strong cleanser. Atmospheric conditions may play some part in discoloration.

Foxing. Fox spots may sometimes be observed on old notes, especially those of the pre-1890 era, just as on old paper in general. They seem more common to foreign currency than American, but their presence on our notes is certainly not rare. These are tiny brownish-red dots, caused by an infestation of lice attacking the paper fibers.

Holes. Holes are more likely to be encountered in early paper money than specimens of recent origin. In early years it was customary for Federal Reserve Banks to use wire clips in making up bundles of notes for distribution to banking organizations, and these clips or staples often pierced the bills. Another common occurrence years ago was the practice of shop clerks and cashiers in general to impale notes upon holders consisting of nails mounted on stands.

Missing pieces. Missing pieces is a highly undesirable defect which, except in the case of rare specimens, renders the item valueless to collectors. Even if only a blank unprinted corner is torn away, this is called a missing-piece note and hardly anyone will give it a second glance.

Stains. Notes sometimes become stained with ink or other liquids. If the specimen is commonplace and easily obtainable in Very Fine or Uncirculated condition, it will be worthless with any kind of stain. In a note of moderate value, its price will be hurt to a greater or lesser degree depending on the stain's intensity, size, nature, and the area it touches. A stain in an outer margin or at a corner is not so objectionable as one occurring at the center or across a signature or serial number. Ink stains, because of their strong color, are generally deemed the worst, but bad staining can also be caused by oil, crayon, "magic marker," and food substances. Pencil markings, which frequently are found on bank notes, will yield to ordinary erasing with a piece of soft "art-gum" worked gently over the surface and brushed away with an artist's camel-hair brush. Most other stains cannot be so easily removed. With ink there is no hope, as any caustic sufficiently strong to remove the ink will also injure the printing and possibly eat through the paper as well. Oil stains can sometimes be lightened, though not removed, by sprinkling the note on both sides (even if the stain shows only on one) with talcum powder or other absorbent powder, placing it between sheets of waxed kitchen paper, and leaving it beneath a heavy weight for several days in a room where the humidity is not unduly high.

Tears. Tears in notes are very common defects, which may be minute or run nearly the whole length of the bill. As a rule the paper on which American currency is printed is fairly rugged and will not tear as readily as most ordinary paper, but given careless or hurried handling anything is possible. An old worn note is more apt to tear in handling than a new one. Repaired tears are more common in the world of paper money collecting than may be generally supposed. A clean tear—one which does not involve loss of surface—can be patched so as to become virtually unnoticed, unless examined against a light or through a strong magnifying glass. X-ray examination will reveal repairs when all else fails.

CONDITION GRADES

The following condition standards have been used throughout this book and, with slight variations depending upon individual interpretation, are generally current in the trade.

Uncirculated—UNC. A specimen that for all appearances has not been handled or passed through general circulation; a crisp fresh note in "bank" condition. There may be minor blemishes, such as a finger smudge or pinhole, but if these are in any respect severe the condition merits description as "Almost Uncirculated." There is not much satisfaction to be taken in a note fresh and crisp that has gaping holes and fingerprints. Obviously, an 1870 Uncirculated note should not be expected to match a 1970 in appearance or feel.

*Uncirculated—***Unc.** An uncirculated "Star Note."

Almost Uncirculated—A.U. In the case of modern or semimodern notes, this is generally taken to mean a specimen that shows no evidence of having passed through general circulation but, because of some detraction, fails to measure up to a rating of Uncirculated. The problem may be finger smudges, counting crinkles, a light crease, a fold along one or more of the corners, or pinholes. But if more than one of these impairments is present, the item would surely not deserve a classification of Almost Uncirculated.

Extremely Fine—X.F. A note exhibiting little evidence of wear from handling, but not so perfect or near-perfect as to qualify for a rating of Uncirculated or Almost Uncirculated.

On a used note issued before 1900 there may be clear evidence of circulation, but no disfiguring marks.

Very Fine—V.F. A Very Fine note has experienced some circulation but escaped without "being mangled." It is still clean and crisp, and its creases are not offensive.

Fine—F. Here the scale begins sliding down. It is obvious that, being the fifth in rank of condition grades, Fine notes are quite a good deal removed from Uncirculated. They have been handed around pretty thoroughly and suffered the normal consequences, but still are without serious blemishes such as tears, missing corners, serious stains, or holes.

Very Good—V.G. A well-circulated note bearing evidence of much folding, creasing, and wrinkling. It may possibly be lightly stained, smudged, or pin punctured, but major defects—such as a torn-off corner—would drop it into an even lower category.

Good—G. Heavily circulated, worn notes that are possibly stained or scribbled on, edges could be frayed or "dog-eared." There may be holes larger than pin punctures, but not on the central portion of design. This is the lowest grade of condition acceptable to a collector, and only when nothing better is available. Unless very rare, such specimens are considered space-fillers only.

Average Buying Prices—A.B.P. The Average Buying Prices given here are the approximate sums paid by retail dealers for specimens in Good condition. As selling prices vary, so do buying prices, and, in fact, they usually vary a bit more.

RECORD KEEPING

For your convenience, we suggest you use the following record-keeping system to note condition of your paper money in the checklist box:

⍂ FAIR	☒ VERY GOOD	◫ VERY FINE	☒ ALMOST UNC
◪ GOOD	⊟ FINE	☒ EXTREMELY FINE	■ UNCIRCULATED

ABOUT THE PRICES IN THIS BOOK

Prices are compiled from offerings made by dealers and from auction sale results. In all cases (except for the Average Buying Price) the prices are retail selling prices. While prices are current at the time of publication, the market can be influenced by buying or selling trends, causing prices to change. All prices, except in the case of seldom-offered rarities, are averages, calculated from numerous sales. The actual prices charged by any individual currency dealer may be slightly higher or lower than those indicated in this book. In any given sale various factors play a role, such as whether the seller is overstocked on notes of that type.

HOW TO USE THIS BOOK

The *Official Blackbook Price Guide to United States Paper Money* provides a convenient reference to prices of all standard U.S. currency, old and new, as well as many unusual issues.

Notes are divided into section by denomination. Within each section can be found the various series of notes for that denomination. The series are arranged chronologically and will vary slightly from section to section, as some notes were issued in one series and not in another. An index page is provided at the beginning of each section.

To familiarize yourself with the various currency terms, the following illustration might be helpful:

To price a note correctly, it is necessary that it be accurately identified and graded. The illustrations will aid in identification, and a grading guide has been provided. In the case of some notes, particularly very old ones, the value depends upon minor details. In all such cases these details have been clearly noted.

Listings include the following information:

Date. This is the "series date," as it appears on the note, and may bear no relation whatsoever to the year in which the note was actually issued. The date of actual issue is not of importance to collectors. If the series date on the note carries a suffix letter, such as 1935A, it will be so indicated in the listing.

Seal. The color of the Treasury Seal will be noted, along with other information if relevant. The following abbreviations are also used: Sm.—small, Lg.—large; w/r—with rays, w/s—with scallops.

Signatures. All U.S. notes carry two signatures, and the names of each signer are given for every note listed. If different signature combinations exist for your note, be sure you refer to the correct signature combination. The listings will show you whether there is just one set of signatures for that note or more than one.

Type. In a small minority of cases, notes were issued in more than one type. For example, a slight change was made in the paper or printing. All recorded types are identified in the listings.

Issuing Bank. This information is provided for Federal Reserve Notes and Federal Reserve Bank Notes only. Check the Federal Reserve seal on your note to identify the issuing bank. In some instances there is a difference in value depending on where the note originated. Space prevents us from listing the numerous local banks issuing National Bank Notes.

A.B.P. The first price column is the A.B.P. or Average Buying Price. This is the approximate sum being paid by dealers for a specimen in the lowest listed grade of condition. The lowest listed grade of condition is the column next to the A.B.P. If the next column is headed "Good," the A.B.P. is for a specimen in Good condition. In all cases the A.B.P. includes the face value of the note. This is an important consideration insofar as U.S. notes, regardless of their age or physical condition, can still be spent as legal tender.

Current Selling Prices. The current selling prices are given in two or three different grades of condition, as indicated at the top of each price column. Different groups of notes are priced in different condition grades, owing to market availability. Some are virtually unobtainable in Uncirculated condition, so it would be pointless to give such a price. Others are of no premium value in less than V.F., hence V.F. is the lowest grade shown.

ONE DOLLAR NOTES

ORDER OF ISSUE

ONE DOLLAR NOTES (1862) UNITED STATES NOTES (ALSO KNOWN AS LEGAL TENDER NOTES)

(Large Size)

Face Design: Portrait of Salmon Portland Chase (1808–73), Secretary of the Treasury under Lincoln, red Treasury Seal, signatures of Chittenden and Spinner, lower right.

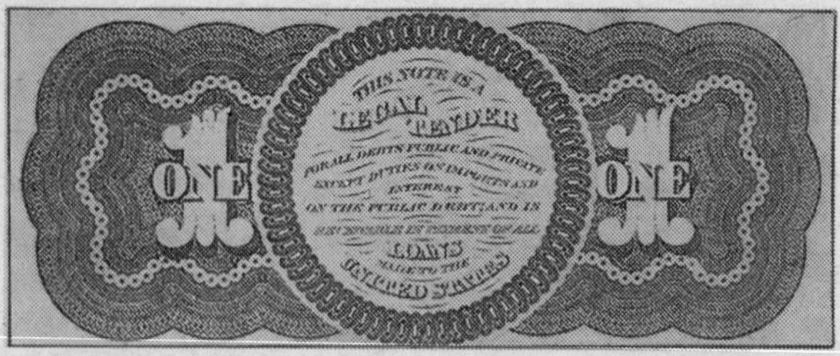

Back Design: Large circle center with legal tender obligation.

SERIES	SIGNATURES	SEAL	A.B.P.	GOOD	V. FINE	UNC.
1862	Chittenden-Spinner					
☐Type I, National Bank Note, American Bank Note without monogram		Red	200.00	375.00	1025.00	3000.00
☐Type II, National Bank Note, American Bank Note with monogram ABNCO		Red	100.00	175.00	725.00	2500.00
☐Type III, National Bank Note, National Bank Note without monogram		Red	100.00	175.00	825.00	2400.00
☐Type IV, National Bank Note, National Bank Note with monogram ABNCO		Red	110.00	200.00	750.00	2400.00

ONE DOLLAR NOTES (1869) UNITED STATES NOTES (ALSO KNOWN AS LEGAL TENDER NOTES)

(Large Size)

Face Design: Portrait of President Washington in the center, large red seal to the right. Scene of Columbus in sight of land to left; also called "Rainbow Note" because of the many colors used in printing. Black ink for main design, red seal and serial numbers, green background for the serial number, green shading in upper-half and blue tint in paper left of portrait to deter counterfeiting.

Back Design: Green, ONE DOLLAR and ONE over "1" center, letters U.S. interwoven to left. Legal tender obligation to right of center.

SERIES	SIGNATURES	SEAL	A.B.P.	GOOD	V. FINE	UNC.
☐1869	Allison-Spinner	Red	110.00	200.00	900.00	3500.00
☐1869	Allison-Spinner Water Mark Paper		110.00	200.00	2000.00	3650.00

ONE DOLLAR NOTES (1874–1917)
UNITED STATES NOTES
(ALSO KNOWN AS LEGAL TENDER NOTES)

(Large Size)

Back Design: Large green "X" with UNITED STATES OF AMERICA in the center. Legal tender obligation and counterfeiting warning to right.
Face Design: No blue or green shading and tinting.

SERIES	SIGNATURES	SEAL	A.B.P.	GOOD	V. FINE	UNC.
☐1874	Allison-Spinner	Sm. Red	65.00	80.00	425.00	1800.00
☐1875	Allison-New	Sm. Red	65.00	80.00	425.00	1450.00
☐1875	Same Series A	Sm. Red	155.00	350.00	1050.00	3250.00
☐1875	Same Series B	Sm. Red	155.00	350.00	1050.00	3250.00
☐1875	Same Series C	Sm. Red	165.00	350.00	1400.00	3500.00
☐1875	Same Series D	Sm. Red	200.00	450.00	1200.00	3400.00
☐1875	Same Series E	Sm. Red	310.00	645.00	1400.00	3500.00
☐1875	Allison-Wyman	Sm. Red	65.00	80.00	375.00	1400.00
☐1878	Allison-Gilfillan	Sm. Red	65.00	85.00	375.00	1400.00
☐1878	Allison-Gilfillan	Water Marked Paper	60.00	120.00	525.00	1850.00
☐1880	Scofield-Gilfillan	Lg. Brown	45.00	100.00	425.00	1250.00
☐1880	Bruce-Gilfillan	Lg. Brown	45.00	100.00	425.00	1250.00
☐1880	Bruce-Wyman	Lg. Brown	44.00	100.00	425.00	1200.00
☐1880	Rosecrans-Huston	Lg. Red	120.00	255.00	1000.00	5000.00
☐1880	Rosecrans-Huston	Lg. Brown	110.00	200.00	1000.00	4500.00
☐1880	Rosecrans-Nebeker	Lg. Brown	110.00	200.00	1000.00	4600.00
☐1880	Rosecrans-Nebeker	Sm. Red	40.00	75.00	300.00	1200.00
☐1880	Tillman-Morgan	Sm. Red	40.00	75.00	300.00	1200.00
☐1917	Tehee-Burke	Sm. Red	40.00	75.00	125.00	400.00

Sm.—Small Seal, Lg.—Large Seal
*This note with signatures of Burke and Elliott is an error issue. The regular procedure was to have the signature of the Register of the Treasury on the left, and that of the Treasurer to the right. The signatures were transposed in this instance.

SERIES	SIGNATURES	SEAL	A.B.P.	GOOD	V. FINE	UNC.
□1917	Elliott-Burke	Sm. Red	25.00	50.00	150.00	400.00
□1917	Burke-Elliott*	Sm. Red	85.00	115.00	530.00	1650.00
□1917	Elliott-White	Sm. Red	25.00	60.00	200.00	575.00
□1917	Speelman-White	Sm. Red	25.00	60.00	150.00	450.00

ONE DOLLAR NOTES (1923) UNITED STATES NOTES (ALSO KNOWN AS LEGAL TENDER NOTES)

(Large Size)

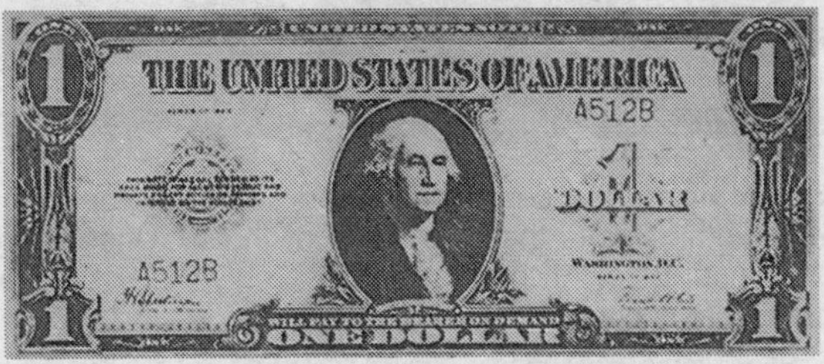

Face Design: Portrait of President Washington in center. Red seal to left, red "1" to the right, red serial numbers.

Back Design: UNITED STATES OF AMERICA and ONE DOLLAR in center. Figures "1" to right and left. This was the last issue of Large Size ONE DOLLAR United States Notes. The last series of Large Size Notes was kept in use until 1929 when the first issue of Small Size Notes was released.

SERIES	SIGNATURES	SEAL	A.B.P.	GOOD	V. FINE	UNC.
□1923	Speelman-White	Red	35.00	75.00	225.00	850.00

ONE DOLLAR NOTES (1928) UNITED STATES NOTES (ALSO KNOWN AS LEGAL TENDER NOTES)

(Small Size)

Face Design: Red seal to left—red serial numbers, large ONE to right. This is the only issue of the $1 United States Note, Small Size. At the present time only the $100 United States Note is current.

Back Design: Large ONE in center with ONE DOLLAR overprint, back printed in green.

SERIES	SIGNATURES	SEAL	A.B.P.	GOOD	V. FINE	UNC.	★UNC.
□1928	Woods-Woodin	Red	30.00	50.00	300.00	550.00	RARE

*Star Notes: Damaged or unsatisfactory notes were replaced at the Bureau of Engraving with new notes bearing a star (★) in place of the first letter and preceding the serial no. Example: *12345678A

ONE DOLLAR NOTES (1863–1875)
NATIONAL BANK NOTES
FIRST CHARTER PERIOD (Large Size)

Face Design: Name of National Bank top center, maidens at altar below.

Back Design: Landing of Pilgrims center, State Seal of state issuing bank to left, eagle and flag.

SERIES	SIGNATURES	SEAL	A.B.P.	GOOD	V. FINE	UNC.
□Original*	Colby-Spinner	Red w/r	145.00	200.00	1200.00	3800.00
□Original*	Jeffries-Spinner	Red w/r	200.00	535.00	1450.00	5500.00
□Original*	Allison-Spinner	Red w/r	145.00	225.00	1200.00	3800.00
□1875	Allison-New	Red w/s	145.00	225.00	1200.00	3800.00
□1875	Allison-Wyman	Red w/s	145.00	225.00	1200.00	3800.00
□1875	Allison-Gilfillan	Red w/s	145.00	225.00	1200.00	3800.00
□1875	Scofield-Gilfillan	Red w/s	145.00	225.00	1200.00	3800.00

w/r—with Rays, w/s—with Scallops

*Early notes of the First Charter Period did not have the series imprinted on them. They are known by the date on the bill which was usually the date of charter or organization, or as the Original Series. These notes had a seal with rays or small notches. In 1875 the series was imprinted in red, and the seal was changed to have scallops around the border. The charter number was added to later issues of notes of the original series and to all notes of the 1875 series.

ONE DOLLAR NOTES (1886) SILVER CERTIFICATES
(Large Size)

SERIES	SIGNATURES	SEAL	A.B.P.	GOOD	V. FINE	UNC.
□1886	Rosecrans-Jordan	Sm. Red	100.00	175.00	675.00	2200.00
□1886	Rosecrans-Hyatt	Sm. Red	100.00	175.00	675.00	2200.00
□1886	Rosecrans-Hyatt	Lg. Red	100.00	175.00	675.00	2400.00
□1886	Rosecrans-Huston	Lg. Red	100.00	175.00	675.00	2400.00
□1886	Rosecrans-Huston	Lg. Brown	100.00	175.00	675.00	2100.00
□1886	Rosecrans-Nebeker	Lg. Brown	100.00	175.00	675.00	2100.00
□1886	Rosecrans-Nebeker	Sm. Red	100.00	175.00	675.00	2200.00

ONE DOLLAR NOTES (1891) SILVER CERTIFICATES
(Large Size)

Back Design

Face Design: Same as 1886 note.

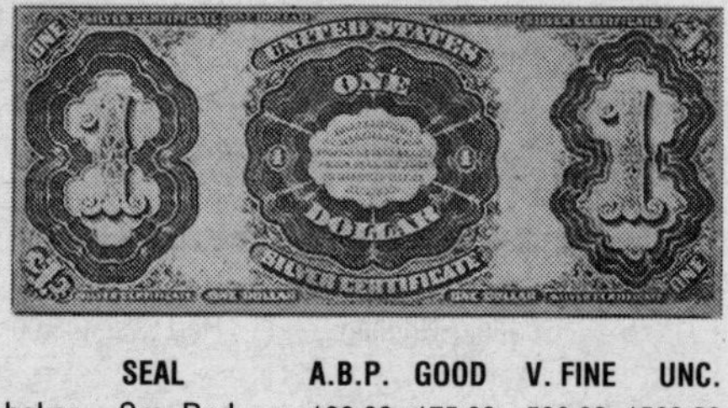

SERIES	SIGNATURES	SEAL	A.B.P.	GOOD	V. FINE	UNC.
□1891	Rosecrans-Nebeker	Sm. Red	100.00	175.00	500.00	1500.00
□1891	Tillman-Morgan	Sm. Red	100.00	175.00	575.00	1500.00

ONE DOLLAR NOTES (1896) SILVER CERTIFICATES
(Large Size)

Face Design: History instructing youth. To the right, panoramic view of the Capitol and Washington Monument. Constitution on tablet, names of famous Americans on top and side borders.

Back Design: Portrait of Martha Washington to left and President Washington to right with large numeral "1" in center.

There is a story that when this note was issued people objected to it because they said No. "1" (ONE) shouldn't stand between George and Martha Washington. The set consists of $1, $2, and $5 denominations. They all have very beautiful engravings, and they are truly the most beautiful notes ever issued by our government. They were first released in 1896 and replaced by a new issue in 1899. They were short-lived because of objections to the unclad female on the $5 Note.

SERIES	SIGNATURES	SEAL	A.B.P.	GOOD	V. FINE	UNC.
□1896	Tillman-Morgan	Red	200.00	350.00	1400.00	3750.00
□1896	Bruce-Roberts	Red	200.00	350.00	1400.00	3750.00

ONE DOLLAR NOTES (1899) SILVER CERTIFICATES (Large Size)

Face Design: Eagle on flag and Capitol background over portraits of Presidents Lincoln and Grant.

Back Design

SERIES	SIGNATURES	SEAL	A.B.P.	GOOD	V. FINE	UNC.
	SERIES OF 1899 (above upper right serial number)					
□1899	Lyons-Roberts	Blue	45.00	65.00	150.00	700.00
	SERIES OF 1899 (below upper right serial number)					
□1899	Lyons-Roberts	Blue	35.00	45.00	225.00	625.00
□1899	Lyons-Treat	Blue	35.00	45.00	225.00	625.00
□1899	Vernon-Treat	Blue	35.00	60.00	225.00	625.00
□1899	Vernon-McClung	Blue	35.00	60.00	225.00	625.00
	SERIES OF 1899 (vertical to right of blue seal)					
□1899	Napier-McClung	Blue	34.00	50.00	135.00	575.00
□1899	Napier-Thompson	Blue	50.00	75.00	350.00	1500.00
□1899	Parker-Burke	Blue	50.00	65.00	155.00	550.00
□1899	Teehee-Burke	Blue	50.00	65.00	155.00	550.00
□1899	Elliott-Burke	Blue	30.00	65.00	155.00	550.00
□1899	Elliott-White	Blue	30.00	65.00	155.00	550.00

SERIES	SIGNATURES	SEAL	A.B.P.	GOOD	V. FINE	UNC.
□1899	Speelman-White	Blue	30.00	50.00	165.00	450.00

ONE DOLLAR NOTES (1923) SILVER CERTIFICATES
(Large Size)

Face Design: Portrait of President Washington in center, blue seal left, blue 1 DOLLAR right, blue numbers.

Back Design: Same as 1923 note.

SERIES	SIGNATURES	SEAL	A.B.P.	GOOD	V. FINE	UNC.
□1923	Speelman-White	Blue	20.00	30.00	50.00	185.00
□1923	Woods-White	Blue	20.00	30.00	100.00	185.00
□1923	Woods-Tate	Blue	25.00	45.00	500.00	1000.00

ONE DOLLAR NOTES (1928) SILVER CERTIFICATES (Small Size)

Face Design: Portrait of President Washington, blue seal to the left, ONE to right, blue seal and numbers. ONE SILVER DOLLAR under portrait.

Back Design

First issue of Series 1928. U.S. paper money was reduced in 1928 from the old Large Size to the size presently in use. This was mostly an economy measure. Unlike Large Size Notes, the Small Notes have a letter designation after the date to denote a minor change in design or change of one or both signatures.

SERIES	SIGNATURES	SEAL	A.B.P.	GOOD	V. FINE	UNC.	★UNC.
☐ 1928	Tate-Mellon	Blue	12.00	20.00	25.00	140.00	700.00
☐ 1928A	Woods-Mellon	Blue	12.00	20.00	25.00	140.00	600.00
☐ 1928B	Woods-Mills	Blue	12.00	20.00	25.00	140.00	1750.00
☐ 1928C	Woods-Woodin	Blue	28.00	70.00	300.00	750.00	RARE
☐ 1928D	Julian-Woodin	Blue	22.00	50.00	100.00	500.00	RARE
☐ 1928E	Julian-Morgenthau	Blue	80.00	200.00	625.00	2650.00	RARE

ONE DOLLAR NOTES (1934) SILVER CERTIFICATES

(Small Size)

Face Design: Portrait of President Washington, blue "1" to left. ONE and blue seal to right. ONE DOLLAR IN SILVER under portrait.

Back Design: Same as 1928 note.

SERIES	SIGNATURES	SEAL	A.B.P.	GOOD	V. FINE	UNC.	★UNC.
□1934	Julian-Morgenthau	Blue	7.00	20.00	35.00	200.00	2200.00

ONE DOLLAR NOTES (1935) SILVER CERTIFICATES

(Small Size)

Face Design: Portrait of President Washington in center. Gray "1" to left, blue seal right, and blue numbers. ONE DOLLAR IN SILVER under portrait.

The following notes are without IN GOD WE TRUST on back.

SERIES	SIGNATURES	SEAL	A.B.P.	GOOD	V. FINE	UNC.	★UNC.
□1935	Julian-Morgenthau	Blue	3.00	4.50	12.00	75.00	725.00
□1935A	Julian-Morgenthau	Blue	2.00	4.00	12.00	30.00	200.00
□1935A	Julian-Morgenthau	Brown	6.00	10.00	40.00	185.00	2000.00

This note was a special issue for use in war zones in the Pacific area during World War II. Brown serial numbers and HAWAII stamped on front and back.

ONE DOLLAR NOTES (1935) SILVER CERTIFICATES (Small Size)

SERIES	SIGNATURES	SEAL	A.B.P.	GOOD	V. FINE	UNC.	★UNC.
□1935A	Julian-Morgenthau	Yellow	12.00	20.00	40.00	175.00	2750.00

The above note was a special issue for use in war zones in the North African and European areas during World War II. Blue serial numbers and yellow seal.

□1935A	Julian-Morgenthau	Blue	20.00	35.00	130.00	425.00	RARE

Red "R" between the Treasury Seal and signature of Morgenthau. This was an experimental issue to test wearing qualities of differently treated paper.

□1935A	Julian-Morgenthau	Blue	25.00	50.00	80.00	425.00	RARE

Above note with red "S" between Treasury Seal and signature of Morgenthau. Experimental issue "R" was for regular paper, "S" for special paper.

□1935B	Julian-Vinson	Blue	2.50	4.00	8.00	20.00	325.00
□1935C	Julian-Snyder	Blue	2.50	4.00	8.00	15.00	100.00
□1935D	Clark-Snyder	Blue	2.50	4.00	8.00	15.00	85.00

Wide design on back. This and all notes of 1935 prior to this have the wide design. See Fig I.

□1935D	Clark-Snyder	Blue	2.00	3.00	4.00	15.00	75.00

Narrow design on back. This and all $1 Notes following have narrow design. See Fig. II.

Figure I

Figure II

ONE DOLLAR NOTES (1935) SILVER CERTIFICATES
(Small Size)

SERIES	SIGNATURES	SEAL	A.B.P.	GOOD	V. FINE	UNC.	★UNC.
□1935E	Priest-Humphrey	Blue	1.50	3.00	6.00	18.00	35.00
□1935F	Priest-Anderson	Blue	1.50	3.00	6.00	18.00	35.00
□1935G	Smith-Dillon	Blue	1.50	3.00	6.00	14.00	35.00

IN GOD WE TRUST added. All notes following have the motto.

□1935G	Smith-Dillon	Blue	3.00	5.00	15.00	50.00	300.00
□1935H	Granahan-Dillon	Blue	2.00	3.50	8.00	15.00	60.00

ONE DOLLAR NOTES (1957) SILVER CERTIFICATES
(Small Size)

The following three notes are the last issue of the $1 Silver Certificates. The reason for the change in series from 1935H to 1957 was due to printing improvements. The 1935 Series, up until the issue of Clark and Snyder, was printed in sheets of twelve subjects to a sheet. During the term of Clark and Snyder notes were printed eighteen subjects to a sheet. Starting with Series 1957, new high-speed rotary presses were installed and notes were printed thirty-two subjects to a sheet.

SERIES	SIGNATURES	SEAL	A.B.P.	GOOD	V. FINE	UNC.	★UNC.
□1957	Priest-Anderson	Blue	1.50	2.00	4.00	9.00	30.00
□1957A	Smith-Dillon	Blue	1.50	2.00	4.00	9.00	20.00
□1957B	Granahan-Dillon	Blue	1.50	2.00	4.00	9.00	17.00

The redemption of Silver Certificates by the U.S. Treasury Department ended on June 24, 1968. These notes are now worth only their face value, plus the numismatic value to collectors. Notes in used condition are not regarded as collectors' items.

ONE DOLLAR NOTES (1890)
TREASURY OR COIN NOTES

(Large Size)

Face Design: Portrait of Stanton, Secretary of War during the Civil War.

Back Design: Green large ornate ONE. Entire back is beautifully engraved.

SERIES	SIGNATURES	SEAL	A.B.P.	GOOD	V. FINE	UNC.
□1890	Rosecrans-Huston	Brown	150.00	200.00	1100.00	3800.00
□1890	Rosecrans-Nebeker	Brown	150.00	200.00	1100.00	3800.00
□1890	Rosecrans-Nebeker	Red	150.00	200.00	1100.00	3800.00

ONE DOLLAR NOTES (1891)
TREASURY OR COIN NOTES

(Large Size)

Face Design: Is similar to 1890 note.

Back Design: More unengraved area, numerous ONES and "1"s.

SERIES	SIGNATURES	SEAL	A.B.P.	GOOD	V. FINE	UNC.
□1891	Rosecrans-Nebeker	Red	80.00	160.00	300.00	1750.00
□1891	Tillman-Morgan	Red	80.00	160.00	300.00	1650.00
□1891	Bruce-Roberts	Red	80.00	160.00	300.00	1650.00

ONE DOLLAR NOTES (1918)
FEDERAL RESERVE BANK NOTES

(Large Size)

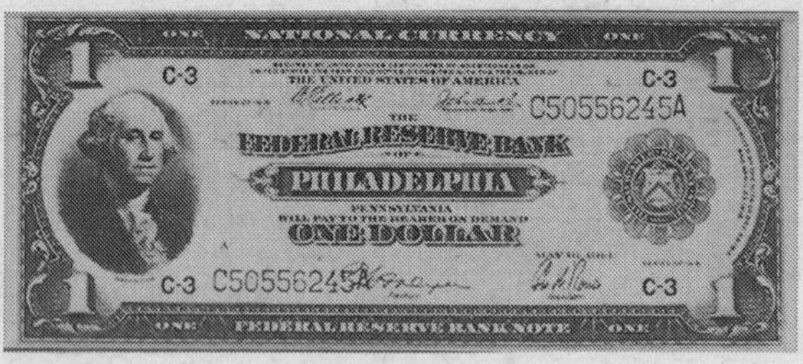

Face Design: Portrait of President Washington, signature to left of center. Bank and city center, blue seal to right. Signatures of government officials above. Signatures of bank officials below. Federal Reserve district letter and numbers in four corners.

Back Design: Flying eagle and flag in center. All are Series 1918 and have blue seals and blue numbers.

BANK	GOV'T SIGNATURES	BANK SIGNATURES	A.B.P.	GOOD	V. FINE	UNC.
☐ Boston	Teehee-Burke	Bullen-Morss	60.00	100.00	185.00	410.00
☐ Boston	Teehee-Burke	Willet-Morss	60.00	100.00	185.00	625.00
☐ Boston	Elliot-Burke	Willet-Morss	60.00	100.00	185.00	410.00

BANK	GOV'T SIGNATURES	BANK SIGNATURES	A.B.P.	GOOD	V. FINE	UNC.
☐ New York	Teehee-Burke	Sailer-Strong	35.00	50.00	200.00	385.00
☐ New York	Teehee-Burke	Hendricks-Strong	35.00	50.00	200.00	385.00
☐ New York	Elliott-Burke	Hendricks-Strong	35.00	50.00	200.00	385.00
☐ Philadelphia	Teehee-Burke	Hardt-Passmore	35.00	50.00	165.00	385.00
☐ Philadelphia	Teehee-Burke	Dyer-Passmore	35.00	50.00	165.00	385.00
☐ Philadelphia	Elliott-Burke	Dyer-Passmore	49.00	75.00	325.00	1000.00
☐ Philadelphia	Elliott-Burke	Dyer-Norris	35.00	50.00	170.00	485.00
☐ Cleveland	Teehee-Burke	Baxter-Fancher	35.00	50.00	170.00	485.00
☐ Cleveland	Teehee-Burke	Davis-Fancher	35.00	50.00	160.00	485.00
☐ Cleveland	Elliott-Burke	Davis-Fancher	35.00	50.00	160.00	485.00
☐ Richmond	Teehee-Burke	Keesee-Seay	35.00	50.00	160.00	485.00
☐ Richmond	Elliott-Burke	Keesee-Seay	35.00	50.00	160.00	485.00
☐ Atlanta	Teehee-Burke	Pike-McCord	35.00	50.00	160.00	485.00
☐ Atlanta	Teehee-Burke	Bell-McCord	50.00	70.00	350.00	1100.00
☐ Atlanta	Teehee-Burke	Bell-Wellborn	54.00	70.00	325.00	925.00
☐ Atlanta	Elliott-Burke	Bell-Wellborn	35.00	55.00	155.00	460.00
☐ Chicago	Teehee-Burke	McCloud-McDougal	35.00	50.00	165.00	460.00
☐ Chicago	Teehee-Burke	Cramer-McDougal	35.00	50.00	165.00	460.00
☐ Chicago	Elliott-Burke	Cramer-McDougal	35.00	50.00	165.00	460.00
☐ St. Louis	Teehee-Burke	Attebery-Wells	35.00	50.00	165.00	460.00
☐ St. Louis	Teehee-Burke	Attebery-Biggs	50.00	70.00	310.00	950.00

BANK	GOV'T SIGNATURES	BANK SIGNATURES	A.B.P.	GOOD	V. FINE	UNC.
☐ St. Louis	Elliott-Burke	Attebery-Biggs	45.00	75.00	320.00	900.00
☐ St. Louis	Elliott-Burke	White-Biggs	35.00	75.00	160.00	385.00
☐ Minneapolis	Teehee-Burke	Cook-Wold	40.00	75.00	160.00	385.00
☐ Minneapolis	Teehee-Burke	Cook-Young	100.00	230.00	575.00	1400.00
☐ Minneapolis	Elliott-Burke	Cook-Young	36.00	75.00	175.00	510.00
☐ Kansas City	Teehee-Burke	Anderson-Miller	35.00	75.00	175.00	510.00
☐ Kansas City	Elliott-Burke	Anderson-Miller	35.00	75.00	175.00	510.00
☐ Kansas City	Elliott-Burke	Helm-Miller	35.00	75.00	175.00	510.00
☐ Dallas	Teehee-Burke	Talley-VanZandt	35.00	75.00	175.00	510.00
☐ Dallas	Elliott-Burke	Talley-VanZandt	45.00	60.00	200.00	510.00
☐ Dallas	Elliott-Burke	Lawder-VanZandt	35.00	55.00	175.00	385.00
☐ San Francisco	Teehee-Burke	Clerk-Lynch	35.00	55.00	175.00	385.00
☐ San Francisco	Teehee-Burke	Clerk-Calkins	50.00	100.00	260.00	725.00
☐ San Francisco	Elliott-Burke	Clerk-Calkins	45.00	65.00	185.00	525.00
☐ San Francisco	Elliott-Burke	Ambrose-Calkins	45.00	65.00	175.00	385.00

ONE DOLLAR NOTES (1963)
FEDERAL RESERVE NOTES

(Small Size)

Face Design: Portrait of President Washington in center, black Federal Reserve seal with city and district letter to left, green Treasury Seal to right. Green serial numbers, Federal Reserve numbers in four corners.
Back Design: Same as all $1 Notes from 1935.

SERIES OF 1963, GRANAHAN-DILLON, GREEN SEAL

DISTRICT	A.B.P.	UNC.	★UNC.	DISTRICT	A.B.P.	UNC.	★UNC.
□1A Boston	3.00	6.00	10.00	□7G Chicago	5.00	9.00	12.00
□2B New York	3.00	6.00	8.00	□8H St. Louis	5.00	9.00	12.00
□3C Philadelphia	3.00	6.00	9.00	□9I Minneapolis	5.00	9.00	15.00
□4D Cleveland	3.00	6.00	9.00	□10J Kansas City	5.00	9.00	12.00
□5E Richmond	3.00	6.00	8.00	□11K Dallas	5.00	9.00	12.00
□6F Atlanta	3.00	6.00	8.00	□12L San Francisco	5.00	9.00	15.00
District Sets (12 notes)		100.00					

The Dallas note of this series as shown, with the letter "K" in the black seal and the number "11" in the four corners, does not have any more significance or value than any other notes with their respective district letter and corresponding number.

A false rumor was circulated several years ago that the "K" was for Kennedy, the "11" was for November (the month in which he was assassinated), and that the note was issued by the Dallas Bank to commemorate the occasion. The entire story is apocryphal.

This note is in no way associated with the late President Kennedy. The notes were authorized by the Act of June 4, 1963. This was five months before Kennedy was assassinated. The Federal Reserve district for Dallas is K-11.

SERIES OF 1963A, GRANAHAN-FOWLER, GREEN SEAL

DISTRICT	A.B.P.	UNC.	★UNC.	DISTRICT	A.B.P.	UNC.	★UNC.
□1A Boston	3.00	5.00	10.00	□7G Chicago	3.50	6.00	12.00
□2B New York	3.00	5.00	10.00	□8H St. Louis	3.50	6.00	12.00
□3C Philadelphia	3.00	5.00	10.00	□9I Minneapolis	3.50	6.00	12.00
□4D Cleveland	3.00	5.00	10.00	□10J Kansas City	3.50	6.00	12.00
□5E Richmond	3.00	5.00	10.00	□11K Dallas	3.50	6.00	12.00
□6F Atlanta	3.00	5.00	10.00	□12L San Francisco	3.50	6.00	10.00
District Sets (12 notes)			100.00				

ONE DOLLAR NOTES (1963-B) FEDERAL RESERVE (WITH SIGNATURE OF JOSEPH W. BARR)

(Small Size)

Joseph W. Barr served as Secretary of the Treasury from December 20, 1968, to January 20, 1969, filling the unexpired term of Henry H. Fowler. His signature appears on the $1 Federal Reserve Notes of the Series of 1963-B only.

During the one-month term of Joseph W. Barr, about 471 million notes were printed with his signature. These notes were for the following Federal Reserve Banks.

	REGULAR NUMBERS	A.B.P.	UNC.	★UNC.
□2B New York	123,040,000	4.00	6.00	22.00
□5E Richmond	93,600,000	4.00	6.00	22.00
□7G Chicago	91,040,000	4.00	6.00	22.00
□10J Kansas City	44,800,000	4.00	6.00	22.00
□12L San Francisco	106,400,000	4.00	6.00	22.00
District Sets (5 notes)				85.00

ONE DOLLAR NOTES (1969)
FEDERAL RESERVE NOTES
(WORDING IN GREEN, TREASURY SEAL CHANGED FROM LATIN TO ENGLISH)

FORMER DESIGN:
The former design had the Latin inscription: *"Thesaur. Amer. Septent. Sigil.,"* which has several translations. It was the Seal of the North American Treasury.

NEW DESIGN:
This new design drops the Latin and states *"The Department of The Treasury, 1789."* First used on the $100 Note of the Series 1966.

ONE DOLLAR NOTES (1969)
FEDERAL RESERVE NOTES

(Small Size)

SERIES OF 1969, SIGNATURES OF ELSTON-KENNEDY, GREEN SEAL

BANK	A.B.P.	V.FINE	UNC.	★UNC.	BANK	A.B.P.	V.FINE	UNC.	★UNC.
☐ Boston	—	1.25	5.75	10.00	☐ Chicago	—	1.50	5.75	10.00
☐ New York	—	1.25	5.75	10.00	☐ St. Louis	—	1.50	5.75	10.00
☐ Philadelphia	—	1.25	5.75	10.00	☐ Minneapolis	—	1.50	5.75	10.00
☐ Cleveland	—	1.25	5.75	10.00	☐ Kansas City	—	1.50	5.75	10.00
☐ Richmond	—	1.25	5.75	10.00	☐ Dallas	—	1.50	5.75	10.00
☐ Atlanta	—	1.25	5.75	10.00	☐ San Francisco	—	1.50	5.75	10.00

SERIES OF 1969A, SIGNATURES OF KABIS-KENNEDY, GREEN SEAL

BANK	A.B.P.	V.FINE	UNC.	★UNC.	BANK	A.B.P.	V.FINE	UNC.	★UNC.
☐ Boston	—	1.25	5.35	10.00	☐ Chicago	—	1.50	6.00	10.00
☐ New York	—	1.25	5.35	10.00	☐ St. Louis	—	1.50	6.00	10.00
☐ Philadelphia	—	1.25	5.35	10.00	☐ Minneapolis	—	1.50	6.00	10.00
☐ Cleveland	—	1.25	5.35	10.00	☐ Kansas City	—	1.50	6.00	10.00
☐ Richmond	—	1.25	5.35	10.00	☐ Dallas	—	1.50	6.00	10.00
☐ Atlanta	—	1.25	5.35	10.00	☐ San Francisco	—	1.50	6.00	10.00

SERIES OF 1969B, SIGNATURES OF KABIS-CONNALLY, GREEN SEAL

BANK	A.B.P.	V.FINE	UNC.	★UNC.	BANK	A.B.P.	V.FINE	UNC.	★UNC.
☐ Boston	—	1.25	6.00	10.00	☐ Chicago	—	1.25	6.00	10.00
☐ New York	—	1.25	6.00	10.00	☐ St. Louis	—	1.25	6.00	10.00
☐ Philadelphia	—	1.25	6.00	10.00	☐ Minneapolis	—	1.25	6.00	10.00
☐ Cleveland	—	1.25	6.00	10.00	☐ Kansas City	—	1.25	6.00	10.00
☐ Richmond	—	1.25	6.00	10.00	☐ Dallas	—	1.25	6.00	10.00
☐ Atlanta	—	1.25	6.00	10.00	☐ San Francisco	—	1.25	6.00	10.00

SERIES OF 1969C, SIGNATURES OF BANUELOS-CONNALLY, GREEN SEAL

BANK	A.B.P.	V.FINE	UNC.	★UNC.	BANK	A.B.P.	V.FINE	UNC.	★UNC.
☐ New York	—	1.25	5.75	—	☐ Chicago	—	1.25	5.75	40.00
☐ Cleveland	—	1.25	5.75	40.00	☐ St. Louis	—	1.25	5.75	40.00
☐ Richmond	—	1.25	5.75	45.00	☐ Minneapolis	—	1.25	5.75	40.00
☐ Atlanta	—	1.25	5.75	40.00	☐ Kansas City	—	1.25	5.75	40.00
					☐ Dallas	—	1.25	5.75	40.00
					☐ San Francisco	—	1.25	5.75	30.00

SERIES OF 1969D, SIGNATURES OF BANUELOS-SHULTZ, GREEN SEAL

BANK	A.B.P.	V.FINE	UNC.	★UNC.	BANK	A.B.P.	V.FINE	UNC.	★UNC.
☐ Boston	—	1.25	6.00	14.00	☐ Chicago	—	1.25	6.00	14.00
☐ New York	—	1.25	6.00	14.00	☐ St. Louis	—	1.25	6.00	14.00
☐ Philadelphia	—	1.25	6.00	14.00	☐ Minneapolis	—	1.25	6.00	14.00
☐ Cleveland	—	1.25	6.00	14.00	☐ Kansas City	—	1.25	6.00	14.00
☐ Richmond	—	1.25	6.00	14.00	☐ Dallas	—	1.25	6.00	14.00
☐ Atlanta	—	1.25	6.00	14.00	☐ San Francisco	—	1.25	6.00	14.00

SERIES OF 1974, SIGNATURES OF NEFF-SIMON, GREEN SEAL

BANK	A.B.P.	V.FINE	UNC.	★UNC.	BANK	A.B.P.	V.FINE	UNC.	★UNC.
☐ Boston	—	1.25	4.75	10.00	☐ Chicago	—	1.25	4.75	7.25
☐ New York	—	1.25	4.75	8.00	☐ St. Louis	—	1.25	4.75	7.25
☐ Philadelphia	—	1.25	4.75	8.00	☐ Minneapolis	—	1.25	4.75	40.00
☐ Cleveland	—	1.25	4.75	20.00	☐ Kansas City	—	1.25	4.75	7.25
☐ Richmond	—	1.25	4.75	8.00	☐ Dallas	—	1.25	4.75	10.00
☐ Atlanta	—	1.25	4.75	6.00	☐ San Francisco	—	1.25	4.75	7.25

SERIES OF 1977, SIGNATURES OF MORTON-BLUMENTHAL, GREEN SEAL

BANK	A.B.P.	V.FINE	UNC.	★UNC.	BANK	A.B.P.	V.FINE	UNC.	★UNC.
☐ Boston	—	1.25	7.00	11.00	☐ Chicago	—	1.25	7.00	11.00
☐ New York	—	1.25	7.00	11.00	☐ St. Louis	—	1.25	7.00	11.00
☐ Philadelphia	—	1.25	7.00	11.00	☐ Minneapolis	—	1.25	7.00	11.00
☐ Cleveland	—	1.25	7.00	11.00	☐ Kansas City	—	1.25	7.00	11.00
☐ Richmond	—	1.25	7.00	11.00	☐ Dallas	—	1.25	7.00	11.00
☐ Atlanta	—	1.25	7.00	11.00	☐ San Francisco	—	1.25	7.00	11.00

SERIES OF 1977A, SIGNATURES OF MORTON-MILLER, GREEN SEAL

BANK	A.B.P.	V.FINE	UNC.	★UNC.	BANK	A.B.P.	V.FINE	UNC.	★UNC.
☐ Boston	—	1.10	6.00	9.00	☐ Chicago	—	1.10	6.00	9.00
☐ New York	—	1.10	6.00	9.00	☐ St. Louis	—	1.10	6.00	9.00
☐ Philadelphia	—	1.10	6.00	9.00	☐ Minneapolis	—	1.10	6.00	25.00
☐ Cleveland	—	1.10	6.00	9.00	☐ Kansas City	—	1.10	6.00	9.00
☐ Richmond	—	1.10	6.00	9.00	☐ Dallas	—	1.10	6.00	9.00
☐ Atlanta	—	1.10	6.00	9.00	☐ San Francisco	—	1.10	6.00	9.00

SERIES OF 1981, SIGNATURES OF BUCHANAN-REGAN, GREEN SEAL

BANK	A.B.P.	V.FINE	UNC.	★UNC.	BANK	A.B.P.	V.FINE	UNC.	★UNC.
☐ Boston	—	1.10	6.00	14.00	☐ Chicago	—	1.10	6.00	14.00
☐ New York	—	1.10	6.00	14.00	☐ St. Louis	—	1.10	6.00	15.00
☐ Philadelphia	—	1.10	6.00	50.00	☐ Minneapolis	—	1.10	6.00	15.00
☐ Cleveland	—	1.10	6.00	14.00	☐ Kansas City	—	1.10	6.00	14.00
☐ Richmond	—	1.10	6.00	14.00	☐ Dallas	—	1.10	6.00	15.00
☐ Atlanta	—	1.10	6.00	14.00	☐ San Francisco	—	1.10	6.00	14.00

SERIES OF 1981A, SIGNATURES OF ORTEGA-REGAN, GREEN SEAL

BANK	A.B.P.	V.FINE	UNC.	★UNC.	BANK	A.B.P.	V.FINE	UNC.	★UNC.
☐ Boston	—	—	7.00	16.00	☐ St. Louis	—	—	7.00	16.00
☐ New York	—	1.10	7.00	16.00	☐ Minneapolis	—	—	7.00	16.00
☐ Philadelphia	—	—	7.00	16.00	☐ Kansas City	—	—	7.00	16.00
☐ Cleveland	—	—	7.00	16.00	☐ Chicago	—	1.10	7.00	16.00
☐ Richmond	—	1.10	7.00	16.00	☐ Dallas	—	1.10	7.00	1100.00
☐ Atlanta	—	—	7.00	16.00	☐ San Francisco	—	1.10	7.00	16.00

SERIES OF 1981A or 1985 (REVERSE #129 LEFT), SIGNATURES OF ORTEGA-REGAN, GREEN SEAL

BANK	A.B.P.	V.FINE	UNC.	★UNC.	BANK	A.B.P.	V.FINE	UNC.	★UNC.
☐ Boston	—	25.00	60.00	—	☐ Chicago	—	25.00	60.00	—
☐ New York	—	25.00	60.00	—	☐ St. Louis	—	25.00	60.00	—
☐ Philadelphia	—	25.00	60.00	—	☐ Minneapolis	—	25.00	60.00	—
☐ Cleveland	—	25.00	60.00	—	☐ Kansas City	—	25.00	60.00	—
☐ Richmond	—	25.00	60.00	—	☐ Dallas	—	25.00	60.00	—
☐ Atlanta	—	25.00	60.00	—	☐ San Francisco	—	25.00	60.00	—

SERIES OF 1985, SIGNATURES OF ORTEGA-BAKER, GREEN SEAL

★Notes not issued for all banks

BANK	A.B.P.	V.FINE	UNC.	★UNC.	BANK	A.B.P.	V.FINE	UNC.	★UNC.
☐ Boston	—	1.10	5.50	—	☐ Chicago	—	1.10	5.50	12.00
☐ New York	—	1.10	5.50	—	☐ St. Louis	—	1.10	5.50	12.00
☐ Philadelphia	—	1.10	5.50	—	☐ Minneapolis	—	1.10	5.50	12.00
☐ Cleveland	—	1.10	5.50	—	☐ Kansas City	—	1.10	5.50	—
☐ Richmond	—	1.10	5.50	12.00	☐ Dallas	—	1.10	5.50	12.00
☐ Atlanta	—	1.10	5.50	—	☐ San Francisco	—	1.10	5.50	12.00

SERIES OF 1985 (REVERSE #129 LEFT), SIGNATURES OF ORTEGA-BAKER, GREEN SEAL

BANK	A.B.P.	V.FINE	UNC.	★UNC.	BANK	A.B.P.	V.FINE	UNC.	★UNC.
☐ Boston	—	25.00	42.00	—	☐ Chicago	—	25.00	42.00	—
☐ New York	—	25.00	42.00	—	☐ St. Louis	—	25.00	42.00	—
☐ Philadelphia	—	25.00	42.00	—	☐ Minneapolis	—	25.00	42.00	—
☐ Cleveland	—	25.00	42.00	—	☐ Kansas City	—	25.00	42.00	—
☐ Richmond	—	25.00	42.00	—	☐ Dallas	—	25.00	42.00	—

SERIES OF 1988, SIGNATURES OF ORTEGA-BRADY, GREEN SEAL

★Notes not issued for all banks

BANK	A.B.P.	V.FINE	UNC.	★UNC.	BANK	A.B.P.	V.FINE	UNC.	★UNC.
☐ Boston	—	1.10	6.00	12.00	☐ Chicago	—	1.10	6.00	—
☐ New York	—	1.10	6.00	12.00	☐ St. Louis	—	1.10	6.00	—
☐ Philadelphia	—	1.10	6.00	—	☐ Minneapolis	—	1.10	6.00	—
☐ Cleveland	—	1.10	6.00	—	☐ Kansas City	—	1.10	6.00	12.00
☐ Richmond	—	1.10	6.00	12.00	☐ Dallas	—	1.10	6.00	12.00
☐ Atlanta	—	1.10	6.00	12.00	☐ San Francisco	—	1.10	6.00	12.00

SERIES OF 1988A, SIGNATURES OF VILLALPANDO-BRADY, GREEN SEAL

★Notes not issued for all banks

BANK	A.B.P.	V.FINE	UNC.	★UNC.	BANK	A.B.P.	V.FINE	UNC.	★UNC.
☐ Boston	—	1.10	4.25	—	☐ Chicago	—	1.10	4.25	14.00
☐ New York	—	1.10	4.25	14.00	☐ St. Louis	—	1.10	4.25	14.00
☐ Philadelphia	—	1.10	4.25	—	☐ Minneapolis	—	1.10	4.25	14.00
☐ Cleveland	—	1.10	4.25	14.00	☐ Kansas City	—	1.10	4.25	—
☐ Richmond	—	1.10	4.25	14.00	☐ Dallas	—	1.10	4.25	14.00
☐ Atlanta	—	1.10	4.25	14.00	☐ San Francisco	—	1.10	4.25	14.00

SERIES OF 1993, SIGNATURES OF WITHROW-BENTSEN, GREEN SEAL

★Notes not issued for all banks

BANK	A.B.P.	V.FINE	UNC.	★UNC.	BANK	A.B.P.	V.FINE	UNC.	★UNC.
☐ Boston	—	1.10	2.25	—	☐ Chicago	—	1.10	2.25	5.50
☐ New York	—	1.10	2.25	5.50	☐ St. Louis	—	1.10	2.25	—
☐ Philadelphia	—	1.10	2.25	225.00	☐ Minneapolis	—	1.10	160.00	—
☐ Cleveland	—	1.10	2.25	—	☐ Dallas	—	1.10	2.25	5.50
☐ Richmond	—	1.10	2.25	—	☐ San Francisco	—	1.10	2.25	—
☐ Atlanta	—	1.10	2.25	5.50					

SERIES OF 1995, SIGNATURES OF WITHROW-RUBIN, GREEN SEAL

★Notes not issued for all banks

BANK	A.B.P.	V.FINE	UNC.	★UNC.	BANK	A.B.P.	V.FINE	UNC.	★UNC.
☐ Boston	—	1.10	2.50	7.25	☐ Chicago	—	1.10	2.50	7.25
☐ New York	—	1.10	2.50	7.25	☐ St. Louis	—	1.10	2.50	—
☐ Philadelphia	—	1.10	2.50	7.25	☐ Minneapolis	—	1.10	2.50	7.25
☐ Cleveland	—	1.10	2.50	7.25	☐ Kansas City	—	1.10	2.50	7.25
☐ Richmond	—	1.10	2.50	7.25	☐ Dallas	—	1.10	250	25.00
☐ Atlanta	—	1.10	2.50	7.25	☐ San Francisco	—	1.10	2.50	7.25

TWO DOLLAR NOTES

ORDER OF ISSUE

TWO DOLLAR NOTES (1862) UNITED STATES NOTES (ALSO KNOWN AS LEGAL TENDER NOTES)

(Large Size)

Face Design: Portrait of Alexander Hamilton (1754–1804), cloverleaf "2"s in upper corners, medallion with "II" in lower left, medallion with "1, 2, 3" right of portrait.

Back Design: "2" in each corner, with "2" motif repeated in scallop circles around obligation; back is printed green.

SERIES	SIGNATURES	SEAL	A.B.P.	GOOD	V. FINE	UNC.
□1862	Chittenden-Spinner Type I, American Banknote Company vertical in left border	Red	150.00	250.00	1650.00	3850.00
□1862	Chittenden-Spinner Type II, National Banknote Company vertical in left border	Red	150.00	250.00	1650.00	3850.00

TWO DOLLAR NOTES (1869) UNITED STATES NOTES (ALSO KNOWN AS LEGAL TENDER NOTES)

(Large Size)

Face Design: Portrait of President Jefferson to left, Capitol in center, large red seal to right.

Back Design: Roman "II" left, arabic "2" center, TWO right. This is the companion note to the $1 "Rainbow Note."

SERIES	SIGNATURES	SEAL	A.B.P.	GOOD	V. FINE	UNC.
□1869	Allison-Spinner	Red	200.00	300.00	1100.00	5000.00
□1869	Allison-Spinner	Water Mark Paper	220.00	425.00	2000.00	5500.00

TWO DOLLAR NOTES (1874) UNITED STATES NOTES (ALSO KNOWN AS LEGAL TENDER NOTES)

(Large Size)

Face Design: Portrait of President Jefferson; same as 1869 note.

Back Design: Completely revised.

SERIES	SIGNATURES	SEAL	A.B.P.	GOOD	V. FINE	UNC.
□1874	Allison-Spinner	Red	105.00	200.00	900.00	2800.00
□1875	Allison-New	Red	110.00	200.00	1200.00	3000.00
□Series A	Allison-New	Red	205.00	350.00	3200.00	6000.00
□Series B	Allison-New	Red	205.00	350.00	3200.00	6000.00
□1875	Allison-Wyman	Red	115.00	200.00	800.00	2400.00
□1878	Allison-Gilfillan	Red	110.00	175.00	800.00	2400.00
□1878	Scofield-Gilfillan	Red	1200.00	1400.00	RARE	RARE
□1880	Scofield-Gilfillan	Brown	65.00	125.00	350.00	1500.00
□1880	Bruce-Gilfillan	Brown	65.00	125.00	345.00	1200.00
□1880	Bruce-Wyman	Brown	65.00	125.00	345.00	1500.00
□1880	Rosecrans-Huston	Red	325.00	675.00	2000.00	7500.00
□1880	Rosecrans-Huston	Brown	690.00	1375.00	3575.00	RARE
□1880	Rosecrans-Nebeker	Red	100.00	150.00	700.00	2200.00
□1880	Tillman-Morgan	Red	70.00	100.00	300.00	900.00

SERIES	SIGNATURES	SEAL	A.B.P.	GOOD	V. FINE	UNC.
□1917	Teehee-Burke	Red	25.00	50.00	110.00	375.00
□1917	Elliott-Burke	Red	25.00	50.00	110.00	375.00
□1917	Elliott-Burke (error)	Red	85.00	110.00	400.00	1250.00
□1917	Elliott-White	Red	25.00	50.00	110.00	375.00
□1917	Speelman-White	Red	25.00	50.00	110.00	375.00

TWO DOLLAR NOTES (1928) UNITED STATES NOTES (ALSO KNOWN AS LEGAL TENDER NOTES)

(Small Size)

Face Design: Portrait of President Jefferson, red seal left, TWO right, red serial numbers.

Back Design: Jefferson Home—Monticello.

SERIES	SIGNATURES	SEAL	A.B.P.	GOOD	V. FINE	UNC.	★UNC.
□1928	Tate-Mellon	Red	5.00	12.00	35.00	200.00	1200.00
□1928A	Woods-Mellon	Red	8.00	20.00	75.00	475.00	8000.00
□1928B	Woods-Mills	Red	36.00	65.00	225.00	1500.00	RARE
□1928C	Julian-Morgenthau	Red	5.00	12.00	20.00	200.00	3000.00
□1928D	Julian-Morgenthau	Red	4.50	7.00	20.00	75.00	600.00
□1928E	Julian-Vinson	Red	4.50	10.00	20.00	150.00	7750.00
□1928F	Julian-Snyder	Red	6.00	8.00	20.00	90.00	700.00
□1928G	Clark-Snyder	Red	6.00	8.00	20.00	90.00	700.00

TWO DOLLAR NOTES (1953) UNITED STATES NOTES (ALSO KNOWN AS LEGAL TENDER NOTES)

(Small Size)

Face Design: Portrait of President Jefferson, gray "2" to left, red seal to right over TWO.

Back Design: Same as 1928 note.

SERIES	SIGNATURES	SEAL	A.B.P.	GOOD	V. FINE	UNC.	★UNC.
☐1953	Priest-Humphrey	Red	3.00	4.00	7.00	28.00	70.00
☐1953A	Priest-Anderson	Red	3.00	4.00	7.00	28.00	95.00
☐1953B	Smith-Dillon	Red	3.00	4.00	7.00	25.00	85.00
☐1953C	Granahan-Dillon	Red	3.00	4.00	7.00	25.00	100.00

Back Design: IN GOD WE TRUST on back.

Face Design: Same as previous note.

SERIES	SIGNATURES	SEAL	A.B.P.	GOOD	V. FINE	UNC.	★UNC.
☐1963	Granahan-Dillon	Red	3.00	4.00	7.00	18.00	60.00
☐1963A	Granahan-Fowler	Red	3.00	4.00	7.00	25.00	65.00

Production of $2 United States Notes was discontinued on August 10, 1966.

TWO DOLLAR NOTES (1875) NATIONAL BANK NOTES
FIRST CHARTER PERIOD (Large Size)

Face Design: This note is known as the "Lazy Two Note" due to the unusual "lying down" shape of the "2" shown on the face. Liberty with flag and red seal.

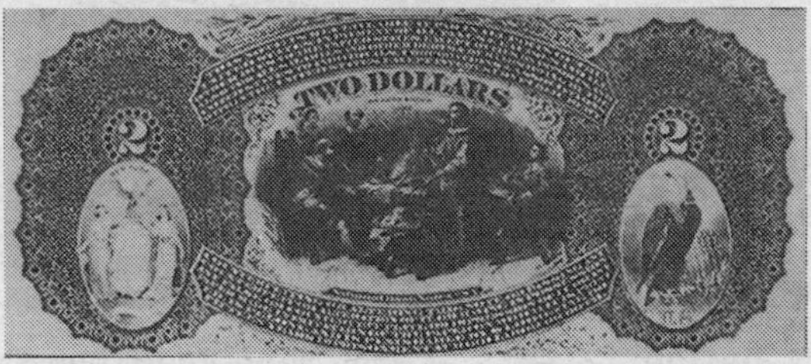

Back Design: Sir Walter Raleigh in England, 1585, exhibiting corn and smoking tobacco from America, State Seal, and eagle.

SERIES	SIGNATURES	SEAL	A.B.P.	GOOD	V. FINE	UNC.
☐Original	Colby-Spinner	Red	600.00	925.00	4000.00	RARE
☐Original	Jeffries-Spinner	Red	1000.00	1400.00	3800.00	12000.00
☐Original	Allison-Spinner	Red	600.00	925.00	4000.00	RARE
☐1875	Allison-New	Red	600.00	925.00	4000.00	RARE
☐1875	Allison-Wyman	Red	600.00	925.00	4000.00	RARE
☐1875	Allison-Gilfillan	Red	600.00	925.00	4000.00	RARE
☐1875	Scofield-Gilfillan	Red	600.00	925.00	4000.00	RARE

TWO DOLLAR NOTES (1886) SILVER CERTIFICATES (Large Size)

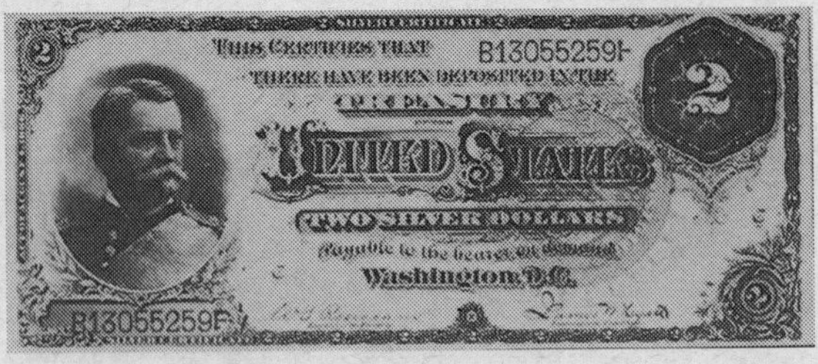

Face Design: General Hancock portrait left. Treasury Seal to the right of center.

Back Design: "2" left and right, very ornate engraving, obligation in center of note. Note is printed in green.

SERIES	SIGNATURES	SEAL	A.B.P.	GOOD	V. FINE	UNC.
□1886	Rosecrans-Jordan	Red	175.00	240.00	1200.00	3500.00
□1886	Rosecrans-Hyatt	Sm.Red	175.00	240.00	1200.00	3500.00
□1886	Rosecrans-Hyatt	Lg.Red	175.00	240.00	1200.00	3500.00
□1886	Rosecrans-Huston	Red	175.00	240.00	1200.00	3500.00
□1886	Rosecrans-Huston	Brown	175.00	240.00	1200.00	3500.00

TWO DOLLAR NOTES (1891) SILVER CERTIFICATES
(Large Size)

Face Design: Portrait of William Windom, Secretary of the Treasury 1881–84 and 1889–91, red seal right.

Back Design: “2” left and right, scalloped design center with obligation, printed in green.

SERIES	SIGNATURES	SEAL	A.B.P.	GOOD	V. FINE	UNC.
□1891	Rosecrans-Nebeker	Red	150.00	250.00	1000.00	4200.00
□1891	Tillman-Morgan	Red	150.00	250.00	1000.00	4200.00

TWO DOLLAR NOTES (1896) SILVER CERTIFICATES
(Large Size)

Face Design: Science presenting Steam and Electricity to Industry and Commerce.

Back Design: Portraits of Robert Fulton and Samuel F.B. Morse.

This is the second note of the popular Educational Series.

SERIES	SIGNATURES	SEAL	A.B.P.	GOOD	V. FINE	UNC.
□1896	Tillman-Morgan	Red	200.00	300.00	1800.00	5000.00
□1896	Bruce-Roberts	Red	200.00	300.00	1800.00	5000.00

TWO DOLLAR NOTES (1899) SILVER CERTIFICATES
(Large Size)

Face Design: Portrait of President Washington between figures of Trade and Agriculture, blue "2" left, blue seal right.

Back Design

SERIES	SIGNATURES	SEAL	A.B.P.	GOOD	V. FINE	UNC.
□1899	Lyons-Roberts	Blue	115.00	150.00	375.00	2200.00
□1899	Lyons-Treat	Blue	115.00	150.00	375.00	2200.00
□1899	Vernon-Treat	Blue	115.00	150.00	375.00	2200.00
□1899	Vernon-McClung	Blue	115.00	150.00	375.00	2200.00
□1899	Napier-McClung	Blue	115.00	150.00	375.00	2200.00
□1899	Napier-Thompson	Blue	115.00	150.00	450.00	4000.00
□1899	Parker-Burke	Blue	115.00	150.00	375.00	2200.00
□1899	Teehee-Burke	Blue	115.00	150.00	375.00	2200.00
□1899	Elliott-Burke	Blue	115.00	150.00	375.00	2200.00
□1899	Speelman-White	Blue	115.00	150.00	375.00	2200.00

TWO DOLLAR NOTES (1890–1891)
TREASURY OR COIN NOTES

(Large Size)

Face Design: Portrait of General James McPherson.

Back Design: Large TWO center, over obligation. Large "2" on engraved background right. Intricate engraving, printed green.

SERIES	SIGNATURES	SEAL	A.B.P.	GOOD	V. FINE	UNC.
□1890	Rosecrans-Huston	Brown	325.00	450.00	3200.00	RARE
□1890	Rosecrans-Nebeker	Brown	325.00	450.00	3200.00	RARE
□1890	Rosecrans-Nebeker	Red	325.00	450.00	3200.00	RARE

TWO DOLLAR NOTES (1890–1891)
TREASURY OR COIN NOTES

(Large Size) **NOTE NO. 30**

Face Design: Similar to 1890–1891 note.
Back Design: Revised.

SERIES	SIGNATURES	SEAL	A.B.P.	GOOD	V. FINE	UNC.
□1891	Rosecrans-Nebeker	Red	150.00	200.00	750.00	3500.00
□1891	Tillman-Morgan	Red	150.00	200.00	750.00	3500.00
□1891	Bruce-Roberts	Red	150.00	200.00	750.00	3500.00

TWO DOLLAR NOTES (1918)
FEDERAL RESERVE BANK NOTES

(Large Size)

Face Design: Portrait of President Jefferson to left, name of bank in center, blue seal to the right, blue numbers, Federal Reserve district letter and number in four corners.

Back Design: American battleship of World War I.

TWO DOLLAR NOTES (1918)
FEDERAL RESERVE BANK NOTES

(Large Size)

BANK	GOV'T SIGNATURES	BANK SIGNATURES	A.B.P.	GOOD	V. FINE	UNC.
☐ Boston	Teehee-Burke	Bullen-Morss	165.00	235.00	675.00	2650.00
☐ Boston	Teehee-Burke	Willet-Morss	165.00	235.00	675.00	2650.00
☐ Boston	Elliot-Burke	Willet-Morss	165.00	235.00	675.00	2650.00
☐ New York	Teehee-Burke	Sailer-Strong	165.00	235.00	675.00	2650.00
☐ New York	Teehee-Burke	Hendricks-Strong	165.00	235.00	675.00	2650.00
☐ New York	Elliott-Burke	Hendricks-Strong	165.00	235.00	675.00	2650.00
☐ Philadelphia	Teehee-Burke	Hardt-Passmore	165.00	235.00	675.00	2650.00
☐ Philadelphia	Teehee-Burke	Dyer-Passmore	165.00	235.00	675.00	2800.00
☐ Philadelphia	Elliott-Burke	Dyer-Passmore	165.00	235.00	1200.00	3500.00
☐ Philadelphia	Elliott-Burke	Dyer-Norris	165.00	235.00	675.00	2650.00
☐ Cleveland	Teehee-Burke	Baxter-Francher	165.00	235.00	675.00	2650.00
☐ Cleveland	Teehee-Burke	Davis-Francher	165.00	235.00	675.00	2650.00
☐ Cleveland	Elliott-Burke	Davis-Francher	165.00	235.00	675.00	2650.00
☐ Richmond	Teehee-Burke	Keesee-Seay	165.00	235.00	675.00	2650.00
☐ Richmond	Elliott-Burke	Keesee-Seay	165.00	235.00	675.00	2650.00
☐ Atlanta	Teehee-Burke	Pike-McCord	165.00	235.00	675.00	2400.00
☐ Atlanta	Teehee-Burke	Bell-McCord	165.00	235.00	1400.00	3200.00
☐ Atlanta	Elliott-Burke	Bell-Wellborn	165.00	235.00	1200.00	3200.00
☐ Chicago	Teehee-Burke	McCloud-McDougal	165.00	235.00	650.00	2200.00

BANK	GOV'T SIGNATURES	BANK SIGNATURES	A.B.P.	GOOD	V. FINE	UNC.
☐ Chicago	Teehee-Burke	Cramer-McDougal	200.00	255.00	625.00	2400.00
☐ Chicago	Elliott-Burke	Cramer-McDougal	200.00	255.00	710.00	2400.00
☐ St. Louis	Teehee-Burke	Attebery-Wells	200.00	255.00	710.00	2400.00
☐ St. Louis	Teehee-Burke	Attebery-Biggs	200.00	255.00	900.00	3250.00
☐ St. Louis	Elliott-Burke	Attebery-Biggs	200.00	255.00	900.00	3250.00
☐ St. Louis	Elliott-Burke	White-Biggs	200.00	255.00	925.00	3250.00
☐ Minneapolis	Teehee-Burke	Cook-Wold	200.00	255.00	650.00	2400.00
☐ Minneapolis	Elliott-Burke	Cook-Young	200.00	255.00	775.00	2275.00
☐ Kansas City	Teehee-Burke	Anderson-Miller	200.00	255.00	650.00	2200.00
☐ Kansas City	Elliott-Burke	Helm-Miller	200.00	255.00	650.00	2200.00
☐ Dallas	Teehee-Burke	Talley-VanZandt	200.00	255.00	775.00	2400.00
☐ Dallas	Elliott-Burke	Talley-VanZandt	200.00	255.00	775.00	2400.00
☐ San Francisco	Teehee-Burke	Clerk-Lynch	200.00	255.00	700.00	2400.00
☐ San Francisco	Elliott-Burke	Clerk-Calkins	200.00	255.00	700.00	2400.00
☐ San Francisco	Elliott-Burke	Ambrose-Calkins	200.00	255.00	700.00	2400.00

TWO DOLLAR NOTES (1976)
FEDERAL RESERVE NOTES

(Small Size)

Face Design: Portrait of President Jefferson.

Back Design: Signing of the Declaration of Independence.

SERIES OF 1976, NEFF-SIMON, GREEN SEAL

DISTRICT	A.B.P.	UNC.	★UNC.	DISTRICT	A.B.P.	UNC.	★UNC.
☐1A Boston	4.00	6.75	25.00	☐7G Chicago	6.00	9.00	90.00
☐2B New York	4.00	6.75	25.00	☐8H St. Louis	6.00	5.50	18.00
☐3C Philadelphia	4.00	6.75	25.00	☐9I Minneapolis	6.00	14.00	250.00
☐4D Cleveland	4.00	7.00	30.00	☐10J Kansas City	6.00	30.00	315.00
☐5E Richmond	4.00	6.75	40.00	☐11K Dallas	6.00	12.00	35.00
☐6F Atlanta	4.00	7.00	25.00	☐12L San Francisco	6.00	12.00	35.00

SERIES OF 1995, GREEN SEAL

DISTRICT	A.B.P.	★UNC.
☐6F Atlanta	12.00	20.00

FIVE DOLLAR NOTES

ORDER OF ISSUE

FIVE DOLLAR NOTES (1861) DEMAND NOTES
(Large Size)

Face Design: Left, Statue of America by Crawford atop United States Capitol. Center, numeral "5" in green. Right, portrait of Alexander Hamilton, statesman, first Secretary of the Treasury.

Back Design: Numerous small "5"s in ovals. This note has no Treasury Seal. The signatures are those of Treasury Department employees who signed for officials.

CITY	A.B.P.	GOOD	V. GOOD
☐Boston (I)	2000.00	3200.00	4850.00
☐New York (I)	2000.00	3200.00	4850.00
☐Philadelphia (I)	2000.00	3200.00	4850.00
☐Cincinnati (I)	5000.00	RARE	RARE
☐St. Louis (I)	5000.00	RARE	RARE
☐Boston (II)	725.00	1000.00	2400.00
☐New York (II)	725.00	1000.00	2400.00
☐Philadelphia (II)	725.00	1000.00	2200.00
☐Cincinnati (II)	4200.00	RARE	RARE
☐St. Louis (II)	4200.00	RARE	RARE

FIVE DOLLAR NOTES (1875–1907)
UNITED STATES NOTES
(ALSO KNOWN AS LEGAL TENDER NOTES)

(Large Size)

Back Design: First Obligation.

Back Design: Second Obligation

SERIES	SIGNATURES	SEAL	A.B.P.	GOOD	V. FINE	UNC.
□1862	Crittenden-Spinner*	Red	175.00	240.00	1100.00	2400.00
□1862	Crittenden-Spinner**	Red	175.00	240.00	1100.00	2400.00
□1863	Crittenden-Spinner**	Red	175.00	240.00	1100.00	2400.00

*First Obligation
**Second Obligation

FIVE DOLLAR NOTES (1869) UNITED STATES NOTES (ALSO KNOWN AS LEGAL TENDER NOTES)

(Large Size)

Face Design: Portrait of President Jackson on left. Pioneer and family in center.

Back Design: Color, green. This is a companion note to the $1 and $2 Notes of 1869 "Rainbow Notes."

SERIES	SIGNATURES	SEAL	A.B.P.	GOOD	V. FINE	UNC.
□1869	Allison-Spinner	Red	80.00	140.00	750.00	2000.00
□1869	Allison-Spinner	Water Marked Paper	100.00	175.00	1450.00	3000.00

FIVE DOLLAR NOTES (1875–1907)
UNITED STATES NOTES
(ALSO KNOWN AS LEGAL TENDER NOTES)

(Large Size)

Back Design: Revised.
Face Design: Similar to 1869 note.

SERIES	SIGNATURES	SEAL	A.B.P.	GOOD	V. FINE	UNC.
☐1875	Allison-New	Red	80.00	120.00	375.00	1850.00
☐1875A	Allison-New	Red	100.00	160.00	525.00	2200.00
☐1875B	Allison-New	Red	80.00	150.00	500.00	1300.00
☐1875	Allison-Wyman	Red	85.00	150.00	500.00	1650.00
☐1878	Allison-Gilfillan	Red	75.00	150.00	450.00	1650.00
☐1880	Scofield-Gilfillan	Brown	325.00	725.00	3525.00	7250.00
☐1880	Bruce-Gilfillan	Brown	110.00	200.00	850.00	2700.00
☐1880	Bruce-Wyman	Brown	80.00	125.00	425.00	2400.00
☐1880	Bruce-Wyman	Red	85.00	150.00	475.00	2150.00
☐1880	Rosecrans-Jordan	Red	80.00	125.00	450.00	1600.00
☐1880	Rosecrans-Hyatt	Red	350.00	750.00	3500.00	7500.00
☐1880	Rosecrans-Huston	Red	85.00	225.00	700.00	2150.00
☐1880	Rosecrans-Huston	Brown	100.00	225.00	700.00	2300.00
☐1880	Rosecrans-Nebeker	Brown	65.00	225.00	650.00	1750.00
☐1880	Rosecrans-Nebeker	Red	55.00	125.00	300.00	1600.00
☐1880	Tillman-Morgan	Red	55.00	125.00	275.00	1600.00
☐1880	Bruce-Roberts	Red	45.00	125.00	250.00	1600.00
☐1880	Lyons-Roberts	Red	65.00	105.00	895.00	2300.00
☐1907	Vernon-Treat	Red	50.00	80.00	275.00	1350.00
☐1907	Vernon-McClung	Red	50.00	80.00	300.00	1250.00
☐1907	Napier-McClung	Red	45.00	60.00	250.00	925.00
☐1907	Napier-Thompson	Red	65.00	125.00	350.00	1050.00
☐1907	Parker-Burke	Red	60.00	75.00	300.00	1050.00
☐1907	Teehee-Burke	Red	60.00	75.00	300.00	1050.00
☐1907	Elliott-Burke	Red	60.00	75.00	250.00	900.00

SERIES	SIGNATURES	SEAL	A.B.P.	GOOD	V. FINE	UNC.
□1907	Elliott-White	Red	45.00	75.00	300.00	725.00
□1907	Speelman-White	Red	50.00	80.00	200.00	575.00
□1907	Woods-White	Red	45.00	75.00	300.00	700.00

FIVE DOLLAR NOTES (1928) UNITED STATES NOTES (ALSO KNOWN AS LEGAL TENDER NOTES)

(Small Size)

Face Design: Portrait of President Lincoln center. Red seal to left, red serial numbers.

Back Design: Lincoln Memorial in Washington, D.C.

SERIES	SIGNATURES	SEAL	A.B.P	GOOD	V. FINE	UNC.	★UNC.
□1928	Woods-Mellon	Red	10.00	15.00	18.00	150.00	2500.00
□1928A	Woods-Mills	Red	10.00	15.00	26.00	200.00	RARE
□1928B	Julian-Morgenthau	Red	10.00	15.00	22.00	95.00	1600.00
□1928C	Julian-Morgenthau	Red	10.00	15.00	22.00	90.00	850.00
□1928D	Julian-Vinson	Red	10.00	15.00	40.00	525.00	3500.00
□1928E	Julian-Snyder	Red	10.00	15.00	22.00	90.00	1150.00
□1928F	Clark-Snyder	Red	10.00	15.00	22.00	95.00	800.00

FIVE DOLLAR NOTES (1953–1963)
UNITED STATES NOTES

(Small Size)

Face Design: Similar to previous note. Portrait of President Lincoln center. Red seal is moved to the right, red numbers.
Back Design: Similar to 1928 note.

SERIES	SIGNATURES	SEAL	A.B.P.	GOOD	V. FINE	UNC.	★UNC.
☐1953	Priest-Humphrey	Red	8.00	10.00	15.00	90.00	360.00
☐1953A	Priest-Anderson	Red	8.00	10.00	16.00	70.00	270.00
☐1953B	Smith-Dillon	Red	8.00	10.00	15.00	50.00	260.00
☐1953C	Granahan-Dillon	Red	8.00	12.00	18.00	85.00	475.00

FIVE DOLLAR NOTES (1953–1963)
UNITED STATES NOTES
(ALSO KNOWN AS LEGAL TENDER NOTES)

(Small Size)

Back Design: The following notes have IN GOD WE TRUST on the back.
Face Design: Similar to 1953–1963 note.

SERIES	SIGNATURES	SEAL	A.B.P.	GOOD	V. FINE	UNC.	★UNC.
☐1963	Granahan-Dillon	Red	7.00	12.00	18.00	45.00	155.00

Production of $5 United States Notes ended in 1967.

FIVE DOLLAR NOTES (1863–1875)
NATIONAL BANK NOTES
FIRST CHARTER PERIOD (Large Size)

Face Design: The Columbus Note. The face shows Columbus in sight of land and Columbus with an Indian princess.

Back Design: Christopher Columbus landing at San Salvador, 1492. Also the State Seal left, and American eagle right.

SERIES	SIGNATURES	SEAL	A.B.P.	GOOD	V. FINE	UNC.
☐Original	Chittenden-Spinner	Red	400.00	600.00	1675.00	RARE
☐Original	Colby-Spinner	Red	400.00	600.00	1675.00	RARE
☐Original	Jeffries-Spinner	Red	600.00	1200.00	4000.00	RARE
☐Original	Allison-Spinner	Red	400.00	600.00	1800.00	RARE
☐1875	Allison-New	Red	400.00	600.00	1800.00	RARE
☐1875	Allison-Wyman	Red	400.00	600.00	1800.00	RARE
☐1875	Allison-Gilfillan	Red	400.00	600.00	1800.00	RARE
☐1875	Scofield-Gilfillan	Red	400.00	600.00	1800.00	RARE
☐1875	Bruce-Gilfillan	Red	400.00	600.00	1800.00	RARE
☐1875	Bruce-Wyman	Red	400.00	600.00	1800.00	RARE
☐1875	Bruce-Jordan	Red		EXTREMELY RARE		
☐1875	Rosecrans-Huston	Red	400.00	600.00	1675.00	RARE
☐1875	Rosecrans-Jordan	Red	400.00	600.00	1675.00	RARE

FIVE DOLLAR NOTES (1882) NATIONAL BANK NOTES
SECOND CHARTER PERIOD (Large Size)

First Issue (Brown seal and brown backs.)
Face Design: Portrait of President Garfield left. Name of bank and city center, brown seal to right. Brown charter number.

Back Design: Brown border design similar to previous note. Center oval now has the bank's charter number in green. The top signatures are those of the Treasury officials. Bottom signatures, usually handwritten or probably rubber-stamped, are bank officials.

SERIES	SIGNATURES	SEAL	A.B.P.	GOOD	V. FINE	UNC.
□1882	Bruce-Gilfillan	Brown	200.00	325.00	875.00	3850.00
□1882	Bruce-Wyman	Brown	200.00	325.00	875.00	3850.00
□1882	Bruce-Jordan	Brown	200.00	325.00	875.00	3850.00
□1882	Rosecrans-Jordan	Brown	200.00	325.00	875.00	3850.00
□1882	Rosecrans-Hyatt	Brown	200.00	325.00	875.00	3850.00
□1882	Rosecrans-Huston	Brown	200.00	325.00	875.00	3850.00
□1882	Rosecrans-Nebeker	Brown	200.00	325.00	825.00	3850.00
□1882	Rosecrans-Morgan	Brown	200.00	325.00	900.00	3500.00
□1882	Tillman-Morgan	Brown	200.00	325.00	875.00	3850.00
□1882	Tillman-Roberts	Brown	200.00	325.00	875.00	3850.00
□1882	Bruce-Roberts	Brown	200.00	325.00	875.00	3850.00
□1882	Lyons-Roberts	Brown	200.00	325.00	875.00	3850.00
□1882	Lyons-Treat		(Unknown in any collection)			
□1882	Vernon-Treat	Brown	200.00	325.00	825.00	3500.00

FIVE DOLLAR NOTES (1882) NATIONAL BANK NOTES
SECOND CHARTER PERIOD, Second Issue (Large Size)

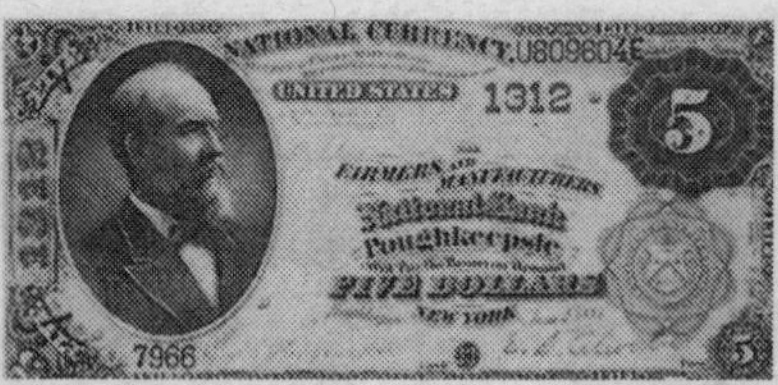

Face Design: Similar to preceding portrait of President Garfield.

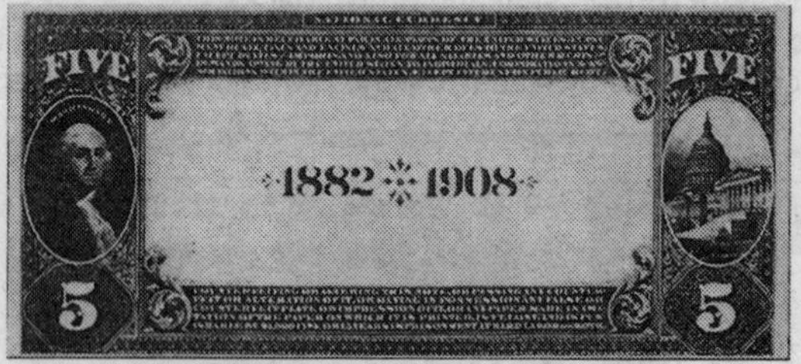

Back Design: Back is now green with date "1882–1908" in center.

SERIES	SIGNATURES	SEAL	A.B.P.	GOOD	V. FINE	UNC.
□1882	Rosecrans-Huston	Blue	135.00	250.00	1400.00	2850.00
□1882	Rosecrans-Nebeker	Blue	135.00	250.00	1400.00	2850.00
□1882	Rosecrans-Morgan	Blue	200.00	350.00	1400.00	3600.00
□1882	Tillman-Morgan	Blue	135.00	250.00	1400.00	2600.00
□1882	Tillman-Roberts	Blue	135.00	250.00	1400.00	2600.00
□1882	Bruce-Roberts	Blue	135.00	250.00	1400.00	2600.00
□1882	Lyons-Roberts	Blue	135.00	250.00	1400.00	2600.00
□1882	Vernon-Treat	Blue	135.00	250.00	1400.00	3250.00
□1882	Vernon-McClung	Blue				RARE
□1882	Napier-McClung	Blue	170.00	315.00	1425.00	3600.00

FIVE DOLLAR NOTES (1882) NATIONAL BANK NOTES
SECOND CHARTER PERIOD, Third Issue (Large Size)

Face Design: Same as 1882 note. Blue seal.

Back Design: Similar to 1882 Second Issue note. FIVE DOLLARS replaces "1882–1908."

SERIES	SIGNATURES	SEAL	A.B.P.	GOOD	V. FINE	UNC.
□1882	Tillman-Morgan	Blue	200.00	300.00	950.00	3750.00
□1882	Tillman-Roberts	Blue	200.00	300.00	950.00	3750.00
□1882	Bruce-Roberts	Blue	200.00	300.00	950.00	3750.00
□1882	Lyons-Roberts	Blue	200.00	300.00	950.00	4000.00
□1882	Vernon-Treat	Blue	200.00	300.00	950.00	3750.00
□1882	Napier-McClung	Blue	200.00	300.00	950.00	3750.00
□1882	Teehee-Burke	Blue			EXTREMELY RARE	

FIVE DOLLAR NOTES (1902) NATIONAL BANK NOTES
THIRD CHARTER PERIOD (Large Size)

First Issue (Red seal and charter numbers.)
Face Design: Portrait of President Harrison left, name of bank and city center, Treasury Seal to right, red seal and charter number.

Back Design: Landing of Pilgrims.

SERIES	SIGNATURES	SEAL	A.B.P.	GOOD	V. FINE	UNC.
☐1902	Lyons-Roberts	Red	200.00	300.00	900.00	RARE
☐1902	Lyons-Treat	Red	200.00	300.00	900.00	RARE
☐1902	Vernon-Treat	Red	200.00	300.00	900.00	RARE

FIVE DOLLAR NOTES (1902) NATIONAL BANK NOTES
THIRD CHARTER PERIOD (Large Size)

SECOND ISSUE

SERIES	SIGNATURES	SEAL	A.B.P.	GOOD	V. FINE	UNC.
☐1902	Lyons-Roberts	Blue	80.00	140.00	525.00	1500.00
☐1902	Lyons-Treat	Blue	80.00	140.00	525.00	1500.00
☐1902	Vernon-Treat	Blue	80.00	140.00	525.00	1500.00
☐1902	Vernon-McClung	Blue	80.00	140.00	525.00	1500.00
☐1902	Napier-McClung	Blue	80.00	140.00	525.00	1500.00
☐1902	Napier-Thompson	Blue	75.00	200.00	525.00	1600.00
☐1902	Napier-Burke	Blue	80.00	140.00	525.00	1500.00
☐1902	Parker-Burke	Blue	80.00	140.00	525.00	1500.00
☐1902	Teehee-Burke	Blue	80.00	140.00	525.00	1500.00

FIVE DOLLAR NOTES (1902) NATIONAL BANK NOTES

THIRD CHARTER PERIOD (Large Size)

Third Issue (Blue seal and numbers.)

The following notes do not have date of "1902–1908" on the back.

SERIES	SIGNATURES	SEAL	A.B.P.	GOOD	V. FINE	UNC.
□1902	Lyons-Roberts	Blue	80.00	150.00	350.00	1275.00
□1902	Lyons-Treat	Blue	80.00	150.00	350.00	1275.00
□1902	Vernon-Treat	Blue	80.00	150.00	350.00	1275.00
□1902	Vernon-McClung	Blue	80.00	150.00	350.00	1275.00
□1902	Napier-McClung	Blue	80.00	150.00	350.00	1275.00
□1902	Napier-Thompson	Blue	80.00	150.00	350.00	1275.00
□1902	Napier-Burke	Blue	80.00	150.00	350.00	1275.00
□1902	Parker-Burke	Blue	80.00	150.00	350.00	1275.00
□1902	Teehee-Burke	Blue	80.00	150.00	350.00	1275.00
□1902	Elliott-Burke	Blue	80.00	150.00	350.00	1275.00
□1902	Elliott-White	Blue	80.00	150.00	350.00	1275.00
□1902	Speelman-White	Blue	80.00	150.00	350.00	1275.00
□1902	Woods-White	Blue	80.00	150.00	350.00	1275.00
□1902	Woods-Tate	Blue	80.00	150.00	350.00	1275.00
□1902	Jones-Woods	Blue	100.00	175.00	550.00	1375.00

FIVE DOLLAR NOTES (1929) NATIONAL BANK NOTES

(Small Size)

TYPE I

TYPE II

Face Design: Portrait of President Lincoln in center, name of bank to left, brown seal to the right. Type I—charter number in black. Type II—similar; charter number added in brown.

Back Design: Lincoln Memorial.

SERIES	SIGNATURES	SEAL	A.B.P.	GOOD	V. FINE	UNC.
□1929	Type I Jones-Woods	Brown	35.00	50.00	135.00	475.00
□1929	Type II Jones-Woods	Brown	60.00	75.00	150.00	425.00

FIVE DOLLAR NOTES (1870)
NATIONAL GOLD BANK NOTES

(Large Size)

Face Design: Vignettes of Columbus sighting land. Presentation of an Indian princess. Red seal. Signatures, Allison-Spinner.

Back Design: California State Seal left, gold coins center, American eagle right.

DATE	BANK	CITY	A.B.P.	GOOD	V. GOOD
□1870	First National Gold Bank	San Francisco	1200.00	2500.00	3700.00
□1872	National Gold Bank and Trust Co.	San Francisco	1200.00	2500.00	3700.00
□1872	National Gold Bank of D.O. Mills and Co.	Sacramento	1600.00	2500.00	3700.00
□1873	First National Gold Bank	Santa Barbara	1600.00	2500.00	3700.00
□1873	First National Gold Bank	Stockton	2000.00	2650.00	4300.00
□1874	Farmers National Gold Bank	San Jose	2000.00	2650.00	4300.00

FIVE DOLLAR NOTES (1886–1891)
SILVER CERTIFICATES

(Large Size)

Face Design: Portrait of President Grant.

Back Design: Five silver dollars.

SERIES	SIGNATURES	SEAL	A.B.P.	GOOD	V. FINE	UNC.
□1886	Rosecrans-Jordan	Red	200.00	285.00	2700.00	RARE
□1886	Rosecrans-Hyatt	Sm. Red	200.00	285.00	2700.00	RARE
□1886	Rosecrans-Hyatt	Lg. Red	200.00	285.00	2700.00	RARE
□1886	Rosecrans-Huston	Lg. Red	200.00	285.00	2700.00	RARE
□1886	Rosecrans-Huston	Brown	200.00	285.00	2700.00	RARE
□1886	Rosecrans-Nebeker	Brown	200.00	285.00	2700.00	RARE
□1886	Rosecrans-Nebeker	Sm. Red	235.00	300.00	2950.00	RARE

FIVE DOLLAR NOTES (1891) SILVER CERTIFICATES (Large Size)

Face Design: Similar to previous note.

Back Design: Revised.

SERIES	SIGNATURES	SEAL	A.B.P.	GOOD	V. FINE	UNC.
□1891	Rosecrans-Nebeker	Red	125.00	200.00	1300.00	4000.00
□1891	Tillman-Morgan	Red	110.00	175.00	1150.00	3500.00

FIVE DOLLAR NOTES (1896) SILVER CERTIFICATES
(Large Size)

Face Design: Portraits of General Grant and General Sheridan.

Back Design: Five females representing Electricity as the dominant force in the world.

This was the last note of the popular Education Series.

SERIES	SIGNATURES	SEAL	A.B.P.	GOOD	V. FINE	UNC.
□1896	Tillman-Morgan	Red	325.00	400.00	2400.00	RARE
□1896	Bruce-Roberts	Red	325.00	400.00	2400.00	RARE
□1896	Lyons-Roberts	Red	325.00	400.00	2400.00	RARE

FIVE DOLLAR NOTES (1899) SILVER CERTIFICATES

(Large Size)

Face Design: Portrait of Indian chief.

Back Design: Green "V" and "5."

SERIES	SIGNATURES	SEAL	A.B.P.	GOOD	V. FINE	UNC.
□1899	Lyons-Roberts	Blue	200.00	275.00	1000.00	3600.00
□1899	Lyons-Treat	Blue	200.00	275.00	1000.00	3600.00
□1899	Vernon-Treat	Blue	200.00	275.00	1000.00	3600.00
□1899	Vernon-McClung	Blue	200.00	275.00	1000.00	3600.00
□1899	Napier-McClung	Blue	200.00	275.00	1000.00	3600.00
□1899	Napier-Thompson	Blue	200.00	275.00	1150.00	4000.00
□1899	Parker-Burke	Blue	200.00	275.00	1000.00	3600.00
□1899	Teehee-Burke	Blue	200.00	275.00	1000.00	3600.00
□1899	Elliott-Burke	Blue	200.00	275.00	1000.00	3600.00
□1899	Elliott-White	Blue	200.00	275.00	1000.00	3600.00
□1899	Speelman-White	Blue	200.00	275.00	1000.00	3600.00

FIVE DOLLAR NOTES (1923) SILVER CERTIFICATES
(Large Size)

Face Design: Portrait of President Lincoln in oval, nickname “Porthole Note,” blue seal left, blue “5” right.

Back Design: Obverse of Great Seal of the United States.

SERIES	SIGNATURES	SEAL	A.B.P.	GOOD	V. FINE	UNC.
□1923	Speelman-White	Blue	300.00	350.00	900.00	3200.00

FIVE DOLLAR NOTES (1934) SILVER CERTIFICATES
(Small Size)

First Issue (Small size of $5 Silver Certificates 1934.)
Face Design: Portrait of President Lincoln, blue "5" to left, blue seal to right.

Back Design: All Small Size $5 Notes have the same back design.

SERIES	SIGNATURES	SEAL	A.B.P.	GOOD	V. FINE	UNC.	★UNC.
□1934	Julian-Morgenthau	Blue	6.00	9.00	15.00	60.00	675.00
□1934A	Julian-Morgenthau	Blue	6.00	8.00	15.00	50.00	500.00
□1934A	Julian-Morgenthau	Yellow	6.50	35.00	75.00	370.00	900.00

This note, with yellow Treasury Seal, was a Special Issue during World War II for military use in combat areas of North Africa and Europe.

SERIES	SIGNATURES	SEAL	A.B.P.	GOOD	V. FINE	UNC.	★UNC.
□1934B	Julian-Vinson	Blue	7.00	10.00	25.00	150.00	600.00
□1934C	Julian-Synder	Blue	7.00	10.00	18.00	40.00	325.00
□1934D	Clark-Snyder	Blue	7.00	10.00	18.00	40.00	350.00

FIVE DOLLAR NOTES (1953) SILVER CERTIFICATES
(Small Size)

Face Design: The following notes are similar to the previous note. The face design has been revised. Gray "5" replaces blue "5" to left of Lincoln. Blue seal is slightly smaller.

Back Design: Same as previous note.

SERIES	SIGNATURES	SEAL	A.B.P.	GOOD	V. FINE	UNC.	★UNC.
□1953	Priest-Humphrey	Blue	8.00	12.00	20.00	75.00	80.00
□1953A	Priest-Anderson	Blue	6.00	10.00	15.00	30.00	40.00
□1953B	Smith-Dillon	Blue	6.00	10.00	15.00	35.00	RARE

Production of $5 Silver Certificates ended in 1962.

FIVE DOLLAR NOTES (1890) TREASURY OR COIN NOTES
(Large Size)

Face Design: Portrait of General George Henry Thomas (1816–70), the "Rock of Chickamauga."

Back Design:

SERIES	SIGNATURES	SEAL	A.B.P.	GOOD	V. FINE	UNC.
☐1890	Rosecrans-Huston	Brown	150.00	235.00	1600.00	RARE
☐1890	Rosecrans-Nebeker	Brown	150.00	235.00	1850.00	RARE
☐1890	Rosecrans-Nebeker	Red	150.00	235.00	1650.00	RARE

Back Design: Second Issue

SERIES	SIGNATURES	SEAL	A.B.P.	GOOD	V.FINE	UNC.
☐1891	Rosecrans-Nebeker	Red	125.00	175.00	700.00	3050.00
☐1891	Tillman-Morgan	Red	125.00	175.00	700.00	3050.00
☐1891	Bruce-Roberts	Red	125.00	175.00	700.00	3050.00
☐1891	Lyons-Roberts	Red	125.00	175.00	700.00	3050.00

FIVE DOLLAR NOTES (1914)
FEDERAL RESERVE NOTES

(Large Size)

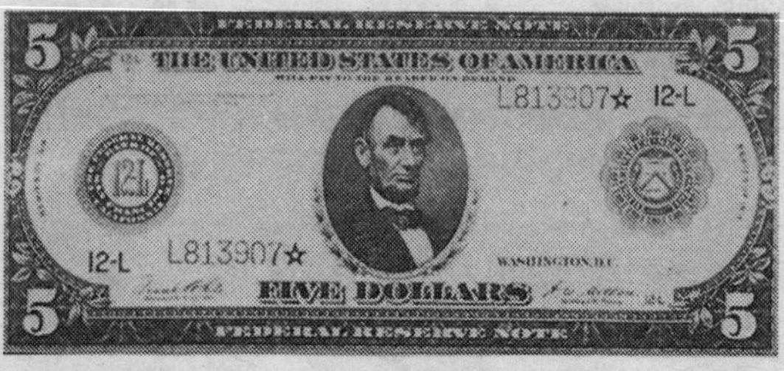

Face Design: Portrait of President Lincoln center, Federal Reserve Seal left, Treasury Seal right.

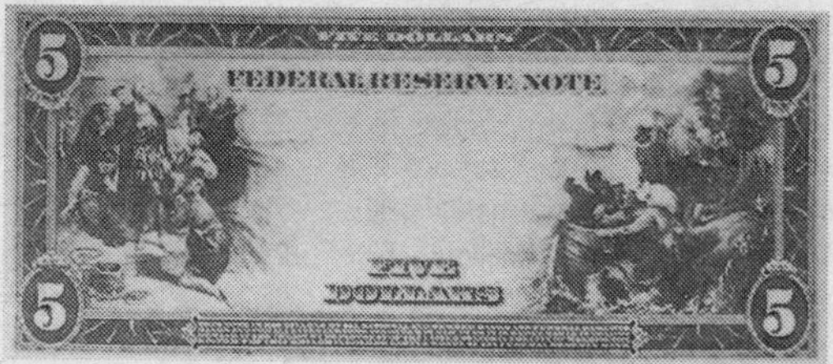

Back Design: Scene of Columbus in sight of land left, landing of Pilgrims right.

SERIES OF 1914, RED TREASURY SEAL AND RED NUMBERS

SERIES	BANK	SIGNATURES	SEAL	A.B.P.	GOOD	V. FINE	UNC.
□1914	Boston	Burke-McAdoo	Red	115.00	160.00	700.00	2600.00
□1914	New York	Burke-McAdoo	Red	115.00	160.00	575.00	2600.00
□1914	Philadelphia	Burke-McAdoo	Red	115.00	160.00	575.00	2600.00
□1914	Cleveland	Burke-McAdoo	Red	115.00	160.00	575.00	2300.00
□1914	Richmond	Burke-McAdoo	Red	115.00	160.00	600.00	2750.00
□1914	Atlanta	Burke-McAdoo	Red	115.00	160.00	575.00	2450.00
□1914	Chicago	Burke-McAdoo	Red	115.00	160.00	750.00	2700.00
□1914	St. Louis	Burke-McAdoo	Red	115.00	160.00	600.00	2450.00
□1914	Minneapolis	Burke-McAdoo	Red	115.00	160.00	650.00	2750.00
□1914	Kansas City	Burke-McAdoo	Red	115.00	160.00	550.00	2500.00
□1914	Dallas	Burke-McAdoo	Red	115.00	160.00	650.00	2600.00
□1914	San Francisco	Burke-McAdoo	Red	115.00	160.00	650.00	2650.00

FIVE DOLLAR NOTES (1914)
FEDERAL RESERVE NOTES

SERIES OF 1914, BLUE TREASURY SEAL AND BLUE NUMBERS

SERIES	BANK	SIGNATURES	SEAL	A.B.P.	GOOD	V. FINE	UNC.
□1914	Boston	Burke-McAdoo	Blue	20.00	65.00	160.00	565.00
□1914	Boston	Burke-Glass	Blue	20.00	65.00	175.00	475.00
□1914	Boston	Burke-Huston	Blue	20.00	65.00	175.00	565.00
□1914	Boston	White-Mellon	Blue	20.00	65.00	175.00	565.00
□1914	New York	Burke-McAdoo	Blue	20.00	65.00	175.00	565.00
□1914	New York	Burke-Glass	Blue	20.00	65.00	150.00	565.00
□1914	New York	Burke-Huston	Blue	20.00	65.00	160.00	465.00
□1914	New York	White-Mellon	Blue	20.00	65.00	140.00	465.00
□1914	Philadelphia	Burke-McAdoo	Blue	20.00	65.00	175.00	575.00
□1914	Philadelphia	Burke-Glass	Blue	20.00	65.00	175.00	650.00
□1914	Philadelphia	Burke-Huston	Blue	20.00	65.00	160.00	465.00

SERIES	BANK	SIGNATURES	SEAL	A.B.P.	GOOD	V. FINE	UNC.
☐1914	Philadelphia	White-Mellon	Blue	22.00	38.00	160.00	450.00
☐1914	Cleveland	Burke-McAdoo	Blue	22.00	38.00	160.00	450.00
☐1914	Cleveland	Burke-Glass	Blue	22.00	38.00	225.00	525.00
☐1914	Cleveland	Burke-Huston	Blue	22.00	38.00	145.00	350.00
☐1914	Cleveland	White-Mellon	Blue	22.00	38.00	145.00	385.00
☐1914	Richmond	Burke-McAdoo	Blue	22.00	38.00	145.00	385.00
☐1914	Richmond	Burke-Glass	Blue	22.00	38.00	220.00	545.00
☐1914	Richmond	Burke-Huston	Blue	22.00	38.00	150.00	485.00
☐1914	Richmond	White-Mellon	Blue	22.00	38.00	150.00	450.00
☐1914	Atlanta	Burke-McAdoo	Blue	22.00	38.00	215.00	525.00
☐1914	Atlanta	Burke-Glass	Blue	22.00	38.00	400.00	825.00
☐1914	Atlanta	Burke-Huston	Blue	22.00	38.00	155.00	350.00
☐1914	Atlanta	White-Mellon	Blue	22.00	38.00	155.00	375.00
☐1914	Chicago	Burke-McAdoo	Blue	22.00	38.00	225.00	525.00
☐1914	Chicago	Burke-Glass	Blue	22.00	38.00	150.00	425.00
☐1914	Chicago	Burke-Huston	Blue	22.00	38.00	150.00	425.00
☐1914	Chicago	White-Mellon	Blue	22.00	38.00	150.00	375.00
☐1914	St. Louis	Burke-McAdoo	Blue	22.00	38.00	145.00	375.00
☐1914	St. Louis	Burke-Glass	Blue	22.00	40.00		385.00
☐1914	St. Louis	Burke-Huston	Blue	22.00	38.00	160.00	360.00
☐1914	St. Louis	White-Mellon	Blue	22.00	38.00	145.00	360.00
☐1914	Minneapolis	Burke-McAdoo	Blue	22.00	38.00	170.00	450.00
☐1914	Minneapolis	Burke-Glass	Blue	22.00	38.00	220.00	475.00
☐1914	Minneapolis	Burke-Huston	Blue	22.00	38.00	165.00	450.00
☐1914	Minneapolis	White-Mellon	Blue	22.00	38.00	165.00	425.00
☐1914	Kansas City	Burke-McAdoo	Blue	22.00	38.00	165.00	445.00
☐1914	Kansas City	Burke-Glass	Blue	22.00	40.00	185.00	475.00
☐1914	Kansas City	Burke-Huston	Blue	22.00	38.00	145.00	450.00
☐1914	Kansas City	White-Mellon	Blue	22.00	38.00	225.00	360.00
☐1914	Dallas	Burke-McAdoo	Blue	22.00	38.00	225.00	400.00
☐1914	Dallas	Burke-Glass	Blue	22.00	38.00	225.00	465.00
☐1914	Dallas	Burke-Huston	Blue	22.00	38.00	225.00	455.00
☐1914	Dallas	White-Mellon	Blue	22.00	38.00	175.00	375.00
☐1914	San Francisco	Burke-McAdoo	Blue	22.00	38.00	235.00	550.00
☐1914	San Francisco	Burke-Glass	Blue	22.00	38.00	280.00	625.00
☐1914	San Francisco	Burke-Huston	Blue	22.00	38.00	215.00	525.00
☐1914	San Francisco	White-Mellon	Blue	22.00	38.00	175.00	365.00

FIVE DOLLAR NOTES (1928)
FEDERAL RESERVE NOTES

(Small Size)

Face Design: Portrait of President Lincoln center, black Federal Reserve Seal with numeral for district in center. City of issuing bank in seal circle. Green Treasury Seal to right.
Back Design: Similar to 1935 note. Lincoln Memorial in Washington, D.C.

SERIES OF 1928, SIGNATURES OF TATE AND MELLON, GREEN SEAL

BANK	A.B.P.	GOOD	V.FINE	UNC.	★UNC.	BANK	A.B.P.	GOOD	V.FINE	UNC.	★UNC.
☐ Boston	8.00	14.00	50.00	400.00	1600.00	☐ Chicago	8.00	14.00	40.00	235.00	1500.00
☐ New York	8.00	14.00	30.00	300.00	875.00	☐ St. Louis	8.00	14.00	40.00	235.00	1600.00
☐ Philadelphia	8.00	14.00	30.00	300.00	875.00	☐ Minneapolis	60.00	80.00	125.00	1000.00	3000.00
☐ Cleveland	8.00	14.00	30.00	300.00	1000.00	☐ Kansas City	8.00	14.00	40.00	275.00	2350.00
☐ Richmond	8.00	14.00	30.00	300.00	1275.00	☐ Dallas	8.00	14.00	35.00	360.00	2350.00
☐ Atlanta	8.00	14.00	30.00	300.00	1525.00	☐ San Francisco	8.00	14.00	35.00	525.00	1650.00

SERIES OF 1928A, SIGNATURES OF WOODS-MELLON, GREEN SEAL

BANK	A.B.P.	GOOD	V.FINE	UNC.	★UNC.	BANK	A.B.P.	GOOD	V.FINE	UNC.	★UNC.
☐ Boston	8.00	15.00	30.00	285.00	1550.00	☐ Chicago	8.00	15.00	30.00	215.00	1250.00
☐ New York	8.00	15.00	30.00	160.00	1050.00	☐ St. Louis	8.00	15.00	30.00	190.00	2700.00
☐ Philadelphia	8.00	15.00	30.00	185.00	1050.00	☐ Minneapolis	8.00	15.00	35.00	265.00	RARE
☐ Cleveland	8.00	15.00	30.00	185.00	1200.00	☐ Kansas City	8.00	15.00	30.00	350.00	RARE
☐ Richmond	8.00	15.00	30.00	185.00	1200.00	☐ Dallas	20.00	35.00	60.00	425.00	2100.00
☐ Atlanta	8.00	15.00	30.00	385.00	2550.00	☐ San Francisco	8.00	15.00	30.00	350.00	1650.00

SERIES OF 1928B, SIGNATURES OF WOODS-MELLON, GREEN SEAL

The black Federal Reserve Seal now has a letter for district in place of the numeral.

BANK	A.B.P.	GOOD	V.FINE	UNC.	★UNC.	BANK	A.B.P.	GOOD	V.FINE	UNC.	★UNC.
☐ Boston	7.00	13.00	23.50	130.00	900.00	☐ Chicago	8.00	15.00	24.00	150.00	1000.00
☐ New York	7.00	13.00	23.50	130.00	900.00	☐ St. Louis	8.00	15.00	24.00	150.00	1000.00
☐ Philadelphia	7.00	13.00	23.50	130.00	900.00	☐ Minneapolis	8.00	15.00	24.00	225.00	1300.00
☐ Cleveland	7.00	13.00	23.50	130.00	900.00	☐ Kansas City	8.00	15.00	24.00	150.00	1300.00
☐ Richmond	7.00	13.00	23.50	130.00	900.00	☐ Dallas	8.00	15.00	24.00	175.00	1300.00
☐ Atlanta	7.00	13.00	23.50	130.00	900.00	☐ San Francisco	8.00	15.00	24.00	150.00	1300.00

SERIES OF 1928C, SIGNATURES OF WOODS-WOODIN, GREEN SEAL

BANK	A.B.P.	GOOD	V.FINE	UNC.	★UNC.
☐ Atlanta	80.00	110.00	600.00	3500.00	RARE

SERIES OF 1928D, SIGNATURES OF WOODS-MILLS, GREEN SEAL

BANK	A.B.P.	GOOD	V.FINE	UNC.	★UNC.
☐ Atlanta	255.00	425.00	1600.00	7500.00	RARE

FIVE DOLLAR NOTES (1934)
FEDERAL RESERVE NOTES
SERIES OF 1934, JULIAN-MORGENTHAU, GREEN SEAL

"Redeemable in Gold" was removed from obligation over Federal Reserve Seal. Also, the green Treasury Seal on this note is known in a light and dark color. The light seal is worth about 10–20 percent more in most cases.

BANK	A.B.P.	V.FINE	UNC.	★UNC.	BANK	A.B.P.	V.FINE	UNC.	★UNC.
☐ Boston	8.00	15.00	70.00	300.00	☐ St. Louis	8.50	17.50	46.50	265.00
☐ New York	8.00	15.00	50.00	300.00	☐ Minneapolis	13.00	21.00	60.00	265.00
☐ Philadelphia	8.00	15.00	60.00	300.00	☐ Kansas City	8.50	17.50	46.50	265.00
☐ Cleveland	8.00	15.00	50.00	300.00	☐ Dallas	8.50	17.50	80.00	265.00
☐ Richmond	8.00	15.00	75.00	300.00	☐ San Francisco	8.50	17.50	46.50	265.00
☐ Atlanta	8.00	15.00	60.00	300.00	☐ San Francisco*	76.50	130.00	800.00	7000.00
☐ Chicago	8.00	15.00	46.50	300.00					

*This note has brown Treasury Seal and is surprinted HAWAII. For use in Pacific area of operations during World War II.

(Small Size)

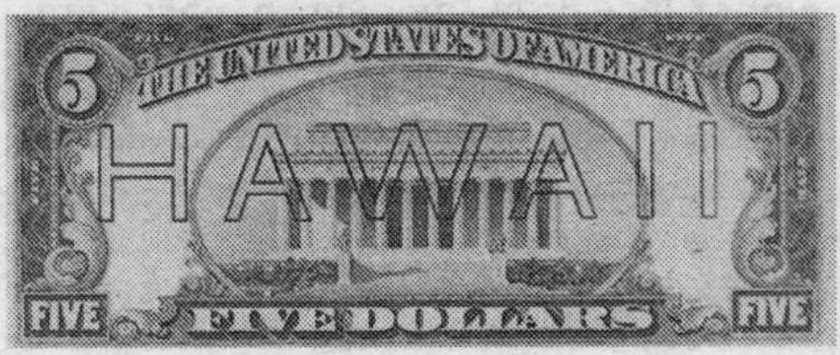

Note—1934A (Julian-Morgenthau) is surprinted HAWAII. It was used in the Pacific area during World War II.

SERIES OF 1934A, JULIAN-MORGENTHAU, GREEN SEAL

BANK	A.B.P.	V.FINE	UNC.	★UNC.	BANK	A.B.P.	V.FINE	UNC.	★UNC.
☐ Boston	7.00	15.50	53.00	350.00	☐ Atlanta	20.00	26.00	80.00	750.00
☐ New York	7.00	15.50	53.00	350.00	☐ Chicago	7.00	16.00	68.00	425.00
☐ Philadelphia	7.00	15.50	53.00	350.00	☐ St. Louis	7.00	16.00	68.00	425.00
☐ Cleveland	7.00	15.50	53.00	525.00	☐ San Francisco	7.00	16.00	68.00	425.00
☐ Richmond	7.00	15.50	53.00	425.00	☐ Hawaii*	20.00	80.00	750.00	15000.00

*This note has brown Treasury Seal and is surprinted HAWAII. For use in Pacific area of operations during World War II.

(Small Size)

SERIES OF 1934B, SIGNATURES OF JULIAN-VINSON, GREEN SEAL

BANK	A.B.P.	V.FINE	UNC.	★UNC.	BANK	A.B.P.	V.FINE	UNC.	★UNC.
☐ Boston	7.00	19.00	57.00	600.00	☐ Chicago	13.00	27.00	65.00	650.00
☐ New York	7.00	19.00	57.00	600.00	☐ St. Louis	13.00	27.00	65.00	650.00
☐ Philadelphia	7.00	19.00	57.00	600.00	☐ Minneapolis	13.00	27.00	65.00	650.00
☐ Cleveland	7.00	19.00	57.00	600.00	☐ Kansas City	650.00	1300.00	2600.00	8200.00
☐ Richmond	7.00	19.00	57.00	600.00	☐ Dallas			NOT ISSUED	
☐ Atlanta	7.00	19.00	57.00	600.00	☐ San Francisco	7.00	26.00	60.00	575.00

SERIES OF 1934C, SIGNATURES OF JULIAN-SNYDER, GREEN SEAL

BANK	A.B.P.	V.FINE	UNC.	★UNC.	BANK	A.B.P.	V.FINE	UNC.	★UNC.
☐ Boston	7.00	17.50	85.00	850.00	☐ Chicago	10.00	17.50	85.00	725.00
☐ New York	7.00	17.50	85.00	700.00	☐ St. Louis	10.00	17.50	85.00	725.00
☐ Philadelphia	7.00	17.50	85.00	750.00	☐ Minneapolis	7.00	17.50	85.00	1300.00
☐ Cleveland	7.00	17.50	85.00	600.00	☐ Kansas City	7.00	17.50	85.00	850.00
☐ Richmond	7.00	17.50	85.00	700.00	☐ Dallas	24.00	31.50	130.00	1700.00
☐ Atlanta	7.00	17.50	85.00	825.00	☐ San Francisco	7.00	17.00	85.00	850.00

SERIES OF 1934D, SIGNATURES OF CLARK-SNYDER, GREEN SEAL

BANK	A.B.P.	V.FINE	UNC.	★UNC.	BANK	A.B.P.	V.FINE	UNC.	★UNC.
☐ Boston	8.00	16.00	80.00	750.00	☐ Chicago	7.00	12.00	65.00	650.00
☐ New York	8.00	16.00	70.00	600.00	☐ St. Louis	7.00	12.00	75.00	850.00
☐ Philadelphia	8.00	16.00	75.00	800.00	☐ Minneapolis	7.00	12.00	75.00	1300.00
☐ Cleveland	8.00	16.00	75.00	850.00	☐ Kansas City	10.00	20.00	80.00	875.00
☐ Richmond	8.00	16.00	115.00	800.00	☐ Dallas	10.00	20.00	150.00	875.00
☐ Atlanta	250.00	600.00	2245.00	4800.00	☐ San Francisco	10.00	20.00	80.00	850.00

FIVE DOLLAR NOTES (1950)
FEDERAL RESERVE NOTES
BLACK FEDERAL RESERVE SEAL AND GREEN TREASURY SEALS ARE NOW SMALLER

(Small Size)

SERIES OF 1950, SIGNATURES OF CLARK-SNYDER, GREEN SEAL

BANK	A.B.P.	V.FINE	UNC.	★UNC.	BANK	A.B.P.	V.FINE	UNC.	★UNC.
☐ Boston	10.00	16.00	45.00	500.00	☐ Chicago	10.00	15.00	35.00	525.00
☐ New York	10.00	16.00	35.00	375.00	☐ St. Louis	10.00	15.00	50.00	525.00
☐ Philadelphia	10.00	16.00	35.00	450.00	☐ Minneapolis	10.00	15.00	75.00	800.00
☐ Cleveland	10.00	16.00	30.00	450.00	☐ Kansas City	10.00	15.00	75.00	475.00
☐ Richmond	10.00	16.00	45.00	535.00	☐ Dallas	10.00	15.00	65.00	650.00
☐ Atlanta	10.00	16.00	45.00	535.00	☐ San Francisco	10.00	15.00	50.00	650.00

SERIES OF 1950A, SIGNATURES OF PRIEST-HUMPHREY, GREEN SEAL

BANK	A.B.P.	V.FINE	UNC.	★UNC.	BANK	A.B.P.	V.FINE	UNC.	★UNC.
☐ Boston	8.00	15.75	26.00	75.00	☐ Chicago	8.00	15.00	30.00	115.00
☐ New York	8.00	15.75	26.00	75.00	☐ St. Louis	8.00	15.00	30.00	160.00
☐ Philadelphia	8.00	15.75	26.00	75.00	☐ Minneapolis	8.00	15.00	30.00	200.00
☐ Cleveland	8.00	15.75	26.00	75.00	☐ Kansas City	8.00	15.00	30.00	120.00
☐ Richmond	8.00	15.75	26.00	80.00	☐ Dallas	8.00	15.00	30.00	180.00
☐ Atlanta	8.00	15.75	26.00	80.00	☐ San Francisco	8.00	15.00	30.00	120.00

SERIES OF 1950B, SIGNATURES OF PRIEST-ANDERSON, GREEN SEAL

BANK	A.B.P.	V.FINE	UNC.	★UNC.	BANK	A.B.P.	V.FINE	UNC.	★UNC.
☐ Boston	8.00	15.75	26.50	65.00	☐ Chicago	8.00	15.00	25.00	70.00
☐ New York	8.00	15.75	26.50	65.00	☐ St. Louis	8.00	15.00	25.00	70.00
☐ Philadelphia	8.00	15.75	26.50	65.00	☐ Minneapolis	8.00	15.00	25.00	70.00
☐ Cleveland	8.00	15.75	26.50	65.00	☐ Kansas City	8.00	15.00	25.00	70.00
☐ Richmond	8.00	15.75	26.50	65.00	☐ Dallas	8.00	15.00	25.00	70.00
☐ Atlanta	8.00	15.75	26.50	65.00	☐ San Francisco	8.00	15.00	25.00	70.00

SERIES OF 1950C, SIGNATURES OF SMITH-DILLON, GREEN SEAL

BANK	A.B.P.	V.FINE	UNC.	★UNC.	BANK	A.B.P.	V.FINE	UNC.	★UNC.
☐ Boston	8.00	15.00	25.00	120.00	☐ Chicago	8.00	15.00	25.00	75.00
☐ New York	8.00	15.00	25.00	85.00	☐ St. Louis	8.00	15.00	25.00	195.00
☐ Philadelphia	8.00	15.00	25.00	115.00	☐ Minneapolis	8.00	15.00	25.00	245.00
☐ Cleveland	8.00	15.00	25.00	95.00	☐ Kansas City	8.00	15.00	25.00	150.00
☐ Richmond	8.00	15.00	25.00	135.00	☐ Dallas	8.00	15.00	25.00	325.00
☐ Atlanta	8.00	15.00	25.00	95.00	☐ San Francisco	8.00	15.00	25.00	330.00

SERIES OF 1950D, SIGNATURES OF GRANAHAN-DILLON, GREEN SEAL

BANK	A.B.P.	V.FINE	UNC.	★UNC.	BANK	A.B.P.	V.FINE	UNC.	★UNC.
☐ Boston	8.00	16.00	27.50	100.00	☐ Chicago	8.00	15.00	16.00	80.00
☐ New York	8.00	16.00	19.00	80.00	☐ St. Louis	8.00	15.00	25.00	140.00
☐ Philadelphia	8.00	16.00	27.50	100.00	☐ Minneapolis	8.00	15.00	30.00	175.00
☐ Cleveland	8.00	16.00	19.00	100.00	☐ Kansas City	8.00	15.00	20.00	140.00
☐ Richmond	8.00	16.00	25.00	100.00	☐ Dallas	8.00	15.00	25.00	195.00
☐ Atlanta	8.00	16.00	25.00	110.00	☐ San Francisco	8.00	15.00	16.00	135.00

SERIES OF 1950E, SIGNATURES OF GRANAHAN-FOWLER, GREEN SEAL

BANK	A.B.P.	V.FINE	UNC.	★UNC.
☐Chicago	8.00	13.00	90.00	250.00
☐New York	8.00	13.00	55.00	110.00
☐San Francisco	8.00	13.00	75.00	250.00

FIVE DOLLAR NOTES (1963)
FEDERAL RESERVE NOTES
(IN GOD WE TRUST IS ADDED ON BACK)

SERIES OF 1963, SIGNATURES OF GRANAHAN-DILLON, GREEN SEAL

BANK	A.B.P.	V.FINE	UNC.	★UNC.	BANK	A.B.P.	V.FINE	UNC.	★UNC.
☐ Boston	8.00	16.00	26.00	70.00	☐ Chicago	8.00	16.00	19.00	70.00
☐ New York	8.00	16.00	21.50	70.00	☐ St. Louis	8.00	16.00	27.50	90.00
☐ Philadelphia	8.00	16.00	21.50	70.00	☐ Minneapolis	8.00	16.00	27.50	90.00
☐ Cleveland	8.00	16.00	21.50	70.00	☐ Kansas City	8.00	16.00	27.50	90.00
☐ Richmond	8.00	16.00	21.50	70.00	☐ Dallas	8.00	16.00	27.50	90.00
☐ Atlanta	8.00	16.00	21.50	70.00	☐ San Francisco	8.00	16.00	27.50	70.00

SERIES OF 1963A, SIGNATURES OF GRANAHAN-FOWLER, GREEN SEAL

BANK	A.B.P.	V.FINE	UNC.	★UNC.	BANK	A.B.P.	V.FINE	UNC.	★UNC.
☐ Boston	7.00	13.00	19.00	43.50	☐ Chicago	7.00	13.00	19.00	43.50
☐ New York	7.00	13.00	19.00	43.50	☐ St. Louis	7.00	13.00	19.00	43.50
☐ Philadelphia	7.00	13.00	19.00	43.50	☐ Minneapolis	7.00	13.00	19.00	43.50
☐ Cleveland	7.00	13.00	19.00	43.50	☐ Kansas City	7.00	13.00	19.00	43.50
☐ Richmond	7.00	13.00	19.00	43.50	☐ Dallas	7.00	13.00	19.00	43.50
☐ Atlanta	7.00	13.00	19.00	43.50	☐ San Francisco	7.00	13.00	19.00	43.50

FIVE DOLLAR NOTES (1969)
FEDERAL RESERVE NOTES
(WORDING IN GREEN TREASURY SEAL IS CHANGED FROM LATIN TO ENGLISH)

SERIES OF 1969, SIGNATURES OF ELSTON-KENNEDY, GREEN SEAL

BANK	A.B.P.	V.FINE	UNC.	★UNC.	BANK	A.B.P.	V.FINE	UNC.	★UNC.
☐ Boston	5.00	9.00	21.00	40.00	☐ Chicago	5.00	9.00	21.00	40.00
☐ New York	5.00	9.00	21.00	40.00	☐ St. Louis	5.00	9.00	21.00	40.00
☐ Philadelphia	5.00	9.00	21.00	40.00	☐ Minneapolis	5.00	9.00	21.00	40.00
☐ Cleveland	5.00	9.00	21.00	40.00	☐ Kansas City	5.00	9.00	21.00	40.00
☐ Richmond	5.00	9.00	21.00	40.00	☐ Dallas	5.00	9.00	21.00	40.00
☐ Atlanta	5.00	9.00	21.00	40.00	☐ San Francisco	5.00	9.00	21.00	40.00

SERIES OF 1969A, SIGNATURES OF KABIS-CONNALLY, GREEN SEAL

BANK	A.B.P.	V.FINE	UNC.	★UNC.	BANK	A.B.P.	V.FINE	UNC.	★UNC.
☐ Boston	5.00	9.00	32.00	65.00	☐ Chicago	5.00	9.00	32.00	65.00
☐ New York	5.00	9.00	32.00	65.00	☐ St. Louis	5.00	9.00	32.00	65.00
☐ Philadelphia	5.00	9.00	32.00	65.00	☐ Minneapolis	5.00	9.00	32.00	65.00
☐ Cleveland	5.00	9.00	32.00	65.00	☐ Kansas City	5.00	9.00	32.00	65.00
☐ Richmond	5.00	9.00	32.00	65.00	☐ Dallas	5.00	9.00	32.00	65.00
☐ Atlanta	5.00	9.00	32.00	65.00	☐ San Francisco	5.00	9.00	32.00	65.00

SERIES OF 1969B, SIGNATURES OF BANUELOS-CONNALLY, GREEN SEAL

BANK	A.B.P.	V.FINE	UNC.	★UNC.	BANK	A.B.P.	V.FINE	UNC.	★UNC.
☐ Boston	7.00	16.00	75.00	—	☐ Chicago	7.00	16.00	53.00	200.00
☐ New York	7.00	16.00	57.50	150.00	☐ St. Louis	7.00	16.00	90.00	—
☐ Philadelphia	7.00	16.00	57.50	—	☐ Minneapolis	7.00	16.00	90.00	—
☐ Cleveland	7.00	16.00	57.50	—	☐ Kansas City	7.00	16.00	80.00	195.00
☐ Richmond	7.00	16.00	57.50	175.00	☐ Dallas	7.00	16.00	57.50	—
☐ Atlanta	7.00	16.00	57.50	185.00	☐ San Francisco	7.00	16.00	57.50	195.00

SERIES OF 1969C, SIGNATURES OF BANUELOS-SHULTZ, GREEN SEAL

BANK	A.B.P.	V.FINE	UNC.	★UNC.	BANK	A.B.P.	V.FINE	UNC.	★UNC.
☐ Boston	5.00	7.50	17.00	57.50	☐ Chicago	5.00	7.75	16.00	—
☐ New York	5.00	7.50	17.00	57.50	☐ St. Louis	5.00	7.75	16.00	57.50
☐ Philadelphia	5.00	7.50	17.00	57.50	☐ Minneapolis	5.00	7.75	16.00	57.50
☐ Cleveland	5.00	7.50	17.00	57.50	☐ Kansas City	5.00	7.75	16.00	57.50
☐ Richmond	5.00	7.50	17.00	57.50	☐ Dallas	5.00	7.75	16.00	57.50
☐ Atlanta	5.00	7.50	17.00	57.50	☐ San Francisco	5.00	7.75	16.00	57.50

FIVE DOLLAR NOTES (1974)
FEDERAL RESERVE NOTES

SERIES OF 1974, SIGNATURES OF NEFF-SIMON, GREEN SEAL

BANK	A.B.P.	V.FINE	UNC.	★UNC.	BANK	A.B.P.	V.FINE	UNC.	★UNC.
☐ Boston	—	9.00	16.00	37.50	☐ Chicago	—	9.00	16.00	37.50
☐ New York	—	9.00	16.00	37.50	☐ St. Louis	—	9.00	16.00	37.50
☐ Philadelphia	—	9.00	16.00	37.50	☐ Minneapolis	—	9.00	16.00	37.50
☐ Cleveland	—	9.00	16.00	37.50	☐ Kansas City	—	9.00	16.00	37.50
☐ Richmond	—	9.00	16.00	37.50	☐ Dallas	—	9.00	16.00	37.50
☐ Atlanta	—	9.00	16.00	37.50	☐ San Francisco	—	9.00	16.00	37.50

FIVE DOLLAR NOTES (1977)
FEDERAL RESERVE NOTES

SERIES OF 1977, SIGNATURES OF MORTON-BLUMENTHAL, GREEN SEAL

★Notes not issued for all banks

BANK	A.B.P.	V.FINE	UNC.	★UNC.	BANK	A.B.P.	V.FINE	UNC.	★UNC.
☐ Boston	—	9.00	16.00	65.00	☐ Chicago	—	9.00	16.00	42.00
☐ New York	—	9.00	16.00	32.50	☐ St. Louis	—	9.00	16.00	60.00
☐ Philadelphia	—	9.00	16.00	45.00	☐ Kansas City	—	9.00	16.00	52.50
☐ Cleveland	—	9.00	16.00	45.00	☐ Dallas	—	9.00	16.00	52.50
☐ Richmond	—	9.00	16.00	45.00	☐ San Francisco	—	9.00	16.00	52.50
☐ Atlanta	—	9.00	16.00	45.00					

SERIES OF 1977A, SIGNATURES OF MORTON-BLUMENTHAL, GREEN SEAL

BANK	A.B.P.	V.FINE	UNC.	★UNC.	BANK	A.B.P.	V.FINE	UNC.	★UNC.
☐ Boston	—	9.00	16.00	80.00	☐ Chicago	—	9.00	16.00	45.00
☐ New York	—	9.00	16.00	37.50	☐ St. Louis	—	9.00	16.00	80.00
☐ Philadelphia	—	9.00	16.00	37.50	☐ Minneapolis	—	9.00	16.00	85.00
☐ Cleveland	—	9.00	16.00	52.00	☐ Kansas City	—	9.00	16.00	65.00
☐ Richmond	—	9.00	16.00	100.00	☐ Dallas	—	9.00	16.00	53.00
☐ Atlanta	—	9.00	16.00	40.00	☐ San Francisco	—	9.00	16.00	42.00

FIVE DOLLAR NOTES (1981)
FEDERAL RESERVE NOTES

SERIES OF 1981, SIGNATURES OF BUCHANAN-REGAN, GREEN SEAL

★Notes not issued for all banks

BANK	A.B.P.	V.FINE	UNC.	★UNC.	BANK	A.B.P.	V.FINE	UNC.	★UNC.
☐ Boston	—	9.00	17.00	—	☐ Chicago	—	9.00	17.00	65.00
☐ New York	—	9.00	17.00	65.00	☐ St. Louis	—	9.00	17.00	65.00
☐ Philadelphia	—	9.00	17.00	65.00	☐ Minneapolis	—	9.00	17.00	65.00
☐ Cleveland	—	9.00	17.00	65.00	☐ Kansas City	—	9.00	17.00	65.00
☐ Richmond	—	9.00	17.00	65.00	☐ Dallas	—	9.00	17.00	65.00
☐ Atlanta	—	9.00	17.00	65.00	☐ San Francisco	—	9.00	17.00	65.00

SERIES OF 1981A, SIGNATURES OF ORTEGA-REGAN, GREEN SEAL

★Notes not issued for all banks

BANK	A.B.P.	V.FINE	UNC.	★UNC.	BANK	A.B.P.	V.FINE	UNC.	★UNC.
☐ Boston	—	10.00	27.50	—	☐ Chicago	—	11.00	27.00	—
☐ New York	—	10.00	27.50	60.00	☐ St. Louis	—	11.00	27.00	—
☐ Philadelphia	—	10.00	27.50	—	☐ Minneapolis	—	11.00	27.00	—
☐ Cleveland	—	10.00	27.50	—	☐ Kansas City	—	11.00	27.00	—
☐ Richmond	—	10.00	27.50	—	☐ Dallas	—	11.00	27.00	—
☐ Atlanta	—	10.00	27.50	—	☐ San Francisco	—	11.00	27.00	65.00

FIVE DOLLAR NOTES (1985)
FEDERAL RESERVE NOTES

SERIES OF 1985, SIGNATURES OF ORTEGA-BAKER, GREEN SEAL

★Notes not issued for all banks

BANK	A.B.P.	V.FINE	UNC.	★UNC.	BANK	A.B.P.	V.FINE	UNC.	★UNC.
☐ Boston	—	9.00	20.00	37.00	☐ Chicago	—	9.00	19.00	37.00
☐ New York	—	9.00	20.00	37.00	☐ St. Louis	—	9.00	19.00	37.00
☐ Philadelphia	—	9.00	20.00	37.00	☐ Minneapolis	—	9.00	19.00	37.00
☐ Cleveland	—	9.00	20.00	37.00	☐ Kansas City	—	9.00	19.00	37.00
☐ Richmond	—	9.00	20.00	37.00	☐ Dallas	—	9.00	19.00	37.00
☐ Atlanta	—	9.00	20.00	37.00	☐ San Francisco	—	9.00	19.00	37.00

FIVE DOLLAR NOTES (1988)
FEDERAL RESERVE NOTES
SERIES OF 1988, SIGNATURES OF ORTEGA-BRADY, GREEN SEAL

★Notes not issued for all banks

BANK	A.B.P.	V.FINE	UNC.	★UNC.	BANK	A.B.P.	V.FINE	UNC.	★UNC.
☐ Boston	—	8.00	16.00	27.00	☐ Chicago	—	8.00	16.00	27.00
☐ New York	—	8.00	16.00	27.00	☐ St. Louis	—	8.00	16.00	27.00
☐ Philadelphia	—	8.00	16.00	27.00	☐ Minneapolis	—	8.00	16.00	27.00
☐ Cleveland	—	8.00	16.00	27.00	☐ Kansas City	—	8.00	16.00	27.00
☐ Richmond	—	8.00	16.00	27.00	☐ Dallas	—	8.00	16.00	27.00
☐ Atlanta	—	8.00	16.00	27.00	☐ San Francisco	—	8.00	16.00	27.00

SERIES OF 1988A, SIGNATURES OF VILLALPANDO-BRADY, GREEN SEAL

★Notes not issued for all banks

BANK	A.B.P.	V.FINE	UNC.	★UNC.	BANK	A.B.P.	V.FINE	UNC.	★UNC.
☐ Boston	—	8.00	13.00	28.00	☐ Chicago	—	8.00	13.00	27.00
☐ New York	—	8.00	13.00	28.00	☐ St. Louis	—	8.00	13.00	27.00
☐ Philadelphia	—	8.00	13.00	28.00	☐ Minneapolis	—	8.00	13.00	27.00
☐ Cleveland	—	8.00	13.00	28.00	☐ Kansas City	—	8.00	13.00	27.00
☐ Richmond	—	8.00	13.00	28.00	☐ Dallas	—	8.00	13.00	27.00
☐ Atlanta	—	8.00	13.00	28.00	☐ San Francisco	—	8.00	13.00	27.00

FIVE DOLLAR NOTES (1993)
FEDERAL RESERVE NOTES
SERIES OF 1993, SIGNATURES OF WITHROW-BENTSEN, GREEN SEAL

★Notes not issued for all banks

BANK	A.B.P.	V.FINE	UNC.	★UNC.	BANK	A.B.P.	V.FINE	UNC.	★UNC.
☐ Boston	—	8.00	13.00	27.00	☐ Chicago	—	8.00	13.00	27.00
☐ New York	—	8.00	13.00	27.00	☐ St. Louis	—	8.00	13.00	27.00
☐ Philadelphia	—	8.00	13.00	27.00	☐ Minneapolis	—	8.00	13.00	27.00
☐ Cleveland	—	8.00	13.00	27.00	☐ Kansas City	—	8.00	13.00	27.00
☐ Richmond	—	8.00	13.00	27.00	☐ Dallas	—	8.00	13.00	27.00
☐ Atlanta	—	8.00	13.00	27.00	☐ San Francisco	—	8.00	13.00	27.00

FIVE DOLLAR NOTES (1995)
FEDERAL RESERVE NOTES
SERIES OF 1995, SIGNATURES OF WITHROW-RUBIN, GREEN SEAL

★Notes not issued for all banks

BANK	A.B.P.	V.FINE	UNC.	★UNC.	BANK	A.B.P.	V.FINE	UNC.	★UNC.
☐ Boston	—	8.00	11.00	21.00	☐ Chicago	—	8.00	11.00	21.00
☐ New York	—	8.00	11.00	21.00	☐ St. Louis	—	8.00	11.00	21.00
☐ Philadelphia	—	8.00	11.00	21.00	☐ Minneapolis	—	8.00	11.00	21.00
☐ Cleveland	—	8.00	11.00	21.00	☐ Kansas City	—	8.00	11.00	21.00
☐ Richmond	—	8.00	11.00	21.00	☐ Dallas	—	8.00	11.00	21.00
☐ Atlanta	—	8.00	11.00	21.00	☐ San Francisco	—	8.00	11.00	21.00

FIVE DOLLAR NOTES (1918)
FEDERAL RESERVE BANK NOTES
(ALL WITH BLUE SEAL AND BLUE SERIAL NUMBERS)

(Large Size)

Face Design: Portrait of President Lincoln with Reserve City in center.

Back Design: Same as 1914 note.

BANK	SERIES	GOV'T SIGNATURES	BANK SIGNATURES	A.B.P.	GOOD	V. FINE	UNC.
☐Boston	1918	Teehee-Burke	Bullen-Morse	75.00	135.00	1550.00	4000.00
☐New York	1918	Teehee-Burke	Hendricks-Strong	75.00	135.00	465.00	2100.00
☐Philadelphia	1918	Teehee-Burke	Hardt-Passmore	75.00	135.00	465.00	2100.00
☐Philadelphia	1918	Teehee-Burke	Dyer-Passmore	75.00	135.00	465.00	2100.00
☐Cleveland	1918	Teehee-Burke	Dyer-Fancher	75.00	135.00	460.00	1900.00
☐Cleveland	1918	Teehee-Burke	Davis-Fancher	75.00	135.00	460.00	1900.00
☐Cleveland	1918	Elliott-Burke	Davis-Fancher	75.00	135.00	460.00	1900.00
☐Atlanta	1915	Teehee-Burke	Bell-Wellborn	75.00	135.00	1500.00	3500.00
☐Atlanta	1915	Teehee-Burke	Pike-McCord	75.00	135.00	465.00	1900.00
☐Atlanta	1918	Teehee-Burke	Pike-McCord	75.00	135.00	525.00	1900.00
☐Atlanta	1918	Teehee-Burke	Bell-Wellborn	75.00	135.00	550.00	2000.00

BANK	SERIES	GOV'T SIGNATURES	BANK SIGNATURES	A.B.P.	GOOD	V. FINE	UNC.
□Atlanta	1918	Elliott-Burke	Bell-Wellborn	55.00	115.00	400.00	1550.00
□Chicago	1915	Teehee-Burke	McLallen-McDougal	55.00	115.00	375.00	1550.00
□Chicago	1918	Teehee-Burke	McCloud-McDougal	55.00	115.00	360.00	1550.00
□Chicago	1918	Teehee-Burke	Cramer-McDougal	55.00	115.00	425.00	1600.00
□St. Louis	1918	Teehee-Burke	Attebery-Wells	55.00	115.00	395.00	1550.00
□St. Louis	1918	Teehee-Burke	Attebery-Biggs	55.00	115.00	395.00	1625.00
□St. Louis	1918	Elliott-Burke	White-Biggs	55.00	115.00	395.00	1300.00
□Minneapolis	1918	Teehee-Burke	Cook-Wold	55.00	115.00	375.00	1550.00
□Kansas City	1915	Teehee-Burke	Anderson-Miller	45.00	100.00	375.00	1500.00
□Kansas City	1915	Teehee-Burke	Cross-Miller	45.00	100.00	385.00	1500.00
□Kansas City	1915	Teehee-Burke	Helm-Miller	45.00	100.00	1425.00	3000.00
□Kansas City	1918	Teehee-Burke	Anderson-Miller	45.00	100.00	375.00	1550.00
□Kansas City	1918	Elliott-Burke	Helm-Miller	45.00	100.00	375.00	1550.00
□Dallas	1915	Teehee-Burke	Hoopes-VanZandt	45.00	100.00	375.00	1550.00
□Dallas	1915	Teehee-Burke	Talley-VanZandt	45.00	100.00	545.00	1550.00
□Dallas	1918	Teehee-Burke	Talley-VanZandt	45.00	100.00	1500.00	3750.00
□San Francisco	1915	Teehee-Burke	Clerk-Lynch	45.00	100.00	1200.00	3000.00
□San Francisco	1918	Teehee-Burke	Clerk-Lynch	45.00	100.00	1975.00	3800.00

FIVE DOLLAR NOTES (1929)
FEDERAL RESERVE BANK NOTES

(Small Size)
Face Design: Portrait of President Lincoln.

SERIES 1929, BROWN SEAL

BANK & CITY	SIGNATURES	A.B.P.	GOOD	V.FINE	UNC.	*UNC.
☐Boston	Jones-Woods	12.00	16.00	45.00	220.00	3900.00
☐New York	Jones-Woods	12.00	16.00	45.00	200.00	3800.00
☐Philadelphia	Jones-Woods	12.00	16.00	45.00	200.00	3800.00
☐Cleveland	Jones-Woods	12.00	16.00	45.00	200.00	3800.00
☐Atlanta	Jones-Woods	12.00	16.00	45.00	375.00	3750.00
☐Chicago	Jones-Woods	12.00	16.00	45.00	200.00	3800.00
☐St. Louis	Jones-Woods	12.00	16.00	215.00	3200.00	3900.00
☐Minneapolis	Jones-Woods	12.00	16.00	75.00	1150.00	3800.00
☐Kansas City	Jones-Woods	12.00	16.00	40.00	300.00	RARE
☐Dallas	Jones-Woods	12.00	16.00	40.00	200.00	RARE
☐San Francisco	Jones-Woods	150.00	250.00	835.00	—	RARE

TEN DOLLAR NOTES

ORDER OF ISSUE

TEN DOLLAR NOTES (1861) DEMAND NOTES (NO TREASURY SEAL)

(Large Size)

Face Design: Portrait of President Lincoln left, female figure with sword and shield.

Back Design: Ornate designs of TEN.

PAYABLE AT	A.B.P.	GOOD	V. GOOD	FINE
☐Boston (I)	1400.00	3500.00	RARE	RARE
☐New York (I)	1400.00	3500.00	RARE	RARE
☐Philadelphia (I)	1400.00	3500.00	RARE	RARE
☐Cincinnati (I)	1740.00	3800.00	RARE	RARE
☐St. Louis (I)	1540.00	3800.00	RARE	RARE
☐Boston (II)	765.00	1250.00	2000.00	4500.00
☐New York (II)	750.00	1500.00	2200.00	4800.00
☐Philadelphia (II)	750.00	1500.00	2200.00	4800.00
☐Cincinnati (II)	4200.00	—	—	RARE
☐St. Louis (II)	4500.00	—	—	RARE

TEN DOLLAR NOTES (1862–1863) UNITED STATES NOTES (ALSO KNOWN AS LEGAL TENDER NOTES)

(Large Size)

Back Design

Face Design: Similar to 1861 note.

SERIES	SIGNATURES	SEAL	A.B.P.	GOOD	V.FINE	UNC.
□1862	Chittenden-Spinner*	Red	300.00	450.00	2000.00	RARE
□1862	Chittenden-Spinner**	Red	300.00	450.00	2000.00	RARE
□1863	Chittenden-Spinner**	Red	300.00	450.00	2000.00	RARE

* First Obligation: Similar to 1875–1907 $5 note.
** Second Obligation: Shown above.

TEN DOLLAR NOTES (1869) UNITED STATES NOTES

(Large Size)

Face Design: Portrait of Daniel Webster left, presentation of Indian princess right. (This note is nicknamed "Jackass Note," because the EAGLE between the signatures resembles a donkey when it is held upside down.)

SERIES	SIGNATURES	SEAL	A.B.P.	GOOD	V.FINE	UNC.
□1869	Allison-Spinner	Red	250.00	400.00	1250.00	RARE

TEN DOLLAR NOTES (1875–1880)
UNITED STATES NOTES

(Large Size)

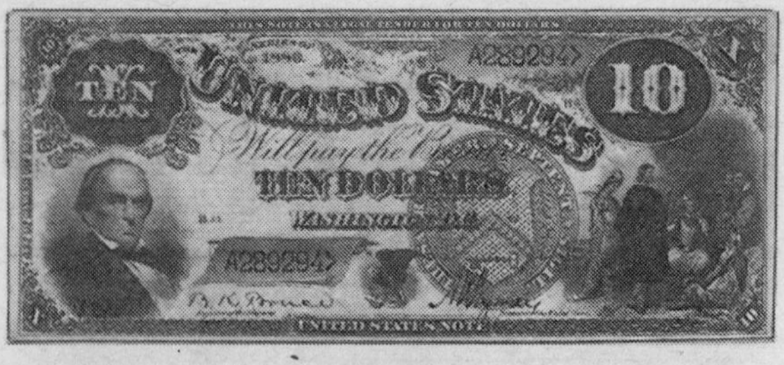

Face Design: Similar to 1869 note.

Back Design: Revised.

SERIES	SIGNATURES	SEAL	A.B.P.	GOOD	V.FINE	UNC.
□1875	Allison-New	Red	150.00	265.00	850.00	RARE
□Same as above, Series A		Red	200.00	265.00	1250.00	RARE
□1878	Allison-Gilfillan	Red	150.00	265.00	1400.00	RARE
□1880	Scofield-Gilfillan	Brown	150.00	265.00	1200.00	2400.00
□1880	Bruce-Gilfillan	Brown	150.00	265.00	1200.00	3000.00
□1880	Bruce-Wyman	Brown	150.00	265.00	1200.00	3000.00
□1880	Bruce-Wyman	Red Plain	135.00	265.00	1200.00	2600.00
□1880	Rosecrans-Jordan	Red Plain	135.00	265.00	1200.00	3400.00
□1880	Rosecrans-Hyatt	Red Plain	135.00	265.00	1200.00	3000.00
□1880	Rosecrans-Hyatt	Red Spikes	135.00	265.00	1200.00	2800.00
□1880	Rosecrans-Huston	Red Spikes	135.00	265.00	1200.00	2800.00
□1880	Rosecrans-Huston	Brown	180.00	265.00	1200.00	3200.00
□1880	Rosecrans-Nebeker	Brown	650.00	2100.00	4600.00	RARE
□1880	Rosecrans-Nebeker	Red	300.00	425.00	600.00	2200.00
□1880	Tillman-Morgan	Red	300.00	425.00	600.00	2200.00

SERIES	SIGNATURES	SEAL	A.B.P.	GOOD	V.FINE	UNC.
□1880	Bruce-Roberts	Red	200.00	250.00	650.00	2750.00
□1880	Lyons-Roberts	Red	200.00	250.00	650.00	2750.00

TEN DOLLAR NOTES (1901) UNITED STATES NOTES (Large Size)

Face Design: American bison (buffalo) center, portrait of Lewis left, portrait of Clark right.

Back Design: Female allegorical figure in arch.

SERIES	SIGNATURES	SEAL	A.B.P.	GOOD	V.FINE	UNC.
□1901	Lyons-Roberts	Red	300.00	425.00	1200.00	4850.00
□1901	Lyons-Treat	Red	300.00	425.00	1200.00	4850.00
□1901	Vernon-Treat	Red	300.00	425.00	1200.00	4850.00
□1901	Vernon-McClung	Red	300.00	425.00	1200.00	4850.00
□1901	Napier-McClung	Red	300.00	425.00	1200.00	4850.00
□1901	Parker-Burke	Red	300.00	425.00	1200.00	4850.00
□1901	Teehee-Burke	Red	300.00	425.00	1200.00	4850.00
□1901	Elliott-White	Red	300.00	425.00	1200.00	4850.00
□1901	Speelman-White	Red	300.00	425.00	1200.00	4850.00

TEN DOLLAR NOTES (1923) UNITED STATES NOTES
(Large Size)

Face Design: Portrait of President Jackson center, red seal left, red "X" to right.

Back Design

SERIES	SIGNATURES	SEAL	A.B.P.	GOOD	V.FINE	UNC.
□1923	Speelman-White	Red	375.00	600.00	2500.00	RARE

TEN DOLLAR NOTES (1863–1875)
NATIONAL BANK NOTES
FIRST CHARTER PERIOD (Large Size)

Face Design: Benjamin Franklin and kite left, name of bank and city center. Effigy of Liberty and eagle right.

Back Design: Border green, center black. DeSoto on horseback at Mississippi River.

SERIES	SIGNATURES	SEAL	A.B.P.	GOOD	V.FINE	UNC.
□Original	Chittenden-Spinner	Red	240.00	375.00	2200.00	RARE
□Original	Colby-Spinner	Red	240.00	375.00	2200.00	RARE
□Original	Jeffries-Spinner	Red	350.00	650.00	2500.00	RARE
□Original	Allison-Spinner	Red	240.00	375.00	2200.00	RARE
□1875	Allison-New	Red	240.00	375.00	2200.00	RARE
□1875	Allison-Wyman	Red	240.00	375.00	2200.00	RARE
□1875	Allison-Gilfillan	Red	240.00	375.00	2200.00	RARE
□1875	Scofield-Gilfillan	Red	240.00	375.00	2200.00	RARE
□1875	Bruce-Gilfillan	Red	240.00	375.00	2200.00	RARE
□1875	Bruce-Wyman	Red	240.00	375.00	2200.00	RARE
□1875	Rosecrans-Huston	Red	240.00	375.00	2200.00	RARE
□1875	Rosecrans-Nebeker	Red	240.00	375.00	2200.00	RARE

TEN DOLLAR NOTES (1882) NATIONAL BANK NOTES
SECOND CHARTER PERIOD (Large Size)

First Issue (Brown seal and brown backs)
Face Design: Similar to 1863–1875 note.
Back Design: Similar to 1882 $5 note. Border in brown with green Charter Number.

SERIES	SIGNATURES	SEAL	A.B.P.	GOOD	V.FINE	UNC.
□1882	Bruce-Gilfillan	Brown	275.00	325.00	1250.00	3500.00
□1882	Bruce-Wyman	Brown	275.00	325.00	1250.00	3500.00
□1882	Bruce-Jordan	Brown	275.00	325.00	1250.00	3500.00
□1882	Rosecrans-Jordan	Brown	275.00	325.00	1250.00	3500.00
□1882	Rosecrans-Hyatt	Brown	275.00	325.00	1250.00	3500.00
□1882	Rosecrans-Huston	Brown	275.00	325.00	1250.00	3500.00
□1882	Rosecrans-Nebeker	Brown	275.00	325.00	1250.00	3500.00
□1882	Rosecrans-Morgan	Brown	275.00	325.00	1250.00	3500.00
□1882	Tillman-Morgan	Brown	275.00	325.00	1250.00	3500.00
□1882	Tillman-Roberts	Brown	275.00	325.00	1250.00	3500.00

SERIES	SIGNATURES	SEAL	A.B.P.	GOOD	V.FINE	UNC.
□1882	Bruce-Roberts	Brown	275.00	340.00	1400.00	3800.00
□1882	Lyons-Roberts	Brown	275.00	340.00	1400.00	3800.00
□1882	Lyons-Treat	Brown	275.00	340.00	1400.00	3800.00
□1882	Vernon-Treat	Brown	275.00	340.00	1400.00	3800.00

Second Issue (Blue seal, green back with date "1882–1908")
Face Design: Similar to 1863–1875 note.
Back Design: Similar to 1882 $5 Second Issue note.
(Large Size)

SERIES	SIGNATURES	SEAL	A.B.P.	GOOD	V.FINE	UNC.
□1882	Rosecrans-Huston	Blue	250.00	325.00	1500.00	3000.00
□1882	Rosecrans-Nebeker	Blue	250.00	325.00	1500.00	3000.00
□1882	Rosecrans-Morgan	Blue	265.00	325.00	1500.00	3200.00
□1882	Tillman-Morgan	Blue	250.00	325.00	1500.00	3200.00
□1882	Tillman-Roberts	Blue	250.00	325.00	1500.00	3200.00
□1882	Bruce-Roberts	Blue	250.00	325.00	1500.00	3200.00
□1882	Lyons-Roberts	Blue	250.00	325.00	1500.00	3200.00
□1882	Vernon-Treat	Blue	250.00	325.00	1500.00	3200.00
□1882	Vernon-McClung	Blue	250.00	325.00	1500.00	3200.00
□1882	Napier-McClung	Blue	250.00	325.00	1500.00	3200.00

TEN DOLLAR NOTES (1882) NATIONAL BANK NOTES
(Large Size)

Third Issue (Blue seal, green back with value in block letters)
Face Design: Similar to previous notes. (*see* 1863–1875 note).
Back Design: Similar to 1882 $500 Third Issue note.

SERIES	SIGNATURES	SEAL	A.B.P.	GOOD	V. FINE	UNC.
□1882	Tillman-Roberts	Blue	375.00	450.00	1650.00	4750.00
□1882	Lyons-Roberts	Blue	375.00	450.00	1650.00	4750.00
□1882	Vernon-Treat	Blue	375.00	450.00	1650.00	4750.00
□1882	Napier-McClung	Blue	375.00	450.00	1650.00	4750.00

These notes may exist with other signatures, but are very rare.

TEN DOLLAR NOTES (1902) NATIONAL BANK NOTES
THIRD CHARTER PERIOD (Large Size)

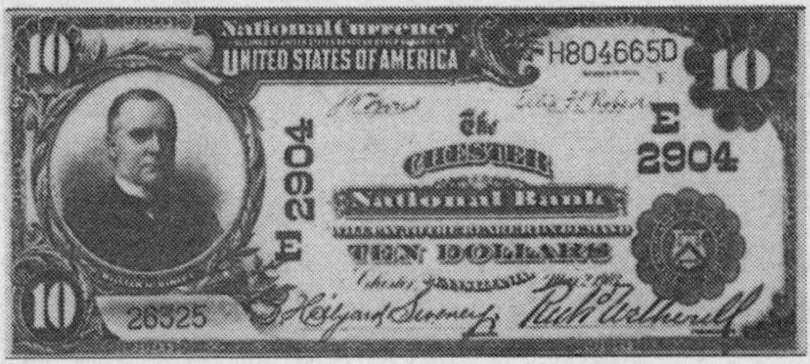

First Issue (Red seal and red Charter Numbers)
Face Design: Portrait of President McKinley left, name of bank and city in center.

SERIES	SIGNATURES	SEAL	A.B.P.	GOOD	V.FINE	UNC.
□1902	Lyons-Roberts	Red	200.00	275.00	1200.00	3200.00
□1902	Lyons-Treat	Red	200.00	275.00	1500.00	3800.00
□1902	Vernon-Treat	Red	200.00	275.00	1500.00	3800.00

TEN DOLLAR NOTES (1902) NATIONAL BANK NOTES
THIRD CHARTER PERIOD (Large Size)

Second Issue (Blue seal and numbers, "1902–1908" on the back)
Face Design: Same as 1882 Third Issue note.
Back Design: Same as 1882 Second Issue note. Date 1902–1908.

SERIES	SIGNATURES	SEAL	A.B.P.	GOOD	V.FINE	UNC.
□1902	Lyons-Roberts	Blue	85.00	125.00	300.00	800.00
□1902	Lyons-Treat	Blue	85.00	125.00	300.00	800.00
□1902	Vernon-Treat	Blue	85.00	125.00	300.00	800.00
□1902	Vernon-McClung	Blue	85.00	125.00	300.00	800.00

□1902	Napier-McClung	Blue	65.00	125.00	210.00	1750.00

SERIES	SIGNATURES	SEAL	A.B.P.	GOOD	V.FINE	UNC.
□1902	Napier-Thompson	Blue	70.00	100.00	275.00	1800.00
□1902	Napier-Burke	Blue	65.00	100.00	300.00	800.00
□1902	Parker-Burke	Blue	65.00	100.00	300.00	800.00
□1902	Teehee-Burke	Blue	65.00	100.00	300.00	1750.00

Third Issue (Blue seal and numbers, without date on back.)

SERIES	SIGNATURES	SEAL	A.B.P.	GOOD	V.FINE	UNC.
□1902	Lyons-Roberts	Blue	75.00	125.00	300.00	1200.00
□1902	Lyons-Treat	Blue	75.00	125.00	300.00	1200.00
□1902	Vernon-Treat	Blue	75.00	125.00	300.00	1200.00
□1902	Vernon-McClung	Blue	75.00	125.00	300.00	1200.00
□1902	Napier-McClung	Blue	75.00	125.00	300.00	1550.00
□1902	Napier-Thompson	Blue	75.00	125.00	300.00	1200.00
□1902	Napier-Burke	Blue	75.00	125.00	300.00	1200.00
□1902	Parker-Burke	Blue	75.00	125.00	300.00	1200.00
□1902	Teehee-Burke	Blue	75.00	125.00	300.00	1200.00
□1902	Elliott-Burke	Blue	75.00	125.00	300.00	1200.00
□1902	Elliott-White	Blue	75.00	125.00	300.00	1200.00
□1902	Speelman-White	Blue	75.00	125.00	300.00	1200.00
□1902	Woods-White	Blue	75.00	125.00	300.00	1200.00
□1902	Woods-Tate	Blue	75.00	125.00	300.00	1200.00
□1902	Jones-Woods	Blue	100.00	140.00	500.00	2500.00

TEN DOLLAR NOTES (1929) NATIONAL BANK NOTES

(Small Size)

Face Design, Type I: Portrait of Hamilton center, name of bank left, brown seal right, Charter Number black.

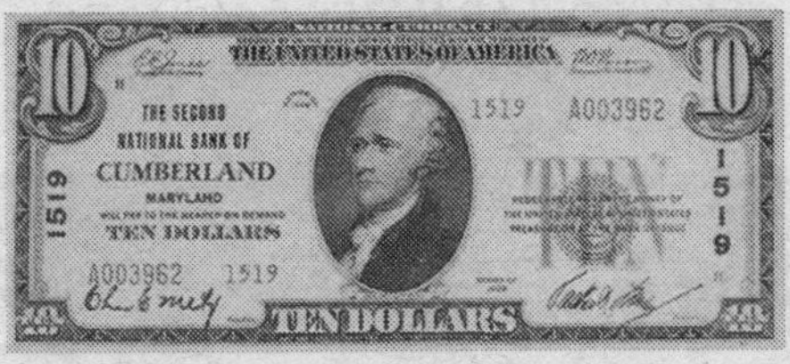

Face Design, Type II: Charter Number added in brown.

Back Design: United States Treasury Building.

SERIES	SIGNATURES	SEAL	A.B.P.	GOOD	V.FINE	UNC.
□1929, Type I	Jones-Woods	Brown	40.00	65.00	125.00	275.00
□1929, Type II	Jones-Woods	Brown	40.00	65.00	125.00	275.00

TEN DOLLAR NOTES (1870–1875)
NATIONAL GOLD BANK NOTES

(Large Size)

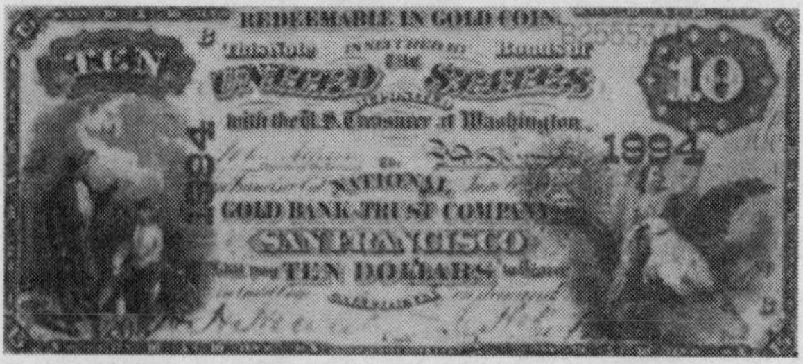

Face Design: Similar to 1863–1875 First Charter Period note.

Back Design: State Seal left, gold coins center, American eagle right.

The following have signatures of Allison-Spinner and a red Treasury Seal.

DATE	BANK	CITY	A.B.P.	GOOD	V. GOOD
□1870	First National Gold Bank	San Francisco	1200.00	2000.00	3750.00
□1872	National Gold Bank and Trust Co.	San Francisco	1200.00	2000.00	3750.00
□1872	National Gold Bank of D.O. Mills and Co.	Sacramento	2200.00	3000.00	RARE
□1873	First National Gold Bank	Santa Barbara	2200.00	3000.00	RARE
□1873	First National Gold Bank	Stockton	2200.00	3000.00	RARE
□1874	Farmers Nat'l Gold Bank	San Jose	2200.00	3000.00	RARE
□1874	First National Gold Bank	Petaluma	3000.00	3500.00	RARE
□1875	First National Gold Bank	Oakland	3000.00	3500.00	RARE

TEN DOLLAR NOTES (1880) SILVER CERTIFICATES
(Large Size)

Face Design: Portrait of Robert Morris left.

Back Design: Printed in black ink, SILVER in large letters.

SERIES	SIGNATURES	SEAL	A.B.P.	GOOD	V.FINE	UNC.
□1880	Scofield-Gilfillan	Brown	575.00	800.00	4000.00	RARE
□1880	Bruce-Gilfillan	Brown	575.00	800.00	4000.00	RARE
□1880	Bruce-Wyman	Brown	575.00	800.00	4000.00	RARE
□1880	Bruce-Wyman	Red	700.00	1000.00	4500.00	RARE

TEN DOLLAR NOTES (1886) SILVER CERTIFICATES

(Large Size)

SERIES	SIGNATURES	SEAL	A.B.P.	GOOD	V.FINE	UNC.
□1886	Rosencrans-Jordan	Sm. Red	300.00	600.00	3500.00	RARE
□1886	Rosecrans-Hyatt	Sm. Red	400.00	500.00	2500.00	RARE
□1886	Rosecrans-Hyatt	Lg. Red	400.00	500.00	2500.00	RARE
□1886	Rosecrans-Huston	Lg. Red	400.00	500.00	2500.00	RARE
□1886	Rosecrans-Huston	Lg. Brown	400.00	500.00	2500.00	RARE
□1886	Rosecrans-Nebeker	Lg. Brown	400.00	500.00	2500.00	RARE
□1886	Rosecrans-Nebeker	Sm. Red	500.00	600.00	2800.00	RARE

TEN DOLLAR NOTES (1891–1908) SILVER CERTIFICATES

(Large Size)

Face Design: Same as 1886 note.
Back Design

SERIES	SIGNATURES	SEAL	A.B.P.	GOOD	V.FINE	UNC.
□1891	Rosecrans-Nebeker	Red	165.00	225.00	1800.00	RARE
□1891	Tillman-Morgan	Red	165.00	225.00	1800.00	RARE
□1891	Bruce-Roberts	Red	165.00	225.00	1800.00	RARE
□1891	Lyons-Roberts	Red	165.00	225.00	1800.00	RARE
□1891	Vernon-Treat	Blue	165.00	225.00	1800.00	RARE
□1891	Vernon-McClung	Blue	145.00	200.00	1750.00	4500.00
□1891	Parker-Burke	Blue	145.00	200.00	1750.00	4500.00

TEN DOLLAR NOTES (1933) SILVER CERTIFICATES
(Small Size)

Face Design: Portrait of Alexander Hamilton center. Blue seal to left, blue numbers.

Back Design: Green United States Treasury Building.

SERIES	SIGNATURES	SEAL	A.B.P.	GOOD	V.FINE	UNC.
□1933	Julian-Woodin	Blue	2800.00	3500.00	—	RARE

TEN DOLLAR NOTES (1934) SILVER CERTIFICATES
(Small Size)

Face Design: Blue "10" to left of portrait, Treasury Seal is now to right.
Back Design: Similar to 1933 issue.

TEN DOLLAR NOTES (1934) SILVER CERTIFICATES
(Small Size)

SERIES	SIGNATURES	SEAL	A.B.P.	GOOD	V.FINE	UNC.	★UNC.
□1934	Julian-Morgenthau	Blue	15.00	25.00	60.00	250.00	1800.00
□1934	Julian-Morgenthau*	Yellow	500.00	750.00	4000.00	25000.00	RARE
□1934A	Julian-Morgenthau	Blue	15.00	20.00	60.00	350.00	2600.00
□1934A	Julian-Morgenthau*	Yellow	15.00	25.00	60.00	350.00	2600.00
□1934B	Julian-Vinson	Blue	20.00	50.00	300.00	5000.00	14000.00
□1934C	Julian-Snyder	Blue	15.00	25.00	50.00	350.00	2200.00
□1934D	Clark-Snyder	Blue	15.00	25.00	50.00	350.00	3250.00

* Silver Certificates with a yellow seal were a special issue for use in combat areas of North Africa and Europe during World War II.

TEN DOLLAR NOTES (1953) SILVER CERTIFICATES
(Small Size)

Face Design: Gray "10" to left of portrait. Treasury Seal is smaller.
Back Design: Back similar to previous note.

SERIES	SIGNATURES	SEAL	A.B.P.	GOOD	V.FINE	UNC.	★UNC.
□1953	Priest-Humphrey	Blue	10.00	16.00	35.00	350.00	1200.00
□1953A	Priest-Anderson	Blue	12.00	20.00	50.00	400.00	1500.00
□1953B	Smith-Dillon	Blue	10.00	18.00	40.00	225.00	NONE

Regarding the 1953 note, there were 720,000 issued. This was the last issue of $10 Silver Certificates. These were not issued with IN GOD WE TRUST on the back. Production ended in 1962.

TEN DOLLAR (1879) REFUNDING CERTIFICATES

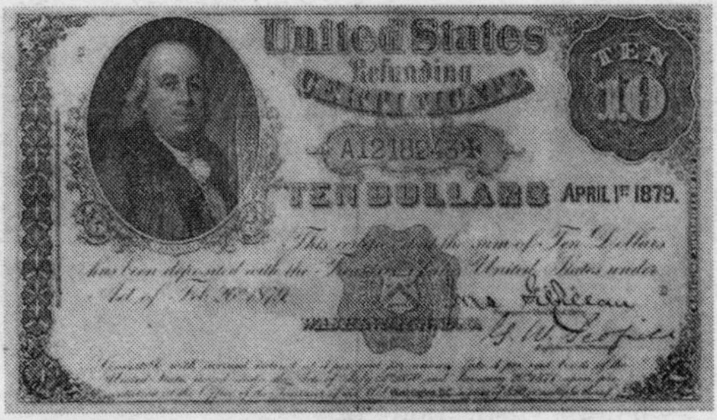

Face Design: Portrait of Benjamin Franklin.

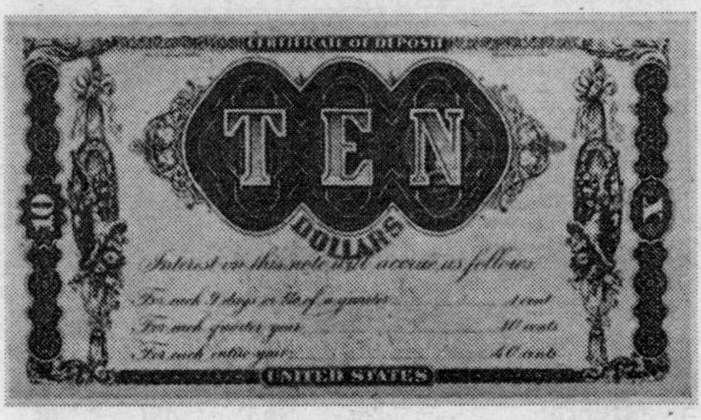

Back Design: Large TEN, ornate cornucopia border.

SERIES	SIGNATURES	SEAL	A.B.P.	GOOD	V.FINE	UNC.
□1879	Scofield-Gilfillan PAY TO ORDER	Red			VERY RARE	
□1879	Scofield-Gilfillan PAY TO BEARER	Red	1000.00	1500.00	2750.00	RARE

TEN DOLLAR NOTES (1907) GOLD CERTIFICATES (Large Size)

Face Design: Portrait of Hillegas center, yellow x left, yellow seal right, yellow numbers.

Back Design: The backs are a bright yellow color.

SERIES	SIGNATURES	SEAL	A.B.P.	GOOD	V.FINE	UNC.
□1907	Vernon-Treat	Gold	80.00	125.00	325.00	1650.00
□1907	Vernon-McClung	Gold	80.00	125.00	325.00	1800.00
□1907	Napier-McClung (1882)	Gold	80.00	125.00	325.00	1200.00
□1907	Napier-McClung (1907)	Gold	80.00	125.00	335.00	1900.00
□1907	Napier-Thompson (1882)	Gold	80.00	125.00	360.00	1900.00
□1907	Napier-Thompson (1907)	Gold	80.00	125.00	400.00	2000.00
□1907	Parker-Burke (1882)	Gold	80.00	125.00	350.00	1850.00
□1907	Teehee-Burke	Gold	80.00	125.00	350.00	1850.00
□1922	Speelman-White	Gold	80.00	125.00	350.00	1000.00

TEN DOLLAR NOTES (1928) GOLD CERTIFICATES
(Small Size)

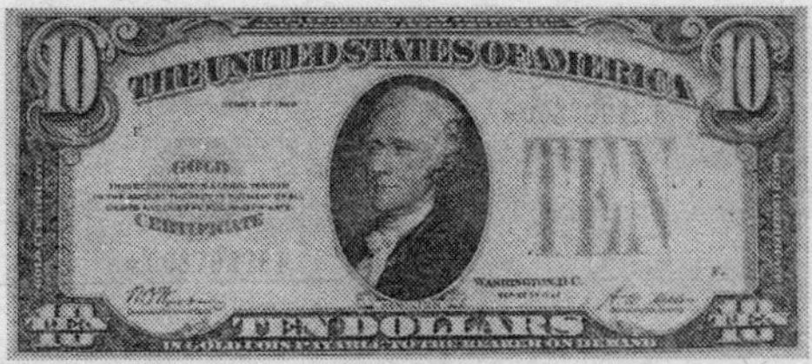

Face Design: Portrait of Alexander Hamilton center, yellow seal to left, yellow numbers.

Back Design: Printed in green ink.

SERIES	SIGNATURES	SEAL	A.B.P.	GOOD	V.FINE	UNC.
□1928	Woods-Mellon	Gold	50.00	75.00	225.00	900.00

TEN DOLLAR NOTES (1890) TREASURY OR COIN NOTES
(Large Size)

Face Design: Portrait of General Philip Sheridan.

Back Design:
Very ornate
large TEN.

SERIES	SIGNATURES	SEAL	A.B.P.	GOOD	V.FINE	UNC.
□1890	Rosecrans-Huston	Lg. Brown	375.00	450.00	2500.00	RARE
□1890	Rosecrans-Nebeker	Lg. Brown	375.00	450.00	2500.00	RARE
□1890	Rosecrans-Nebeker	Sm. Red	375.00	450.00	2500.00	RARE

TEN DOLLAR NOTES (1891) TREASURY OR COIN NOTES
(Large Size)

Face Design:
Same as 1890 note.
Back Design:
Ornate small
TEN.

SERIES	SIGNATURES	SEAL	A.B.P.	GOOD	V.FINE	UNC.
□1891	Rosecrans-Nebeker	Sm. Red	275.00	350.00	2000.00	4750.00
□1891	Tillman-Morgan	Sm. Red	275.00	350.00	2000.00	4750.00
□1891	Bruce-Roberts	Sm. Red	275.00	350.00	2000.00	RARE

TEN DOLLAR NOTES (1914)
FEDERAL RESERVE NOTES

(Large Size)

Face Design: Portrait of President Jackson center, Federal Reserve Seal left, Treasury Seal right.

Back Design: Scenes of farming and industry.

The following have signatures of Burke-McAdoo, red seals and red serial numbers.

SERIES	BANK	SEAL	A.B.P.	GOOD	V.FINE	UNC.
☐1914	Boston	Red	175.00	250.00	1400.00	3600.00
☐1914	New York	Red	175.00	250.00	1200.00	2650.00
☐1914	Philadelphia	Red	175.00	250.00	1200.00	3000.00
☐1914	Cleveland	Red	175.00	250.00	1200.00	3600.00
☐1914	Richmond	Red	175.00	250.00	1200.00	3600.00
☐1914	Atlanta	Red	175.00	250.00	1200.00	3600.00
☐1914	Chicago	Red	175.00	250.00	1200.00	3400.00
☐1914	St. Louis	Red	175.00	250.00	1200.00	3400.00
☐1914	Minneapolis	Red	175.00	250.00	1200.00	3400.00
☐1914	Kansas City	Red	175.00	250.00	1200.00	3600.00
☐1914	Dallas	Red	175.00	250.00	1200.00	3200.00
☐1914	San Francisco	Red	175.00	250.00	1200.00	3600.00

TEN DOLLAR NOTES (1914)
FEDERAL RESERVE NOTES

(Large Size)

BANK	SIGNATURES	SEAL	A.B.P.	V.FINE	UNC.
☐Boston	Burke-McAdoo	Blue	50.00	150.00	650.00
☐Boston	Burke-Glass	Blue	50.00	225.00	800.00
☐Boston	Burke-Huston	Blue	50.00	150.00	650.00
☐Boston	White-Mellon	Blue	50.00	150.00	650.00
☐New York	Burke-McAdoo	Blue	50.00	125.00	675.00
☐New York	Burke-Glass	Blue	100.00	150.00	675.00
☐New York	Burke-Huston	Blue	100.00	150.00	625.00
☐New York	White-Mellon	Blue	50.00	150.00	625.00
☐Philadelphia	Burke-McAdoo	Blue	100.00	450.00	2000.00
☐Philadelphia	Burke-Glass	Blue	100.00	450.00	2000.00
☐Philadelphia	Burke-Huston	Blue	100.00	140.00	625.00
☐Philadelphia	White-Mellon	Blue	100.00	140.00	625.00
☐Cleveland	Burke-McAdoo	Blue	100.00	350.00	1800.00
☐Cleveland	Burke-Glass	Blue	100.00	425.00	1825.00
☐Cleveland	Burke-Huston	Blue	100.00	150.00	600.00
☐Cleveland	White-Mellon	Blue	100.00	150.00	600.00
☐Richmond	Burke-McAdoo	Blue	100.00	650.00	1400.00
☐Richmond	Burke-Glass	Blue	100.00	650.00	1400.00
☐Richmond	Burke-Huston	Blue	100.00	140.00	725.00
☐Richmond	White-Mellon	Blue	100.00	140.00	725.00
☐Atlanta	Burke-McAdoo	Blue	50.00	155.00	650.00
☐Atlanta	Burke-Glass	Blue	150.00	850.00	2225.00
☐Atlanta	Burke-Huston	Blue	100.00	530.00	1800.00
☐Atlanta	White-Mellon	Blue	100.00	150.00	1000.00
☐Chicago	Burke-McAdoo	Blue	100.00	150.00	725.00
☐Chicago	Burke-Glass	Blue	100.00	150.00	725.00
☐Chicago	Burke-Huston	Blue	100.00	150.00	600.00
☐Chicago	White-Mellon	Blue	100.00	150.00	600.00
☐St. Louis	Burke-McAdoo	Blue	120.00	330.00	1200.00
☐St. Louis	Burke-Glass	Blue	120.00	450.00	1250.00
☐St. Louis	Burke-Huston	Blue	100.00	150.00	750.00
☐St. Louis	White-Mellon	Blue	100.00	150.00	750.00
☐Minneapolis	Burke-McAdoo	Blue	200.00	375.00	1225.00
☐Minneapolis	Burke-Glass	Blue	50.00	325.00	1275.00
☐Minneapolis	Burke-Huston	Blue	50.00	325.00	1275.00
☐Minneapolis	White-Mellon	Blue	100.00	150.00	850.00
☐Kansas City	Burke-McAdoo	Blue	100.00	150.00	1425.00
☐Kansas City	Burke-Glass	Blue	225.00	425.00	2000.00

BANK	SIGNATURES	SEAL	A.B.P.	V.FINE	UNC.
☐Kansas City	Burke-Huston	Blue	75.00	150.00	800.00
☐Kansas City	White-Mellon	Blue	75.00	150.00	800.00
☐Dallas	Burke-McAdoo	Blue	50.00	150.00	700.00
☐Dallas	Burke-Glass	Blue	400.00	700.00	2000.00
☐Dallas	Burke-Huston	Blue	50.00	150.00	1400.00
☐Dallas	White-Mellon	Blue	50.00	175.00	1600.00
☐San Francisco	Burke-McAdoo	Blue	160.00	400.00	1650.00
☐San Francisco	Burke-Glass	Blue	50.00	250.00	1500.00
☐San Francisco	Burke-Huston	Blue	160.00	300.00	1650.00
☐San Francisco	White Mellon	Blue	50.00	150.00	800.00

TEN DOLLAR NOTES (1928–1928A)
FEDERAL RESERVE NOTES

(Small Size)

Face Design: Portrait of Alexander Hamilton center, black Federal Reserve Seal left, with number over green Treasury Seal to the right.

Back Design: United States Treasury Building.

SERIES OF 1928, SIGNATURES OF TATE-MELLON, GREEN SEAL

BANK	A.B.P.	V.FINE	UNC.	★UNC.	BANK	A.B.P.	V.FINE	UNC.	★UNC.
☐ Boston	17.00	46.00	375.00	1550.00	☐ Chicago	18.00	40.00	500.00	1850.00
☐ New York	17.00	36.00	245.00	1250.00	☐ St. Louis	18.00	55.00	250.00	1600.00
☐ Philadelphia	17.00	41.00	245.00	1250.00	☐ Minneapolis	75.00	100.00	500.00	3000.00
☐ Cleveland	17.00	41.00	245.00	1250.00	☐ Kansas City	18.00	65.00	450.00	1650.00

BANK	A.B.P.	V.FINE	UNC.	★UNC.	BANK	A.B.P.	V.FINE	UNC.	★UNC.
☐ Richmond	35.00	70.00	365.00	2250.00	☐ Dallas	45.00	75.00	350.00	5800.00
☐ Atlanta	35.00	70.00	365.00	2250.00	☐ San Francisco	45.00	75.00	350.00	5800.00

SERIES OF 1928A, SIGNATURES OF WOODS-MELLON, GREEN SEAL

BANK	A.B.P.	V.FINE	UNC.	★UNC.	BANK	A.B.P.	V.FINE	UNC.	★UNC.
☐ Boston	55.00	100.00	600.00	1600.00	☐ Chicago	60.00	110.00	350.00	1600.00
☐ New York	55.00	100.00	375.00	1400.00	☐ St. Louis	60.00	110.00	350.00	1600.00
☐ Philadelphia	55.00	100.00	375.00	1650.00	☐ Minneapolis	100.00	170.00	2000.00	5500.00
☐ Cleveland	55.00	100.00	275.00	1400.00	☐ Kansas City	80.00	175.00	350.00	5500.00
☐ Richmond	80.00	130.00	700.00	2150.00	☐ Dallas	80.00	175.00	650.00	5500.00
☐ Atlanta	55.00	100.00	450.00	1650.00	☐ San Francisco	80.00	175.00	500.00	2200.00

TEN DOLLAR NOTES (1928B–1928C)
FEDERAL RESERVE NOTES

(Small Size)

Face Design: Alexander Hamilton; black Federal Reserve Seal left, has letter instead of number.
Back Design: Same as 1928–1928A note.

SERIES OF 1928B, SIGNATURES OF WOODS-MELLON, GREEN SEAL

BANK	A.B.P.	V.FINE	UNC.	★UNC.	BANK	A.B.P.	V.FINE	UNC.	★UNC.
☐ Boston	15.00	36.00	175.00	975.00	☐ Chicago	18.00	30.00	175.00	1000.00
☐ New York	14.00	26.00	125.00	975.00	☐ St. Louis	18.00	30.00	175.00	1000.00
☐ Philadelphia	15.00	36.00	175.00	975.00	☐ Minneapolis	27.00	60.00	225.00	1000.00
☐ Cleveland	15.00	36.00	185.00	975.00	☐ Kansas City	18.00	30.00	175.00	1000.00
☐ Richmond	22.00	40.00	175.00	975.00	☐ Dallas	27.00	50.00	225.00	1000.00
☐ Atlanta	22.00	40.00	175.00	975.00	☐ San Francisco	24.00	45.00	225.00	1000.00

SERIES OF 1928C, SIGNATURES OF WOOD-MILLS, GREEN SEAL

BANK	A.B.P.	V.FINE	UNC.
☐New York	45.00	150.00	600.00
☐Cleveland	200.00	525.00	4500.00
☐Richmond	1500.00	2500.00	18500.00
☐Chicago	60.00	175.00	675.00

TEN DOLLAR NOTES (1934)
FEDERAL RESERVE NOTES

(Small Size)

SERIES OF 1934,
SIGNATURES OF JULIAN-MORGENTHAU, GREEN SEAL

BANK	A.B.P.	V.FINE	UNC.	★UNC.	BANK	A.B.P.	V.FINE	UNC.	★UNC.
☐ Boston	10.00	15.00	55.00	400.00	☐ Chicago	15.00	25.00	90.00	475.00
☐ New York	12.00	25.00	60.00	575.00	☐ St. Louis	15.00	25.00	90.00	600.00
☐ Philadelphia	12.00	25.00	85.00	575.00	☐ Minneapolis	15.00	25.00	90.00	600.00
☐ Cleveland	12.00	25.00	85.00	575.00	☐ Kansas City	15.00	25.00	90.00	600.00
☐ Richmond	12.00	25.00	85.00	575.00	☐ Dallas	15.00	25.00	90.00	600.00
☐ Atlanta	12.00	25.00	85.00	575.00	☐ San Francisco	15.00	25.00	90.00	600.00

The green Treasury Seal on this note is known in a light and dark color. The light seal is worth about 10–20 percent more in most cases. REDEEMABLE IN GOLD removed from obligation over Federal Reserve Seal.

TEN DOLLAR NOTES (1934)
FEDERAL RESERVE NOTES

(Small Size)

SERIES OF 1934A,
SIGNATURES OF JULIAN-MORGENTHAU, GREEN SEAL

BANK	A.B.P.	V.FINE	UNC.	★UNC.	BANK	A.B.P.	V.FINE	UNC.	★UNC.
☐ Boston	12.00	15.00	65.00	400.00	☐ Chicago	12.00	15.00	75.00	475.00
☐ New York	12.00	15.00	65.00	400.00	☐ St. Louis	12.00	15.00	75.00	475.00
☐ Philadelphia	12.00	15.00	65.00	400.00	☐ Minneapolis	12.00	15.00	75.00	475.00
☐ Cleveland	12.00	15.00	65.00	400.00	☐ Kansas City	12.00	15.00	75.00	475.00
☐ Richmond	12.00	15.00	65.00	400.00	☐ Dallas	15.00	20.00	100.00	450.00
☐ Atlanta	12.00	15.00	65.00	425.00	☐ San Francisco*	15.00	20.00	100.00	450.00

* San Francisco, 1934A, with brown seal and overprinted HAWAII on face and back. Special issue for use in combat areas during World War II. Value in V. FINE $100, value in UNC. $1000. ★UNC $10000.00

SERIES OF 1934B,
SIGNATURES OF JULIAN-VINSON, GREEN SEAL

BANK	A.B.P.	V.FINE	UNC.	★UNC.	BANK	A.B.P.	V.FINE	UNC.	★UNC.
☐ Boston	12.00	25.00	110.00	675.00	☐ Chicago	15.00	25.00	85.00	700.00
☐ New York	12.00	25.00	60.00	675.00	☐ St. Louis	15.00	25.00	85.00	700.00
☐ Philadelphia	12.00	25.00	60.00	675.00	☐ Minneapolis	15.00	25.00	125.00	2000.00
☐ Cleveland	12.00	25.00	100.00	675.00	☐ Kansas City	15.00	25.00	75.00	700.00
☐ Richmond	12.00	25.00	85.00	675.00	☐ Dallas	15.00	25.00	100.00	1525.00
☐ Atlanta	12.00	25.00	85.00	675.00	☐ San Francisco	15.00	25.00	85.00	700.00

SERIES OF 1934C, SIGNATURES OF JULIAN-SNYDER, GREEN SEAL

BANK	A.B.P.	V.FINE	UNC.	★UNC.	BANK	A.B.P.	V.FINE	UNC.	★UNC.
☐ Boston	15.00	25.00	90.00	550.00	☐ Chicago	15.00	25.00	100.00	575.00
☐ New York	15.00	25.00	90.00	550.00	☐ St. Louis	15.00	25.00	100.00	575.00
☐ Philadelphia	15.00	25.00	90.00	550.00	☐ Minneapolis	15.00	25.00	100.00	1025.00
☐ Cleveland	15.00	25.00	90.00	550.00	☐ Kansas City	15.00	25.00	100.00	575.00
☐ Richmond	15.00	25.00	90.00	550.00	☐ Dallas	15.00	25.00	80.00	525.00
☐ Atlanta	15.00	25.00	90.00	550.00	☐ San Francisco	15.00	25.00	100.00	575.00

SERIES OF 1934D, SIGNATURES OF CLARK-SNYDER, GREEN SEAL

BANK	A.B.P.	V.FINE	UNC.	★UNC.	BANK	A.B.P.	V.FINE	UNC.	★UNC.
☐ Boston	15.00	25.00	85.00	575.00	☐ Chicago	15.00	25.00	65.00	575.00
☐ New York	15.00	25.00	85.00	575.00	☐ St. Louis	15.00	25.00	150.00	650.00
☐ Philadelphia	15.00	25.00	85.00	575.00	☐ Minneapolis	15.00	25.00	150.00	1000.00
☐ Cleveland	15.00	25.00	85.00	575.00	☐ Kansas City	15.00	25.00	150.00	1000.00
☐ Richmond	15.00	25.00	85.00	925.00	☐ Dallas	15.00	25.00	150.00	1200.00
☐ Atlanta	15.00	25.00	85.00	575.00	☐ San Francisco	15.00	25.00	150.00	1200.00

TEN DOLLAR NOTES (1950)

FEDERAL RESERVE NOTES

SERIES OF 1950, SIGNATURES OF CLARK-SNYDER, GREEN SEAL

BANK	A.B.P.	V.FINE	UNC.	★UNC.	BANK	A.B.P.	V.FINE	UNC.	★UNC.
☐ Boston	12.00	25.00	150.00	600.00	☐ Chicago	12.00	25.00	140.00	600.00
☐ New York	12.00	25.00	150.00	600.00	☐ St. Louis	12.00	25.00	140.00	600.00
☐ Philadelphia	12.00	25.00	150.00	600.00	☐ Minneapolis	12.00	25.00	140.00	600.00
☐ Cleveland	12.00	25.00	150.00	600.00	☐ Kansas City	12.00	25.00	140.00	600.00
☐ Richmond	12.00	25.00	150.00	600.00	☐ Dallas	12.00	25.00	140.00	600.00
☐ Atlanta	12.00	25.00	150.00	600.00	☐ San Francisco	12.00	25.00	140.00	600.00

(Small Size)

SERIES OF 1950A, SIGNATURES OF PRIEST-HUMPHERY, GREEN SEAL

BANK	A.B.P.	V.FINE	UNC.	★UNC.	BANK	A.B.P.	V.FINE	UNC.	★UNC.
☐ Boston	15.00	30.00	80.00	260.00	☐ Chicago	15.00	30.00	80.00	450.00
☐ New York	15.00	20.00	80.00	260.00	☐ St. Louis	15.00	30.00	80.00	450.00
☐ Philadelphia	15.00	30.00	80.00	260.00	☐ Minneapolis	15.00	30.00	120.00	525.00
☐ Cleveland	15.00	30.00	80.00	350.00	☐ Kansas City	15.00	30.00	80.00	475.00
☐ Richmond	15.00	30.00	80.00	500.00	☐ Dallas	15.00	30.00	80.00	350.00
☐ Atlanta	15.00	30.00	80.00	350.00	☐ San Francisco	15.00	30.00	80.00	350.00

SERIES OF 1950B, SIGNATURES OF PRIEST-ANDERSON, GREEN SEAL

BANK	A.B.P.	V.FINE	UNC.	★UNC.	BANK	A.B.P.	V.FINE	UNC.	★UNC.
☐ Boston	14.00	20.00	75.00	225.00	☐ Chicago	14.00	20.00	75.00	250.00
☐ New York	14.00	20.00	75.00	225.00	☐ St. Louis	14.00	20.00	75.00	250.00
☐ Philadelphia	14.00	20.00	75.00	225.00	☐ Minneapolis	14.00	23.00	75.00	475.00
☐ Cleveland	14.00	20.00	75.00	225.00	☐ Kansas City	14.00	23.00	75.00	250.00
☐ Richmond	14.00	20.00	75.00	225.00	☐ Dallas	14.00	23.00	75.00	500.00
☐ Atlanta	14.00	20.00	75.00	225.00	☐ San Francisco	14.00	20.00	75.00	225.00

SERIES OF 1950C, SIGNATURES OF SMITH-DILLON, GREEN SEAL

BANK	A.B.P.	V.FINE	UNC.	★UNC.	BANK	A.B.P.	V.FINE	UNC.	★UNC.
☐ Boston	14.00	20.00	70.00	450.00	☐ Chicago	14.00	20.00	70.00	450.00
☐ New York	14.00	20.00	70.00	450.00	☐ St. Louis	14.00	20.00	70.00	450.00
☐ Philadelphia	14.00	20.00	70.00	450.00	☐ Minneapolis	15.00	25.00	100.00	450.00
☐ Cleveland	14.00	20.00	70.00	450.00	☐ Kansas City	15.00	25.00	100.00	450.00
☐ Richmond	14.00	20.00	70.00	450.00	☐ Dallas	15.00	25.00	85.00	450.00
☐ Atlanta	14.00	20.00	70.00	450.00	☐ San Francisco	14.00	20.00	85.00	450.00

SERIES OF 1950D, SIGNATURES OF GRANAHAN-DILLON, GREEN SEAL

BANK	A.B.P.	V.FINE	UNC.	★UNC.	BANK	A.B.P.	V.FINE	UNC.	★UNC.
☐ Boston	14.00	25.00	70.00	325.00	☐ Chicago	14.00	35.00	65.00	325.00
☐ New York	14.00	25.00	70.00	325.00	☐ St. Louis	14.00	35.00	65.00	325.00
☐ Philadelphia	14.00	25.00	70.00	325.00	☐ Minneapolis	14.00	35.00	65.00	325.00
☐ Cleveland	14.00	25.00	70.00	325.00	☐ Kansas City	14.00	35.00	65.00	325.00
☐ Richmond	14.00	25.00	70.00	325.00	☐ Dallas	14.00	35.00	65.00	325.00
☐ Atlanta	14.00	25.00	70.00	325.00	☐ San Francisco	14.00	35.00	65.00	325.00

SERIES OF 1950E, SIGNATURES OF GRANAHAN-FOWLER, GREEN SEAL

BANK	A.B.P.	V.FINE	UNC.	★UNC.	BANK	A.B.P.	V.FINE	UNC.	★UNC.
☐ New York	14.00	25.00	100.00	400.00	☐ Chicago	14.00	25.00	95.00	340.00
					☐ San Francisco	14.00	25.00	150.00	525.00

TEN DOLLAR NOTES (1963)
FEDERAL RESERVE NOTES
(IN GOD WE TRUST IS ADDED ON BACK)

SERIES OF 1963, SIGNATURES OF GRANAHAN-DILLON, GREEN SEAL

BANK	A.B.P.	V.FINE	UNC.	★UNC.	BANK	A.B.P.	V.FINE	UNC.	★UNC.
☐ Boston	—	14.00	65.00	175.00	☐ Chicago	—	14.00	65.00	175.00
☐ New York	—	14.00	65.00	175.00	☐ St. Louis	—	14.00	65.00	175.00
☐ Philadelphia	—	14.00	65.00	175.00	☐ Minneapolis	—	14.00	65.00	175.00
☐ Cleveland	—	14.00	65.00	175.00	☐ Kansas City	—	14.00	65.00	175.00
☐ Richmond	—	14.00	65.00	175.00	☐ Dallas	—	14.00	65.00	175.00
☐ Atlanta	—	14.00	65.00	175.00	☐ San Francisco	—	14.00	65.00	175.00

SERIES OF 1963A, SIGNATURES OF GRANAHAN-FOWLER, GREEN SEAL

BANK	A.B.P.	V.FINE	UNC.	★UNC.	BANK	A.B.P.	V.FINE	UNC.	★UNC.
☐ Boston	—	15.00	45.00	150.00	☐ Chicago	—	15.00	45.00	150.00
☐ New York	—	15.00	45.00	150.00	☐ St. Louis	—	15.00	45.00	150.00
☐ Philadelphia	—	15.00	45.00	150.00	☐ Minneapolis	—	15.00	45.00	150.00
☐ Cleveland	—	15.00	45.00	150.00	☐ Kansas City	—	15.00	45.00	150.00
☐ Richmond	—	15.00	45.00	150.00	☐ Dallas	—	15.00	45.00	150.00
☐ Atlanta	—	15.00	45.00	150.00	☐ San Francisco	—	15.00	45.00	150.00

TEN DOLLAR NOTES (1969)
FEDERAL RESERVE NOTES
(WORDING IN GREEN TREASURY SEAL IS CHANGED FROM LATIN TO ENGLISH)

SERIES OF 1969, SIGNATURES OF ELSTON-KENNEDY, GREEN SEAL

BANK	A.B.P.	V.FINE	UNC.	★UNC.	BANK	A.B.P.	V.FINE	UNC.	★UNC.
☐ Boston	—	14.00	45.00	95.00	☐ Chicago	—	14.00	45.00	95.00
☐ New York	—	14.00	45.00	95.00	☐ St. Louis	—	14.00	45.00	95.00
☐ Philadelphia	—	14.00	45.00	95.00	☐ Minneapolis	—	14.00	45.00	95.00
☐ Cleveland	—	14.00	45.00	95.00	☐ Kansas City	—	14.00	45.00	95.00
☐ Richmond	—	14.00	45.00	95.00	☐ Dallas	—	14.00	45.00	95.00
☐ Atlanta	—	14.00	45.00	95.00	☐ San Francisco	—	14.00	45.00	95.00

SERIES OF 1969A, SIGNATURES OF KABIS-CONNALLY, GREEN SEAL

BANK	A.B.P.	V.FINE	UNC.	★UNC.	BANK	A.B.P.	V.FINE	UNC.	★UNC.
☐ Boston	—	14.00	45.00	95.00	☐ Chicago	—	14.00	45.00	95.00
☐ New York	—	14.00	45.00	95.00	☐ St. Louis	—	14.00	45.00	95.00
☐ Philadelphia	—	14.00	45.00	95.00	☐ Minneapolis	—	14.00	45.00	95.00
☐ Cleveland	—	14.00	45.00	95.00	☐ Kansas City	—	14.00	45.00	95.00
☐ Richmond	—	14.00	45.00	95.00	☐ Dallas	—	14.00	45.00	95.00
☐ Atlanta	—	14.00	45.00	95.00	☐ San Francisco	—	14.00	45.00	95.00

SERIES OF 1969B, SIGNATURES OF BANUELOS-CONNALLY, GREEN SEAL

BANK	A.B.P.	V.FINE	UNC.	★UNC.	BANK	A.B.P.	V.FINE	UNC.	★UNC.
☐ Boston	—	22.00	175.00	—	☐ Chicago	—	22.00	175.00	350.00
☐ New York	—	22.00	175.00	335.00	☐ St. Louis	—	22.00	175.00	350.00
☐ Philadelphia	—	22.00	175.00	—	☐ Minneapolis	—	22.00	175.00	—
☐ Cleveland	—	22.00	175.00	—	☐ Kansas City	—	22.00	175.00	335.00
☐ Richmond	—	22.00	175.00	375.00	☐ Dallas	—	22.00	175.00	—
☐ Atlanta	—	22.00	175.00	335.00	☐ San Francisco	—	22.00	175.00	335.00

SERIES OF 1969C, SIGNATURES OF BANUELOS-SHULTZ, GREEN SEAL

BANK	A.B.P.	V.FINE	UNC.	★UNC.	BANK	A.B.P.	V.FINE	UNC.	★UNC.
☐ Boston	—	—	40.00	125.00	☐ Chicago	—	—	40.00	125.00
☐ New York	—	—	40.00	125.00	☐ St. Louis	—	—	40.00	125.00
☐ Philadelphia	—	—	40.00	125.00	☐ Minneapolis	—	—	40.00	125.00
☐ Cleveland	—	—	40.00	125.00	☐ Kansas City	—	—	40.00	125.00
☐ Richmond	—	—	40.00	125.00	☐ Dallas	—	—	40.00	125.00
☐ Atlanta	—	—	40.00	125.00	☐ San Francisco	—	—	40.00	125.00

TEN DOLLAR NOTES (1974)
FEDERAL RESERVE NOTES

SERIES OF 1974, SIGNATURES OF NEFF-SIMON, GREEN SEAL

BANK	A.B.P.	V.FINE	UNC.	★UNC.	BANK	A.B.P.	V.FINE	UNC.	★UNC.
☐ Boston	—	—	30.00	110.00	☐ Chicago	—	—	30.00	110.00
☐ New York	—	—	30.00	110.00	☐ St. Louis	—	—	30.00	110.00
☐ Philadelphia	—	—	30.00	110.00	☐ Minneapolis	—	—	30.00	110.00
☐ Cleveland	—	—	30.00	110.00	☐ Kansas City	—	—	30.00	110.00
☐ Richmond	—	—	30.00	110.00	☐ Dallas	—	—	30.00	110.00
☐ Atlanta	—	—	30.00	110.00	☐ San Francisco	—	—	30.00	110.00

TEN DOLLAR NOTES (1977)
FEDERAL RESERVE NOTES

SERIES OF 1977, SIGNATURES OF MORTON-BLUMENTHAL, GREEN SEAL

BANK	A.B.P.	V.FINE	UNC.	★UNC.	BANK	A.B.P.	V.FINE	UNC.	★UNC.
☐ Boston	—	—	30.00	90.00	☐ Chicago	—	—	30.00	90.00
☐ New York	—	—	30.00	90.00	☐ St. Louis	—	—	30.00	90.00
☐ Philadelphia	—	—	30.00	90.00	☐ Minneapolis	—	—	30.00	90.00
☐ Cleveland	—	—	30.00	90.00	☐ Kansas City	—	—	30.00	90.00
☐ Richmond	—	—	30.00	90.00	☐ Dallas	—	—	30.00	90.00
☐ Atlanta	—	—	30.00	90.00	☐ San Francisco	—	—	30.00	90.00

TEN DOLLAR NOTES (1981)
FEDERAL RESERVE NOTES

SERIES OF 1981, SIGNATURES OF BUCHANAN-REGAN, GREEN SEAL

★Notes not issued for all banks

BANK	A.B.P.	V.FINE	UNC.	★UNC.	BANK	A.B.P.	V.FINE	UNC.	★UNC.
☐ Boston	—	—	28.00	80.00	☐ Chicago	—	—	28.00	80.00
☐ New York	—	—	28.00	80.00	☐ St. Louis	—	—	28.00	80.00
☐ Philadelphia	—	—	28.00	80.00	☐ Minneapolis	—	—	28.00	80.00
☐ Cleveland	—	—	28.00	80.00	☐ Kansas City	—	—	28.00	80.00
☐ Richmond	—	—	28.00	80.00	☐ Dallas	—	—	28.00	80.00
☐ Atlanta	—	—	28.00	80.00	☐ San Francisco	—	—	28.00	80.00

SERIES OF 1981A, SIGNATURES OF ORTEGA-REGAN, GREEN SEAL

★Notes not issued for all banks

BANK	A.B.P.	V.FINE	UNC.	★UNC.	BANK	A.B.P.	V.FINE	UNC.	★UNC.
☐ Boston	—	—	28.00	—	☐ Chicago	—	—	28.00	—
☐ New York	—	—	28.00	125.00	☐ St. Louis	—	—	28.00	—
☐ Philadelphia	—	—	28.00	—	☐ Minneapolis	—	—	28.00	—
☐ Cleveland	—	—	28.00	—	☐ Kansas City	—	—	28.00	—
☐ Richmond	—	—	28.00	—	☐ Dallas	—	—	28.00	—
☐ Atlanta	—	—	28.00	95.00	☐ San Francisco	—	—	28.00	—

TEN DOLLAR NOTES (1985)
FEDERAL RESERVE NOTES

SERIES OF 1985, SIGNATURES OF ORTEGA-BAKER, GREEN SEAL

★Notes not issued for all banks

BANK	A.B.P.	V.FINE	UNC.	★UNC.	BANK	A.B.P.	V.FINE	UNC.	★UNC.
☐ Boston	—	—	25.00	80.00	☐ Chicago	—	—	25.00	—
☐ New York	—	—	25.00	80.00	☐ St. Louis	—	—	25.00	80.00
☐ Philadelphia	—	—	25.00	80.00	☐ Minneapolis	—	—	25.00	80.00
☐ Cleveland	—	—	25.00	80.00	☐ Kansas City	—	—	25.00	80.00
☐ Richmond	—	—	25.00	80.00	☐ Dallas	—	—	25.00	80.00
☐ Atlanta	—	—	25.00	80.00	☐ San Francisco	—	—	25.00	80.00

TEN DOLLAR NOTES (1988)
FEDERAL RESERVE NOTES

SERIES OF 1988A, SIGNATURES OF VILLALPANDO-BRADY, GREEN SEAL

★Notes not issued for all banks

BANK	A.B.P.	V.FINE	UNC.	★UNC.	BANK	A.B.P.	V.FINE	UNC.	★UNC.
☐ Boston	—	—	25.00	150.00	☐ Chicago	—	—	25.00	—
☐ New York	—	—	25.00	150.00	☐ St. Louis	—	—	25.00	—
☐ Philadelphia	—	—	25.00	150.00	☐ Minneapolis	—	—	25.00	—
☐ Cleveland	—	—	25.00	150.00	☐ Kansas City	—	—	25.00	—
☐ Richmond	—	—	25.00	—	☐ Dallas	—	—	25.00	—
☐ Atlanta	—	—	25.00	—	☐ San Francisco	—	—	25.00	150.00

TEN DOLLAR NOTES (1990)
FEDERAL RESERVE NOTES
SERIES OF 1990, SIGNATURES OF VILLALPANDO-BRADY, GREEN SEAL

★Notes not issued for all banks

BANK	A.B.P.	V.FINE	UNC.	★UNC.	BANK	A.B.P.	V.FINE	UNC.	★UNC.
☐ Boston	—	—	18.00	—	☐ Chicago	—	—	18.00	50.00
☐ New York	—	—	18.00	52.00	☐ St. Louis	—	—	18.00	50.00
☐ Philadelphia	—	—	18.00	52.00	☐ Minneapolis	—	—	18.00	—
☐ Cleveland	—	—	18.00	—	☐ Kansas City	—	—	18.00	—
☐ Richmond	—	—	18.00	—	☐ Dallas	—	—	18.00	—
☐ Atlanta	—	—	18.00	—	☐ San Francisco	—	—	18.00	—

TEN DOLLAR NOTES (1993)
FEDERAL RESERVE NOTES
SERIES OF 1993, SIGNATURES OF WITHROW-BENTSEN, GREEN SEAL

★Notes not issued for all banks

BANK	A.B.P.	V.FINE	UNC.	★UNC.	BANK	A.B.P.	V.FINE	UNC.	★UNC.
☐ Boston	—	—	15.00	—	☐ Chicago	—	—	15.00	45.00
☐ New York	—	—	15.00	45.00	☐ St. Louis	—	—	15.00	—
☐ Philadelphia	—	—	15.00	45.00					
☐ Cleveland	—	—	15.00	—	☐ Kansas City	—	—	15.00	—
☐ Atlanta	—	—	15.00	—	☐ San Francisco	—	—	15.00	—

TEN DOLLAR NOTES (1995)
FEDERAL RESERVE NOTES
SERIES OF 1995, SIGNATURES OF WITHROW-RUBIN, GREEN SEAL

★Notes not issued for all banks

BANK	A.B.P.	V.FINE	UNC.	★UNC.	BANK	A.B.P.	V.FINE	UNC.	★UNC.
☐ Boston	—	—	18.00	—	☐ Chicago	—	—	18.00	48.50
☐ New York	—	—	18.00	—	☐ St. Louis	—	—	18.00	48.50
☐ Philadelphia	—	—	18.00	—	☐ Minneapolis	—	—	18.00	48.50
☐ Cleveland	—	—	18.00	48.50	☐ Kansas City	—	—	18.00	48.50
☐ Richmond		—	18.00	48.50	☐ Dallas	—	—	18.00	48.50
☐ Atlanta	—	—	18.00	52.00	☐ San Francisco	—	—	18.00	48.50

TEN DOLLAR NOTES (1915–1918)
FEDERAL RESERVE BANK NOTES

(Large Size)

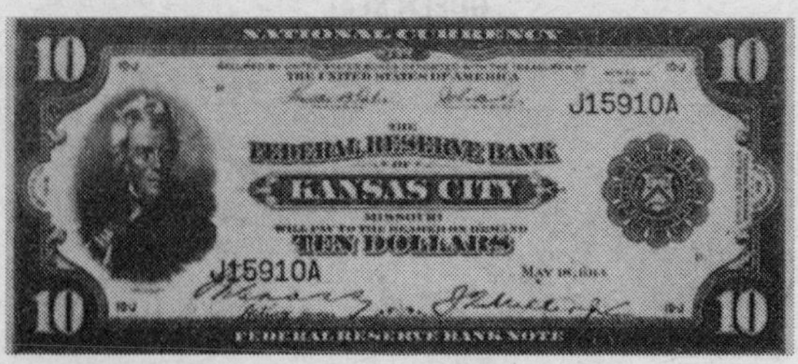

Face Design: Portrait of President Jackson to left, bank and city in center, blue seal to the right.

Back Design: Similar to 1914 note.

BANK	SERIES	GOV'T SIGNATURES	BANK SIGNATURES	A.B.P.	GOOD	V.FINE	UNC.
☐New York	1918	Teehee-Burke	Hendricks-Strong	450.00	750.00	2400.00	RARE
☐Atlanta	1915	Teehee-Burke	Bell-Wellborn	685.00	1200.00	3500.00	RARE
☐Atlanta	1918	Elliott-Burke	Bell-Wellborn	475.00	750.00	2400.00	RARE
☐Chicago	1915	Teehee-Burke	McLallen-McDougal	475.00	750.00	2400.00	RARE
☐Chicago	1918	Teehee-Burke	McCloud-McDougal	475.00	750.00	2400.00	RARE
☐St. Louis	1918	Teehee-Burke	Attebery-Wells	475.00	750.00	2400.00	RARE
☐Kansas City	1915	Teehee-Burke	Anderson-Miller	475.00	750.00	2400.00	RARE

BANK	SERIES	GOV'T SIGNATURES	BANK SIGNATURES	A.B.P.	GOOD	V.FINE	UNC.
☐Kansas City	1915	Teehee-Burke	Cross-Miller	275.00	750.00	2400.00	RARE
☐Kansas City	1915	Teehee-Burke	Helm-Miller	400.00	500.00	3500.00	RARE
☐Dallas	1915	Teehee-Burke	Hoopes-Van Zandt	260.00	660.00	2400.00	RARE
☐Dallas	1915	Teehee-Burke	Gilbert-Van Zandt	400.00	1000.00	3500.00	RARE
☐Dallas	1918	Teehee-Burke	Talley-Van Zandt	260.00	775.00	3500.00	RARE

TEN DOLLAR NOTES (1929)
FEDERAL RESERVE BANK NOTES

(Small Size)

Face Design: Portrait of Alexander Hamilton.

Back Design: Same as all Small Size $10 notes.

SIGNATURES OF JONES-WOODS, BROWN SEAL

BANK	SEAL	A.B.P.	GOOD	V.FINE	UNC.	★UNC.
☐Boston	Brown	15.00	25.00	80.00	300.00	RARE
☐New York	Brown	15.00	25.00	80.00	300.00	3200.00
☐Philadelphia	Brown	15.00	25.00	80.00	300.00	4000.00
☐Cleveland	Brown	15.00	25.00	80.00	300.00	4000.00

BANK	SEAL	A.B.P.	GOOD	V.FINE	UNC.	★UNC.
☐Richmond	Brown	15.00	25.00	60.00	500.00	4200.00
☐Atlanta	Brown	15.00	25.00	60.00	380.00	4500.00
☐Chicago	Brown	15.00	25.00	60.00	425.00	3600.00
☐St. Louis	Brown	15.00	25.00	60.00	450.00	3600.00
☐Minneapolis	Brown	15.00	25.00	60.00	450.00	3600.00
☐Kansas City	Brown	15.00	25.00	60.00	450.00	3600.00
☐Dallas	Brown	200.00	400.00	850.00	2850.00	RARE
☐San Francisco	Brown	15.00	25.00	60.00	1650.00	4500.00

TWENTY DOLLAR NOTES

ORDER OF ISSUE

TWENTY DOLLAR NOTES (1861) DEMAND NOTES (Large Size)

Face Design: Liberty with sword and shield.

Back Design: Intricate design of numerals, "20." Demand Notes have no Treasury Seal.

SERIES	PAYABLE AT	A.B.P.	GOOD	V.GOOD
□1861	Boston (I)	RARE	RARE	RARE
□1861	New York (I)	RARE	RARE	RARE
□1861	Philadelphia (I)	RARE	RARE	RARE
□1861	Cincinnati (I)	RARE	RARE	RARE
□1861	St. Louis (I)	(Unknown in any collection)		
□1861	Boston (II)	RARE	RARE	RARE
□1861	New York (II)	RARE	RARE	RARE
□1861	Philadelphia (II)	RARE	RARE	RARE
□1861	Cincinnati (II)	RARE	RARE	RARE
□1861	St. Louis (II)	(Unknown in any collection)		

Counterfeits exist. Use caution in buying.

TWENTY DOLLAR NOTES (1862–1863)
UNITED STATES NOTES
(ALSO KNOWN AS LEGAL TENDER NOTES)

(Large Size)

Face Design: Liberty with sword and shield.

Back Design: Second obligation. This note was also issued with first obligation on the back.

SERIES	SIGNATURES	SEAL	A.B.P.	GOOD	V.FINE	UNC.
□1862	Chittenden-Spinner*	Red	1100.00	1500.00	RARE	RARE
□1862	Chittenden-Spinner**	Red	1100.00	1500.00	RARE	RARE
□1863	Chittenden-Spinner**	Red	1100.00	1500.00	RARE	RARE

* First Obligation: Similar to 1875–1907 $5 note.
** Second Obligation: Shown above.

TWENTY DOLLAR NOTES (1869)
UNITED STATES NOTES
(ALSO KNOWN AS LEGAL TENDER NOTES)

(Large Size)

SERIES	SIGNATURES	SEAL	A.B.P.	GOOD	V.FINE	UNC.
□1869	Allison-Spinner	Red	425.00	600.00	2800.00	20000.00
	Series Back Design: Revised					
□1875	Allison-New	Red	300.00	475.00	1500.00	RARE
□1878	Allison-Gilfillan	Red	280.00	385.00	1275.00	5000.00
□1878	Watermark Paper		400.00	585.00	2000.00	RARE
□1880	Scofield-Gilfillan	Lg. Brown	640.00	1000.00	3375.00	RARE
□1880	Bruce-Gilfillan	Lg. Brown	240.00	460.00	2775.00	RARE
□1880	Bruce-Wyman	Lg. Brown	300.00	450.00	2300.00	5000.00
□1880	Bruce-Wyman	Lg. Red	600.00	2060.00	2275.00	RARE
□1880	Rosecrans-Jordan	Lg. Red	200.00	315.00	1200.00	5000.00
□1880	Rosecrans-Hyatt	Red Plain	175.00	300.00	1100.00	5000.00
□1880	Rosecrans-Hyatt	Red Spikes	125.00	200.00	875.00	3000.00
□1880	Rosecrans-Huston	Lg. Red	125.00	200.00	1000.00	3000.00
□1880	Rosecrans-Huston	Lg. Brown	125.00	200.00	950.00	3250.00
□1880	Rosecrans-Nebeker	Lg. Brown	125.00	200.00	2400.00	RARE
□1800	Rosecrans-Nebeker	Sm. Red	125.00	200.00	650.00	3000.00
□1880	Tillman-Morgan	Sm. Red	150.00	200.00	650.00	3000.00
□1880	Bruce-Roberts	Sm. Red	150.00	200.00	650.00	3000.00
□1880	Lyons-Roberts	Sm. Red	150.00	200.00	700.00	3000.00
□1880	Vernon-Treat	Sm. Red	150.00	200.00	755.00	3000.00
□1880	Vernon-McClung	Sm. Red	150.00	200.00	700.00	3000.00
□1880	Teehee-Burke	Sm. Red	150.00	200.00	700.00	3000.00
□1880	Elliott-White	Sm. Red	150.00	200.00	625.00	3000.00

TWENTY DOLLAR NOTES (1863–1875)
NATIONAL BANK NOTES
FIRST CHARTER PERIOD (Large Size)

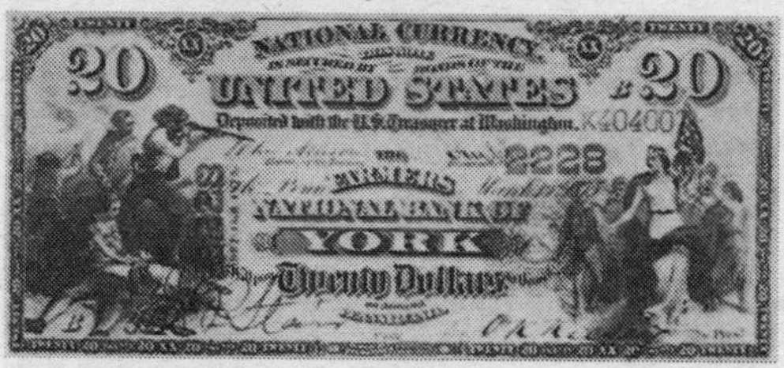

Face Design: Battle of Lexington left, name of bank in center. Columbia with flag right.

Back Design: Green border, black center picture of baptism of Pocahontas.

SERIES	SIGNATURES	SEAL	A.B.P.	GOOD	V.FINE	UNC.
□Original	Chittenden-Spinner	Red	625.00	825.00	3800.00	RARE
□Original	Colby-Spinner	Red	625.00	825.00	3800.00	RARE
□Original	Jeffries-Spinner	Red	585.00	985.00	3800.00	RARE
□Original	Allison-Spinner	Red	625.00	825.00	3800.00	RARE
□1875	Allison-New	Red	625.00	825.00	3800.00	RARE
□1875	Allison-Wyman	Red	625.00	825.00	3800.00	RARE
□1875	Allison-Gilfillan	Red	625.00	825.00	3800.00	RARE
□1875	Scofield-Gilfillan	Red	625.00	825.00	3800.00	RARE
□1875	Bruce-Gilfillan	Red	625.00	825.00	3800.00	RARE
□1875	Bruce-Wyman	Red	625.00	825.00	3800.00	RARE
□1875	Rosecrans-Huston	Red	625.00	825.00	3800.00	RARE
□1875	Rosecrans-Nebeker	Red	625.00	825.00	3800.00	RARE
□1875	Tillman-Morgan	Red	625.00	825.00	3800.00	RARE

TWENTY DOLLAR NOTES (1882)
NATIONAL BANK NOTES

SECOND CHARTER PERIOD (Large Size)

First Issue (Brown seal and brown backs.)
Face Design: Similar to First Charter Period note.
Back Design: Similar to 1882 $5 note. Border is brown, green Charter Number in center.

SERIES	SIGNATURES	SEAL	A.B.P.	GOOD	V.FINE	UNC.
□1882	Bruce-Gilfillan	Brown	550.00	700.00	1750.00	4200.00
□1882	Bruce-Wyman	Brown	550.00	700.00	1750.00	4200.00
□1882	Bruce-Jordan	Brown	550.00	700.00	1750.00	4200.00
□1882	Rosecrans-Jordan	Brown	550.00	700.00	1750.00	4200.00
□1882	Rosecrans-Hyatt	Brown	550.00	700.00	1750.00	4200.00
□1882	Rosecrans-Huston	Brown	550.00	700.00	1750.00	4200.00
□1882	Rosecrans-Nebeker	Brown	550.00	700.00	1750.00	4200.00
□1882	Rosecrans-Morgan	Brown	1820.00	760.00	1750.00	4500.00
□1882	Tillman-Morgan	Brown	550.00	700.00	1750.00	4000.00
□1882	Tillman-Roberts	Brown	550.00	700.00	1750.00	4000.00
□1882	Bruce-Roberts	Brown	550.00	700.00	1750.00	4000.00
□1882	Lyons-Roberts	Brown	550.00	700.00	1750.00	4000.00
□1882	Lyons-Treat	Brown	550.00	700.00	1750.00	4000.00
□1882	Vernon-Treat	Brown	550.00	700.00	1750.00	4000.00

SECOND CHARTER PERIOD, Second Issue

Face Design: Similar to First Charter Period note.
Back Design: Similar to 1882 $5.00 Second Issue note.

SERIES	SIGNATURES	SEAL	A.B.P.	GOOD	V.FINE	UNC.
□1882	Rosecrans-Huston	Blue	500.00	600.00	1600.00	3500.00
□1882	Rosecrans-Nebeker	Blue	500.00	600.00	1600.00	3500.00
□1882	Rosecrans-Morgan	Blue	600.00	765.00	2000.00	4500.00
□1882	Tillman-Morgan	Blue	500.00	600.00	1600.00	3500.00
□1882	Tillman-Roberts	Blue	500.00	600.00	1600.00	3500.00
□1882	Bruce-Roberts	Blue	500.00	600.00	1600.00	3500.00
□1882	Lyons-Roberts	Blue	500.00	600.00	1600.00	3500.00
□1882	Vernon-Treat	Blue	500.00	600.00	1600.00	3500.00
□1882	Napier-McClung	Blue	500.00	600.00	1600.00	3500.00

SECOND CHARTER PERIOD, Third Issue (Large Size)

Face Design: Similar to First Charter Period note with blue seal.
Back Design: Similar to 1882 Third Issue note, green back, value in block letters.

SERIES	SIGNATURES	SEAL	A.B.P.	GOOD	V.FINE	UNC.
□1882	Tillman-Morgan	Blue	750.00	900.00	1850.00	5000.00
□1882	Lyons-Roberts	Blue	600.00	800.00	1850.00	RARE
□1882	Lyons-Treat	Blue	750.00	900.00	1850.00	RARE
□1882	Vernon-Treat	Blue	750.00	900.00	1850.00	5000.00
□1882	Napier-McClung	Blue	750.00	900.00	1850.00	5000.00
□1882	Teehee-Burke	Blue	750.00	900.00	1850.00	5000.00

TWENTY DOLLAR NOTES (1902)
NATIONAL BANK NOTES
THIRD CHARTER PERIOD, First Issue (Large Size)

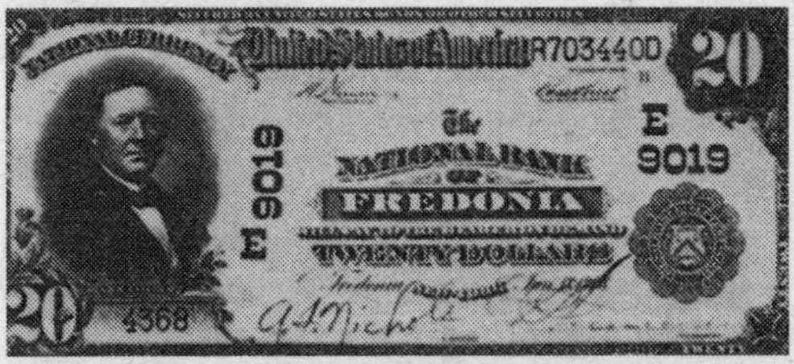

Face Design: Portrait of McCulloch left, name of bank center, Treasury Seal right.

SERIES	SIGNATURES	SEAL	A.B.P.	GOOD	V.FINE	UNC.
□1902	Lyons-Roberts	Red	450.00	550.00	1600.00	4200.00
□1902	Lyons-Treat	Red	450.00	550.00	1600.00	4200.00
□1902	Vernon-Treat	Red	450.00	550.00	1600.00	4200.00

Second Issue (Date "1902–1908" added on back, Treasury Seal and serial numbers blue)

SERIES	SIGNATURES	SEAL	A.B.P.	GOOD	V.FINE	UNC.
□1902	Lyons-Roberts	Blue	60.00	100.00	300.00	875.00
□1902	Lyons-Treat	Blue	60.00	100.00	300.00	875.00
□1902	Vernon-Treat	Blue	60.00	100.00	300.00	875.00
□1902	Vernon-McClung	Blue	60.00	100.00	300.00	875.00
□1902	Napier-McClung	Blue	60.00	100.00	300.00	875.00
□1902	Napier-Thompson	Blue	60.00	100.00	300.00	875.00
□1902	Napier-Burke	Blue	60.00	100.00	300.00	875.00
□1902	Parker-Burke	Blue	60.00	100.00	300.00	875.00

Third Issue (Date "1902–1908" removed from back, seal and serial numbers blue)

SERIES	SIGNATURES	SEAL	A.B.P.	GOOD	V.FINE	UNC.
□1902	Lyons-Roberts	Blue	60.00	100.00	250.00	850.00
□1902	Lyons-Treat	Blue	60.00	100.00	250.00	850.00
□1902	Vernon-Treat	Blue	60.00	100.00	250.00	850.00
□1902	Vernon-McClung	Blue	60.00	100.00	250.00	850.00

SERIES	SIGNATURES	SEAL	A.B.P.	GOOD	V.FINE	UNC.
□1902	Napier-McClung	Blue	60.00	100.00	250.00	850.00
□1902	Napier-Thompson	Blue	60.00	100.00	250.00	850.00
□1902	Napier-Burke	Blue	60.00	100.00	250.00	850.00
□1902	Parker-Burke	Blue	60.00	100.00	250.00	850.00
□1902	Teehee-Burke	Blue	60.00	100.00	250.00	850.00
□1902	Elliott-Burke	Blue	60.00	100.00	250.00	850.00
□1902	Elliott-White	Blue	60.00	100.00	250.00	850.00
□1902	Speelman-White	Blue	60.00	100.00	250.00	850.00
□1902	Woods-White	Blue	60.00	100.00	250.00	850.00
□1902	Woods-Tate	Blue	55.00	100.00	325.00	1200.00
□1902	Jones-Woods	Blue	63.00	650.00	1500.00	RARE

TWENTY DOLLAR NOTES (1929)
NATIONAL BANK NOTES

(Small Size)

Face Design, Type I: Portrait of President Jackson in center, name of bank to left, brown seal right. Charter number in black.

Face Design, Type II.

Back Design: The White House, similar to all $20 Small Notes.

SERIES	SIGNATURES	SEAL	A.B.P.	GOOD	V.FINE	UNC.
□1929, Type I	Jones-Woods	Brown	55.00	80.00	175.00	475.00
□1929, Type II	Jones-Woods	Brown	55.00	80.00	175.00	475.00

TWENTY DOLLAR NOTES (1880)
SILVER CERTIFICATES

(Large Size)

Face Design: Portrait of Stephen Decatur right. TWENTY SILVER DOLLARS in center.

Back Design: SILVER in large block letters.

SERIES	SIGNATURES	SEAL	A.B.P.	GOOD	V.FINE	UNC.
□1880	Scofield-Gilfillan	Brown	1200.00	1500.00		RARE
□1880	Bruce-Gilfillan	Brown	1200.00	1500.00		RARE
□1880	Bruce-Wyman	Brown	1200.00	1500.00		RARE
□1880	Bruce-Wyman	Sm. Red	1400.00	1800.00		RARE

This note was also issued in the Series of 1878. They are very rare.

TWENTY DOLLAR NOTES (1886)
SILVER CERTIFICATES

(Large Size)

Face Design: Portrait of Daniel Manning center, Agriculture left, Industry right.

Back Design: Double-diamond design center.

SERIES	SIGNATURES	SEAL	A.B.P.	GOOD	V.FINE	UNC.
□1886	Rosecrans-Hyatt	Lg. Red	1750.00	2500.00	RARE	RARE
□1886	Rosecrans-Huston	Lg. Brown	1750.00	2500.00	RARE	RARE
□1886	Rosecrans-Nebeker	Lg. Brown	1750.00	2500.00	RARE	RARE
□1886	Rosecrans-Nebeker	Sm. Red	1000.00	1500.00	RARE	RARE

TWENTY DOLLAR NOTES (1891)
SILVER CERTIFICATES
(NOT ISSUED IN SMALL SIZE NOTES)

(Large Size)

Face Design: Same as 1886 note.

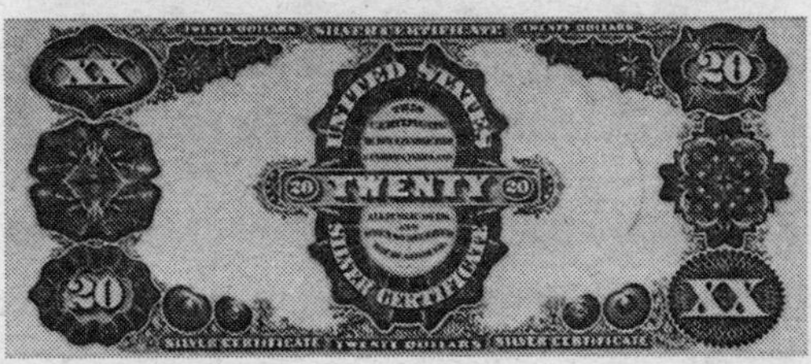

Back Design: Revised.

SERIES	SIGNATURES	SEAL	A.B.P.	GOOD	V.FINE	UNC.
□1891	Rosecrans-Nebeker	Red	300.00	400.00	2200.00	RARE
□1891	Tillman-Morgan	Red	300.00	400.00	2200.00	RARE
□1891	Bruce-Roberts	Red	300.00	400.00	2200.00	RARE
□1891	Lyons-Roberts	Red	300.00	400.00	2200.00	RARE
□1891	Parker-Burke	Blue	300.00	400.00	2200.00	RARE
□1891	Teehee-Burke	Blue	300.00	400.00	2200.00	RARE

TWENTY DOLLAR NOTES (1882) GOLD CERTIFICATES
(Large Size)

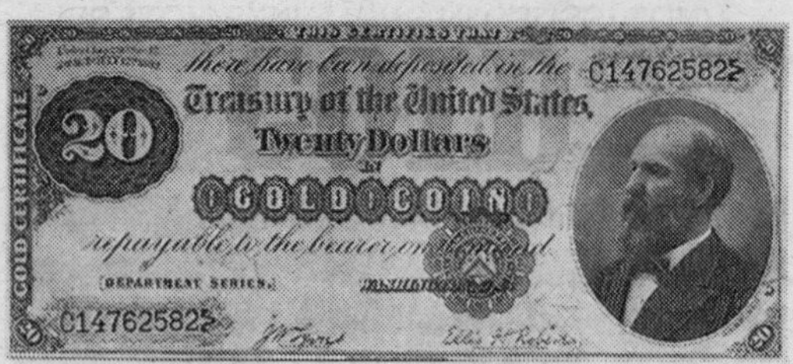

Face Design: Portrait of President Garfield right, TWENTY DOLLARS IN GOLD COIN center.

Back Design: Large "20" left, eagle and arrows center, bright orange color.

SERIES	SIGNATURES	SEAL	A.B.P.	GOOD	V.FINE	UNC.
□1882*	Bruce-Gilfillan	Brown	3550.00	RARE	RARE	RARE
□1882	Bruce-Gilfillan	Brown	2850.00	5000.00	RARE	RARE
□1882	Bruce-Wyman	Brown	1550.00	2200.00	RARE	RARE
□1882	Rosecrans-Huston	Brown	1850.00	2850.00	RARE	RARE
□1882	Lyons-Roberts	Red	225.00	400.00	2500.00	6000.00

*This note has a countersigned signature.

TWENTY DOLLAR NOTES (1905) GOLD CERTIFICATES
(Large Size)

Face Design: Portrait of President Washington center, "XX" left, Treasury Seal right.

Back Design: Eagle and shield center, printed in bright orange color.

SERIES	SIGNATURES	SEAL	A.B.P.	GOOD	V.FINE	UNC.
□1905	Lyons-Roberts	Red	350.00	450.00	3500.00	RARE
□1905	Lyons-Treat	Red	350.00	450.00	3500.00	RARE
□1906	Vernon-Treat	Gold	75.00	150.00	650.00	3150.00
□1906	Vernon-McClung	Gold	75.00	150.00	650.00	3150.00
□1906	Napier-McClung	Gold	75.00	150.00	650.00	3150.00
□1906	Napier-Thompson	Gold	110.00	175.00	800.00	3150.00
□1906	Parker-Burke	Gold	75.00	150.00	650.00	3150.00
□1906	Tehee-Burke	Gold	75.00	150.00	650.00	3150.00
□1922	Speelman-White	Gold	75.00	150.00	650.00	2500.00

TWENTY DOLLAR NOTES (1928) GOLD CERTIFICATES (Small Size)

Face Design: Portrait of President Jackson center, gold seal left, gold serial numbers.

Back Design: The White House, printed green, similar to all Small Size $20 Notes.

SERIES	SIGNATURES	SEAL	A.B.P.	V.FINE	UNC.
□1928	Woods-Mellon	Gold	150.00	275.00	1450.00

TWENTY DOLLAR NOTES (1890) TREASURY NOTES (Large Size)

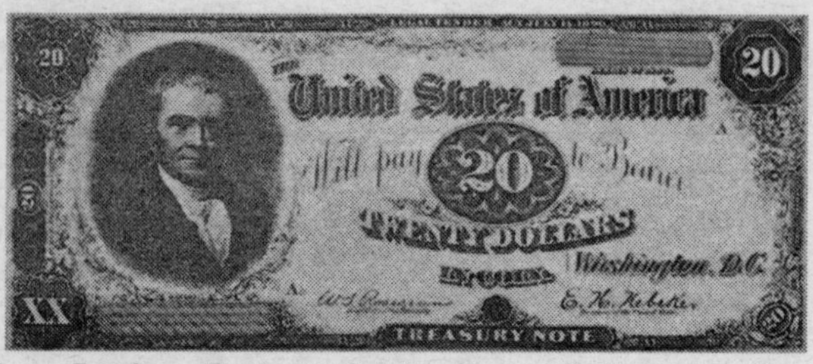

Face Design: Portrait of John Marshall, Supreme Court Chief Justice, left, "20" center.

Back Design

SERIES	SIGNATURES	SEAL	A.B.P.	GOOD	V.FINE	UNC.
□1890	Rosecrans-Huston	Brown	1000.00	1500.00	RARE	RARE
□1890	Rosecrans-Nebeker	Brown	1000.00	1500.00	RARE	RARE
□1890	Rosecrans-Nebeker	Red	1000.00	1500.00	RARE	RARE

(Large Size)

Back Design

Face Design: Same as previous note.

SERIES	SIGNATURES	SEAL	A.B.P.	GOOD	V.FINE	UNC.
□1891	Tillman-Morgan	Red	800.00	1500.00	RARE	RARE
□1891	Bruce-Roberts	Red	800.00	1500.00	RARE	RARE

TWENTY DOLLAR NOTES (1914)
FEDERAL RESERVE NOTES

(Large Size)

Face Design: Portrait of President Cleveland center, Federal Reserve Seal left, Treasury Seal right.

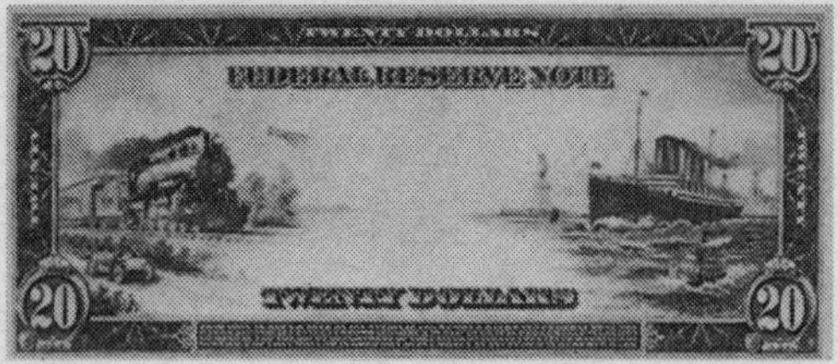

Back Design: Scenes of transportation. Locomotive left, steamship right.

(Small Size)

SERIES OF 1914, SIGNATURES OF BURKE-McADOO, RED TREASURY SEAL

BANK	A.B.P.	V.FINE	UNC.	BANK	A.B.P.	V.FINE	UNC.
☐ Boston	150.00	700.00	2500.00	☐ Chicago	150.00	1650.00	RARE
☐ New York	150.00	700.00	2500.00	☐ St. Louis	150.00	1650.00	RARE
☐ Philadelphia	150.00	1450.00	2500.00	☐ Minneapolis	150.00	1650.00	RARE
☐ Cleveland	150.00	1450.00	2500.00	☐ Kansas City	150.00	1650.00	RARE
☐ Richmond	150.00	1450.00	2500.00	☐ Dallas	150.00	1650.00	RARE
☐ Atlanta	150.00	1450.00	2500.00	☐ San Francisco	150.00	1650.00	RARE

SERIES OF 1914, BLUE TREASURY SEAL AND BLUE SERIAL NUMBERS

(Small Size)

This note was issued with signatures of Burke-McAdoo, Burke-Glass, Burke-Huston, and White-Mellon.

TWENTY DOLLAR NOTES (1914)
FEDERAL RESERVE NOTES
1914, BLUE TREASURY SEAL AND BLUE NUMBERS

DATE	CITY	SIGNATURES	SEAL	A.B.P.	GOOD	V.FINE	UNC.
1914	Boston	Burke-McAdoo	Blue	40.00	55.00	230.00	675.00
1914	Boston	Burke-Glass	Blue	40.00	60.00	230.00	2000.00
1914	Boston	Burke-Huston	Blue	40.00	55.00	230.00	1200.00
1914	Boston	White-Mellon	Blue	40.00	55.00	230.00	1200.00
1914	New York	Burke-McAdoo	Blue	40.00	55.00	230.00	1200.00
1914	New York	Burke-Glass	Blue	40.00	55.00	230.00	1200.00
1914	New York	Burke-Huston	Blue	40.00	55.00	230.00	1200.00
1914	New York	White-Mellon	Blue	40.00	55.00	230.00	675.00
1914	Phila.	Burke-McAdoo	Blue	40.00	52.00	230.00	700.00
1914	Phila.	Burke-Glass	Blue	40.00	55.00	735.00	1650.00
1914	Phila.	Burke-Huston	Blue	40.00	55.00	230.00	675.00
1914	Phila.	White-Mellon	Blue	40.00	55.00	230.00	675.00
1914	Cleveland	Burke-McAdoo	Blue	40.00	55.00	230.00	700.00

DATE	CITY	SIGNATURES	SEAL	A.B.P.	GOOD	V.FINE	UNC.
1914	Cleveland	Burke-Glass	Blue	40.00	60.00	725.00	1600.00
1914	Cleveland	Burke-Huston	Blue	40.00	55.00	450.00	1600.00
1914	Cleveland	White-Mellon	Blue	40.00	55.00	200.00	700.00
1914	Richmond	Burke-McAdoo	Blue	40.00	60.00	725.00	1675.00
1914	Richmond	Burke-Glass	Blue	40.00	60.00	850.00	1675.00
1914	Richmond	Burke-Huston	Blue	40.00	57.00	275.00	1200.00
1914	Richmond	White-Mellon	Blue	40.00	55.00	200.00	550.00
1914	Atlanta	Burke-McAdoo	Blue	40.00	55.00	245.00	1200.00
1914	Atlanta	Burke-Glass	Blue	150.00	200.00	1200.00	2000.00
1914	Atlanta	Burke-Huston	Blue	40.00	55.00	200.00	750.00
1914	Atlanta	White-Mellon	Blue	40.00	60.00	725.00	1475.00
1914	Chicago	Burke-McAdoo	Blue	40.00	55.00	150.00	750.00
1914	Chicago	Burke-Glass	Blue	40.00	55.00	200.00	750.00
1914	Chicago	Burke-Huston	Blue	40.00	55.00	300.00	750.00
1914	Chicago	White-Mellon	Blue	40.00	55.00	300.00	750.00
1914	St. Louis	Burke-McAdoo	Blue	40.00	55.00	300.00	750.00
1914	St. Louis	Burke-Glass	Blue	40.00	60.00	725.00	1250.00
1914	St. Louis	Burke-Huston	Blue	40.00	55.00	155.00	750.00
1914	St. Louis	White-Mellon	Blue	40.00	55.00	300.00	750.00
1914	Minneapolis	Burke-McAdoo	Blue	40.00	55.00	200.00	750.00
1914	Minneapolis	Burke-Glass	Blue	50.00	75.00	875.00	2000.00
1914	Minneapolis	Burke-Huston	Blue	40.00	55.00	250.00	725.00
1914	Minneapolis	White-Mellon	Blue	40.00	55.00	200.00	725.00
1914	Kansas City	Burke-McAdoo	Blue	40.00	55.00	300.00	725.00
1914	Kansas City	Burke-Glass	Blue	40.00	75.00	200.00	750.00
1914	Kansas City	Burke-Huston	Blue	40.00	55.00	200.00	725.00
1914	Kansas City	White-Mellon	Blue	44.00	60.00	725.00	1200.00
1914	Dallas	Burke-McAdoo	Blue	40.00	55.00	800.00	1200.00
1914	Dallas	Burke-Glass	Blue	40.00	60.00	725.00	1625.00
1914	Dallas	Burke-Huston	Blue	40.00	55.00	555.00	1000.00
1914	Dallas	White-Mellon	Blue	40.00	55.00	200.00	1000.00
1914	San Fran.	Burke-McAdoo	Blue	40.00	55.00	455.00	1000.00
1914	San Fran.	Burke-Glass	Blue	40.00	55.00	475.00	725.00
1914	San Fran.	Burke-Huston	Blue	40.00	55.00	300.00	825.00
1914	San Fran.	White-Mellon	Blue	40.00	55.00	155.00	725.00

TWENTY DOLLAR NOTES (1928)

FEDERAL RESERVE NOTES

(Small Size)

Face Design: Portrait of President Jackson center, black Federal Reserve Seal with numeral for district in center. City of issuing bank in Seal circle. Green Treasury Seal right.

Back Design: Picture of the White House, similar to all Small Size $20 Notes.

(Small Size)

SERIES OF 1928, SIGNATURES OF TATE-MELLON, GREEN SEAL

BANK	A.B.P.	V.FINE	UNC.	★UNC.	BANK	A.B.P.	V.FINE	UNC.	★UNC.
☐ Boston	32.00	55.00	295.00	2200.00	☐ Chicago	32.00	50.00	350.00	2200.00
☐ New York	32.00	45.00	255.00	1650.00	☐ St. Louis	32.00	55.00	350.00	2850.00
☐ Philadelphia	32.00	55.00	355.00	2000.00	☐ Minneapolis	32.00	55.00	500.00	2850.00
☐ Cleveland	32.00	75.00	345.00	1800.00	☐ Kansas City	60.00	85.00	325.00	2200.00
☐ Richmond	32.00	75.00	355.00	3150.00	☐ Dallas	60.00	85.00	420.00	7500.00
☐ Atlanta	32.00	65.00	420.00	3000.00	☐ San Francisco	60.00	85.00	375.00	2400.00

(Small Size)

SERIES OF 1928A, SIGNATURES OF WOODS-MELLON, GREEN SEAL

CITY	A.B.P.	V.FINE	UNC.	★UNC.	CITY	A.B.P.	V.FINE	UNC.	★UNC.
☐ Boston	33.00	65.00	400.00	4300.00	☐ Chicago	50.00	80.00	550.00	RARE
☐ New York	33.00	65.00	335.00	4375.00	☐ St. Louis	50.00	80.00	550.00	RARE
☐ Philadelphia	33.00	70.00	335.00	4375.00	☐ Minneapolis	NOT ISSUED			
☐ Cleveland	33.00	75.00	335.00	4375.00	☐ Kansas City	45.00	85.00	750.00	RARE
☐ Richmond	25.00	55.00	340.00	4450.00	☐ Dallas	40.00	75.00	650.00	RARE
☐ Atlanta	33.00	65.00	340.00	4450.00	☐ San Francisco	NOT ISSUED			

TWENTY DOLLAR NOTES (1928)
FEDERAL RESERVE NOTES

(Small Size)

SERIES OF 1928B, SIGNATURES OF WOODS-MELLON, GREEN SEAL

The face and back design are similar to previous note. Numeral in Federal Reserve Seal is now changed to a letter.

BANK	A.B.P.	V.FINE	UNC.	★UNC.	BANK	A.B.P.	V.FINE	UNC.	★UNC.
☐ Boston	24.00	48.00	275.00	1250.00	☐ Chicago	22.00	40.00	325.00	1550.00
☐ New York	24.00	48.00	275.00	1250.00	☐ St. Louis	22.00	52.00	325.00	1550.00
☐ Philadelphia	24.00	48.00	275.00	1250.00	☐ Minneapolis	22.00	52.00	300.00	1525.00
☐ Cleveland	24.00	32.00	275.00	1250.00	☐ Kansas City	22.00	37.00	325.00	1550.00
☐ Richmond	24.00	37.00	275.00	1250.00	☐ Dallas	22.00	70.00	325.00	1550.00
☐ Atlanta	24.00	22.00	275.00	1250.00	☐ San Francisco	22.00	37.00	325.00	1550.00

SERIES OF 1928C, SIGNATURES OF WOODS-MILLS, GREEN SEAL

Only two banks issued this note.

BANK	A.B.P.	V.FINE	UNC.	★UNC.	BANK	A.B.P.	V.FINE	UNC.	★UNC.
☐ Chicago	100.00	825.00	2850.00	NONE	☐ San Francisco	800.00	1400.00	5250.00	NONE

TWENTY DOLLAR NOTES (1934)
FEDERAL RESERVE NOTES

(Small Size)

SIGNATURES OF JULIAN-MORGENTHAU, GREEN SEAL

Face and back design are similar to previous note. "Redeemable in Gold" removed from obligation over Federal Reserve Seal.

BANK	A.B.P.	V.FINE	UNC.	★UNC.	BANK	A.B.P.	V.FINE	UNC.	★UNC.
☐ Boston	22.00	35.50	120.00	655.50	☐ St. Louis	22.00	38.50	135.00	675.00
☐ New York	22.00	35.50	120.00	655.50	☐ Minneapolis	22.00	38.50	135.00	675.00
☐ Philadelphia	22.00	35.50	120.00	655.50	☐ Kansas City	22.00	38.50	135.00	675.00
☐ Cleveland	22.00	35.50	120.00	655.50	☐ Dallas	22.00	38.50	135.00	675.00
☐ Richmond	22.00	35.50	120.00	655.50	☐ San Francisco	22.00	38.50	135.00	675.00
☐ Atlanta	22.00	35.50	155.00	655.50	☐ San Francisco*				
☐ Chicago	22.00	35.50	120.00	655.50	(HAWAII)	37.00	150.00	2500.00	12000.00

* The San Francisco Federal Reserve Note with brown seal and brown serial numbers, and overprinted HAWAII on face and back, was a special issue for the armed forces in the Pacific area during World War II.

TWENTY DOLLAR NOTES (1934A)
FEDERAL RESERVE NOTES

(Small Size)

SERIES OF 1934A, SIGNATURES OF JULIAN-MORGENTHAU

BANK	A.B.P.	V.FINE	UNC.	★UNC.	BANK	A.B.P.	V.FINE	UNC.	★UNC.
☐ Boston	22.00	30.00	75.00	535.00	☐ St. Louis	22.00	38.00	90.00	570.00
☐ New York	22.00	30.00	90.00	535.00	☐ Minneapolis	30.00	48.00	115.00	570.00
☐ Philadelphia	22.00	30.00	90.00	535.00	☐ Kansas City	22.00	38.00	110.00	570.00
☐ Cleveland	22.00	30.00	75.00	535.00	☐ Dallas	22.00	38.00	110.00	570.00
☐ Richmond	22.00	30.00	100.00	535.00	☐ San Francisco	22.00	30.00	110.00	570.00
☐ Atlanta	22.00	30.00	80.00	535.00	☐ San Francisco*				
☐ Chicago	22.00	30.00	125.00	535.00	(HAWAII)	28.00	75.00	1500.00	10000.00

* The San Francisco Federal Reserve Note with brown seal and brown serial numbers, and overprinted HAWAII on face and back, was a special issue for the armed forces in the Pacific area during World War II.

(Small Size)

SERIES OF 1934B,
SIGNATURES OF JULIAN-VINSON, GREEN SEAL

BANK	A.B.P.	V.FINE	UNC.	★UNC.	BANK	A.B.P.	V.FINE	UNC.	★UNC.
☐ Boston	25.00	32.50	135.00	1025.00	☐ Chicago	25.00	35.50	165.00	1250.00
☐ New York	25.00	32.50	135.00	1025.00	☐ St. Louis	25.00	35.50	165.00	1250.00
☐ Philadelphia	25.00	32.50	135.00	1025.00	☐ Minneapolis	25.00	35.50	165.00	1250.00
☐ Cleveland	25.00	32.50	135.00	1025.00	☐ Kansas City	25.00	35.50	165.00	1250.00
☐ Richmond	25.00	32.50	135.00	1025.00	☐ Dallas	25.00	35.50	165.00	1250.00
☐ Atlanta	25.00	32.50	135.00	1025.00	☐ San Francisco	25.00	35.50	165.00	1250.00

SERIES OF 1934C, SIGNATURES OF JULIAN-SNYDER, GREEN SEAL

Back Design: This has been modified with this series, with or without balcony added to the White House.

BANK	A.B.P.	V.FINE	UNC.	★UNC.	BANK	A.B.P.	V.FINE	UNC.	★UNC.
☐ Boston	22.00	32.50	130.00	750.00	☐ Chicago	22.00	32.50	150.00	660.00
☐ New York	22.00	32.50	130.00	750.00	☐ St. Louis	22.00	32.50	150.00	660.00
☐ Philadelphia	22.00	32.50	130.00	750.00	☐ Minneapolis	22.00	32.50	150.00	660.00
☐ Cleveland	22.00	32.50	130.00	750.00	☐ Kansas City	22.00	32.50	150.00	660.00
☐ Richmond	22.00	32.50	130.00	750.00	☐ Dallas	22.00	32.50	150.00	660.00
☐ Atlanta	22.00	32.50	130.00	750.00	☐ San Francisco	22.00	32.50	150.00	660.00

SERIES OF 1934D, SIGNATURES OF CLARK-SNYDER, GREEN SEAL

BANK	A.B.P.	V.FINE	UNC.	★UNC.	BANK	A.B.P.	V.FINE	UNC.	★UNC.
☐ Boston	22.00	30.00	100.00	835.00	☐ Chicago	22.00	30.00	125.00	750.00
☐ New York	22.00	30.00	100.00	635.00	☐ St. Louis	22.00	30.00	125.00	750.00
☐ Philadelphia	22.00	30.00	100.00	635.00	☐ Minneapolis	22.00	30.00	125.00	900.00
☐ Cleveland	22.00	30.00	100.00	835.00	☐ Kansas City	22.00	30.00	125.00	900.00
☐ Richmond	22.00	30.00	100.00	635.00	☐ Dallas	22.00	30.00	125.00	900.00
☐ Atlanta	22.00	30.00	100.00	835.00	☐ San Francisco	22.00	30.00	125.00	750.00

TWENTY DOLLAR NOTES (1950)
FEDERAL RESERVE NOTES

(Small Size)

SERIES OF 1950, SIGNATURES OF CLARK-SNYDER, GREEN SEAL

The black Federal Seal and green Treasury Seal are slightly smaller.

BANK	A.B.P.	V.FINE	UNC.	★UNC.	BANK	A.B.P.	V.FINE	UNC.	★UNC.
☐ Boston	22.00	30.00	140.00	535.00	☐ Chicago	22.00	30.00	150.00	550.00
☐ New York	22.00	30.00	140.00	535.00	☐ St. Louis	22.00	30.00	150.00	550.00
☐ Philadelphia	22.00	30.00	140.00	535.00	☐ Minneapolis	22.00	30.00	150.00	550.00
☐ Cleveland	22.00	30.00	140.00	535.00	☐ Kansas City	22.00	30.00	150.00	550.00

BANK	A.B.P.	V.FINE	UNC.	★UNC.	BANK	A.B.P.	V.FINE	UNC.	★UNC.
□ Richmond	22.00	30.00	150.00	550.00	□ Dallas	26.00	30.00	150.00	550.00
□ Atlanta	22.00	30.00	150.00	550.00	□ San Francisco	26.00	30.00	150.00	550.00

SERIES OF 1950A, SIGNATURES OF PRIEST-HUMPHERY, GREEN SEAL

BANK	A.B.P.	V.FINE	UNC.	★UNC.	BANK	A.B.P.	V.FINE	UNC.	★UNC.
□ Boston	22.00	25.00	120.00	250.00	□ Chicago	22.00	25.00	120.00	250.00
□ New York	22.00	25.00	120.00	250.00	□ St. Louis	22.00	25.00	120.00	250.00
□ Philadelphia	22.00	25.00	120.00	250.00	□ Minneapolis	22.00	25.00	120.00	250.00
□ Cleveland	22.00	25.00	120.00	250.00	□ Kansas City	22.00	25.00	120.00	250.00
□ Richmond	22.00	25.00	120.00	350.00	□ Dallas	22.00	25.00	120.00	250.00
□ Atlanta	22.00	25.00	120.00	250.00	□ San Francisco	22.00	25.00	120.00	250.00

SERIES OF 1950B, SIGNATURES OF PRIEST-ANDERSON, GREEN SEAL

BANK	A.B.P.	V.FINE	UNC.	★UNC.	BANK	A.B.P.	V.FINE	UNC.	★UNC.
□ Boston	22.00	25.00	100.00	350.00	□ Chicago	22.00	25.00	100.00	350.00
□ New York	22.00	25.00	100.00	350.00	□ St. Louis	22.00	25.00	100.00	350.00
□ Philadelphia	22.00	25.00	100.00	350.00	□ Minneapolis	22.00	25.00	100.00	350.00
□ Cleveland	22.00	25.00	100.00	350.00	□ Kansas City	22.00	25.00	100.00	350.00
□ Richmond	22.00	25.00	100.00	350.00	□ Dallas	22.00	25.00	100.00	350.00
□ Atlanta	22.00	25.00	100.00	350.00	□ San Francisco	22.00	25.00	100.00	350.00

SERIES OF 1950C, SIGNATURES OF SMITH-DILLON, GREEN SEAL

BANK	A.B.P.	V.FINE	UNC.	★UNC.	BANK	A.B.P.	V.FINE	UNC.	★UNC.
□ Boston	22.00	25.00	100.00	425.00	□ Chicago	22.00	25.00	100.00	425.00
□ New York	22.00	25.00	100.00	425.00	□ St. Louis	22.00	25.00	100.00	425.00
□ Philadelphia	22.00	25.00	100.00	425.00	□ Minneapolis	22.00	25.00	100.00	425.00
□ Cleveland	22.00	25.00	100.00	425.00	□ Kansas City	22.00	25.00	100.00	425.00
□ Richmond	22.00	25.00	100.00	425.00	□ Dallas	22.00	25.00	100.00	425.00
□ Atlanta	22.00	25.00	100.00	425.00	□ San Francisco	22.00	25.00	100.00	425.00

SERIES OF 1950D, SIGNATURES OF GRANAHAN-DILLON, GREEN SEAL

BANK	A.B.P.	V.FINE	UNC.	★UNC.	BANK	A.B.P.	V.FINE	UNC.	★UNC.
□ Boston	22.00	28.50	100.00	325.00	□ Chicago	22.00	28.50	100.00	325.00
□ New York	22.00	28.50	100.00	325.00	□ St. Louis	22.00	28.50	100.00	325.00
□ Philadelphia	22.00	28.50	100.00	325.00	□ Minneapolis	22.00	28.50	100.00	325.00
□ Cleveland	22.00	28.50	100.00	325.00	□ Kansas City	22.00	28.50	100.00	325.00
□ Richmond	22.00	28.50	100.00	325.00	□ Dallas	22.00	28.50	100.00	325.00
□ Atlanta	22.00	28.50	100.00	325.00	□ San Francisco	22.00	28.50	100.00	325.00

SERIES OF 1950E, SIGNATURES OF GRANAHAN-FOWLER, GREEN SEAL

BANK	A.B.P.	V.FINE	UNC.	★UNC.	BANK	A.B.P.	V.FINE	UNC.	★UNC.
☐ Boston	22.00	30.00	200.00	800.00	☐ Chicago	22.00	25.00	200.00	850.00
					☐ San Francisco	22.00	25.00	200.00	850.00

TWENTY DOLLAR NOTES (1963)
FEDERAL RESERVE NOTES

SERIES OF 1963, SIGNATURES OF GRANAHAN-FOWLER, GREEN SEAL

BANK	A.B.P.	V.FINE	UNC.	★UNC.	BANK	A.B.P.	V.FINE	UNC.	★UNC.
☐ Boston	22.00	25.00	100.00	175.00	☐ Chicago	22.00	25.00	100.00	175.00
☐ New York	22.00	25.00	100.00	175.00	☐ St. Louis	22.00	25.00	100.00	175.00
☐ Cleveland	22.00	25.00	100.00	175.00	☐ Kansas City	22.00	25.00	100.00	175.00
☐ Richmond	22.00	25.00	100.00	175.00	☐ Dallas	22.00	25.00	100.00	175.00
☐ Atlanta	22.00	25.00	100.00	175.00	☐ San Francisco	22.00	25.00	100.00	175.00

SERIES OF 1963A, SIGNATURES OF GRANAHAN-FOWLER, GREEN SEAL

BANK	A.B.P.	V.FINE	UNC.	★UNC.	BANK	A.B.P.	V.FINE	UNC.	★UNC.
☐ Boston	22.00	25.00	85.00	150.00	☐ Chicago	22.00	25.00	85.00	150.00
☐ New York	22.00	25.00	85.00	150.00	☐ St. Louis	22.00	25.00	85.00	150.00
☐ Philadelphia	22.00	25.00	85.00	150.00	☐ Minneapolis	22.00	25.00	85.00	150.00
☐ Cleveland	22.00	25.00	85.00	150.00	☐ Kansas City	22.00	25.00	85.00	150.00
☐ Richmond	22.00	25.00	85.00	150.00	☐ Dallas	22.00	25.00	85.00	150.00
☐ Atlanta	22.00	25.00	85.00	150.00	☐ San Francisco	22.00	25.00	85.00	150.00

TWENTY DOLLAR NOTES (1969)
FEDERAL RESERVE NOTES

SERIES OF 1969, SIGNATURES OF ELSTON-KENNEDY, GREEN SEAL

BANK	A.B.P.	V.FINE	UNC.	★UNC.	BANK	A.B.P.	V.FINE	UNC.	★UNC.
☐ Boston	—	25.00	60.00	145.00	☐ Chicago	—	25.00	60.00	145.00
☐ New York	—	25.00	60.00	145.00	☐ St. Louis	—	25.00	60.00	145.00
☐ Philadelphia	—	25.00	60.00	145.00	☐ Minneapolis	—	25.00	60.00	145.00
☐ Cleveland	—	25.00	60.00	145.00	☐ Kansas City	—	25.00	60.00	145.00
☐ Richmond	—	25.00	60.00	145.00	☐ Dallas	—	25.00	60.00	145.00
☐ Atlanta	—	25.00	60.00	145.00	☐ San Francisco	—	25.00	60.00	145.00

SERIES OF 1969A, SIGNATURES OF KABIS-CONNALLY, GREEN SEAL

BANK	A.B.P.	V.FINE	UNC.	★UNC.	BANK	A.B.P.	V.FINE	UNC.	★UNC.
☐ Boston	—	22.00	75.00	130.00	☐ Chicago	—	22.00	75.00	130.00
☐ New York	—	22.00	75.00	130.00	☐ St. Louis	—	22.00	75.00	130.00
☐ Philadelphia	—	22.00	75.00	130.00	☐ Minneapolis	—	22.00	75.00	130.00
☐ Cleveland	—	22.00	75.00	130.00	☐ Kansas City	—	22.00	75.00	130.00
☐ Richmond	—	22.00	75.00	130.00	☐ Dallas	—	22.00	75.00	130.00
☐ Atlanta	—	22.00	75.00	130.00	☐ San Francisco	—	22.00	75.00	130.00

SERIES OF 1969B, SIGNATURES OF BANUELOS-CONNALLY, GREEN SEAL

BANK	A.B.P.	V.FINE	UNC.	★UNC.	BANK	A.B.P.	V.FINE	UNC.	★UNC.
☐ New York	—	22.00	150.00	550.00	☐ Chicago	—	22.00	200.00	550.00
☐ Cleveland	—	22.00	170.00	550.00	☐ St. Louis	—	22.00	200.00	550.00
☐ Richmond	—	22.00	170.00	550.00	☐ Minneapolis	—	22.00	240.00	550.00
☐ Atlanta	—	22.00	170.00	550.00	☐ Kansas City	—	22.00	240.00	550.00
					☐ Dallas	—	22.00	200.00	550.00
					☐ San Francisco	—	22.00	165.00	550.00

SERIES OF 1969C, SIGNATURES OF BANUELOS-SHULTZ, GREEN SEAL

BANK	A.B.P.	V.FINE	UNC.	★UNC.	BANK	A.B.P.	V.FINE	UNC.	★UNC.
☐ Boston	—	22.00	85.00	200.00	☐ Chicago	—	22.00	85.00	200.00
☐ New York	—	22.00	85.00	200.00	☐ St. Louis	—	22.00	85.00	200.00
☐ Philadelphia	—	22.00	85.00	200.00	☐ Minneapolis	—	22.00	85.00	200.00
☐ Cleveland	—	22.00	85.00	200.00	☐ Kansas City	—	22.00	85.00	200.00
☐ Richmond	—	22.00	85.00	200.00	☐ Dallas	—	22.00	85.00	200.00
☐ Atlanta	—	22.00	85.00	200.00	☐ San Francisco	—	22.00	85.00	200.00

TWENTY DOLLAR NOTES (1974)
FEDERAL RESERVE NOTES

SERIES OF 1974, SIGNATURES OF NEFF-SIMON, GREEN SEAL

BANK	A.B.P.	V.FINE	UNC.	★UNC.	BANK	A.B.P.	V.FINE	UNC.	★UNC.
☐ Boston	—	22.00	75.00	150.00	☐ Chicago	—	22.00	75.00	150.00
☐ New York	—	22.00	75.00	150.00	☐ St. Louis	—	22.00	75.00	150.00
☐ Philadelphia	—	22.00	75.00	150.00	☐ Minneapolis	—	25.00	75.00	150.00
☐ Cleveland	—	22.00	75.00	150.00	☐ Kansas City	—	25.00	75.00	150.00
☐ Richmond	—	22.00	75.00	150.00	☐ Dallas	—	25.00	75.00	150.00
☐ Atlanta	—	22.00	75.00	150.00	☐ San Francisco	—	22.00	75.00	150.00

TWENTY DOLLAR NOTES (1977)
FEDERAL RESERVE NOTES
SERIES OF 1977, SIGNATURES OF MORTON-BLUMENTHAL, GREEN SEAL

BANK	A.B.P.	V.FINE	UNC.	★UNC.	BANK	A.B.P.	V.FINE	UNC.	★UNC.
☐ Boston	—	25.00	60.00	150.00	☐ Chicago	—	25.00	60.00	150.00
☐ New York	—	25.00	60.00	150.00	☐ St. Louis	—	25.00	60.00	150.00
☐ Philadelphia	—	25.00	60.00	150.00	☐ Minneapolis	—	25.00	60.00	150.00
☐ Cleveland	—	25.00	60.00	150.00	☐ Kansas City	—	25.00	60.00	150.00
☐ Richmond	—	25.00	60.00	150.00	☐ Dallas	—	25.00	60.00	150.00
☐ Atlanta	—	25.00	60.00	150.00	☐ San Francisco	—	25.00	60.00	150.00

TWENTY DOLLAR NOTES (1981)
FEDERAL RESERVE NOTES
SERIES OF 1981, SIGNATURES OF BUCHANAN-REGAN, GREEN SEAL

BANK	A.B.P.	V.FINE	UNC.	★UNC.	BANK	A.B.P.	V.FINE	UNC.	★UNC.
☐ Boston	—	25.00	85.00	175.00	☐ Chicago	—	25.00	85.00	175.00
☐ New York	—	25.00	85.00	175.00	☐ St. Louis	—	25.00	85.00	175.00
☐ Philadelphia	—	25.00	85.00	175.00	☐ Minneapolis	—	25.00	85.00	250.00
☐ Cleveland	—	25.00	85.00	175.00	☐ Kansas City	—	25.00	85.00	175.00
☐ Richmond	—	25.00	85.00	175.00	☐ Dallas	—	25.00	85.00	200.00
☐ Atlanta	—	25.00	85.00	175.00	☐ San Francisco	—	25.00	85.00	175.00

SERIES OF 1981A, SIGNATURES OF ORTEGA-REGAN, GREEN SEAL

★Notes not issued for all banks

BANK	A.B.P.	V.FINE	UNC.	★UNC.	BANK	A.B.P.	V.FINE	UNC.	★UNC.
☐ Boston	—	25.00	65.00	—	☐ Chicago	—	25.00	65.00	—
☐ New York	—	25.00	65.00	—	☐ St. Louis	—	25.00	65.00	—
☐ Philadelphia	—	25.00	65.00	—	☐ Minneapolis	—	25.00	65.00	—
☐ Cleveland	—	25.00	65.00	125.00	☐ Kansas City	—	25.00	65.00	—
☐ Richmond	—	25.00	65.00	225.00	☐ Dallas	—	25.00	65.00	—
☐ Atlanta	—	25.00	65.00	150.00	☐ San Francisco	—	25.00	65.00	150.00

TWENTY DOLLAR NOTES (1985)
FEDERAL RESERVE NOTES
SERIES OF 1985, SIGNATURES OF ORTEGA-BAKER, GREEN SEAL

★Notes not issued for all banks

BANK	A.B.P.	V.FINE	UNC.	★UNC.	BANK	A.B.P.	V.FINE	UNC.	★UNC.
☐ Boston	—	22.00	60.00	85.00	☐ Chicago	—	22.00	60.00	90.00
☐ New York	—	22.00	60.00	85.00	☐ St. Louis	—	22.00	60.00	90.00
☐ Philadelphia	—	22.00	60.00	85.00	☐ Minneapolis	—	22.00	60.00	90.00
☐ Cleveland	—	22.00	60.00	90.00	☐ Kansas City	—	22.00	60.00	85.00
☐ Richmond	—	22.00	60.00	90.00	☐ Dallas	—	22.00	60.00	85.00
☐ Atlanta	—	22.00	60.00	90.00	☐ San Francisco	—	22.00	60.00	85.00

TWENTY DOLLAR NOTES (1988)
FEDERAL RESERVE NOTES
SERIES OF 1988A, SIGNATURES OF VILLALPANDO-BRADY, GREEN SEAL

★Notes not issued for all banks

BANK	A.B.P.	V.FINE	UNC.	★UNC.	BANK	A.B.P.	V.FINE	UNC.	★UNC.
☐ Boston	—	22.00	58.50	—	☐ Chicago	—	22.00	58.50	125.00
☐ New York	—	22.00	58.50	125.00	☐ St. Louis	—	22.00	58.50	110.00
☐ Philadelphia	—	22.00	58.50	125.00	☐ Minneapolis	—	22.00	58.50	110.00
☐ Cleveland	—	22.00	58.50	125.00	☐ Kansas City	—	22.00	58.50	110.00
☐ Richmond	—	22.00	58.50	125.00	☐ Dallas	—	22.00	58.50	125.00
☐ Atlanta	—	22.00	58.50	125.00	☐ San Francisco	—	22.00	58.50	—

TWENTY DOLLAR NOTES (1990)
FEDERAL RESERVE NOTES
SERIES OF 1990, SIGNATURES OF VILLALPANDO-BRADY, GREEN SEAL

★Notes not issued for all banks

BANK	A.B.P.	V.FINE	UNC.	★UNC.	BANK	A.B.P.	V.FINE	UNC.	★UNC.
☐ Boston	—	22.00	55.00	82.50	☐ Chicago	—	22.00	55.00	82.50
☐ New York	—	22.00	55.00	82.50	☐ St. Louis	—	22.00	55.00	82.50
☐ Philadelphia	—	22.00	55.00	82.50	☐ Minneapolis	—	22.00	55.00	82.50
☐ Cleveland	—	22.00	55.00	80.00	☐ Kansas City	—	22.00	55.00	—
☐ Richmond	—	22.00	55.00	80.00	☐ Dallas	—	22.00	55.00	—
☐ Atlanta	—	22.00	55.00	80.00	☐ San Francisco	—	22.00	55.00	—

TWENTY DOLLAR NOTES (1993)
FEDERAL RESERVE NOTES
SERIES OF 1993, SIGNATURES OF WITHROW-BENTSEN, GREEN SEAL

★Notes are not issued for all banks

BANK	A.B.P.	V.FINE	UNC.	★UNC.	BANK	A.B.P.	V.FINE	UNC.	★UNC.
☐ Boston	—	22.00	55.00	80.00	☐ Chicago	—	22.00	55.00	—
☐ New York	—	22.00	55.00	80.00	☐ St. Louis	—	22.00	55.00	—
☐ Philadelphia	—	22.00	55.00	80.00	☐ Kansas City	—	22.00	55.00	—
☐ Cleveland	—	22.00	55.00	80.00	☐ Dallas	—	22.00	55.00	—
☐ Richmond	—	22.00	55.00	80.00	☐ San Francisco	—	22.00	55.00	75.00
☐ Atlanta	—	22.00	55.00	80.00					

TWENTY DOLLAR NOTES (1995)
FEDERAL RESERVE NOTES
SERIES OF 1995, SIGNATURES OF WITHROW-RUBIN, GREEN SEAL

★Notes not issued for all banks

BANK	A.B.P.	V.FINE	UNC.	★UNC.	BANK	A.B.P.	V.FINE	UNC.	★UNC.
☐ Boston	—	22.00	42.50	72.50	☐ Chicago	—	22.00	42.50	75.00
☐ New York	—	22.00	42.50	72.50	☐ St. Louis	—	22.00	42.50	72.50
☐ Philadelphia	—	22.00	42.50	72.50	☐ Minneapolis	—	22.00	42.50	72.50
☐ Cleveland	—	22.00	42.50	75.00	☐ Kansas City	—	22.00	42.50	72.50
☐ Richmond	—	22.00	42.50	75.00	☐ Dallas	—	22.00	42.50	75.00
☐ Atlanta	—	22.00	42.50	75.00	☐ San Francisco	—	22.00	42.50	75.00

TWENTY DOLLAR NOTES (1915–1918)
FEDERAL RESERVE BANK NOTES
(ALL HAVE BLUE SEALS)

(Large Size)

Face Design: Portrait of President Cleveland left, name of bank and city center, blue seal right.

Back Design: Locomotive and steamship, similar to 1914 note.

BANK	SERIES	GOV'T SIGNATURES	BANK SIGNATURES	A.B.P.	GOOD	V.FINE	UNC.
☐Atlanta	1915	Teehee-Burke	Bell-Wellborn	635.00	1200.00	4200.00	RARE
	1915	Teehee-Burke	Pike-McCord	835.00	1200.00	4000.00	RARE
☐Atlanta	1918	Elliott-Burke	Bell-Wellborn	475.00	1200.00	3500.00	RARE
☐Chicago	1915	Teehee-Burke	McLallen-McDougal	475.00	1200.00	3500.00	RARE
☐St. Louis	1918	Teehee-Burke	Attebery-Wells	475.00	1200.00	3500.00	RARE

BANK	SERIES	GOV'T SIGNATURES	BANK SIGNATURES	A.B.P.	GOOD	V.FINE	UNC.
☐Kansas City	1915	Teehee-Burke	Anderson-Miller	425.00	800.00	3200.00	RARE
☐Kansas City	1915	Teehee-Burke	Cross-Miller	475.00	800.00	3200.00	RARE
☐Dallas	1915	Teehee-Burke	Hoopes-Van Zandt	475.00	800.00	3200.00	RARE
☐Dallas	1915	Teehee-Burke	Gilbert-Van Zandt	500.00	875.00	5000.00	RARE
☐Dallas	1915	Teehee-Burke	Talley-Van Zandt	500.00	875.00	4550.00	RARE

TWENTY DOLLAR NOTES (1929)
FEDERAL RESERVE BANK NOTES

(Small Size)

Face Design: Portrait of President Jackson center, name of bank and city left, blue seal right.

Back Design: The White House.

BANK	A.B.P.	V.FINE	UNC.	★UNC.	BANK	A.B.P.	V.FINE	UNC.	★UNC.
☐ Boston	25.00	100.00	340.00	4250.00	☐ Chicago	60.00	100.00	475.00	3850.00
☐ New York	25.00	100.00	325.00	3225.00	☐ St. Louis	60.00	100.00	475.00	3850.00
☐ Philadelphia	25.00	100.00	310.00	3800.00	☐ Minneapolis	60.00	100.00	475.00	4400.00
☐ Cleveland	25.00	100.00	310.00	4250.00	☐ Kansas City	60.00	100.00	1650.00	4400.00
☐ Richmond	25.00	100.00	475.00	3650.00	☐ Dallas	125.00	225.00	1650.00	RARE
☐ Atlanta	25.00	100.00	650.00	4250.00	☐ San Francisco	40.00	80.00	1650.00	RARE

FIFTY DOLLAR NOTES

ORDER OF ISSUE

FIFTY DOLLAR NOTES (1862–1863)
UNITED STATES NOTES
(ALSO KNOWN AS LEGAL TENDER NOTES)

(Large Size)

Face Design: Portrait of Hamilton to left.

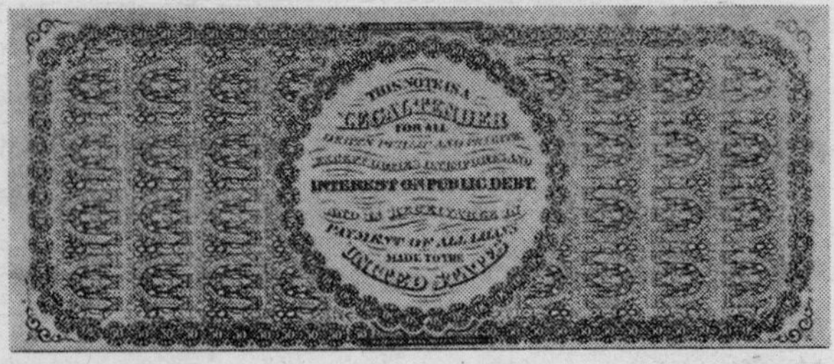

Back Design

SERIES	SIGNATURES	SEAL	A.B.P.	GOOD	V.FINE	UNC.
☐1862	Chittenden-Spinner*	Red	4500.00	—	—	RARE
☐1862	Chittenden-Spinner**	Red	4500.00	—	—	RARE
☐1863	Chittenden-Spinner**	Red	4500.00	—	—	RARE

*First Obligation: Similar to 1862 $5 note.
**Second Obligation: Shown above.

FIFTY DOLLAR NOTES (1869) UNITED STATES NOTES (ALSO KNOWN AS LEGAL TENDER NOTES)

(Large Size)

Face Design: Portrait of Henry Clay to right.

Back Design

SERIES	SIGNATURES	SEAL	A.B.P.	GOOD	V.FINE	UNC.
□1869	Allison-Spinner	Red	4500.00	—	—	RARE

Only twenty-four pieces of this note remain unredeemed.

FIFTY DOLLAR NOTES (1874–1880)
UNITED STATES NOTES

(Large Size)

Face Design: Franklin to left.

Back Design

SERIES	SIGNATURES	SEAL	A.B.P.	GOOD	V.FINE	UNC.
□1874	Allison-Spinner	Sm. Red	1500.00	3000.00	RARE	RARE
□1875	Allison-Wyman	Sm. Red	1000.00	RARE	RARE	
□1878	Allison-Gilfillan	Sm. Red	1500.00	2000.00	RARE	RARE
□1880	Bruce-Gilfillan	Lg. Brown	1100.00	1650.00	RARE	RARE
□1880	Bruce-Wyman	Lg. Brown	2000.00	3200.00	RARE	RARE
□1880	Rosecrans-Jordan	Lg. Red	2000.00	3200.00	RARE	RARE
□1880	Rosecrans-Hyatt	Red Plain	VERY RARE			
□1880	Rosecrans-Hyatt	Red Spike	1600.00	2200.00	RARE	RARE
□1880	Rosecrans-Huston	Lg. Red	1500.00	3000.00	RARE	RARE
□1880	Rosecrans-Huston	Lg. Brown	1250.00	2000.00	RARE	RARE
□1880	Tillman-Morgan	Sm. Red	1650.00	2200.00	RARE	RARE
□1880	Bruce-Roberts	Sm. Red	5050.00	RARE	RARE	RARE
□1880	Lyons-Roberts	Sm. Red	1200.00	1750.00	RARE	RARE

FIFTY DOLLAR NOTES (1875) NATIONAL BANK NOTES

FIRST CHARTER PERIOD (Large Size)

Face Design: Washington crossing Delaware left, Washington at Valley Forge, right.

Back Design: Embarkation of the Pilgrims.

SERIES	SIGNATURES	SEAL	A.B.P.	GOOD	V.FINE	UNC.
☐ Original	Chittenden-Spinner	Red w/r	3500.00	7500.00	RARE	RARE
☐ Original	Colby-Spinner	Red w/r	3500.00	7500.00	RARE	RARE
☐ Original	Allison-Spinner	Red w/r	3500.00	7500.00	RARE	RARE
☐ 1875	Allison-New	Red w/s	3500.00	7500.00	RARE	RARE
☐ 1875	Allison-Wyman	Red w/s	3500.00	7500.00	RARE	RARE
☐ 1875	Allison-Gilfillan	Red w/s	3500.00	7500.00	RARE	RARE
☐ 1875	Scofield-Gilfillan	Red w/s	3500.00	7500.00	RARE	RARE
☐ 1875	Bruce-Gilfillan	Red w/s	3500.00	7500.00	RARE	RARE
☐ 1875	Bruce-Wyman	Red w/s	3500.00	7500.00	RARE	RARE
☐ 1875	Rosecrans-Huston	Red w/s	3500.00	7500.00	RARE	RARE
☐ 1875	Rosecrans-Nebeker	Red w/s	3500.00	7500.00	RARE	RARE
☐ 1875	Tillman-Morgan	Red w/s	3500.00	7500.00	RARE	RARE

FIFTY DOLLAR NOTES (1882) NATIONAL BANK NOTES
SECOND CHARTER PERIOD (Large Size)

First Issue (Brown seal and brown back)
Back Design
Face Design: Similar to First Charter Period note.

SERIES	SIGNATURES	SEAL	A.B.P.	GOOD	V.FINE	UNC.
□1882	Bruce-Gilfillan	Brown	1000.00	2500.00	RARE	RARE
□1882	Bruce-Wyman	Brown	1000.00	2500.00	RARE	RARE
□1882	Bruce-Jordan	Brown	1000.00	2500.00	RARE	RARE
□1882	Rosecrans-Jordan	Brown	1000.00	2500.00	RARE	RARE
□1882	Rosecrans-Hyatt	Brown	1000.00	2500.00	RARE	RARE
□1882	Rosecrans-Huston	Brown	1000.00	2500.00	RARE	RARE
□1882	Rosecrans-Nebeker	Brown	1000.00	2500.00	RARE	RARE
□1882	Rosecrans-Morgan	Brown	1000.00	2800.00	RARE	RARE
□1882	Tillman-Morgan	Brown	1000.00	2500.00	RARE	RARE
□1882	Tillman-Roberts	Brown	1000.00	2500.00	RARE	RARE
□1882	Bruce-Roberts	Brown	1000.00	2500.00	RARE	RARE
□1882	Lyons-Roberts	Brown	1000.00	2500.00	RARE	RARE
□1882	Vernon-Treat	Brown	1000.00	2500.00	RARE	RARE

FIFTY DOLLAR NOTES (1882) NATIONAL BANK NOTES
SECOND CHARTER PERIOD (Large Size)

Second Issue (Blue seal, green back with date "1882–1908".)
Face Design: Washington crossing Delaware left, Washington at Valley Forge right.

Back Design

SERIES	SIGNATURES	SEAL	A.B.P.	GOOD	V.FINE	UNC.
☐1882	Rosecrans-Huston	Blue	2400.00	3200.00	RARE	RARE
☐1882	Rosecrans-Nebeker	Blue	2400.00	3200.00	RARE	RARE
☐1882	Tillman-Morgan	Blue	2400.00	3200.00	RARE	RARE
☐1882	Tillman-Roberts	Blue	2400.00	3200.00	RARE	RARE
☐1882	Bruce-Roberts	Blue	2400.00	3200.00	RARE	RARE
☐1882	Lyons-Roberts	Blue	2400.00	3200.00	RARE	RARE
☐1882	Vernon-Treat	Blue	2400.00	3200.00	RARE	RARE
☐1882	Napier-McClung	Blue	2400.00	3200.00	RARE	RARE

Third Issue (As above, "FIFTY DOLLARS" replaces 1882–1908—excessively rare!)

☐1882	Lyons-Roberts		RARE	RARE	RARE	RARE

FIFTY DOLLAR NOTES (1902) NATIONAL BANK NOTES
THIRD CHARTER PERIOD (Large Size)

First Issue (Red seal and numbers)
Face Design: Portrait of Sherman left. Name of bank center. Treasury Seal and numbers.

SERIES	SIGNATURES	SEAL	A.B.P.	GOOD	V.FINE	UNC.
□1902	Lyons-Roberts	Red	1000.00	1800.00	RARE	RARE
□1902	Lyons-Treat	Red	1000.00	1800.00	RARE	RARE
□1902	Vernon-Treat	Red	1000.00	1800.00	RARE	RARE

Second Issue (Treasury Seal)
Numbers remain blue, date "1902–1908" added on back.

□1902	Lyons-Roberts	Blue	800.00	2000.00	3500.00	RARE
□1902	Lyons-Treat	Blue	800.00	2000.00	3500.00	RARE
□1902	Vernon-Treat	Blue	800.00	2000.00	3500.00	RARE
□1902	Vernon-McClung	Blue	800.00	2000.00	3500.00	RARE
□1902	Napier-McClung	Blue	800.00	2000.00	3500.00	RARE
□1902	Napier-Thompson	Blue	800.00	2000.00	3500.00	RARE
□1902	Napier-Burke	Blue	800.00	2000.00	3500.00	RARE
□1902	Parker-Burke	Blue	800.00	2000.00	3500.00	RARE
□1902	Teehee-Burke	Blue	800.00	2000.00	3500.00	RARE

Third Issue (Treasury Seal)
Numbers remain blue, date "1902–1908" removed from back.

□1902	Lyons-Roberts	Blue	500.00	800.00	2500.00	RARE
□1902	Lyons-Treat	Blue	500.00	800.00	2500.00	RARE
□1902	Vernon-Treat	Blue	500.00	800.00	2500.00	RARE
□1902	Vernon-McClung	Blue	500.00	800.00	2500.00	RARE
□1902	Napier-McClung	Blue	500.00	800.00	2500.00	RARE
□1902	Napier-Thompson	Blue	500.00	800.00	2500.00	RARE
□1902	Napier-Burke	Blue	500.00	800.00	2500.00	RARE
□1902	Parker-Burke	Blue	500.00	800.00	2500.00	RARE
□1902	Teehee-Burke	Blue	500.00	800.00	2500.00	RARE
□1902	Elliott-Burke	Blue	500.00	800.00	2500.00	RARE
□1902	Elliott-White	Blue	500.00	800.00	2500.00	RARE

SERIES	SIGNATURES	SEAL	A.B.P.	GOOD	V.FINE	UNC.
□1902	Speelman-White	Blue	200.00	375.00	2500.00	RARE
□1902	Woods-White	Blue	200.00	375.00	2500.00	RARE

FIFTY DOLLAR NOTES (1929) NATIONAL BANK NOTES
(Small Size)

Face Design: Portrait of President Grant center. Bank left, brown seal right. Brown serial numbers, black Charter Numbers.

Back Design: The Capitol.

SERIES	SIGNATURES	SEAL	A.B.P.	V.FINE	UNC.
□1929, Type I*	Jones-Wood	Brown	325.00	600.00	1000.00
□1929, Type II*	Jones-Wood	Brown	350.00	600.00	1400.00

*See Page 92. Type I—Charter Number in black. Type II—Similar. Charter Number added in brown.

FIFTY DOLLAR NOTES (1878–1880)
SILVER CERTIFICATES

(Large Size)

Face Design: Portrait of Edward Everett.

Back Design

SERIES	SIGNATURES	SEAL	A.B.P.	GOOD	V.FINE	UNC.
☐ 1878	Varied	Red		—	VERY RARE	
☐ 1880	Scofield-Gilfillan	Brown	—	—	VERY RARE	VERY RARE
☐ 1880	Bruce-Gilfillan	Brown	—	—	45000.00	UNKNOWN
☐ 1880	Bruce-Wyman	Brown	—	—	—	RARE
☐ 1880	Rosecrans-Huston	Brown	3500.00	—	—	RARE
☐ 1880	Rosecrans-Nebeker	Red	3000.00	—	—	RARE

FIFTY DOLLAR NOTES (1891) SILVER CERTIFICATES
(Large Size)

Face Design: Portrait of Edward Everett.

Back Design

SERIES	SIGNATURES	SEAL	A.B.P.	GOOD	V.FINE	UNC.
□1891	Rosecrans-Nebeker	Red	800.00	3550.00	RARE	RARE
□1891	Tillman-Morgan	Red	800.00	1500.00	RARE	RARE
□1891	Bruce-Roberts	Red	800.00	1500.00	RARE	RARE
□1891	Lyons-Roberts	Red	800.00	1500.00	RARE	RARE
□1891	Vernon-Treat	Red	800.00	1500.00	RARE	RARE
□1891	Parker-Burke	Blue	750.00	1000.00	RARE	RARE

FIFTY DOLLAR NOTES (1882) GOLD CERTIFICATES (Large Size)

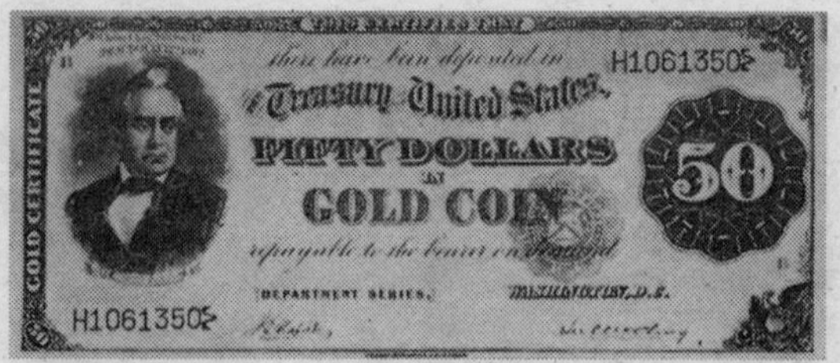

Face Design: Portrait of Silas Wright to left.

Back Design: Bright yellow color.

SERIES	SIGNATURES	SEAL	A.B.P.	GOOD	V.FINE	UNC.
□1882	Bruce-Gilfillan	Brown	2750.00	4500.00		RARE
□1882	Bruce-Wyman	Brown	2750.00	4500.00		RARE
□1882	Rosecrans-Hyatt	Red	1500.00	2000.00		RARE
□1882	Rosecrans-Huston	Brown	6200.00	8050.00		RARE
□1882	Lyons-Roberts	Red	2650.00	5000.00		RARE
□1882	Lyons-Treat	Red	600.00	1200.00		RARE
□1882	Vernon-Treat	Red	600.00	1200.00		RARE
□1882	Vernon-McClung	Red	600.00	1200.00		RARE
□1882	Napier-McClung	Red	475.00	650.00	2500.00	RARE

FIFTY DOLLAR NOTES (1913) GOLD CERTIFICATES
(Large Size)

Face Design: Portrait of President Grant.

Back Design: Bright yellow color.

SERIES	SIGNATURES	SEAL	A.B.P.	GOOD	V.FINE	UNC.
□1913	Parker-Burke	Gold	600.00	1000.00	2500.00	RARE
□1913	Teehee-Burke	Gold	650.00	800.00	1750.00	RARE
□1922	Speelman-White	Gold	650.00	800.00	1750.00	RARE

FIFTY DOLLAR NOTES (1928) GOLD CERTIFICATES
(Small Size)

Back Design: Same as 1929 note.

SERIES	SIGNATURES	SEAL	A.B.P.	GOOD	V.FINE	UNC.
☐1928	Woods-Mellon	Gold	500.00	850.00	—	RARE

FIFTY DOLLAR NOTES (1891) TREASURY OR COIN NOTES
(Large Size)

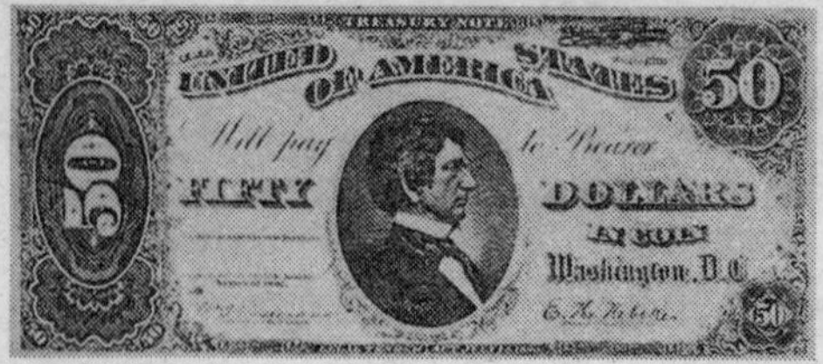

Face Design: Portrait of William H. Seward. Only twenty-five pieces remain unredeemed.
Back Design: Green.

SERIES	SIGNATURES	SEAL	A.B.P.	GOOD	V.FINE	UNC.
☐1891	Rosecrans-Nebeker	Red	—	—	RARE	

FIFTY DOLLAR NOTES (1914)
FEDERAL RESERVE NOTES

(Large Size)

SERIES OF 1914, SIGNATURES OF BURKE-McADOO, RED SEAL AND RED SERIAL NUMBERS

BANK	A.B.P.	V.FINE	UNC.	CITY	A.B.P.	V.FINE	UNC.
☐Boston	475.00	2000.00	RARE	☐ Chicago	1800.00	3250.00	RARE
☐New York	475.00	2000.00	RARE	☐ St. Louis	1800.00	3250.00	RARE
☐Philadelphia	475.00	2000.00	RARE	☐ Minneapolis	1800.00	3250.00	RARE
☐Cleveland	475.00	2000.00	RARE	☐ Kansas City	1800.00	3250.00	RARE
☐Richmond	475.00	2000.00	RARE	☐ Dallas	1800.00	3250.00	RARE
☐Atlanta	475.00	2000.00	RARE	☐ San Francisco	1800.00	3250.00	RARE

FIFTY DOLLAR NOTES (1914)
FEDERAL RESERVE NOTES
1914, BLUE TREASURY SEAL AND BLUE NUMBERS

DATE	BANK	SIGNATURES	SEAL	A.B.P.	GOOD	V.FINE	UNC.
1914	Boston	Burke-McAdoo	Blue	105.00	200.00	800.00	3000.00
1914	Boston	Burke-Glass	Blue	105.00	150.00	575.00	3000.00
1914	Boston	Burke-Huston	Blue	210.00	375.00	2150.00	RARE
1914	Boston	White-Mellon	Blue	105.00	140.00	600.00	2750.00
1914	New York	Burke-McAdoo	Blue	105.00	150.00	800.00	4200.00
1914	New York	Burke-Glass	Blue	105.00	140.00	1200.00	3750.00
1914	New York	Burke-Huston	Blue	105.00	160.00	800.00	3750.00
1914	New York	White-Mellon	Blue	105.00	160.00	800.00	3750.00

DATE	BANK	SIGNATURES	SEAL	A.B.P.	GOOD	V.FINE	UNC.
1914	Philadelphia	Burke-McAdoo	Blue	105.00	150.00	875.00	4500.00
1914	Philadelphia	Burke-Glass	Blue	105.00	175.00	1225.00	4500.00
1914	Philadelphia	Burke-Huston	Blue	105.00	150.00	600.00	3200.00
1914	Philadelphia	White-Mellon	Blue	105.00	150.00	600.00	3200.00
1914	Cleveland	Burke-McAdoo	Blue	105.00	150.00	600.00	3200.00
1914	Cleveland	Burke-Glass	Blue	105.00	175.00	800.00	4200.00
1914	Cleveland	Burke-Huston	Blue	105.00	155.00	875.00	4000.00
1914	Cleveland	White-Mellon	Blue	105.00	150.00	400.00	3500.00
1914	Richmond	Burke-McAdoo	Blue	105.00	175.00	1125.00	4200.00
1914	Richmond	Burke-Glass	Blue	105.00	300.00	1000.00	4300.00
1914	Richmond	Burke-Huston	Blue	105.00	150.00	450.00	3200.00
1914	Richmond	White-Mellon	Blue	105.00	200.00	1200.00	3200.00
1914	Atlanta	Burke-McAdoo	Blue	105.00	175.00	1000.00	3200.00
1914	Atlanta	Burke-Glass	Blue	150.00	275.00	1500.00	4500.00
1914	Atlanta	Burke-Huston	Blue	105.00	135.00	400.00	3500.00
1914	Atlanta	White-Mellon	Blue	105.00	250.00	700.00	4200.00
1914	Chicago	Burke-McAdoo	Blue	105.00	150.00	600.00	3200.00
1914	Chicago	Burke-Glass	Blue	105.00	150.00	600.00	3200.00
1914	Chicago	Burke-Huston	Blue	105.00	200.00	600.00	3200.00
1914	Chicago	White-Mellon	Blue	105.00	200.00	600.00	3200.00
1914	St. Louis	Burke-McAdoo	Blue	105.00	200.00	2000.00	3200.00
1914	St. Louis	Burke-Glass	Blue	105.00	150.00	1000.00	3200.00
1914	St. Louis	Burke-Huston	Blue	105.00	135.00	600.00	2500.00
1914	St. Louis	White-Mellon	Blue	175.00	500.00	2200.00	RARE
1914	Minneapolis	Burke-McAdoo	Blue	105.00	175.00	800.00	3500.00
1914	Minneapolis	Burke-Glass	Blue	175.00	375.00	1500.00	RARE
1914	Minneapolis	Burke-Huston	Blue	150.00	325.00	2200.00	RARE
1914	Minneapolis	White-Mellon	Blue	175.00	355.00	700.00	3500.00
1914	Kansas City	Burke-McAdoo	Blue	105.00	155.00	1000.00	3800.00
1914	Kansas City	White-Mellon	Blue		ONLY 1 KNOWN—RARE		
1914	Dallas	Burke-McAdoo	Blue	105.00	175.00	1200.00	4000.00
1914	Dallas	Burke-Glass	Blue	175.00	450.00	1200.00	6000.00
1914	Dallas	Burke-Huston	Blue	175.00	450.00	1200.00	6000.00
1914	Dallas	White Mellon	Blue	175.00	450.00	1200.00	4200.00
1914	San Francisco	Burke-McAdoo	Blue	105.00	150.00	500.00	3750.00
1914	San Francisco	Burke-Glass	Blue	175.00	400.00	3200.00	3750.00
1914	San Francisco	Burke-Huston	Blue	105.00	150.00	475.00	4200.00
1914	San Francisco	White-Mellon	Blue	105.00	170.00	575.00	3800.00

FIFTY DOLLAR NOTES (1928)
FEDERAL RESERVE NOTES

(Small Size)

Face Design: Portrait of President Grant center. Black Federal Reserve Seal with number to left. Green Treasury Seal to right.

Back Design: Same as 1929 note.

FIFTY DOLLAR NOTES (1928)
FEDERAL RESERVE NOTES

SERIES OF 1928, SIGNATURES OF WOODS-MELLON, GREEN SEAL

BANK	A.B.P.	V.FINE	UNC.	★UNC.	BANK	A.B.P.	V.FINE	UNC.	★UNC.
☐ Boston	100.00	200.00	1250.00	—	☐ Chicago	100.00	175.00	1250.00	—
☐ New York	100.00	200.00	1250.00	—	☐ St. Louis	100.00	200.00	1250.00	—
☐ Philadelphia	100.00	200.00	1250.00	—	☐ Minneapolis	100.00	300.00	1450.00	—
☐ Cleveland	100.00	200.00	1250.00	—	☐ Kansas City	100.00	200.00	1250.00	—
☐ Richmond	100.00	200.00	1250.00	—	☐ Dallas	100.00	200.00	1450.00	—
☐ Atlanta	100.00	200.00	1250.00	—	☐ San Francisco	100.00	200.00	1250.00	—

SERIES OF 1928A, SIGNATURES OF WOODS-MELLON, GREEN SEAL

BANK	A.B.P.	V.FINE	UNC.	★UNC.	BANK	A.B.P.	V.FINE	UNC.	★UNC.
☐ Boston	65.00	125.00	500.00	—	☐ Chicago	65.00	125.00	500.00	—
☐ New York	65.00	125.00	500.00	—	☐ St. Louis	65.00	125.00	500.00	—
☐ Philadelphia	65.00	125.00	500.00	—	☐ Minneapolis	65.00	125.00	500.00	—
☐ Cleveland	65.00	125.00	500.00	—	☐ Kansas City	65.00	125.00	500.00	—
☐ Richmond	65.00	125.00	500.00	—	☐ Dallas	65.00	125.00	500.00	—
☐ Atlanta	65.00	150.00	500.00	—	☐ San Francisco	65.00	125.00	500.00	—

FIFTY DOLLAR NOTES (1934)
FEDERAL RESERVE NOTES

SERIES OF 1934, SIGNATURES OF JULIAN-MORGENTHAU, GREEN SEAL

BANK	A.B.P.	V.FINE	UNC.	★UNC.	BANK	A.B.P.	V.FINE	UNC.	★UNC.
☐ Boston	60.00	100.00	300.00	875.00	☐ Chicago	60.00	100.00	300.00	875.00
☐ New York	60.00	100.00	300.00	875.00	☐ St. Louis	60.00	100.00	300.00	875.00
☐ Philadelphia	60.00	100.00	300.00	875.00	☐ Minneapolis	60.00	100.00	300.00	875.00
☐ Cleveland	60.00	100.00	300.00	875.00	☐ Kansas City	60.00	100.00	300.00	875.00
☐ Richmond	60.00	100.00	300.00	875.00	☐ Dallas	60.00	100.00	300.00	875.00
☐ Atlanta	60.00	100.00	300.00	875.00	☐ San Francisco	60.00	100.00	300.00	875.00

SERIES OF 1934A, SIGNATURES OF JULIAN-MORGENTHAU, GREEN SEAL

BANK	A.B.P.	V.FINE	UNC.	★UNC.	BANK	A.B.P.	V.FINE	UNC.	★UNC.
☐ Boston	60.00	110.00	550.00	1800.00	☐ Chicago	60.00	110.00	550.00	1500.00
☐ New York	60.00	110.00	350.00	1800.00	☐ St. Louis	60.00	110.00	550.00	1500.00
☐ Philadelphia	60.00	110.00	550.00	1400.00	☐ Minneapolis	60.00	120.00	550.00	1500.00
☐ Cleveland	60.00	110.00	550.00	1400.00	☐ Kansas City	60.00	120.00	550.00	1500.00
☐ Richmond	60.00	110.00	550.00	1400.00	☐ Dallas	60.00	120.00	550.00	1500.00
☐ Atlanta	60.00	110.00	550.00	1400.00	☐ San Francisco	60.00	110.00	550.00	1500.00

SERIES OF 1934B, SIGNATURES OF JULIAN-VINSON, GREEN SEAL

BANK	A.B.P.	V.FINE	UNC.	★UNC.	BANK	A.P.B.	V.FINE	UNC.	★UNC.
					☐ Chicago	55.00	125.00	650.00	—
					☐ St. Louis	55.00	125.00	650.00	—
☐ Philadelphia	60.00	105.00	450.00	4500.00	☐ Minneapolis	65.00	200.00	650.00	—
☐ Cleveland	60.00	125.00	450.00	4500.00	☐ Kansas City	65.00	200.00	650.00	4500.00
☐ Richmond	60.00	125.00	450.00	4500.00	☐ Dallas	65.00	225.00	650.00	—
☐ Atlanta	60.00	125.00	650.00	—	☐ San Francisco	55.00	125.00	650.00	—

SERIES OF 1934C, SIGNATURES OF JULIAN-SNYDER, GREEN SEAL

BANK	A.B.P.	V.FINE	UNC.	★UNC.	BANK	A.B.P.	V.FINE	UNC.	★UNC.
☐ Boston	60.00	150.00	335.00	—	☐ Chicago	60.00	110.00	335.00	2200.00
☐ New York	60.00	110.00	335.00	2200.00	☐ St. Louis	60.00	110.00	335.00	2200.00
☐ Philadelphia	60.00	125.00	335.00	2200.00	☐ Minneapolis	60.00	110.00	335.00	2200.00
☐ Cleveland	60.00	105.00	335.00	2200.00	☐ Kansas City	60.00	105.00	335.00	2200.00
☐ Richmond	60.00	105.00	335.00	2200.00	☐ Dallas	60.00	105.00	335.00	2200.00
☐ Atlanta	60.00	150.00	335.00	—					

SERIES OF 1934D, SIGNATURES OF CLARK-SNYDER, GREEN SEAL

BANK	A.B.P.	V.FINE	UNC.	★UNC.	BANK	A.B.P.	V.FINE	UNC.	★UNC.
☐ Boston	70.00	150.00	450.00	4500.00	☐ Chicago	55.00	100.00	450.00	5000
☐ New York	53.00	100.00	450.00	4500.00					
☐ Philadelphia	53.00	100.00	450.00	4000.00	☐ Minneapolis	55.00	200.00	750.00	—
☐ Richmond	70.00	150.00	450.00	—	☐ Dallas	65 .00	125.00	450.00	—
☐ Atlanta	70.00	150.00	450.00	4500.00					

FIFTY DOLLAR NOTES (1950)
FEDERAL RESERVE NOTES

SERIES OF 1950, SIGNATURES OF CLARK-SNYDER, GREEN SEAL

BANK	A.B.P.	V.FINE	UNC.	★UNC.	BANK	A.P.B.	V.FINE	UNC.	★UNC.
☐ Boston	75.00	125.00	350.00	1400.00	☐ Chicago	75.00	125.00	350.00	1200.00
☐ New York	75.00	125.00	350.00	1200.00	☐ St. Louis	75.00	125.00	350.00	1200.00
☐ Philadelphia	75.00	125.00	350.00	1400.00	☐ Minneapolis	75.00	125.00	550.00	1800.00
☐ Cleveland	75.00	125.00	350.00	1200.00	☐ Kansas City	75.00	125.00	350.00	1600.00
☐ Richmond	75.00	125.00	350.00	1200.00	☐ Dallas	75.00	125.00	350.00	1200.00
☐ Atlanta	75.00	125.00	350.00	1200.00	☐ San Francisco	75.00	125.00	350.00	1200.00

SERIES OF 1950A, SIGNATURES OF PRIEST-HUMPHERY, GREEN SEAL

BANK	A.B.P.	V.FINE	UNC.	★UNC.	BANK	A.B.P.	V.FINE	UNC.	★UNC.
☐ Boston	55.00	90.00	250.00	650.00	☐ Chicago	55.00	80.00	250.00	650.00
☐ New York	55.00	90.00	250.00	650.00	☐ St. Louis	55.00	80.00	250.00	650.00
☐ Philadelphia	55.00	90.00	250.00	650.00	☐ Minneapolis	55.00	80.00	250.00	650.00
☐ Cleveland	55.00	90.00	250.00	650.00	☐ Kansas City	55.00	80.00	250.00	650.00
☐ Richmond	55.00	90.00	250.00	650.00	☐ Dallas	55.00	80.00	250.00	650.00
☐ Atlanta	55.00	90.00	250.00	650.00	☐ San Francisco	55.00	80.00	250.00	650.00

SERIES OF 1950B, SIGNATURES OF PRIEST-ANDERSON, GREEN SEAL

BANK	A.B.P.	V.FINE	UNC.	★UNC.	BANK	A.B.P.	V.FINE	UNC.	★UNC.
☐ Boston	52.00	85.00	275.00	550.00	☐ Chicago	52.00	85.00	275.00	750.00
☐ New York	52.00	85.00	275.00	450.00	☐ St. Louis	52.00	85.00	275.00	750.00
☐ Philadelphia	52.00	85.00	275.00	550.00	☐ Minneapolis	52.00	85.00	275.00	750.00
☐ Cleveland	52.00	85.00	275.00	550.00	☐ Kansas City	52.00	85.00	275.00	750.00
☐ Richmond	52.00	85.00	275.00	750.00	☐ Dallas	52.00	85.00	275.00	750.00
☐ Atlanta	52.00	85.00	275.00	750.00	☐ San Francisco	52.00	85.00	275.00	750.00

SERIES OF 1950C, SIGNATURES OF SMITH-DILLON, GREEN SEAL

BANK	A.B.P.	V.FINE	UNC.	★UNC.	BANK	A.B.P.	V.FINE	UNC.	★UNC.
☐ Boston	52.00	85.00	200.00	750.00	☐ Chicago	52.00	85.00	200.00	750.00
☐ New York	52.00	85.00	200.00	750.00	☐ St. Louis	52.00	85.00	200.00	750.00
☐ Philadelphia	52.00	85.00	200.00	750.00	☐ Minneapolis	52.00	85.00	200.00	950.00
☐ Cleveland	52.00	85.00	200.00	750.00	☐ Kansas City	52.00	85.00	200.00	750.00
☐ Richmond	52.00	85.00	200.00	750.00	☐ Dallas	52.00	85.00	200.00	750.00
☐ Atlanta	52.00	85.00	200.00	750.00	☐ San Francisco	52.00	85.00	200.00	750.00

SERIES OF 1950D, SIGNATURES OF GRANAHAN-DILLON, GREEN SEAL

BANK	A.B.P.	V.FINE	UNC.	★UNC.	BANK	A.B.P.	V.FINE	UNC.	★UNC.
☐ Boston	75.00	125.00	250.00	650.00	☐ Chicago	58.00	125.00	150.00	550.00
☐ New York	75.00	125.00	250.00	650.00	☐ St. Louis	58.00	125.00	150.00	650.00
☐ Philadelphia	75.00	125.00	250.00	650.00	☐ Minneapolis	58.00	125.00	250.00	850.00
☐ Cleveland	58.00	110.00	150.00	650.00	☐ Kansas City	58.00	125.00	150.00	650.00
☐ Richmond	58.00	110.00	150.00	650.00	☐ Dallas	65.00	125.00	250.00	750.00
☐ Atlanta	58.00	110.00	150.00	650.00	☐ San Francisco	65.00	125.00	250.00	650.00

SERIES OF 1950E, SIGNATURES OF GRANAHAN-FOWLER, GREEN SEAL

BANK	A.B.P.	V.FINE	UNC.	★UNC.
☐ Chicago	75.00	200.00	600.00	2500.00
☐ New York	75.00	200.00	400.00	1500.00
☐ San Francisco	80.00	150.00	500.00	1500.00

FIFTY DOLLAR NOTES (1963)
FEDERAL RESERVE NOTES
SERIES OF 1963,
(THERE WERE NOT ANY NOTES PRINTED FOR THIS SERIES.)

SERIES OF 1963A, SIGNATURES OF GRANAHAN-FOWLER, GREEN SEAL

BANK	A.B.P.	V.FINE	UNC.	BANK	A.B.P.	V.FINE	UNC.
☐ Boston	52.00	125.00	350.00	☐ Chicago	52.00	125.00	350.00
☐ New York	52.00	125.00	350.00	☐ St. Louis	52.00	125.00	350.00
☐ Philadelphia	52.00	125.00	350.00	☐ Minneapolis	52.00	125.00	350.00
☐ Cleveland	52.00	125.00	350.00	☐ Kansas City	52.00	125.00	350.00
☐ Richmond	52.00	125.00	350.00	☐ Dallas	52.00	125.00	350.00
☐ Atlanta	52.00	125.00	350.00	☐ San Francisco	52.00	125.00	350.00

FIFTY DOLLAR NOTES (1969)
FEDERAL RESERVE NOTES
(WORDING IN GREEN TREASURY SEAL IS CHANGED FROM LATIN TO ENGLISH)

SERIES OF 1969, SIGNATURES OF ELSTON-KENNEDY, GREEN SEAL

BANK	A.B.P.	V.FINE	UNC.	BANK	A.B.P.	V.FINE	UNC.
☐ Boston	52.00	80.00	225.00	☐ Chicago	52.00	80.00	225.00
☐ New York	52.00	80.00	225.00	☐ St. Louis	52.00	80.00	225.00
☐ Philadelphia	52.00	80.00	225.00	☐ Minneapolis	52.00	80.00	225.00
☐ Cleveland	52.00	80.00	225.00	☐ Kansas City	52.00	80.00	225.00
☐ Richmond	52.00	80.00	225.00	☐ Dallas	52.00	80.00	225.00
☐ Atlanta	52.00	80.00	225.00	☐ San Francisco	52.00	80.00	225.00

SERIES OF 1969A, SIGNATURES OF KABIS-CONNALLY, GREEN SEAL

BANK	A.B.P.	V.FINE	UNC.	BANK	A.B.P.	V.FINE	UNC.
☐ Boston	52.00	75.00	155.00	☐ Chicago	52.00	75.00	155.00
☐ New York	52.00	75.00	155.00	☐ St. Louis	52.00	75.00	155.00
☐ Philadelphia	52.00	75.00	155.00	☐ Minneapolis	52.00	75.00	155.00
☐ Cleveland	52.00	75.00	155.00	☐ Kansas City	52.00	75.00	155.00
☐ Richmond	52.00	75.00	155.00	☐ Dallas	52.00	75.00	155.00
☐ Atlanta	52.00	75.00	155.00	☐ San Francisco	52.00	75.00	155.00

SERIES OF 1969B, SIGNATURES OF BANUELOS-CONNALLY, GREEN SEAL

BANK	A.B.P.	V.FINE	UNC.	BANK	A.B.P.	V.FINE	UNC.
☐ Boston	52.00	275.00	850.00	☐ Chicago	52.00	275.00	850.00
☐ New York	52.00	275.00	850.00				
☐ Richmond	52.00	275.00	850.00	☐ Dallas	52.00	275.00	850.00
☐ Atlanta	52.00	275.00	850.00				

SERIES OF 1969C, SIGNATURES OF BANUELOS-SHULTZ, GREEN SEAL

BANK	A.B.P.	V.FINE	UNC.	BANK	A.B.P.	V.FINE	UNC.
☐ Boston	52.00	70.00	125.00	☐ Chicago	52.00	70.00	125.00
☐ New York	52.00	70.00	125.00	☐ St. Louis	52.00	70.00	125.00
☐ Philadelphia	52.00	70.00	125.00	☐ Minneapolis	52.00	70.00	125.00
☐ Cleveland	52.00	70.00	125.00	☐ Kansas City	52.00	70.00	125.00
☐ Richmond	52.00	70.00	125.00	☐ Dallas	52.00	70.00	125.00
☐ Atlanta	52.00	70.00	125.00	☐ San Francisco	52.00	70.00	125.00

FIFTY DOLLAR NOTES (1974)
FEDERAL RESERVE NOTES

SERIES OF 1974, SIGNATURES OF NEFF-SIMON, GREEN SEAL

BANK	A.B.P.	V.FINE	UNC.	BANK	A.B.P.	V.FINE	UNC.
☐ Boston	52.00	70.00	130.00	☐ Chicago	52.00	70.00	200.00
☐ New York	52.00	70.00	125.00	☐ St. Louis	52.00	70.00	200.00
☐ Philadelphia	52.00	70.00	130.00	☐ Minneapolis	52.00	70.00	175.00
☐ Cleveland	52.00	70.00	125.00	☐ Kansas City	52.00	70.00	150.00
☐ Richmond	52.00	70.00	130.00	☐ Dallas	52.00	70.00	150.00
☐ Atlanta	52.00	70.00	130.00	☐ San Francisco	52.00	70.00	150.00

FIFTY DOLLAR NOTES (1977)
FEDERAL RESERVE NOTES

SERIES OF 1977, SIGNATURES OF MORTON-BLUMENTHAL, GREEN SEAL

BANK	A.B.P.	V.FINE	UNC.	BANK	A.B.P.	V.FINE	UNC.
☐ Boston	—	65.00	100.00	☐ Chicago	—	65.00	95.00
☐ New York	—	65.00	95.00	☐ St. Louis	—	65.00	150.00
☐ Philadelphia	—	65.00	95.00	☐ Minneapolis	—	65.00	125.00
☐ Cleveland	—	65.00	95.00	☐ Kansas City	—	65.00	125.00
☐ Richmond	—	65.00	95.00	☐ Dallas	—	65.00	125.00
☐ Atlanta	—	65.00	95.00	☐ San Francisco	—	65.00	95.00

FIFTY DOLLAR NOTES (1981)
FEDERAL RESERVE NOTES

SERIES OF 1981, SIGNATURES OF BUCHANAN-REGAN, GREEN SEAL

BANK	A.B.P.	V.FINE	UNC.	BANK	A.B.P.	V.FINE	UNC.
☐ Boston	—	60.00	100.00	☐ Chicago	—	60.00	100.00
☐ New York	—	60.00	100.00	☐ St. Louis	—	60.00	100.00
☐ Philadelphia	—	60.00	100.00	☐ Minneapolis	—	60.00	100.00
☐ Cleveland	—	60.00	100.00	☐ Kansas City	—	60.00	100.00
☐ Richmond	—	60.00	100.00	☐ Dallas	—	60.00	100.00
☐ Atlanta	—	60.00	100.00	☐ San Francisco	—	60.00	100.00

SERIES OF 1981A, SIGNATURES OF ORTEGA-REGAN, GREEN SEAL

BANK	A.B.P.	V.FINE	UNC.	BANK	A.B.P.	V.FINE	UNC.
☐ Boston	—	70.00	100.00	☐ Chicago	—	70.00	100.00
☐ New York	—	70.00	100.00	☐ St. Louis	—	70.00	100.00
☐ Philadelphia	—	70.00	100.00	☐ Minneapolis	—	70.00	100.00
☐ Cleveland	—	70.00	100.00	☐ Kansas City	—	70.00	100.00
☐ Richmond	—	70.00	100.00	☐ Dallas	—	70.00	100.00
☐ Atlanta	—	70.00	100.00	☐ San Francisco	—	70.00	100.00

FIFTY DOLLAR NOTES (1985)

FEDERAL RESERVE NOTES

SERIES OF 1985, SIGNATURES OF ORTEGA-BAKER, GREEN SEAL

BANK	A.B.P.	V.FINE	UNC.	BANK	A.B.P.	V.FINE	UNC.
☐ Boston	—	60.00	100.00	☐ Chicago	—	60.00	100.00
☐ New York	—	60.00	100.00	☐ St. Louis	—	60.00	100.00
☐ Philadelphia	—	60.00	100.00	☐ Minneapolis	—	60.00	100.00
☐ Cleveland	—	60.00	100.00	☐ Kansas City	—	60.00	100.00
☐ Richmond	—	60.00	100.00	☐ Dallas	—	60.00	100.00
☐ Atlanta	—	60.00	100.00	☐ San Francisco	—	60.00	100.00

FIFTY DOLLAR NOTES (1988)

FEDERAL RESERVE NOTES

SERIES OF 1988, SIGNATURES OF ORTEGA-BRADY, GREEN SEAL

BANK	A.B.P.	V.FINE	UNC.	BANK	A.B.P.	V.FINE	UNC.
☐ Boston	—	55.00	100.00	☐ Chicago	—	55.00	100.00
☐ New York	—	55.00	100.00	☐ St. Louis	—	55.00	100.00
☐ Philadelphia	—	55.00	100.00	☐ Minneapolis	—	55.00	100.00
☐ Cleveland	—	55.00	100.00	☐ Kansas City	—	55.00	100.00
☐ Richmond	—	55.00	100.00	☐ Dallas	—	55.00	100.00
☐ Atlanta	—	55.00	100.00	☐ San Francisco	—	55.00	100.00

FIFTY DOLLAR NOTES (1990)

FEDERAL RESERVE NOTES

SERIES OF 1990, SIGNATURES OF VILLALPANDO-BRADY, GREEN SEAL

BANK	A.B.P.	V.FINE	UNC.	BANK	A.B.P.	V.FINE	UNC.
☐ Boston	—	55.00	95.00	☐ Chicago	—	55.00	95.00
☐ New York	—	55.00	95.00	☐ St. Louis	—	55.00	95.00
☐ Philadelphia	—	55.00	95.00	☐ Minneapolis	—	55.00	95.00
☐ Cleveland	—	55.00	95.00	☐ Kansas City	—	55.00	95.00
☐ Richmond	—	55.00	95.00	☐ Dallas	—	55.00	95.00
☐ Atlanta	—	55.00	95.00	☐ San Francisco	—	55.00	95.00

FIFTY DOLLAR NOTES (1993)
FEDERAL RESERVE NOTES
SERIES OF 1993, SIGNATURES OF WITHROW-BENTSEN, GREEN SEAL

BANK	A.B.P.	V.FINE	UNC.	BANK	A.B.P.	V.FINE	UNC.
☐ Boston	—	55.00	95.00	☐ Chicago	—	55.00	95.00
☐ New York	—	55.00	95.00	☐ St. Louis	—	55.00	95.00
☐ Philadelphia	—	55.00	95.00	☐ Minneapolis	—	55.00	95.00
☐ Cleveland	—	55.00	95.00	☐ Kansas City	—	55.00	95.00
☐ Richmond	—	55.00	95.00	☐ Dallas	—	55.00	95.00
☐ Atlanta	—	55.00	95.00	☐ San Francisco	—	55.00	95.00

FIFTY DOLLAR NOTES (1996)
FEDERAL RESERVE NOTES
SERIES OF 1995, SIGNATURES OF WITHROW-BENTSEN, GREEN SEAL

BANK	A.B.P.	V.FINE	UNC.	BANK	A.B.P.	V.FINE	UNC.
☐ Boston	—	55.00	85.00	☐ Chicago	—	55.00	85.00
☐ New York	—	55.00	85.00	☐ St. Louis	—	55.00	85.00
☐ Philadelphia	—	55.00	85.00	☐ Minneapolis	—	55.00	85.00
☐ Cleveland	—	55.00	85.00	☐ Kansas City	—	55.00	85.00
☐ Richmond	—	55.00	85.00	☐ Dallas	—	55.00	85.00
☐ Atlanta	—	55.00	85.00	☐ San Francisco	—	55.00	85.00

FIFTY DOLLAR NOTES (1918)

FEDERAL RESERVE BANK NOTES

(Large Size)

Face Design: Portrait of President Grant to left, Federal Reserve Bank in center, blue seal right.

Back Design: Female figure of Panama between merchant ship and battleship. Plates were made for all twelve Federal Reserve Districts. Only St. Louis bank issued. Less than thirty notes are known today.

BANK	SERIES	GOV'T SIGNATURES	BANK SIGNATURES	A.B.P.	V. FINE	UNC.
☐St. Louis	1918	Teehee-Burke	Attebery-Wells	RARE	RARE	RARE

FIFTY DOLLAR NOTES (1929)

FEDERAL RESERVE BANK NOTES

(Small Size)

Face Design: Portrait of Grant center, name of bank left, brown serial numbers, black letter for Federal Reserve District.

Back Design: Same as 1929 $50 note.

BANK	SERIES	SIGNATURES	SEAL	A.B.P.	V.FINE	UNC.	★UNC.
☐ New York	1929	Jones-Woods	Brown	70.00	150.00	450.00	RARE
☐ Cleveland	1929	Jones-Woods	Brown	75.00	140.00	450.00	RARE
☐ Chicago	1929	Jones-Woods	Brown	70.00	150.00	500.00	RARE
☐ Minneapolis	1929	Jones-Woods	Brown	70.00	150.00	600.00	RARE
☐ Kansas City	1929	Jones-Woods	Brown	105.00	200.00	400.00	RARE
☐ Dallas	1929	Jones-Woods	Brown	75.00	155.00	2850.00	RARE
☐ San Francisco	1929	Jones-Woods	Brown	100.00	250.00	400.00	RARE

ONE HUNDRED DOLLAR NOTES

ORDER OF ISSUE

ONE HUNDRED DOLLAR NOTES (1862–1863)
UNITED STATES NOTES
(ALSO KNOWN AS LEGAL TENDER NOTES)

(Large Size)

Face Design: Eagle with spread wings left, three discs with "100," red seal numbers.

Back Design: Green, two variations of the wording in obligation.

SERIES	SIGNATURES	SEAL	A.B.P.	GOOD	V.FINE	UNC.
□1862	Chittenden-Spinner*	Red	—	—	—	RARE
□1862	Chittenden-Spinner**	Red	—	—	—	RARE
□1863	Chittenden-Spinner**	Red	—	—	—	RARE

*First Obligation: Similar to 1875–1907 $5 note.
**Second Obligation: Shown above.

ONE HUNDRED DOLLAR NOTES (1869–1880)
UNITED STATES NOTES

(Large Size)

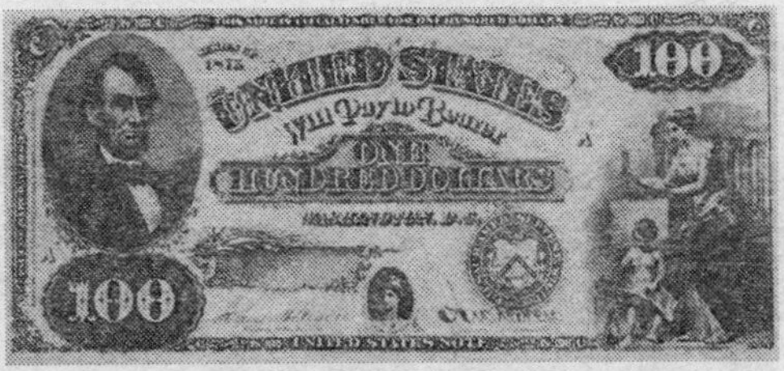

Face Design: Portrait of President Lincoln.

Back Design: First Issue

Back Design: Second Issue.

SERIES	SIGNATURES	SEAL	A.B.P.	GOOD	V.FINE	UNC.
□1869	Allison-Spinner	Red	3800.00			RARE

The following notes have a modified back design.

(Small Size)

Second Issue

SERIES	SIGNATURES	SEAL	A.B.P.	GOOD	V.FINE	UNC.
□1875	Allison-New	Sm. Red	3000.00	4500.00	RARE	RARE
□1875	Allison-Wyman	Sm. Red	4500.00	6000.00	RARE	RARE
□1878	Allison-Gilfillan	Sm. Red	2200.00	3200.00	RARE	RARE
□1880	Bruce-Gilfillan	Lg. Brown	1700.00	2400.00	RARE	RARE
□1880	Bruce-Wyman	Lg. Brown	1700.00	2500.00	RARE	RARE
□1880	Rosecrans-Jordan	Lg. Red	1700.00	2400.00	RARE	RARE
□1880	Rosecrans-Hyatt	Red Plain	2200.00	3500.00	RARE	RARE
□1880	Rosecrans-Hyatt	Red Spike	1800.00	2500.00	RARE	RARE
□1880	Rosecrans-Huston	Lg. Red	1800.00	2500.00	RARE	RARE
□1880	Rosecrans-Huston	Lg. Brown	1800.00	2700.00	RARE	RARE
□1880	Tillman-Morgan	Sm. Red	1600.00	2000.00	RARE	RARE
□1880	Bruce-Roberts	Sm. Red	1600.00	2000.00	RARE	RARE
□1880	Lyons-Roberts	Sm. Red	1600.00	2000.00	RARE	RARE

ONE HUNDRED DOLLAR NOTES (1966) U.S. NOTES (ALSO KNOWN AS LEGAL TENDER NOTES)

(Small Size)

Face Design: Portrait of Franklin, red seal, red serial numbers.

Back Design: Independence Hall.

SERIES	SIGNATURES	SEAL	A.B.P.	V.FINE	UNC.	*UNC
☐1966*	Granahan-Fowler	Red	135.00	200.00	1000.00	3000.00
☐1966A	Elston-Kennedy	Red	175.00	275.00	1600.00	—

*This is the first note to be issued with the new Treasury Seal with wording in English instead of Latin.

ONE HUNDRED DOLLAR NOTES (1875)
NATIONAL BANK NOTES

FIRST CHARTER PERIOD (Large Size)

Face Design: Perry leaving the Saint Lawrence, left.

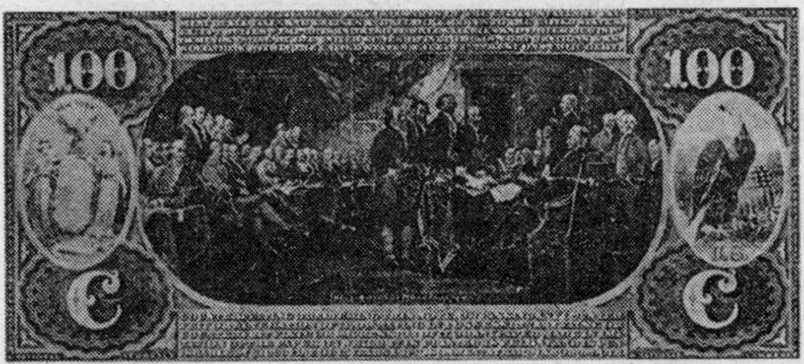

Back Design: Border green, center black, signing of the Declaration of Independence.

SERIES	SIGNATURES	SEAL	A.B.P.	GOOD	V.FINE	UNC.
☐Original	Chittenden-Spinner	Red	RARE	RARE	RARE	RARE
☐Original	Colby-Spinner	Red	RARE	RARE	RARE	RARE
☐Original	Allison-Spinner	Red	RARE	RARE	RARE	RARE
☐1875	Allison-New	Red	RARE	RARE	RARE	RARE
☐1875	Allison-Wyman	Red	RARE	RARE	RARE	RARE
☐1875	Allison-Gilfillan	Red	RARE	RARE	RARE	RARE
☐1875	Scofield-Gilfillan	Red	RARE	RARE	RARE	RARE
☐1875	Bruce-Gilfillan	Red	RARE	RARE	RARE	RARE
☐1875	Bruce-Wyman	Red	RARE	RARE	RARE	RARE
☐1875	Rosecrans-Huston	Red	RARE	RARE	RARE	RARE
☐1875	Tillman-Morgan	Red	RARE	RARE	RARE	RARE

ONE HUNDRED DOLLAR NOTES (1882)
NATIONAL BANK NOTES

SECOND CHARTER PERIOD (Large Size)

First Issue (Brown seal and brown backs.)

SERIES	SIGNATURES	SEAL	A.B.P.	GOOD	V.FINE	UNC.
□1882	Bruce-Gilfillan	Brown	2500.00	3500.00	RARE	RARE
□1882	Bruce-Wyman	Brown	2500.00	3500.00	RARE	RARE
□1882	Bruce-Jordan	Brown	2500.00	3500.00	RARE	RARE
□1882	Rosecrans-Jordan	Brown	2500.00	3500.00	RARE	RARE
□1882	Rosecrans-Hyatt	Brown	2500.00	3500.00	RARE	RARE
□1882	Rosecrans-Huston	Brown	2500.00	3500.00	RARE	RARE
□1882	Rosecrans-Nebeker	Brown	2500.00	3500.00	RARE	RARE
□1882	Rosecrans-Morgan	Brown	2500.00	3500.00	RARE	RARE
□1882	Tillman-Morgan	Brown	2500.00	3500.00	RARE	RARE
□1882	Tillman-Roberts	Brown	2500.00	3500.00	RARE	RARE
□1882	Bruce-Roberts	Brown	2500.00	3500.00	RARE	RARE
□1882	Lyons-Roberts	Brown	2500.00	3500.00	RARE	RARE

SECOND CHARTER PERIOD (Large Size)

Second Issue (Blue seal, green back with date "1882–1908")

Back Design: Green with date "1882–1908" center.

SERIES	SIGNATURES	SEAL	A.B.P.	GOOD	V.FINE	UNC.
□1882	Rosecrans-Huston	Blue	2400.00	3000.00	RARE	RARE
□1882	Rosecrans-Nebeker	Blue	2400.00	3000.00	RARE	RARE
□1882	Tillman-Morgan	Blue	2400.00	3000.00	RARE	RARE
□1882	Tillman-Roberts	Blue	2400.00	3000.00	RARE	RARE
□1882	Bruce-Roberts	Blue	2400.00	3000.00	RARE	RARE
□1882	Lyons-Roberts	Blue	2400.00	3000.00	RARE	RARE
□1882	Vernon-Treat	Blue	2400.00	3000.00	RARE	RARE
□1882	Napier-McClung	Blue	2400.00	3000.00	RARE	RARE

This note was also issued with (value) ONE HUNDRED DOLLARS on the back. Very rare. —

ONE HUNDRED DOLLAR NOTES (1902)
NATIONAL BANK NOTES
THIRD CHARTER PERIOD (Large Size)

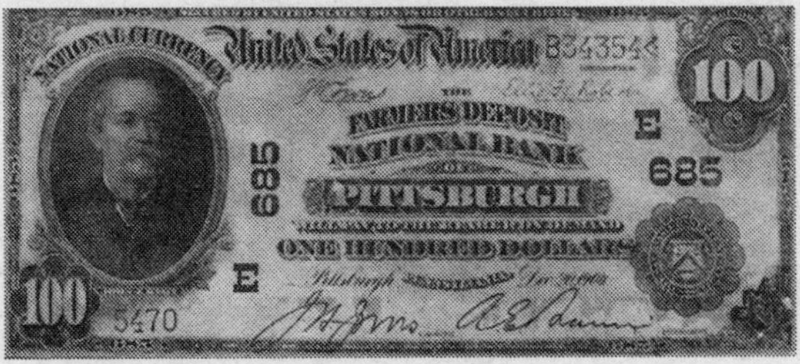

Face Design: Portrait of John J. Knox left.

Back Design: Male figures with shield and flags.

First Issue (Red seal)

SERIES	SIGNATURES	SEAL	A.B.P.	GOOD	V.FINE	UNC.
□1902	Lyons-Roberts	Red	2200.00	3000.00	RARE	RARE
□1902	Lyons-Treat	Red	2200.00	3000.00	RARE	RARE
□1902	Vernon-Treat	Red	2200.00	3000.00	RARE	RARE

Second Issue*

Design is similar to previous note. Seal and serial numbers are now blue; back of note has date "1902–1908" added.

SERIES	SIGNATURES	SEAL	A.B.P.	GOOD	V.FINE	UNC.
		Blue	600.00	1000.00	3000.00	RARE

Third Issue*

Design continues as previous notes. Seal and serial numbers remain blue, date "1902–1908" removed from back.

SERIES	SIGNATURES	SEAL	A.B.P.	GOOD	V.FINE	UNC.
		Blue	550.00	850.00	3200.00	RARE

* The notes of the **Second and Third Issue** appeared with various signatures: Lyons-Roberts, Lyons-Treat, Vernon-Treat, Vernon-McClung, Napier-McClung, Parker-Burke, Teehee-Burke, Elliott-Burke, Elliott-White, Speelman-White, Woods-White.

ONE HUNDRED DOLLAR NOTES (1929)
NATIONAL BANK NOTES

(Small Size)

Face Design: Portrait of Franklin center. Name of bank and city left. Brown seal right.

SERIES	SIGNATURES	SEAL	A.B.P.	V.FINE	UNC.
□1929	Type I Jones-Woods	Brown	155.00	450.00	1200.00
□1929	Type II Jones-Woods	Brown	200.00	625.00	1750.00

ONE HUNDRED DOLLAR NOTES (1878)
SILVER CERTIFICATES

SERIES	SIGNATURES	SEAL	A.B.P.	V.FINE	UNC.
□1878	Scofield-Gilfillan-White	Red			UNIQUE
□1878	Scofield-Gilfillan-Hopper	Red	NO SPECIMENS KNOWN		
□1878	Scofield-Gilfillan-Hillhouse	Red	NO SPECIMENS KNOWN		
□1878	Scofield-Gilfillan-Anthony	Red			UNIQUE
□1878	Scofield-Gilfillan-Wyman (printed signature of Wyman)	Red	NO SPECIMENS KNOWN		
□1878	Scofield-Gilfillan	Red			VERY RARE
□1880	Scofield-Gilfillan	Brown	EXTREMELY RARE		
□1880	Bruce-Gilfillan	Brown	25000.00	30000.00	RARE
□1880	Bruce-Wyman	Brown	25000.00	30000.00	RARE
□1880	Rosecrans-Huston	Brown	25000.00	30000.00	RARE
□1880	Rosecrans-Nebeker	Brown	25000.00	30000.00	RARE

ONE HUNDRED DOLLAR NOTES (1891)
SILVER CERTIFICATES

(Large Size)

Face Design: Portrait of President Monroe.

SERIES	SIGNATURES	SEAL	A.B.P.	GOOD	V.FINE	UNC.
□1891	Rosecrans-Nebeker	Red	4000.00			VERY RARE
□1891	Tillman-Morgan	Red	4000.00			VERY RARE

This note was also issued in the Series of 1878 and 1880. They are very rare.

ONE HUNDRED DOLLAR NOTES (1882–1922)
GOLD CERTIFICATES

(Large Size)

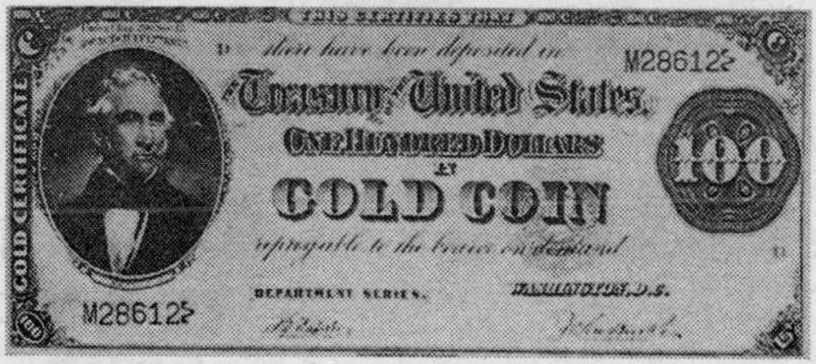

Face Design: Portrait of Thomas H. Benton.

SERIES	SIGNATURES	SEAL	A.B.P.	GOOD	V.FINE	UNC.
□1882	Bruce-Gilfillan	Brown	1840.00	2985.00	25000.00	RARE
□1882	Bruce-Wyman	Brown	3800.00	7500.00	RARE	RARE
□1882	Rosecrans-Hyatt	Lg. Red	3800.00	6100.00	RARE	RARE
□1882	Rosecrans-Huston	Lg. Brown	3500.00	5100.00	35000.00	RARE
□1882	Lyons-Roberts	Sm. Red	300.00	330.00	2800.00	RARE
□1882	Lyons-Treat	Sm. Red	300.00	540.00	4500.00	RARE
□1882	Vernon-Treat	Sm. Red	300.00	430.00	2800.00	RARE
□1882	Vernon-McClung	Sm. Red	300.00	430.00	2575.00	RARE
□1882	Napier-McClung	Sm. Red	300.00	345.00	2800.00	RARE
□1882	Napier-Thompson	Sm. Red	300.00	450.00	2500.00	RARE
□1882	Napier-Burke	Sm. Red	300.00	425.00	2500.00	RARE
□1882	Parker-Burke	Sm. Red	300.00	425.00	2500.00	RARE
□1882	Teehee-Burke	Sm. Red	300.00	425.00	2500.00	RARE
□1922	Speelman-White	Sm. Red	300.00	425.00	2500.00	RARE

ONE HUNDRED DOLLAR NOTES (1928)
GOLD CERTIFICATES

(Small Size)

Face Design: Portrait of Franklin center. Yellow seal to left. Yellow numbers.

SERIES	SIGNATURES	SEAL	A.B.P.	GOOD	V.FINE	UNC.
□1928	Woods-Mellon	Gold	200.00	350.00	1000.00	4500.00

ONE HUNDRED DOLLAR NOTES (1890–1891)
TREASURY OR COIN NOTES

(Large Size)

Face Design: Portrait of Commodore Farragut to right.

Back Design: Large "100," called "Watermelon Note."

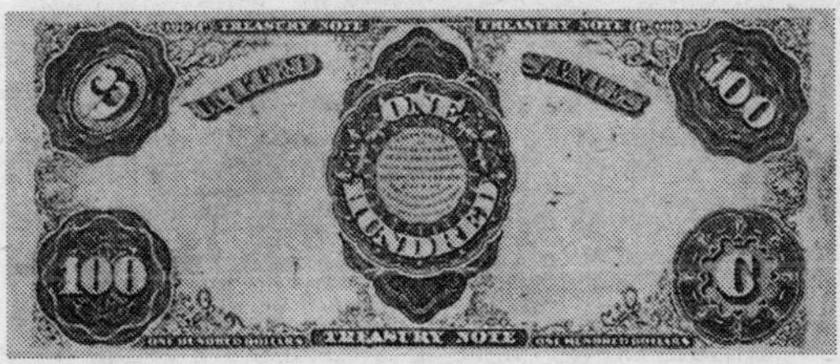

Back Design: ONE HUNDRED in scalloped medallion.

SERIES	SIGNATURES	SEAL	A.B.P.	GOOD	V.FINE	UNC.
□1890	Rosecrans-Huston	Brown			RARE	RARE
□1890	Rosecrans-Nebeker	Red			RARE	RARE

ONE HUNDRED DOLLAR NOTES (1914)
FEDERAL RESERVE NOTES

(Large Size)

Face Design: Portrait of Franklin in center.
Back Design: Group of five allegorical figures.

SERIES OF 1914, SIGNATURES OF BURKE-McADOO, RED SEAL AND RED SERIAL NUMBERS

BANK	A.B.P.	GOOD	V.FINE	UNC.	BANK	A.B.P.	GOOD	V.FINE	UNC.
☐ Boston	800.00	1200.00	RARE	RARE	☐ Chicago	800.00	1200.00	RARE	RARE
☐ New York	800.00	1200.00	RARE	RARE	☐ St. Louis	800.00	1200.00	RARE	RARE
☐ Philadelphia	800.00	1200.00	RARE	RARE	☐ Minneapolis	800.00	1200.00	RARE	RARE
☐ Cleveland	800.00	1200.00	RARE	RARE	☐ Kansas City	800.00	1200.00	RARE	RARE
☐ Richmond	800.00	1200.00	RARE	RARE	☐ Dallas	800.00	1200.00	RARE	RARE
☐ Atlanta	800.00	1200.00	RARE	RARE	☐ San Francisco	800.00	1200.00	RARE	RARE

SERIES OF 1914, DESIGN CONTINUES AS PREVIOUS NOTE, BLUE SEAL AND BLUE SERIAL NUMBERS

This note was issued with various signatures for each bank (Burke-McAdoo, Burke-Glass, Burke-Huston, White-Mellon).

BANK	A.B.P.	V.FINE	UNC.	BANK	A.B.P.	V.FINE	UNC.
☐ Boston	375.00	1200.00	2800.00	☐ Chicago	550.00	1200.00	2800.00
☐ New York	375.00	1200.00	2800.00	☐ St. Louis	550.00	1200.00	2800.00
☐ Philadelphia	375.00	1200.00	2800.00	☐ Minneapolis	550.00	1200.00	2800.00
☐ Cleveland	375.00	1400.00	2800.00	☐ Kansas City	550.00	1200.00	2800.00
☐ Richmond	375.00	1200.00	2800.00	☐ Dallas	550.00	1200.00	2800.00
☐ Atlanta	375.00	1400.00	2800.00	☐ San Francisco	550.00	1200.00	2800.00

ONE HUNDRED DOLLAR NOTES (1928)
FEDERAL RESERVE NOTES

(Small Size)

Face Design: Portrait of Franklin, black Federal Reserve Seal left with number, green Treasury Seal right.

SERIES OF 1928, SIGNATURES OF WOODS-MELLON, GREEN SEAL

BANK	A.B.P.	V.FINE	UNC.	BANK	A.B.P.	V.FINE	UNC.
☐Boston	120.00	250.00	725.00	☐ Chicago	120.00	250.00	725.00
☐New York	120.00	250.00	725.00	☐ St. Louis	120.00	250.00	725.00
☐Philadelphia	120.00	250.00	725.00	☐ Minneapolis	120.00	250.00	725.00
☐Cleveland	120.00	250.00	725.00	☐ Kansas City	120.00	250.00	725.00
☐Richmond	120.00	250.00	725.00	☐ Dallas	170.00	250.00	725.00
☐Atlanta	120.00	250.00	725.00	☐ San Francisco	120.00	250.00	725.00

SERIES OF 1928A, SIGNATURES OF WOODS-MELLON, GREEN SEAL

The number is in black and the Federal Reserve Seal is changed to a letter.

(Small Size)

BANK	A.B.P.	V.FINE	UNC.	BANK	A.B.P.	V.FINE	UNC.
☐Boston	120.00	250.00	450.00	☐ Chicago	120.00	250.00	450.00
☐New York	120.00	250.00	450.00	☐ St. Louis	120.00	250.00	450.00
☐Philadelphia	120.00	250.00	450.00	☐ Minneapolis	120.00	250.00	450.00
☐Cleveland	120.00	250.00	450.00	☐ Kansas City	120.00	250.00	450.00
☐Richmond	120.00	250.00	450.00	☐ Dallas	120.00	250.00	450.00
☐Atlanta	170.00	250.00	450.00	☐ San Francisco	120.00	250.00	450.00

ONE HUNDRED DOLLAR NOTES (1934)
FEDERAL RESERVE NOTES

SERIES OF 1934, SIGNATURES OF JULIAN-MORGENTHAU, GREEN SEAL

BANK	A.B.P.	V.FINE	UNC.	BANK	A.B.P.	V.FINE	UNC.
☐ Boston	115.00	175.00	300.00	☐ Chicago	115.00	175.00	300.00
☐ New York	115.00	175.00	300.00	☐ St. Louis	115.00	175.00	300.00

□ Philadelphia	110.00	175.00	325.00	□ Minneapolis	110.00	175.00	325.00
□ Cleveland	110.00	175.00	325.00	□ Kansas City	110.00	175.00	325.00
□ Richmond	110.00	175.00	325.00	□ Dallas	110.00	175.00	325.00
□ Atlanta	110.00	175.00	325.00	□ San Francisco	110.00	175.00	325.00

SERIES OF 1934A, SIGNATURES OF JULIAN-MORGENTHAU, GREEN SEAL

BANK	A.B.P.	V.FINE	UNC.	BANK	A.B.P.	V.FINE	UNC.
□ Boston	110.00	200.00	300.00	□ Chicago	110.00	200.00	300.00
□ New York	110.00	200.00	300.00	□ St. Louis	110.00	200.00	300.00
□ Philadelphia	110.00	200.00	300.00	□ Minneapolis	110.00	200.00	300.00
□ Cleveland	110.00	200.00	300.00	□ Kansas City	110.00	200.00	300.00
□ Richmond	110.00	200.00	300.00	□ Dallas	110.00	200.00	300.00
□ Atlanta	110.00	200.00	300.00	□ San Francisco	110.00	200.00	300.00

SERIES OF 1934B, SIGNATURES OF JULIAN-VINSON, GREEN SEAL

BANK	A.B.P.	V.FINE	UNC.	BANK	A.B.P.	V.FINE	UNC.
□ Boston	120.00	180.00	400.00	□ Chicago	120.00	180.00	400.00
□ New York	120.00	180.00	400.00	□ St. Louis	120.00	180.00	400.00
□ Philadelphia	120.00	180.00	400.00	□ Minneapolis	120.00	180.00	400.00
□ Cleveland	120.00	180.00	400.00	□ Kansas City	120.00	180.00	400.00
□ Richmond	120.00	180.00	400.00	□ Dallas	120.00	180.00	400.00
□ Atlanta	120.00	180.00	400.00	□ San Francisco	120.00	180.00	400.00

SERIES OF 1934C, SIGNATURES OF JULIAN-SNYDER, GREEN SEAL

BANK	A.B.P.	V.FINE	UNC.	BANK	A.B.P.	V.FINE	UNC.
□ Boston	120.00	180.00	400.00	□ Chicago	120.00	180.00	400.00
□ New York	120.00	180.00	400.00	□ St. Louis	120.00	180.00	400.00
□ Philadelphia	120.00	180.00	400.00	□ Minneapolis	120.00	180.00	400.00
□ Cleveland	120.00	180.00	400.00	□ Kansas City	120.00	180.00	400.00
□ Richmond	120.00	180.00	400.00	□ Dallas	120.00	180.00	400.00
□ Atlanta	120.00	180.00	400.00	□ San Francisco	120.00	180.00	400.00

SERIES OF 1934D, SIGNATURES OF JULIAN-SNYDER, GREEN SEAL

BANK	A.B.P.	V.FINE	UNC.	BANK	A.B.P.	V.FINE	UNC.
□ New York	2000.00	5000.00	8500.00	□ St. Louis	175.00	325.00	1000.00
□ Philadelphia	175.00	325.00	1000.00	□ Dallas	175.00	325.00	1000.00
□ Atlanta	175.00	325.00	1000.00				
□ Chicago	175.00	325.00	1000.00				

ONE HUNDRED DOLLAR NOTES (1950)
FEDERAL RESERVE NOTES
SERIES OF 1950, SIGNATURES OF CLARK-SNYDER, GREEN SEAL

BANK	A.B.P.	V.FINE	UNC.	UNC.★	BANK	A.B.P.	V.FINE	UNC.	UNC.★
☐ Boston	110.00	175.00	350.00	1800.00	☐ Chicago	110.00	175.00	350.00	1800.00
☐ New York	110.00	175.00	350.00	1800.00	☐ St. Louis	110.00	175.00	350.00	1800.00
☐ Philadelphia	105.00	175.00	350.00	1800.00	☐ Minneapolis	110.00	175.00	350.00	1800.00
☐ Cleveland	110.00	175.00	350.00	1800.00	☐ Kansas City	110.00	175.00	350.00	1800.00
☐ Richmond	110.00	175.00	350.00	1800.00	☐ Dallas	110.00	175.00	350.00	1800.00
☐ Atlanta	110.00	175.00	350.00	1800.00	☐ San Francisco	110.00	175.00	350.00	1800.00

SERIES OF 1950A, SIGNATURES OF PRIEST-HUMPHERY, GREEN SEAL

BANK	A.B.P.	V.FINE	UNC.	UNC.★	BANK	A.B.P.	V.FINE	UNC.	UNC.★
☐ Boston	105.00	120.00	300.00	825.00	☐ Chicago	105.00	120.00	300.00	825.00
☐ New York	105.00	120.00	300.00	825.00	☐ St. Louis	105.00	120.00	300.00	825.00
☐ Philadelphia	105.00	120.00	300.00	825.00	☐ Minneapolis	105.00	120.00	300.00	825.00
☐ Cleveland	105.00	120.00	300.00	825.00	☐ Kansas City	105.00	120.00	300.00	825.00
☐ Richmond	105.00	120.00	300.00	825.00	☐ Dallas	105.00	120.00	300.00	825.00
☐ Atlanta	105.00	120.00	300.00	825.00	☐ San Francisco	105.00	120.00	300.00	825.00

SERIES OF 1950B, SIGNATURES OF PRIEST-ANDERSON, GREEN SEAL

BANK	A.B.P.	V.FINE	UNC.	UNC.★	BANK	A.B.P.	V.FINE	UNC.	UNC.★
☐ Boston	110.00	120.00	200.00	850.00	☐ Chicago	110.00	120.00	200.00	850.00
☐ New York	110.00	120.00	200.00	850.00	☐ St. Louis	110.00	120.00	200.00	850.00
☐ Philadelphia	100.00	120.00	200.00	850.00	☐ Minneapolis	110.00	120.00	200.00	850.00
☐ Cleveland	110.00	120.00	200.00	850.00	☐ Kansas City	110.00	120.00	200.00	850.00
☐ Richmond	110.00	120.00	200.00	850.00	☐ Dallas	110.00	120.00	200.00	850.00
☐ Atlanta	110.00	120.00	200.00	850.00	☐ San Francisco	110.00	120.00	200.00	850.00

SERIES OF 1950C, SIGNATURES OF SMITH-DILLON, GREEN SEAL

BANK	A.B.P.	V.FINE	UNC.	UNC.★	BANK	A.B.P.	V.FINE	UNC.	UNC.★
☐ Boston	105.00	110.00	200.00	750.00	☐ Chicago	105.00	110.00	200.00	750.00
☐ New York	105.00	110.00	200.00	750.00	☐ St. Louis	105.00	110.00	200.00	750.00
☐ Philadelphia	105.00	110.00	200.00	750.00	☐ Minneapolis	105.00	110.00	200.00	750.00
☐ Cleveland	105.00	110.00	200.00	750.00	☐ Kansas City	105.00	110.00	200.00	750.00
☐ Richmond	105.00	110.00	200.00	750.00	☐ Dallas	105.00	110.00	200.00	750.00
☐ Atlanta	105.00	110.00	200.00	750.00	☐ San Francisco	105.00	110.00	200.00	750.00

SERIES OF 1950D, SIGNATURES OF GRANAHAN-DILLON, GREEN SEAL

BANK	A.B.P.	V.FINE	UNC.	UNC.★	BANK	A.B.P.	V.FINE	UNC.	UNC.★
☐ Boston	110.00	125.00	250.00	1200.00	☐ Chicago	110.00	125.00	250.00	1200.00
☐ New York	110.00	125.00	250.00	1200.00	☐ St. Louis	110.00	125.00	250.00	1200.00
☐ Philadelphia	110.00	125.00	250.00	1200.00	☐ Minneapolis	110.00	125.00	250.00	1200.00
☐ Cleveland	110.00	125.00	250.00	1200.00	☐ Kansas City	110.00	125.00	250.00	1200.00
☐ Richmond	110.00	125.00	250.00	1200.00	☐ Dallas	110.00	125.00	250.00	1200.00
☐ Atlanta	110.00	125.00	250.00	1200.00	☐ San Francisco	100.00	125.00	250.00	1200.00

SERIES OF 1950E, SIGNATURES OF GRANAHAN-FOWLER, GREEN SEAL

BANK	A.B.P.	V.FINE	UNC.
☐ Chicago	150.00	200.00	1500.00
☐ New York	150.00	235.00	1000.00
☐ San Francisco	150.00	235.00	1500.00

ONE HUNDRED DOLLAR NOTES (1963)

FEDERAL RESERVE NOTES

SERIES OF 1963, (THERE WERE NOT ANY NOTES PRINTED FOR THIS SERIES.)

SERIES OF 1963A, SIGNATURES OF GRANAHAN-FOWLER, GREEN SEAL

BANK	A.B.P.	V.FINE	UNC.	UNC.★	BANK	A.B.P.	V.FINE	UNC.	UNC.★
☐ Boston	—	110.00	225.00	700.00	☐ Chicago	—	110.00	225.00	700.00
☐ New York	—	110.00	225.00	700.00	☐ St. Louis	—	110.00	225.00	700.00
☐ Philadelphia	—	110.00	225.00	700.00	☐ Minneapolis	—	110.00	225.00	700.00
☐ Cleveland	—	110.00	225.00	700.00	☐ Kansas City	—	110.00	225.00	700.00
☐ Richmond	—	110.00	225.00	700.00	☐ Dallas	—	110.00	225.00	700.00
☐ Atlanta	—	110.00	225.00	700.00	☐ San Francisco	—	110.00	225.00	700.00

ONE HUNDRED DOLLAR NOTES (1969)

FEDERAL RESERVE NOTES

SERIES OF 1969, SIGNATURES OF ELSTON-KENNEDY, GREEN SEAL

BANK	A.B.P.	V.FINE	UNC.	UNC.★	BANK	A.B.P.	V.FINE	UNC.	UNC.★
☐ Boston	—	110.00	200.00	450.00	☐ Chicago	—	110.00	200.00	450.00
☐ New York	—	110.00	200.00	450.00	☐ St. Louis	—	110.00	200.00	450.00
☐ Philadelphia	—	110.00	200.00	450.00	☐ Minneapolis	—	110.00	200.00	450.00
☐ Cleveland	—	110.00	200.00	450.00	☐ Kansas City	—	110.00	200.00	450.00
☐ Richmond	—	110.00	200.00	450.00	☐ Dallas	—	110.00	200.00	450.00
☐ Atlanta	—	110.00	200.00	450.00	☐ San Francisco	—	110.00	200.00	450.00

SERIES OF 1969A, SIGNATURES OF KABIS-CONNALLY, GREEN SEAL

BANK	A.B.P.	V.FINE	UNC.	UNC.★	BANK	A.B.P.	V.FINE	UNC.	UNC.★
☐ Boston	—	110.00	200.00	450.00	☐ Chicago	—	110.00	200.00	450.00
☐ New York	—	110.00	200.00	450.00	☐ St. Louis	—	110.00	200.00	450.00
☐ Philadelphia	—	110.00	200.00	450.00	☐ Minneapolis	—	110.00	200.00	450.00
☐ Cleveland	—	110.00	200.00	450.00	☐ Kansas City	—	110.00	200.00	450.00
☐ Richmond	—	110.00	200.00	450.00	☐ Dallas	—	110.00	200.00	450.00
☐ Atlanta	—	110.00	200.00	450.00	☐ San Francisco	—	110.00	200.00	450.00

SERIES OF 1969B (THERE WERE NO NOTES PRINTED FOR THIS SERIES.)

SERIES OF 1969C, SIGNATURES OF BANUELOS-SHULTZ, GREEN SEAL

BANK	A.B.P.	V.FINE	UNC.	UNC.★	BANK	A.B.P.	V.FINE	UNC.	UNC.★
☐ Boston	—	110.00	225.00	425.00	☐ Chicago	—	110.00	225.00	425.00
☐ New York	—	110.00	225.00	425.00	☐ St. Louis	—	110.00	225.00	425.00
☐ Philadelphia	—	110.00	225.00	425.00	☐ Minneapolis	—	110.00	225.00	425.00
☐ Cleveland	—	110.00	225.00	425.00	☐ Kansas City	—	110.00	225.00	425.00
☐ Richmond	—	110.00	225.00	425.00	☐ Dallas	—	110.00	225.00	425.00
☐ Atlanta	—	110.00	225.00	425.00	☐ San Francisco	—	110.00	225.00	425.00

ONE HUNDRED DOLLAR NOTES (1974)
FEDERAL RESERVE NOTES

SERIES OF 1974, SIGNATURES OF NEFF-SIMON, GREEN SEAL

BANK	A.B.P.	V.FINE	UNC.	UNC.★	BANK	A.B.P.	V.FINE	UNC.	UNC.★
☐ Boston	—	110.00	180.00	400.00	☐ Chicago	—	110.00	180.00	400.00
☐ New York	—	110.00	180.00	400.00	☐ St. Louis	—	110.00	180.00	400.00
☐ Philadelphia	—	110.00	180.00	400.00	☐ Minneapolis	—	110.00	180.00	400.00
☐ Cleveland	—	110.00	180.00	400.00	☐ Kansas City	—	110.00	180.00	400.00
☐ Richmond	—	110.00	180.00	400.00	☐ Dallas	—	110.00	180.00	400.00
☐ Atlanta	—	110.00	180.00	400.00	☐ San Francisco	—	110.00	180.00	400.00

ONE HUNDRED DOLLAR NOTES (1977)
FEDERAL RESERVE NOTES

SERIES OF 1977, SIGNATURES OF MORTON-BLUMENTHAL, GREEN SEAL

BANK	A.B.P.	V.FINE	UNC.	UNC.★	BANK	A.B.P.	V.FINE	UNC.	UNC.★
☐ Boston	—	110.00	200.00	375.00	☐ Chicago	—	110.00	200.00	375.00
☐ New York	—	110.00	200.00	375.00	☐ St. Louis	—	110.00	200.00	375.00
☐ Philadelphia	—	110.00	200.00	375.00	☐ Minneapolis	—	110.00	200.00	375.00
☐ Cleveland	—	110.00	200.00	375.00	☐ Kansas City	—	110.00	200.00	375.00
☐ Richmond	—	110.00	200.00	375.00	☐ Dallas	—	110.00	200.00	375.00
☐ Atlanta	—	110.00	200.00	375.00	☐ San Francisco	—	110.00	200.00	375.00

ONE HUNDRED DOLLAR NOTES (1981)
FEDERAL RESERVE NOTES
SERIES OF 1981, SIGNATURES OF BUCHANAN-REGAN, GREEN SEAL

BANK	A.B.P.	V.FINE	UNC.	BANK	A.B.P.	V.FINE	UNC.
☐ Boston	—	110.00	250.00	☐ Chicago	—	110.00	235.00
☐ New York	—	110.00	235.00	☐ St. Louis	—	110.00	235.00
☐ Philadelphia	—	110.00	235.00	☐ Minneapolis	—	110.00	235.00
☐ Cleveland	—	110.00	235.00	☐ Kansas City	—	110.00	235.00
☐ Richmond	—	110.00	235.00	☐ Dallas	—	110.00	235.00
☐ Atlanta	—	110.00	235.00	☐ San Francisco	—	110.00	235.00

SERIES OF 1981A, SIGNATURES OF ORTEGA-REGAN, GREEN SEAL

BANK	A.B.P.	V.FINE	UNC.	BANK	A.B.P.	V.FINE	UNC.
☐ Boston	—	110.00	225.00	☐ Chicago	—	110.00	225.00
☐ New York	—	110.00	225.00	☐ St. Louis	—	110.00	225.00
☐ Philadelphia	—	110.00	225.00	☐ Minneapolis	—	110.00	225.00
☐ Cleveland	—	110.00	225.00	☐ Kansas City	—	110.00	225.00
☐ Richmond	—	110.00	225.00	☐ Dallas	—	110.00	225.00
☐ Atlanta	—	110.00	225.00	☐ San Francisco	—	110.00	225.00

ONE HUNDRED DOLLAR NOTES (1985)
FEDERAL RESERVE NOTES
SERIES OF 1985, SIGNATURES OF ORTEGA-REGAN, GREEN SEAL

BANK	A.B.P.	V.FINE	UNC.	BANK	A.B.P.	V.FINE	UNC.
☐ Boston	—	110.00	200.00	☐ Chicago	—	110.00	200.00
☐ New York	—	110.00	200.00	☐ St. Louis	—	110.00	200.00
☐ Philadelphia	—	110.00	200.00	☐ Minneapolis	—	110.00	200.00
☐ Cleveland	—	110.00	200.00	☐ Kansas City	—	110.00	200.00
☐ Richmond	—	110.00	200.00	☐ Dallas	—	110.00	200.00
☐ Atlanta	—	110.00	200.00	☐ San Francisco	—	110.00	200.00

ONE HUNDRED DOLLAR NOTES (1988)
FEDERAL RESERVE NOTES
SERIES OF 1988, SIGNATURES OF ORTEGA-BRADY, GREEN SEAL

BANK	A.B.P.	V.FINE	UNC.	BANK	A.B.P.	V.FINE	UNC.
☐ Boston	—	110.00	200.00	☐ Chicago	—	110.00	200.00
☐ New York	—	110.00	200.00	☐ St. Louis	—	110.00	200.00
☐ Philadelphia	—	110.00	200.00	☐ Minneapolis	—	110.00	200.00
☐ Cleveland	—	110.00	200.00	☐ Kansas City	—	110.00	200.00
☐ Richmond	—	110.00	200.00	☐ Dallas	—	110.00	200.00
☐ Atlanta	—	110.00	200.00	☐ San Francisco	—	110.00	200.00

ONE HUNDRED DOLLAR NOTES (1990)
FEDERAL RESERVE NOTES
SERIES OF 1990, SIGNATURES OF VILLALPANDO-BRADY, GREEN SEAL

BANK	A.B.P.	V.FINE	UNC.	BANK	A.B.P.	V.FINE	UNC.
☐ Boston	—	—	200.00	☐ Chicago	—	—	200.00
☐ New York	—	—	200.00	☐ St. Louis	—	—	200.00
☐ Philadelphia	—	—	200.00	☐ Minneapolis	—	—	200.00
☐ Cleveland	—	—	200.00	☐ Kansas City	—	—	200.00
☐ Richmond	—	—	200.00	☐ Dallas	—	—	200.00
☐ Atlanta	—	—	200.00	☐ San Francisco	—	—	200.00

ONE HUNDRED DOLLAR NOTES (1993)
FEDERAL RESERVE NOTES
SERIES OF 1993, SIGNATURES OF WITHROW-BENTSEN, GREEN SEAL

BANK	A.B.P.	V.FINE	UNC.	BANK	A.B.P.	V.FINE	UNC.
☐ Boston	—	—	175.00	☐ Chicago	—	—	175.00
☐ New York	—	—	175.00	☐ St. Louis	—	—	175.00
☐ Philadelphia	—	—	175.00	☐ Minneapolis	—	—	175.00
☐ Cleveland	—	—	175.00	☐ Kansas City	—	—	175.00
☐ Richmond	—	—	175.00	☐ Dallas	—	—	175.00
☐ Atlanta	—	—	175.00	☐ San Francisco	—	—	175.00

ONE HUNDRED DOLLAR NOTES (1996)
FEDERAL RESERVE NOTES
SERIES OF 1996, SIGNATURES OF WITHROW-RUBIN, GREEN SEAL

BANK	A.B.P.	V.FINE	UNC.	BANK	A.B.P.	V.FINE	UNC.
☐ Boston	—	—	150.00	☐ Chicago	—	—	150.00
☐ New York	—	—	150.00	☐ St. Louis	—	—	150.00
☐ Philadelphia	—	—	150.00	☐ Minneapolis	—	—	150.00
☐ Cleveland	—	—	150.00	☐ Kansas City	—	—	150.00
☐ Richmond	—	—	150.00	☐ Dallas	—	—	150.00
☐ Atlanta	—	—	150.00	☐ San Francisco	—	—	150.00

ONE HUNDRED DOLLAR NOTES (1929)
FEDERAL RESERVE BANK NOTES
(ISSUED ONLY IN SERIES OF 1929)

(Small Size)

Face Design: Portrait of Franklin, brown seal and numbers.

Back Design

BANK & CITY	SIGNATURES	SEAL	A.B.P.	V.FINE	UNC.
☐New York	Jones-Woods	Brown	175.00	250.00	625.00
☐Cleveland	Jones-Woods	Brown	175.00	250.00	625.00
☐Richmond	Jones-Woods	Brown	120.00	200.00	850.00
☐Chicago	Jones-Woods	Brown	175.00	250.00	625.00
☐Minneapolis	Jones-Woods	Brown	175.00	250.00	625.00
☐Kansas City	Jones-Woods	Brown	120.00	145.00	675.00
☐Dallas	Jones-Woods	Brown	120.00	210.00	2200.00

FIVE HUNDRED, ONE THOUSAND, FIVE THOUSAND, AND TEN THOUSAND DOLLAR NOTES

(Production of notes in denominations above one hundred dollars was discontinued in 1969.)

FEDERAL RESERVE
FIVE HUNDRED DOLLAR NOTES

	A.B.P.	V.FINE	UNC.	BANK
☐ 1928	700.00	1200.00	3750.00	ALL BANKS
☐ 1934	700.00	1200.00	3750.00	ALL BANKS
☐ 1934A	700.00	1200.00	2750.00	ALL BANKS EXCEPT BOSTON/ATLANTA
☐ 1934B	—	RARE	RARE	ATLANTA ONLY
☐ 1934C	—	RARE	RARE	BOSTON ONLY
▼Gold Certs.				
☐ 1928	1000.00	5000.00	25000.00	

ONE THOUSAND DOLLAR NOTES

	A.B.P.	V.FINE	UNC.
☐ 1928	1200.00	2500.00	5000.00
☐ 1934	1200.00	2500.00	4500.00
☐ 1934A	1200.00	2500.00	4500.00
▼Gold:			
☐ 1928	1200.00	6000.00	RARE
☐ 1934		ALL RARE	

FIVE THOUSAND DOLLAR NOTES

	A.B.P.	V.FINE	UNC.	BANK
☐ 1928			RARE	
☐ 1934			RARE	
☐ 1934A		ALL RARE		ST. LOUIS ONLY
☐ 1934B		ALL RARE		NEW YORK
☐ Gold Certs.			VERY RARE	

TEN THOUSAND DOLLAR NOTES

	A.B.P.	V.FINE	UNC.	BANK
☐ 1928		RARE	RARE	
☐ 1934			RARE	
☐ 1934A	—	RARE		CHICAGO ONLY
☐ Gold Certs.			VERY RARE	

WESTERN SCRIP & OBSOLETES

First a word regarding these western notes. Paper was generally despised in the West where gold was the main source of exchange. However, certain realities dictated the use of paper currency. Notes listed here fall into nine categories;

1) SUTLER NOTES (S); Forts in the military west needed a traceable form of barter payable between paydays.

2) PRIVATE BANK NOTES (B); Western banks isolated from the eastern monetary sources couldn't wait months for gold delivery when their daily existence was tenable at best.

3) MERCHANT SCRIP (M); Businesses needed a means to pay their workers and issue credits to customers. Companies also used scrip to ensure that wages were spent at their company store.

4) BUSINESS COLLEGE NOTES (C); These were printed for use within the classes to facilitate the handling of currency. A large number of these notes were readily accepted in city commerce.

5) WARRANTS (W); These are notes issued by government authority. They may be Federal, State, County, City, and have been issued for Postmasters, School, Roads, Juror pay, or a wide variety of other reasons. City, County, and State governments needed a medium to pay for services where non-existent funds still required the continuance of local government. They were notes with the "promise" of money.

6) COMMUNAL SCRIP (CS); Civic Groups and rural areas needed a way to trade or barter labor, necessities or agriculture goods. Storehouses were maintained and deposits made which were exchanged for notes that could be returned later for items needed as they became available. Includes U.S. Government.

7) ADVERTISING NOTES (A); These represented promises to the holder and either had a face value or were printed on other notes such as Private Bank or CSA notes. Some were printed as close copies of U.S. Federal Currency.

8) PANIC or DEPRESSION SCRIP (D); Widespread runs on banks (1907) or the closing of all banks (1933) necessitated a form of currency that could keep commerce operating while Federal notes were in short supply. It should be noted that the Federal Gov't welcomed these notes and ignored currency laws banning them.

9) CERTIFICATE OF DEPOSIT (CD); Negotiable Deposits were placed in Banks and Certificates issued that could be used in lieu of cash. These were bearer items. Some are quite valuable today.

Comments or information regarding existing unlisted or listed issues is encouraged and should be sent to Bill Rindone, P.O. Box 790, Aurora, OR 97002 or emailed to bnnw@bnnw.net. Scans and data may be submitted for the states/territories listed. This listing of Western Scrip is part of an ongoing research project.

Prices listed are for the most common of the denominations shown and for the condition most frequently found. A short glossary of terms can be found after the listings.

ALASKA

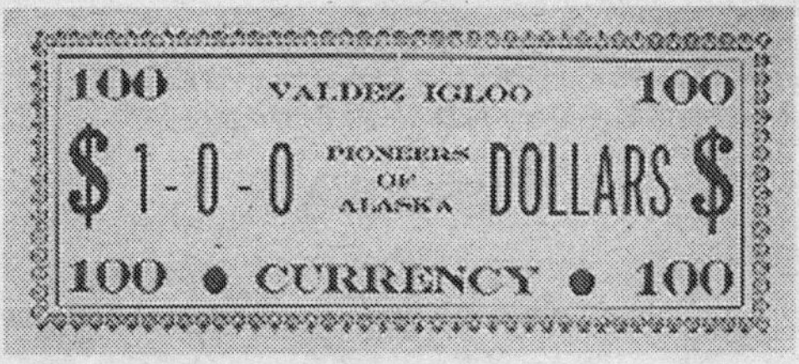

1920 $100 Valdez Igloo of Pioneers of Alaska

DENOMINATION	PRICE
1820 Russian-America - 50K Russian-American Company. "Seal Skin" money.	$6000
1954 Alaska Terr. - $100 Black Diamond Certificate (A)	$75
1916 Alaska - $1, $5, $10, $50 Klondyke Koin Scrip.	$300
1847–52 Aleutians, AT-10 Kopeks 1 Rouble, etc. Russian-America Sealskin Money (M)	$6000
1922c Anchorage, AT - $5 Finley Shoes. Poll Parrot (M)	$195
1950 Anchorage, AT - $1, 5, 10, 20, Bi-Lo Grocery Alaska (M)	$11
1954 Anchorage - $100 Black Diamond Certificate, Territorial.	$50
1923c Chichagoff - 5¢, 10¢, 25¢, 50¢ Chicagoff Development (Chichagoff Gold Mine) Scrip (M)	$125
19-- Dillingham 5¢, 10¢, 25¢, 50¢ Fisherman's Co-Op Trading Post and Roadhouse (M)	Set $18
1900c Eagle - 5c, 10c, 25c Eagle Trading Company, founded 1897.	$75
1908 Fairbanks, AT - $1 United States Construction Co.	$375

DENOMINATION	PRICE
1915 Fairbanks, AT - $1 Fraternal Order of Eagles, March 26, 1915.	$775
1907c Fairbanks, AT - 25¢ 50¢ Salchaket Trading Co. Scrip (M)	$8500
19-- ND Fairbanks - 1 share Alaska-Colonial Currency (A)	$38
1910 Iditarod - Miners and Merchants Bank Certificate of Deposit.	$175
1900 Juneau - $800 Var.$ First Nat'l Bank of Juneau Cert. of Deposit (B)	$550
19-- Juneau - 5¢, 10¢, 25¢, 50¢ Juneau Hotel Scrip (M)	$20
1939 Ketchikan - $20 Tongass Trading Co. (M)	$425
1939 Ketchikan - $20 Cordell Transfer Co. (M)	$400
1894 Kodiak - 2¢. U.S. Postal Note. Alaska was a U.S. district in 1894 (US)	$9775
1960 Kodiak - $1 Snowflake Certificate (A)	$30
1894 Sitka. 2¢ U.S. Postal note. This is one of only three recorded Alaska notes. (US)	$10000
1907 Nome, AT - $1, $2, $5, $10, $20, $50, $100 Nome Clearing House (D)	$9000
1916 Skagway - 50 Bunk Money reads, "50 - W.P.A.C."	$240
1920–33 Skagway, AT - $5 $10 $20 $50 White Pass Dance Hall (Issue #1 pictoral) (A)	$450
1920–33 Skagway, AT - $5 $10 $20 $50 White Pass Dance Hall (#2 Black on color paper) (A)	$250
1920–33 Skagway, AT - $5 $10 $20 $50 White Pass Dance Hall (#3 Colored Ink) (A)	$250
1902–43 - Skagway - 1 Meal Ticket round card, Pullen House. Famous hotel that burned in 1943	$37
1916c Thane - 5c Gastineau Mining Co. Scrip chits (M)	$75
1920 Valdez, AT - $10 $20 $50 $100 Valdez Igloo, Pioneers of Alaska (A)	$105
1954 Anchorage - $100 Black Diamond Certificate, Territorial.	$45

ARIZONA

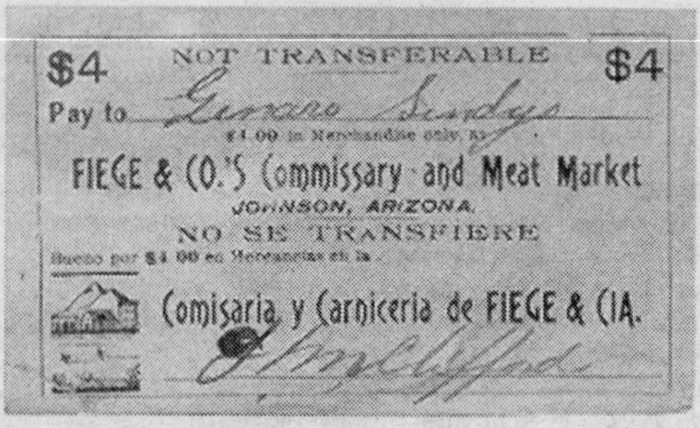

1902 $4 Fiege & Company, Arizona Territory

DENOMINATION	PRICE
1933 Arizona - 50¢ $1.00 Arizona Grocery Co. (no city shown) (D)	$725
1924–?? ND Arizona - 1¢ 5¢ 10¢ 25¢ 50¢ Arizona State Hospital Script (M)	$45
1907 Benson - $1 Bank of Benson (D)	$1750
1907 Bisbee, AT - $1 Miner's and Merchants Bank (D)	$1600

DENOMINATION	PRICE
1913 Bisbee - 25¢ Bank of Bisbee/Mercantile Bank of Cananea (B)	$780
1913 Bisbee - $50, $100 Miner's and Merchants Bank CD (B)	$1400
1933 Buckeye - 5¢ 10¢ 25¢ 50¢ Buckeye Merchants (D)	$2150
1880s Clifton - 10c Longfellow Mining Co. store (M)	$1700
1880s Clifton - 25c Arizona Copper Co. at the Clifton Store	$1250
1913 Douglas - 25c Bank of Bisbee, for the Moctezuma Copper Co. (M)	$600
1933 Flagstaff - 50¢ Arizona State Teachers College (D)	$365
1880s Evans Point - 50c Evans-Van Hecke Mining Co. Cardboard R7 (M)	$4,025
1907 Globe, AT - $1 Old Dominion Commercial Company (D)	$600
1879 Hackberry AT - $2.50 Hackberry Mill & Mining Co. (M)	$5000
1880c Hampden, AT - 25¢ 50¢, $1, $2 Territorial Script of F S Collins & Co. (M)	$7000
1904 Harshaw, AT - $3 $7 (var.) Mowry Mines, American Industrial Development Co. (M)	$1000
1904 Holbrook - $10 Arizona Co-Operative Mercantile Institution (M)	$2000
1933c - 25¢/25¢ Ritz Theatre. for Civilian Conservation Corp. (D)	$105
1900–04 Johnson City, AT - $1, 2, 3, 4 Fiege & Co. Commisary & Meat Market. (M)	$1750
1862c Mesilla - 50c William D. Skillman "Redeemable in Confederate" (M)	RARE
1933 Nogales - $1 Nogales Herald Newspaper (D)	$525
1933 Phoenix - $1, $5, $10, $20, $50, $100 Phoenix Clearing House Certificate (D)	$600
1933 Phoenix - $1 Arizona Republic and Phoenix Gazette Newspapers (D)	$700
1933 Phoenix - 50¢, $1 Arizona Grocery Co. (D)	$700
1887 Pima Cnty - $150 Pima County Bank Certificate of Deposit	$500
1880s Pinal - $1 Pinal Gold & Silver Mining Co., Office in SF & Arizona. (M)	$6,500
1900–03 Russellville, AT - $1, $2, $3, $4 Fiege Co. Commisary & Meat Market (M)	$1750
1878 Smith's Mill - 25c A. T. Smith's Mill Store. (M)	$3000
1901 Snowflake - $4.50 Arizona Co-Op Mercantile (M)	$1200
1881 Tombstone - $1000 Agency Pima County (CD)	$140
1883 Tucson - 1¢. U.S. Postal Note uncancelled. (US)	$2185
1890c Tucson, AT - 25¢ 50¢ L. Zeckendorf & Co. (M)	$9500
1870–81c Tuscon, AT - 5c 25c 50c $1 $5 Lord & Williams, Arizona Terr (M)	$12000
1895c Tucson, AT - 5¢ Lord & Williams, Arizona Territory (M)	$9500
1907 Tucson, AT - $1 Arizona Nat'l Bank (D)	$625
1933 Tucson - $20 Consolidated National Bank (D)	$525
1933 Tucson - $1 Arizona Daily Star Newspaper (D)	$500
1940 Tucson - 10¢, 25¢, 50¢ Old Tucson issued during filming of "ARIZONA" (A)	$85
1880c Tucson, AT - $10, $20 Safford, Hudson & Co. Bankers Scrip (B)	$125
1890s Tucson, AT - 50c L. Zeckendorf & Co. (M)	$6500
1905c Twin Buttes, AT - $2.50, $5, $10 Twin Buttes Mining and Smelting Scrip (M)	$140
1933 Tucson - 1 Bit, Wolfeville - Tucson Lodge 385, B.P.O.E.	$475

CALIFORNIA

1880 Stockton - 50¢ E.E. Washburn Commission Scrip

DENOMINATION	PRICE
19-- ND State of California - $1 Colonization of Sanguine People. (A)	$105
1933 State - Var.$ State of California Warrant (W)	$125
1933 Alameda - 25¢ Unemployed Relief Assoc. (D)	$495
1922 Anaheim - $500 $1000 Chamber of Comm. Valencia Orange Show (W)	$375
1933 Anaheim - $1 Anaheim Emergency Voucher (D)	$200
1933 Anaheim - $1 Emergency Plan Voucher (D)	$170
1933 Anderson-Cottonwood - $1 A-C Irrigation District . . . (D)	$100
1929 Angels Camp - $10 $25 Gold, Jumping Frog Jubilee (A)	$100
1948 Angels Camp - 5 Skins, Calaveras County Fair - Jumping Frog Jubilee (A)	$25
1865–85 Contra Costa County - 5¢ 10¢ Black Diamond Mining Co. (M)	$600
1869–76 Bakersfield - $25 Kernville Stage, Valley Express Co. (M)	$800
1880's Bakersfield - Var.$ Board of Supervisors of Kern County (W)	$60
1933 Barstow - 25¢ 50¢ $1 Barstow Printer Scrip (D)	$150
1907 Berkeley - $5 $10 The First National Bank (D)	$2000
1933 Berkeley - $1 Chamber of Commerce clear envelope (D)	$30
1879 Bodie - $55 The Bodie Bank. Cert. of Deposit (CD)	$175
1933 Burlingame - $1 $2.50 City of Burlingame (D)	$165
1933 Carmel - $1 Carmel-by-the Sea Business Assoc. (D)	$85
1933 Chico - $1 Chico Chamber of Commerce (D)	$100
1932 Chula Vista - $1 Emergency Relief Voucher (D)	$190
1865 Colusa - Var.$ $35 Treasurer of Colusa County (W)	$125
1933 Compton - Time Barter, Unemployed Co-Operative Relief (D)	$40
1933 Crescent City - 25¢ Clamshell, B & A Steamship Co. (D)	$450
1933 Crescent City - 10¢ 25¢ Clamshell, Chamber of Commerce	$450
1933 Crescent City - 50¢ Clamshell, Cleanatorium Odorless Cleaners (D)	$500
1933 Crescent City - 25¢ Clamshell, Electric Shop (D)	$425
1933 Crescent City - 10¢ Clamshell, Public Utilities Office (D)	$425
1933 Crescent City - 50¢ (paper), Davis' Associated Service Station (D)	$765
1870s Darwin - $20 The Defiance Mining Co at Office in Darwin, Inyo	$3500
1870s Darwin - 25c New Coso Mining Company at Office in Darwin, Inyo	$725
18-- Downieville - Var$ Banking House of PA Lamping & Co. Cert of Deposit. (B)	$130
1876 Eureka District, Tulare County, - $3 Settlers' Ditch Script (W) . . .	$40

DENOMINATION	PRICE
1860c Fort Jones - 25¢ Adam B. Carlock Store (M)	$1800
1907 Fresno - $1 Fresno Clearing House (D)	$1500
1880c Fresno - $3 Kutner, Goldstein & Co. General Merchandise & Grain (A)	$80
1907 Fresno - $1 Fresno Clearing House (D)	$750
191_ Greenville - $10 C.E. Young, payable at Indian Valley Bank. (M)	$100
1933 Hollywood - Var.$ Hollywood Cooperative Exchange (D)	$100
1965 Hollywood - Advertising film Major Dundee on back of 1862 U.S. $5 (A)	$22
1880s Humboldt Cty - $100 Humboldt County School Bank (W)	$40
1900c Jackson - 2¢ Redlick's Standard Goods (A)	$25
1933–34 Lancaster - 50¢ $1 $5 Lancaster Chamber of Commerce (D)	$85
1878 Los Angeles - $25 Silver. LA County Bank. Depression bearer note. (B)	$160
1880s Los Angeles - $1000 Woodbury's College Bank R-7 (C)	$625
1890 Los Angeles - First Nat'l Bank of Los Angeles ABNCo Specimen (CD)	$275
1908 Los Angeles - Wm. H. Carlson $5 July 1, 1908 (M)	$265
1914 Los Angeles, - $1000 Los Angeles Clearing House (B)	$2800
1933 Los Angeles - $1, 5, 10, 20, 50, 100 Los Angeles Clearing House Certificate (D)	$90
1933 Los Angeles - Var.$, $5 L.A Cooperative Exchange (D)	$45
1933 Los Angeles - 10¢ U.C.L.A. Associated Students (C)	$40
1933 Los Angeles - 5¢ U.S.C. Book Store and Cafe (D)	$35
1933 Los Angeles - $1 U.S. Spring & Bumper Co. (D)	$57
ND Maltermoro - $5 St. George Vineyard at Stores, (Fresno County)	$850
1852 Marysville - Var.$ Treasurer of Yuba County Warrant (W)	$445
1860–70s Marysville - Var.$ George North & Company Due Bill (W)	$150
1880c Marysville - $3 Eastman & Wright, watchmaker and engraver (A)	$65
1932 Merced - $1 Merced Merchants Trade-At-Home Scrip (D)	$85
1933 Merced - 50¢ City of Merced Depression Scrip (D)	$45
1935 Merced - Var.$ Merced Sun-Star Scrip (D)	$80
1910 Modesto - 1¢, 2¢. 3¢ 50¢ Lewis Shoe Co., The Stork System of Savings, (M)	$100
1910 Modesto - 1¢ 2¢ 3¢ 4¢ Latz's, Trustee, Stork Savings (M)	$105
1910 Modesto - 1¢ 2¢ 3¢ 4¢ The Osvald Hardware Co. Stork Savings (M)	$300
1932 Modesto - 1c 2c Modesto Bank of America - Stork Savings (D)	$165
1933 Monterey - Monterey Peninsula Convention, Tourist & Publicity Bureau (D)	$90
1933 Monterey-Pacific Grove - 50¢ $1 Trade Warrant (D)	$100
1860c Napa - $1000 Napa Collegiate Institute R-7 (C)	$1050
1886–90's Oakland - $10 DePue & Aydelotte Business College (C)	$1050
1871–80 Oakland - 50¢ Golden Gate Academy Commerical College Bank (A)	$875
1877 Oakland - $5 Oakland Business College (C)	$400
1880's Oakland - $5 W. Wilson Commission scrip (M)	$75
1894 Oakland - 2¢. U.S. Postal note dated May 12, 1894. (US)	$740
1899 Oakland - Central Cyclery, reverse of CSA facsimile. (A)	$160
1933 Oakland - 5¢. 10¢, 25¢, 50¢, $1 Natural Development Assoc. (Chits) (D)	$30
1933 Oakland - $1 $5 $10 $20 Oakland Clearing House Assoc. (D)	$250
1880c Oroville - C.A. Parlin, watchmaker and jeweler Ad Note (A)	$150
1933 Oxnard - 25¢ City of Oxnard Depression (D)	$75
1932 Pacific Grove - $1 Pacific Grove Tribune RARE (D)	$250
1870s Panamint - 50c Surprise Valley Mill & Water Co., Inyo Co. (M)	$1,200
1933 Pasadena - 25¢ 50¢ $1 $5 Hunting Hotel Company (D)	$90
1933 Petaluma - 10¢ Cochrane Lumber Co. RARE (D)	$250

DENOMINATION	PRICE
19-- ND Perris - Perris Market, M.A. Wolcott, Proprietor (A)	$25
1933 Pismo Beach - $1 Clamshell, Beach Camp (D)	$450
1933 Pismo Beach - 25¢, 50¢, $1 Clamshell, Beach Store AA Erhart (D)	$495
1933 Pismo Beach - 25¢, 50¢, $1 Clamshell, California Market (D)	$475
1933 Pismo Beach - $1 Clamshell, Pismo Beach Chamber of Commerce (D)	$575
1933 Pismo Beach - 25¢, 50¢ Clamshell, Harter Drug Co. (D)	$500
1933 Pismo Beach - 25¢, 50¢, $1 Clamshell, Henderson's Drug Store (D)	$475
1933 Pismo Beach - 25¢, 50¢, $1 Clamshell, Hi-way Cigar Store (D)	$525
1933 Pismo Beach - 25¢, 50¢, $1 Clamshell, Leiter's Pharmacy (D)	$500
1933 Pismo Beach - 25¢, 50¢, $1 Clamshell, Philipps' Tidewater Service Stn (D)	$750
1933 Pismo Beach - 25¢, 50¢, $1 Clamshell, Restwell Cabins (D)	$625
1933 Pismo Beach - $1 $5 $10 Clamshell, Wolverton Sign Company (D)	$850
1897 Portersville - $2 Labor Exchange Branch No. 136.	$400
1907 Riverside - $5 Associated Banks of Riverside, CA, (D)	$200
1933 Riverside - $1 $5 $10 $20 Associated Banks of Riverside Clearing House (D)	$100
1933 Riverside - $1 Sherman Institute, American Indian school. (D)	$450
1863 Sacramento - $50 California and Salt Lake Mail Line (M)	RARE
1865 Sacramento - Var $ Controller's Office - Soldiers Relief . . . (W)	$220
1852 Sacramento - $100 Rhodes & Lusk Banking & Express (B)	$450
1877 Sacramento - $3 A.M. Smith June, 1st Ad Note (A)	$350
1880c Sacramento - $10 Elite Theater Ad Note (A)	$95
1880 Sacramento - Var$ Treasurer of State, Controllers Warrant (W)	$70
1880c Sacramento - $1 $5 Business College Bank - (C)	$275
1883 Sacramento - Store at N.W. Corner 9th and J Sts. One Dollar Gold Note. (M)	$1500
1887c Sacramento - Sacramento Shirt Factory baseball Ad Note (A)	$1500
1887 Sacramento - $3 R.E. Gogings, apothecary Ad Note (A)	$150
19-- ND Sacramento - Reliance Lithograph Company . . . (A)	$20
1887 Sacramento - Fred. Mason 1887 Ad Note (A)	$4100
1877 Sacramento - $3 A.M. Smith June, 1st (A)	$295
1887 Sacramento - $5 California School Bank (C)	$850
1887c San Diego - 5% K.C. Naylor, Jewelers, baseball Ad Note (A) %	$1400
1893 San Diego - $1 San Diego and Phoenix Railroad Co. (M)	$3,000
1933 San Diego - $1 $5 $10 $20 San Diego Clearing House (D)	$30
1935 San Diego - 1, 5 Nuggets Gold Gulch, San Diego Exposition (A)	$30
1935 San Diego - 1, 5, 10, 20 Jardin de Plaisir, San Diego Expo (A)	$30
1849 San Francisco - $1 $5 The Miner's Bank, One Dollar on Demand. (B)	$18,000
1850 St. Francisco - 25¢ 50¢ $1 Miner's Bank of Savings of Alta California (N)	$2200
1850 San Francisco - $1000 Banking House of F. Argenti & Co., (B)	$19,000
1850s San Francisco - 25c, $20 Burgoyne & Co., San Francisco (B)	$3,750
1853 San Francisco - $50 California, N.Y. & European Steamship Co. (C)	$7500
1853 San Francisco - $50 California, N.Y. & European Steamship Co. (A)	$7500
1854 San Francisco - Var $ Bacon & Page Duplicate of Exchange (B)	$450
1859 San Francisco - $100 Pacific Loan & Security Bank. Cert. of Deposit. (CD)	$650
1867 San Francisco - $1 $3 $5 $10 $50 $100 $500 $1000 Pacific Business College (D)	$250
18-- ND San Francisco, - H. Van Valkenburgh (The San Francisco Gold Dust Office) . . . (M)	$1380
18-- San Francisco - $10 $20 Manly & Orr Style Unissued Scrip (M)	$300

DENOMINATION	PRICE
1867 San Francisco - $1 $5 $100 $1000 Union Business College (C)	$300
1860s–80s SF - 5, 10 Black Diamond Mining Company.	$400
1870 San Francisco - 10¢ Bank of Lower California pay in Gold Coin (CB)	$550
1870s San Francisco - $1 Gold, Amador Canal & Mining Company. (M)	$5000
1873 San Francisco. - $5 Thalia Verein. Liberty, eagle and shield. German text. (A)	$850
1874 San Francisco - $1 Bradley & Rulofson Advertising Note (A)	$550
1876 San Franciso - 50 cents. $5 Imperial Government of NORTON I. (A)	$15,500
ND San Francisco - $2 Ivanpah Consolidated Mill & Mining Company (M)	$1,600
ND San Francisco - $1 Pinal Gold & Silver Mining Co., Offices SF & Ariz. (M)	$6,000
ND San Francisco - $10 Bank of New York	$12,650
ND San Francisco - 50c R. H. Taylor & Co., Upper California. (M)	$550
1877 San Francisco - $5 Thalia Verein April 3, 1877 (M)	$100
1880s San Francisco, - $500 St. Mary's College (C)	$1250
1880s San Francisco, - Josiah J. Lecount Ad Note (A)	$400
1880s San Francisco. $100 Crane & Brigham. Perry's special corn & bunion cure. (A)	$650
1880s San Francisco - $5 Davis & Son. San Francisco Loan Office. (A)	$350
1880s San Francisco - $10/$3 O'Meara & Painter. 10 & 3. Eagle flanked by Xs.	$375
1880c San Francisco - $5 Brooks & Capp. The Golden Era. (A)	$345
1886 San Francisco. - $4.20 June 12, 1886. A rare cashed note. (US)	$720
1890s San Francisco - $20 William G. Badger, Commission Scrip. (M)	$650
1893 San Francisco, - 125,000 Pacific Bank, Feb. 23, 1893 (A)	$345
1894 San Francisco - $10 Dr. L. C. Harmon. $10. Savings bond look alike. (A)	$100
1890s San Francisco, - Rosenstock, Price & Co. Ad Note (A)	$460
1898 San Francisco - Labor Exchange 1 Unit 1898 (W)	$300
1900c San Francisco - $1 $5 $10 $20 $50 $1000 Heald's Business College (C)	$275
1915 San Francisco - $10 $50 Panama Pacific Exposition, 49 Camp (A)	$150
1915 San Francisco - 1, Native Sons & Native Daughters of the Golden West (A)	$150
1931 San Francisco - One Meal. Depression Scrip "The Kitchen" good for one meal. (D)	$80
1907 San Francisco - $1 $5 $10 $20 San Francisco Clearing House Certificate (D)	$65
1907 San Francisco - $1 Northern Electric Company (D)	$750
1907 San Francisco - $5 $10 $20 Northern Electric Company (D)	$1250
1922 San Francisco - $1 The Johnson Studio (A)	$150
1933 San Francisco - $1 $5 $10 Standard Oil Company of California (D)	$175
1933 San Francisco - $1 San Francisco Clearing House Certificate (D)	$650
1907 San Francisco, - $50 Ocean Shore Railway Company (D)	$1495
1865 San Joaquin - Var.$ San Joaquin County Warrant (W)	$165
18-- San Jose - $1 $5 $10 $20 $50 $100 San Jose High School Bank (C)	$185
1870, 80's San Jose - Var.$ Trearurer for Santa Clara County (W)	$90
1880c ND San Jose - Wilcox Silver Tipped Shoes. Knight on horse. (A)	$250
1928 San Jose - 2 ½¢ The Bit House, yellow chit. (A)	$90
1937 San Jose - $1 & Var.$ American Revolving Finance Co. (D)	$90
1937 San Jose - 5¢ 10¢ 25¢ 50¢ American Revolving Finance Co. (D)	$135
1934–36 San Jose - 25¢ 50¢ $1 California Market (D)	$70
1934–36 San Jose - $5 $10 $20 $50 $100 $500 $1000 California Market (D)	$85
1933 San Jose - 5¢ Ralph Mitchell, Wood flat. (A)	$18
1880c San Jose - B McIllriach, Grocer - Tiffany Commission Scrip (M)	$275

DENOMINATION	PRICE
1770s San Joaquin - $500 San Joaquin Valley College Bank (C)	$195
1907 San Luis Obispo - $5 San Luis Obispo County Bankers (D)	$450
1939 San Luis Obispo - $1 American Revolving Finance Co. (D)	$160
1887c Santa Barbara - 5 IXL Store baseball Ad Note (A)	$1450
1884 Santa Cruz - 25¢ 50¢ $1 $20 $100 Chestnutwood's College Bank (C)	$250
1933 Santa Cruz - $1 Santa Cruz Trade Warrant (D)	$50
1897 Santa Maria - 5¢ Labor Exchange Branch 177 (W)	$350
1933 Santa Monica - 50¢ Santa Monica Bureau of Relief (D)	$90
1907 Santa Rosa, - $1 $10 $20 $1000 Sonoma County Clearing House . . . (D)	$1150
1880c Stockton - $2 Stockton Business College (C)	$750
1880c Stockton - 50¢ E.E. Washburn Commission Scrip (A)	$475
1887c Stockton - J. Glick Reliable Jeweler and Watchmaker	$1250
1907 Stockton - $5 $10 $20 $500 $1000 Stocking Clearing House (D)	$500
1933 Stockton - $1 "Pefferbill" reprint (D)	$30
1866 Taylorsville - $5 Sincerity Lodge. (M)	$250
1866 Taylorsville - $10 C.E. Young, General Merchandise. (M)	$85
1933 Truckee - 50¢ $1 Truckee Chamber of Commerce (D)	$350
1933 Tulare - 50¢ $1 City of Tular Relief Certificate (D)	$200
1907 Ventura $1 $2 $5 $10 $20 San Luis Obispo County Bankers (D)	$400
1932 Watsonville - $2.50 Pajaro Valley National Bank (4 known) (D)	$3200
1907c Weed - 30¢ Weed Lumber Co. good for one 30x meal. (D)	$80
1885 Woodbridge - $500 San Joaquin Valley College Bank (C)	$800
1850s Steamship Brother Jonathan 2nd Cabin Ticket. Homeward. Ca. (M)	$3,500
1880s American Exchange in Europe, Limited, London. $10 or One Share.	$185
1854 Calif. - 25c Adams & Co's Express. Cardboard Chit. Ca. 1845 Mint.	$165
1860c Arapahoe, Ct - $5 Oregon State Bank at Arapahoe (B)	$3500

COLORADO

DENOMINATION	PRICE
1896 Aspen - 5/100 1/4 $5 Labor Exchange Aspen Colorado (W)	$800
1896 Aspen - 5/100, 1/4, $5 Labor Exchange Aspen Colorado (G)	$800
1863 Black Hawk Pt, CT - 15c Gov's Tobacco & Cigar Store, (M)	$19,000
1909 ND Boyero - 1¢ 5¢ HF Davis, General Merchandise (M)	$650
1933 Castle Rock - ($ various) Douglas County Treasurer's Warrant (D)	$170
1930c Canon City - 25¢ Batchelor Dairy (Orange) (A)	$35
1933 Castle Rock - ($ various) Douglas County Treasurer's (W)	$195
1863 Central City - 20c Central City Bakery, Colo. Territory. 20c. (M)	$7500
1880s Cerro - 5c Arizona Mining Co. Office or Store (M)	$15,000
1911 Cokedale - 5c 10c Gottlieb Mercantile. (M)	$700
1880c Colorado Springs - $3 Geo. Fechter Advertising Note (A)	$950

DENOMINATION	PRICE
1883 Colorado Spgs. - 5c U.S. Postal Note. Sept 4, 1883. (US)	$3000
19-- ND Colorado Springs - Pelta's Department Store Premium Scrip (A)	$75
1907 Colorado Springs - $2 $5 $10 $20 Commercial Bank & Trust (Clearing House) (D)	$180
1907 Colorado Springs - $1, 5, 10 First Nat'l Bank (Clearing House) (D)	$200
1933 Crede - 50¢, $1 Town of Crede (D)	$135
1933 Delta - ($ various) - Natural Development Assoc. (D)	$150
1859 Denver - $5, $25 Treas of the Territory of Jefferson, Denver (G)	$19,000
1859c Denver - $5 Clark, Gruber & Co. with Bison (B)	RARE
1860 Denver - 50¢ Woolworth & Co. (M)	$1750
1860 Denver - $5 Clark, Gruber & Co, Terr. of Jefferson. Pikes Peak Gold. (B)	$950
1861–63 Denver, CT - 10c 20c 25c 50c $1 Banking House CA Cook & Co. (B)	$10,000
1867 Denver - One Sack of Flour or $10, First Nat'l Bank of Denver. (B)	$1500
1877 Denver - $2 $5 $100 Business College Bank of Colorado (C)	$1200
1887 Denver - $5 J. Thorrington, Boots & Shoes baseball Ad Note (A)	$2600
1890 Denver - 5c. Colorado Telephone Co.	$795
1897 Denver - 1/10, 1/4, 1/2, 1, 2 Labor Exchange #158. Good for hours of labor (W)	$150
1899 Denver - $1. Colorado Supply Co. (M)	$1500
1900c Denver - 25c Hindman Mercantile (M)	$700
1900 Denver $1 Western Trading & Supply Co., Denver, Colorado. (M)	$700
1900 Denver - 25c State Mercantile Company. Existence Not Confirmed	
1901 Denver - 10¢ 25¢ The Miner's Trading Company (M)	$1600
1901–05 Denver 5¢, 10¢, 25¢. Colorado Supply Co. (M)	$175
1901–10 Denver $1, $2, $5 Colorado Supply Co. (M)	$375
1904 Denver - 5c Hensley Supply Co. (M)	$600
1905 Denver 5¢ Rocky Mountain Supply Co. (M)	$750
1905–07 Denver - 5¢, 25¢ Western Stores Co. (M)	$500
1905c Denver - 50¢, $1 Western Trading & Supply (M)	$400
1905 Denver - 25c South Canon Supply Co. Red "25" center (M)	$1250
1905 Denver - $1 Sunnyside Coal Mining Co. (M)	$1550
1907 Denver - $5, $10 Colorado Nat'l Bank (D)	$250
1907 Denver - $5 Denver Nat'l Bank Panic of '07 cashiers check (D)	$500
1907 Denver - $5, $10, $20 Capitol Nat'l Bank of Denver (D)	$225
1907 Denver - $5, $10, $20 First Nat'l Bank of Denver (D)	$225
1907 Denver - $5, $10, $20 Nat'l Bank of Commerce (D)	$250
1907 Denver - $5, $10 United States Nat'l Bank (D)	$225
1910 Denver. - $5 Colorado Supply Co. Red FIVE (M)	$6800
1910 Denver - $5, $10 Gem City Business College R7 Discovery notes	$1250
1921 Denver - $1 Askin & Marine Company, Green and Gold (A)	$385
1933 Denver - $5, $10, $20 The International Trust Company (D)	$175
1933 Denver - $2.50 trade scrip booklet from the State Theatre (M)	$85
1933 (ND) Durango - 5¢, 10¢, 25¢ Community Council Scrip (D)	$225
1922 Elizabeth - $1 Elizabeth Mercantile Co. $1 or 100 pds wheat. (G)	$375
1907 Fort Collins - $2, $5, $10 Ft. Collins Clearing House (D)	$140
1907 Fort Collins - $2, $5 Commercial Bank & Trust (D)	$150
1907 Fort Collins - $5, $10 Poudre Valley Nat'l Bank of Ft. Collins (D)	$250
1907 Fort Collins - $5, $10 First Nat'l Bank of Ft. Collins (D)	$230

DENOMINATION	PRICE
1912 Fort Collins - 1c 2c 3c 4c 5c 10c Edmonds Dry Goods, Stork (M)	$150
1912 Fort Collins - 1c 2c 3c 4c 5c 10c Collins Cash Clothing, Stork (M)	$150
1912 Fort Collins - 1c 2c 3c 4c 5c 10c Lowell-Moore Hardware, Stork (M)	$175
1933 Fort Collins - 1¢, 2¢, 3¢, 4¢, 5¢, 10¢ Edmonds Dry Goods, Stork Savings (D)	$165
1933 Fort Collins - 1¢, 2¢, 3¢, 4¢, 5¢, 10¢ Collins Cash Clothing Co., Stork (D)	$175
1933 Fort Collins - 1¢, 2¢, 3¢, 4¢, 5¢, 10¢ Lowell-Moore Hardware Co., Stork (D)	$150
1860s Fort Lyon - 10c 50c $1 $2 Sutler's Check, Fort Lyon, Col. Ter. (S)	$6,250
1897 Fruita - 1/10, 1/4, 1/2, 1, 2 Labor Exchange. Good for hours of labor (W)	$550
1896 Garrison - 5/100 Labor Exchange # 153.	$550
1884 Georgetown - 7¢. U.S. Postal note. Only nine Colorado notes known (US)	$2250
1906 Gold Boulder - $1.50 Gold Boulder Mining Co, Punch card. (M)	$1,000
1933 Golden - $1 Golden Welfare Association (D)	$160
1915 Goldfield - $2, $50 (var.) City of Goldfield Colorado (W)	$70
1896 Hotchkiss - 1/10, 1/2 Labor Exchange #156. (CS)	$450
1933 Hot Sulphur Springs - $5 First State Bank (D)	$300
1933 Julesburg - $1 Town of Julesburg (D)	$175
1933 Kremmling - $1 Bank of Kremmling (D)	$185
1924 Leadville - $50 Days of '79. Leadville Lodge B.P.O.E. (A)	$170
1907 Loveland - $1 $20 Loveland National Bank (D)	$525
1907 Loveland - $1, $5 Larimer County Bank (D)	$440
1900c Ludlow - 5c Woodward Brothers, Merchandise (M)	$1625
1860s Missouri City, CT - Treas of Consolidated Ditch Co. (M)	$16,000
1899 Pueblo - 25c 50c $1. Colorado Supply Co. (M)	$650
1900c Pueblo - 5¢ Herman & Shloss, General Merchandise (M)	$700
1910 Pueblo - 5c 10c 25c 50c The Union Trading Company. (M)	$850
1933 Pueblo - Depression Scrip, existence unconfirmed (D)	
1907 Rocky Ford - $1, $5, $10, $20 State Bank of Rocky Ford (D)	$450
19?? Rocky Ford - 50c, $1 Clarks Corner (A)	$21
1949 Rocky Ford - 5¢ Watermelon Day - Cloth Watermelon (A)	$40
1885c Ruby City - Var$ The Bank of Ruby City. ABNCo. (CD)	$350
1859 St. Vrain - $5.67 St. Vrain, Golden City & Colo. Wagon-Road Co (W)	$750
1880c Salida - $3 New York Clothing House Adv. Note (A)	$600
1933 Springfield - Various, Baca County Treasurer's Warrant (D)	$350
1933 Sterling - $1, $5, $10 Commercial Savings Bank (D)	$150
1933 Sterling - $1 Sterling, City of, Scrip Certificate (D)	$150
1933 Sterling - $1 Sterling Lions Club (D)	$250
1933 Sterling - $1 $5 Sterling Security State Bank (D)	$135
1935 Sterling - 10¢, 25¢ Logan County Fair (A)	$35
1892 Trinidad - $1 Trinidad Fuel Co	$650
1894 Trinidad - 5c Victor Coal & Coke Co. (M)	$700
1905 Trinidad - 10c Chicosa Mercantile Co.	$700
1912 Trinidad - $1 The Aiello Mercantile Company (M)	$1000
1933 Trinidad - Depression Scrip, existence unconfirmed (D)	

DAKOTA TERRITORY

1868 $50 First Empire City Outfitting Store

DENOMINATION	PRICE
1868 Territory - US Treasury payroll for Territorial civil servants (W)	$475
1888 Canton, DT - (var) Town Treasurer Canton D.T. (W)	$100
1870s Central City, DT, Black Hills - $1 Dorr Heffleman, First Central Bank.	$17,500
1868 Cheyenne, DT - $50 First Empire City Outfitting Store (A)	$16,500
1888c Deadwood, DT - Chase's Clothing, Boots, Shoes baseball Ad Note (A)	$4300
1888 Deadwood, DT - I.H. Chase 1888 Baseball Adv. Note (A)	$10,000
1888 Devil's Lake, DT - 1¢ US Postal note. Only 5 recorded DT. (G)	$9200
1871 Ft. Rice, DT - $55 U.S. Infantry Pay Voucher (W)	$500
1861–64 Fort Abercrombie, D. T. - 5c J.M. Stone & Co, Proprietor Sutler's Store. (S)	$14,775
19-- ND Holabird - Var.$ County of Hyde, Holabird School Township (W)	$195
1880s–90s Watertown DT - $5 Chalmers Bonded Investment Co., (A)	$16,500
1889 ND Holabird - Var.$ County of Hyde, Holabird School Township (W)	$200
1885–89 Watertown - $5 Chalmers Bonded Investment Co., Watertown N B (A)	$3500

HAWAII

1933 $1 Honolulu Clearing House Certificate, Hawaii Territory

DENOMINATION	PRICE
1879 Hawaiian Islands - $50 Department of Finance. Certificate of Deposit	$1500
192- Honokaa - Vars $ The Bank of Hawaii, Certificate of Deposit	$1000
1874 Honolulu - $100 Hawaiian Treasury Certificate of Deposit	$6570
1887 Honolulu - $10 $20 $50 $100 Bank of Claus Spreckels (B)	$7500
18-- Hawaiian Islands $10 $20 $50 $100 Certificate of Deposit. (B)	$10,000

DENOMINATION	PRICE
1922c Honolulu - 5c Orange Lantern Ball Room. 1st at A st. (M)	$200
1933 Honolulu - $1 Honolulu Clearing House Certificate, Hawaii (D)	$135
1933 Honolulu - $5 Honolulu Clearing House Certificate, Hawaii (D)	$350
1933 Honolulu - $10 Honolulu Clearing House Certificate, Hawaii (D)	$575
1974 Honolulu - $2 Windjammer Cruises	$20
1942 Kahuilui, Maui - $3 Naval Air Station NASKA (S)	$150
1835 Kaua'i - Hapawalu (12.5c), Hapaha (25c) Hapalua (50c) Sm chits $	7000
1839 Kaua'i - $3 $5 Ladd & Company scrip ($3) Whaling ($5) Ships $	RARE
1911 Kona - $3 Kona & Kau Railway Company Coupon (W)	$80
1840c Lahaina - 50c Lahainaluna Seminary Business College. (C)	$9900
1843 Maui - 3c to $1 Rev. Lorrin Andrews of the Lahainaluna Seminary.	$25,000
1844 Wailuku - 6 1/4c Edward Bailey for Wailuku Female Seminary.	$14,000

IDAHO

1885 $5 Coeur D'Alene Water Supply Company Territorial

DENOMINATION	PRICE
1888 Alturas County, IT - Idaho Territorial School Warrant. Green (W)	$350
1867 Boise City, IT - $10, $20, $50, $100 Du Rell & Moore, First Nat'l Bank of Idaho (B)	$3500
1883 Boise City, IT - Treasurer of Idaho Territory Warrant (W)	$295
1928 Boise - 100 Boldts Restaurants - Battleship USS Idaho at Bremerton (A)	$275
1907 Boise - $1, $20, $10 First Nat'l Bank of Idaho (D)	$375
1933 Boise - 5¢, 10¢ Farmer-Labor Exchange (D)	$750
1933 Boise - $5 $20 Chamber of Commerce - Nat'l Grange Harvest Festival (D)	$500
1933 Boise - $5 Ida-Ha Cafe Scrip card for meals (M)	$75
1943 Boise - 1¢ Retail Merchants Bureau. Minute Man in "V". Blue (M)	$5
1932 Caldwell - $1, $5 Dairymen's Co-Operative. Blue/Gold (D)	$50
1933 Caldwell - $5 Dairymen's Co-Operative. Gold (D)	$60
1935 Caldwell - $1 $5 Dairymen's Co-Operative. Plum (D)	$60
1937 Caldwell - $5 Dairymen's Co-Operative. Green (D)	$60
1885 Coeur D'Alene - $5 Coeur D'Alene Water Supply Company (M)	$950
1907 Coeur D'Alene - $5, $10, $20, $50 American Trust Company (D)	$1200
1860s Devil's Gate - 12 1/2c 50c Devil's Gate Toll Road. Yellow cardboard (M)	$675
1935 Elk River - $1 Civilian Conservation Corp. 590th Co. (D)	$400
1892 Franklin - 5¢, 10¢ Oneida Mercantile Union (M)	$6500
1894 Franklin - 10¢, 25¢ Lowe & Company (M)	$3500
1874 Granite Creek, IT - 25c Alex. Danskin Dealer in Genl Merch. (M)	$7,500

DENOMINATION	PRICE
1867 Idaho City - $10, $20, $50, $100 Du Rell & Moore FNB of Idaho (B)	$3750
1895 Idaho Falls - 1/20 1 Labor Exchange (W)	$1500
1936 Lapwai - 25¢ Idaho Spaulding Centennial. Wood (D)	$135
1864 Laramie, I.T. - $50 (var.$) Asst. Treasurer of the United States (W)	$350
1866c Lewiston - Lewsiton Road, (good for) _ Head of Cattle, Mules or Horses	$765
1933 Malad City - 10¢, 25¢, 50¢ Unbankable Certificate, Malad City, ID (D)	$900
1907 Milner - $1 Twin Falls North-Side Land & Water (W)	$1750
1894 Moscow - 2¢ U.S. Postal note. Only six (6) Idaho notes recorded. (US)	$1700
1915 Moscow - (var.) Latah County Warrant (W)	$90
1890c Preston - 5¢, 10¢, 50¢ W.C. Parkinson & Co. (M)	$3000
1868 Rocky Bar - Alturas County Territorial Warrant (W)	$365
1867 Silver City - $10, $20, $50, $100 Du Rell & Moore First Nat'l Bank of Idaho (B)	$3750
1876–89 Silver City - (various denoms.) Owyhee County Territorial Warrant (W)	$265
1890 Silver City - (var.) Owyhee County Warrant (W)	$100
1863 Virginia City - $1 Tutt & Donnell, !$ Gold Dust. Indian/bison (M)	$17,500

KANSAS

1871 $1 City of Leavenworth, Kansas Territory

DENOMINATION	PRICE
1860's 1st Kansas Cavalry 25c Sutler note (S)	$13,800
1907 Atchison - $1000 Clearing House (D)	$900
1907 Atchison - $1 $2 $5 Atchison State Bank (D)	$475
1907 Atchison - $1, $2, $5 Exchange Nat'l Bank (D)	$250
1907 Atchison - $1 $2 $5 $10 First Nat'l Bank of Atchison (D)	$250
1900c Baileyville - Bailey and Co. Due bill Green (M)	$115
1899 Beauville - 5¢ Beauville mercantile (M)	$500
1890c ND Broken Bow - $10 Broken Bow Business College (B)	$1000
1884 Burlington - 1¢ U.S. Postal note. (US)	$750
1857c Chetopa, KT - $2 City of Chetopa (B)	$675
1933 Clay Center - 5¢, 50¢ Chamber of Commerce (D)	$19
1854 Delaware, KT - $1, $2 Delaware City Bank (B)	$425
1890s Dodge City - $1.00 W. F. DEAN'S GROCERIES and QUEENSWARE (M)	$500
1855 Easton - $1 Easton Bank .. Train. (B)	$650
1890s Florence - $10 "For use in public schools Florence" Ks (C)	$115
1854 Fort Leavenworth, KT - $2, $3, $5, $10 Merchants Bank (B)	$350
1856 Fort Leavenworth, KT - $1 $5 $10 Drovers Bank (B)	$5000

DENOMINATION	PRICE
1880 Fort Scott - 5¢ $50 Kansas Normal College Bank (B)	$950
1898 Freedom - 1/10 Labor Exchange #199. (CS)	$325
1933 Garden City - United States Sugar & Land Co. (D)	$600
1933 Gardner - City of Gardner, KS (D)	$140
1880s Garnett - 1 M. D. Calkins & Co's. 1. Silver Tipped Boots and Shoes (A)	$250
1880c Greenwood - A.W. Sanders Groceries Ad Note ($100 CSA) (A)	$165
1800c Hiawatha - L.S. McNamar Ad Note (A)	$180
1882 Holton - $1, $5, $10 Commercial Institute Bank (B)	$185
1889 Hutchinson - 5 Star Clothiers baseball advertising note (A)	$1495
1907c Independence - $1, $5, $10 Citizen's Nat'l Bank (D)	$385
1907c Independence - $1, $5, $10, $20 Commercial Nat'l Bank (D)	$385
1907c Independence - $1 First Nat'l Bank (D)	$385
1863 Junction City - 25¢ Streeter & Strickler (M)	$1375
1933 Kansas City - (var.) Goodwill Barter and Exchange Centers (D)	$120
1869 Larned - J.H. Dow, General Merchandise, Adv. Note (A)	$325
1880s Lawrence - 50¢ E. A. Skinner, Durfee House "$2 per Day." (A)	$325
18-- Lawrence - $2, $3 The Bank of Wm. H.R. Lykins (B)	$1400
18-- Lawrence - $3 The Lawrence Bank (B)	$3220
1857 Lawrence, KT - $2, $3 Redwing Bank (B)	$1000
1861 Lawrence - Var $ Nat'l Bank of Lawrence Cert. of Deposit (B)	$110
1856 Leavenworth City, KT - $3, $5, $10 Drovers Bank. Ormsby (B)	$1200
1856 Leavenworth City, KT - $1 The City Bank (B)	$375
1856 Leavenworth City, KT - $2, $3 The City Bank (B)	$900
1871 Leavenworth - $1, $2, $3 City of Leavenworth (B)	$385
1862 Leavenworth - $1 Scott, Kerr & Co. (B)	$700
1870s Lawrence - $20 Western Business College Bank (C)	$275
187- Lawrence - $3 Macauley's Commercial Institute (C)	$275
1880's Lawrence - 50c E. A. Skinner. Durfee House. "$2 per Day." (A)	$300
18-- Lawrence - $2 $3 The Bank of Wm. H. R. Lykins (B)	$1400
18-- Lawrence $1 $3 $5 The Lawrence Bank (B)	$3220
18-- Lawrence - 10c The Business College Bank, Lawrence Ks (C)	$280
1861 Lawrence - Var $ Nat'l Bank of Lawrence Cert. of Deposit (CD)	$110
1856 Leavenworth City, KT - $5, $10 Drovers Bank. Ormsby (B)	$1200
1856 Leavenworth City, KT - $2 $3 Drovers Bank. Ormsby (B)	$750
1856 Leavenworth City, KT - $1 The City Bank (B)	$375
1856 Leavenworth City, KT - $2 $3 The City Bank (B)	$900
1871 Leavenworth 0 $1, $2, $3 City of Leavenworth (B)	$375
18-- ND Leavenworth - (var.) Western Business College (C)	$285
1856 Lecompton, KT - $3 The State Bank (B)	$1250
1861 Manhattan - $1 John Pipher & Co. Eagle + ship.	$1500
1933 McPherson - $1 $5 City of McPherson, Kansas, (D)	$415
1933 Neodesha - 5¢ ,10¢, 25¢, 50¢, $1 $5 Chamber of Commerce (D)	$60
1898 Osage City- 1/10 labor Exchange #223. (CS)	$325
1933 Oswego - $5 First Nat'l Bank of Oswego (D)	$135
1933 Parsons - $5 Parson's Commercial Bank (D)	$225
1890s Pittsburg - 10¢ Rogers Coal Co. (M)	$375
1894 Pittsburg - 10¢ The Wear Coal Co. (M)	$375
1901 Pittsburg, etc. - $1 A Hood & Sons Implement Co. (M)	$185

DENOMINATION	PRICE
1907 Pittsburg - $1, $2, $5, $10 Associated Banks of Pittsburg (D)	$235
1905 Rook County - (var.) State of Kansas Warrant (W)	$60
1933 Russell - 50¢ City of Russell (D)	$50
1933 Sedan - 25¢ Sedan Depressio Scrip (D)	$135
18-- ND Seneca - 50¢ Lappin & Scrafford (M)	$650
1880s Topeka - 5 Kansas Pacific Railway. Steer (A)	$1150
1880c Topeka - 10¢ C.C. Andrews and Company (M)	$135
1880s Topeka - 50¢ Karp & Turnbull (M)	$85
1880s Topeka - 10¢ Kore & Hackman (M)	$100
1855 Topeka, KT - $20 The State of Kansas (W)	$750
1867 Topeka - $1 $10 $20 Union Military Scrip. Bare-breasted maid (W)	$225
1867 Topeka - Var$ Union Military Scrip. Penned amts-Plain (G)	$325
1867 Topeka - $100 Union Military Scrip. Lincoln vignette. (W)	$400
1907 Topeka - $2, $5 Associated Banks of Topeka (D)	$400
1933 Trego - $1 County of Trego. Yellow and very ornate. (D)	$375
1915c - 25¢, 50¢, $1, $5 Albert H. Shuler / Citizens State Bank (M)	$50
1880s Wichita - 1¢, $2 $50 Southwestern Business College (C)	$175
1914 Wichita - Wichita Clearing House Assoc. (D)	$125
1933 Wichita - 5¢ Unemployed Trading Post (D)	$250
1933 Wichita - $1 Howard W. Shroeder / Farmers State Bank (M)	$170
1934 Wilmore - 1 Jack, Merchants of Wilmore (D)	$15
18-- Wyandott - $1, $2 Kansas State Savings Bank. Green/black (B)	$230
18-- Wyandott - $3 Kansas State Savings Bank. Green/black (B)	$850
1857c ND 1857c Wyandott - $2 The City of Wyandott (M)	$450
18-- Wyandott - $1 $3 Kansas City Savings Bank. Green overprint. (B)	$500

MISSOURI

DENOMINATION	PRICE
1862 State Issue - $1 $2 $3 $5 $10 $20 STATE OF MISSOURI White or Blue paper (W)	$130
18-- ND State Issue- $1 $3 $3 $.50 $20 $50 $100 MISSOURI DEFENCE BOND (W)	$115
1874 State Issue - Var.$ STATE OF MISSOURI Civil War settlements (W)	$60
1859 Arrow Rock - $20 Bank of the State of Missouri. $20. (Ctf)	$640
18-- ND Carrollton - 50c Henry Myers. Indian chief, left. (M)	$4300
1890 Chillicothe - $5 $10 Chil. Normal School & Business Institute (C)	$200
1907 Doe Run - $1 $2 $5 Doe Run Lead Co. (D)	$22

DENOMINATION	PRICE
1874 Gads Hill - $1 Clear Water Lumber Co. Washington, lower left. (M)	$190
1857 Fayette - $20 Bank of the State of Missouri. Two women seated (Ctf)	$230
1858 Fayetteville - Bank of the State of Missouri. (B)	$350
1862 Granby $1 Leads Mine Scrip. Present at Fort Smith to Major Geo W. Clark (M)	$210
1862 Hannibal - 10c City of Hannibal. RECEIVABLE FOR ALL CITY DUES (W)	$460
1872 Iron Mountain - 10c, $2 American Iron Mountain. U.S. Fractional lookalike. (M)	$315
1933 Jackson - $15 $25 $45 $100 $125 Treas. of Jackson County. Sig Harry Truman (D)	$115
1862 Jefferson - $10 State of Missouri Defence Warrant. State seal, left. Girl, right. (B)	$185
1907 Joplin - $1 $2 $5 Joplin State Bank (D)	$110
1907 Joplin - $1 $5 Miner's Bank of Joplin (D)	$225
1870 Kansas City - $1 $2 City of Kansas (W)	$210
1872 Kansas City - $50 First Nat'l Bank - Spaldings Commercial College. (C)	$200
1880c Kansas City - $2 $10 Student's Bank - Spalding's Comm'l College (C)	$190
1891 Kansas City - 1¢. U.S. Postal note. Aug. 5, 1891. (US)	$550
1898 Kansas City - 5/100 Labor Exchange #199. (CS)	$330
1907 Kansas City - $1 $2 $5 $10 Commerce Trust Company, (D)	$50
1907 Kansas City - $2 $5 $10 Kansas City Clearing House (D)	$60
1907 Kansas City - $1 $2 Union National Bank of Kansas City (D)	$200
1907 Kansas City - $5 Missouri Savings Bank (D)	$300
1897 Marshall - 1/2 Labor Exchange # 183. (W)	$105
18-- LeGendre Mines - $2 Chas. Le Gendre & Co. (M)	$100
1862 Lexington - $1 Farmers Bank of Missouri	$325
1961 Liberty - $1 Farmers Bank of Missouri. Slaves in corn field. (B)	$805
1869 Maramec - 5c Maramec Iron Works, Steer ctr. (M)	$250
1862 Neosho - 50c Roberts & Eppem. Redeemable in CSA Money. (M)	$315
1853 Palmyra - $20 Bank of the State of Missouri. Male portraits in corners. (Ctf)	$325
1880's Paris - W.S. Moore, Shoes, Adv. Note (A)	$70
1871 Pilot Knob - 10c Pilot Knob Iron Company. Train. (M)	$800
1876 Pleasant Hill - 5 W. C. Davis. Clay Bros. Cook stoves. (A)	$130
1818 St. Genevieve. - $3, 10 Bank of Missouri (B)	$750
1865c St. Joseph - $20 $100 First Nat'l Bank - Nat'l Business Colleges	$175
1907 St. Joseph - $1 $2 $5 $10 St. Joseph Clearing House (D)	$225
1907 St. Joseph - $1 $5 Drovers and Merchants Bank (D)	$100
1907 St. Joseph - $1 $2 Merchants Bank (D)	$100
1907 St. Joseph - $1 First National Bank of Saint Joseph (D)	$150
1907 St. Joseph - $2 $5 Burnes National Bank of Saint Joseph (D)	$180
1860 St. Joseph & Hannibal - 50¢ Missouri. Woolworth & Co. (M)	$400
1838 $20 Bank of the State of Missouri. Payable at B of A, N.Y. (B)	RARE
1862 Sarcoxie - $2 Dixon & Nichols Confederate Note. Plow, etc. Pay in CSA notes (M)	$9000
18-- St. Louis - Page, Bacon & Co. Orig Bill of Exch. Danforth proof (B)	$1000
18-- St. Louis - $2 Bank of St. Louis. $2. Horses frightened by storm. (B)	$525
1817 St. Louis - $2 Bank of St. Louis (B)	$3000
1819 St. Louis - $20 Bank of Missouri. Statue of Jefferson, ships beyond. (B)	$1200
18-- St. Louis - $10 Exchange Bank of St. Louis. Girl with scythe. (B)	$1150
1819 St. Louis - $5 Missouri Exchange Bank. (B)	$1900

DENOMINATION	PRICE
1819 St. Louis - 37 1/2¢ Bank of St. Louis. Ornate end panels. (B)	$4025
1820 St. Louis - Bank of Missouri. $1, 5, 10. April 1, 1820. (B)	$230
1829 St. Louis - $5 Bank of the United States (B)	$450
1839 St. Louis - 50c 75c A. T. Crane, Postmaster, "POST OFFICE CHANGE"	$430
1837 St. Louis - 50c 75c Epperand and Hawken. Famous gunmaker. (M)	$460
1859 St. Louis - $10 Merchants Bank of St. Louis (B)	$650
1859 St. Louis - $5 Southern Bank of St. Louis, (B) unk	
1859 St. Louis - $5 Terre Haute, Alton & St. Louis RR Co. (M)	$60
1859 St. Louis - $10 $50 Mechanic's Bank. Three maids/Wash./Ship (B)	$185
1860s St. Louis - $40, $50 North Missouri Railroad Adv. Note (A)	$250
1861 St. Louis - $1 $20 Union Bank of Missouri. (B)	$920
1860s St. Louis - $10 $20 $50 Rohrer's Business College, (C)	$385
1869 St. Louis - $1 Public School Library Society of St. Louis (G)	$350
1873 St. Louis - $1 $2 $3 City of St. Louis (B)	$135
1874 St. Louis - $20 St. Louis & Southeastern Railroad (M)	$175
1870s St. Louis - $1 Dr. J.J. McLean. Adv. note (A)	$160
1880 St. Louis - $100 Butcher's and Drover's Bank (B)	$180
18-- St. Louis - $5 Bank of St. Louis (B)	$400
1880s St. Louis - $10,000 St. Louis Mutual Life Ins. Adv note. (A)	$270
1880s St. Louis - $3 A. B. Mayer. "Dry Buffalo Bones." on $3 Defense Bond.	$375
1887c St. Louis - Nat'l Baseball Assoc. baseball Ad Note (A)	$1250
1887c St. Louis - Thom. Wand, Livery and Boarding Stable baseball Ad Note (A)	$3450
1907 St. Louis - $1 Central Nat'l Bank of St. Louis (D)	$225
1907 St. Louis - $1 $2 $5 $0 $20 Commerce Trust Co. Treasurers (D)	$150
1907 St. Louis - $1 $5 $10 Mechanics-American Nat'l Bank of St. Louis (D)	$170
1907 St. Louis - $1 $5 $10 Nat'l Bank of Commerce in St. Louis (D)	$110
1907 St. Louis - $1 $5 $10 Third Nat'l Bank of St. Louis (D)	$110
1912 St. Louis - 50¢ American Women's League (A)	$25
1880s Savannah - $5 Savannah Business College Bank (C)	$250
1880s Savannah - $10,000 Savannah Business College Bank (C)	$750
1890s Sedalia - $500 Central Business College, on CSA replica (C)	$140
1907 Sedalia - $1 $2 $5 $10 Citizen's Nat'l Bank (D)	$375
1907 Sedalia - $1 $2 $5 $10 Sedalia Trust Co. (D)	$275
1840 Steelville - 10c Steelville. Printed at the Herald. Wheat/scythe ctr (M)	$140

MONTANA

$20 Peoples Nat'l Bank of Helena

DENOMINATION	PRICE
1865 Beaver Head County, MT - (var.) Territorial Warrant	$140
1868 Territory - $100 Interest Bearing Note issued by Territory of Montana . . . (W)	$750
1898 Belt - $1 Labor Exchange #289 (CS)	$1950
1890c Billings - Montana Mining and Business College (C)	$850
1900–07 Butte - 25¢, 50¢, $1 Montana Mining Loan & Investment Co.	$95
1964 Butte - $20 Century of Mining (A)	$22
1933 Conrad - $1 Farmers State Bank of Conrad (D)	$850
1933 Forsyth - 25c, 50c, $1 Forsyth Mercantile (D)	$250
1889 Fort Keogh, M.T. - 25c MacQueen & Young, Post Traders. (S)	$3500
1880c Fort Shaw, MT - $3 J.H. McKnight & Co., Indian Post Trader, (S)	$2250
1905–14 Great Falls - (var.) City of Great Falls, Cascade County (W)	$18
1894 Great Falls - 2c United States Postal Notes, Uncut Pair	$9775
1933 Great Falls - $1 Black Eagle Commandery, Conrad Nat'l Bank on Leather (D)	$1450
1890s Havre - 5c, $1 F.A. Buttrey Company Notes. (M)	$475
1864 Helena - Stebbins&Co. has deposited one purse 54.6 ozs DWT (Gold) CD	$235
1866 Helena, MT - (var.) First Nat'l Bank of Helena (B)	$125
1867 Helena, MT - $50 Var$ Banking House of L.H. Hershfield (B)	$295
1873 Helena, MT - $50 First Nat'l Bank Helena, Territorial CD (B)	$135
18-- ND Helena - $5, $10, $20, $50 Peoples Nat'l Bank of Helena (B)	$1900
1870s Helena - $50 "Queen City of the Rockies." Covered wagon Green (A)	$750
1887 Helena, MT - (var.) Territory of Montana Warrant (Liberty/shield) (W)	$40
1887 Helena - Var $ Holter Hardware Interest bearing Cert. of Deposit. (M)	$95
1893 Helena - (var.) State of Montana Warrant (Liberty/shield) (W)	$35
1901 Helena - $1000 Helena Business College / Jackman Commercial	$950
1869 Helena - Var$ First NB of Helena, MTerr. Orig Bill of Exch.(B)	$1900
1901 Helena - (var.) State of Montana Warrant (State Capitol) (W)	$55
1919 Helena - $10 $20 $100 Helena Commercial Club "Pay Dirt" (A)	$100
1869 Jefferson County, MT - (var.) Treasurer of Jefferson County (W)	$100
1915c Lewistown - $25 Elk's Fair. Green/stag/brown (A)	$65
1920c Lewistown - Elks Monte Carlo. Blue w/Dog (A)	$45
1920c Lewistown - $10, $20, $25 Days of '49 BPOE Brown/blue (A)	$40
1909 Miles City - $5, $10 Bank of Elkville. Heart of the Yellowstone (B)	$350
1910c Missoula - 1c to 50c, $5 to $500 Garden City Commercial College (C)	$350
1910c Missoula - $500 $1000 Garden City Business College (C)	$500
1910c Missoula - $50 $100 Garden City Commercial College (C)	$350
1915c Missoula - $5 Missoula Stampede (A)	$160
1933 Missoula - 5¢, 10¢, 25¢, 50¢, $1, $5, $10 Missoula County Peoples Exchange (D)	$185
1933 Montana - $1 Montana Trade Certificate (D)	$750
1934 Montana - $1 H. A. Stephens - One Dollar for 50 minutes work.	$250
1933 Scobey, Poplar & Glascow - 25¢, $1 St. Pauls Rural Parish (D)	$260
1890s Sheridan 25c 50c R. P. Bateman, Sheridan, Montana. (M)	$2600
1868 Smith River - $10 Holographic scrip (M)	$160
1897 Stevensville - $20 Labor Exchange #207 (CS)	$1500
1860c Virginia - Holladay Overland Mail and Express Co. Unissued (M)	$70
1869 Virginia City, MT - $600 Territorial Revenue, Treasurer's Office MT	$250

NEBRASKA

1857 $5 Brownville Bank & Land Co., Nebraska Territory

DENOMINATION	PRICE
1862 Territory - US Treasury pay for Territorial Governor A Saunders (W)	$170
1933 Aurora - $1 Aurora Scrip Money, Republican-Register Newspaper (D)	$110
1980s Beatrice - $1 $5 $10 $50 Beatrice College Bank R7 (C)	$325
1933 Beatrice - $1, $5 American Legion/Chamber of Commerce (D)	$90
1856 Bellevue, NT - $1, $2, $3, $5, $10 Fontenelle Bank (B)	$200
1885c Blair - 50¢ Haller Proprietary Co. "Haller's Remedies" on CSA (A)	$275
1930s Boy's Town - 5¢, 10¢, 25¢, 50¢, $1 & $5 Boy's Town Currency (M)	$18
1907 Bradshaw - $5 $10 $15 $20 $25 $35 $45 Bradshaw First Nat'l Bank (D)	$42
1900c Broken Bow - $10 Broken Bow Business College rev of CSA (C)	$165
1856 Brownville, NT - $1 $2 $3 $5 $10 Brownville Bank	$325
1856 Brownville, NT - $1, $2, $3, $5, $10 Nemaha Valley Bank (B)	$155
1856 Brownville, NT - $3 $10 Nemaha Valley Bank	$300
1857 Brownville, NT - $1 Nemaha Valley Bk. June 8, Lazy One R7 (B)	$2760
1857 Brownville, NT - $2 Nemaha Valley Bk. June 8, Lazy Two (B)	$975
1859 Dakota City, NT - $1, $2, $5 Bank of Dakota (B)	$2500
1885 Dakota City - (var.) Dakota County Cert. of Account (W)	$70
1857 DeSoto, NT - $1, $2, $3, $5 The Waubeek Bank (B)	$185
1857 DeSoto, NT - $1 Western Land & Exchange Co. (ABNCo) (B)	$1950
1857–63 DeSoto, NT - $1, $2, $3, $5 Bank of DeSoto (B)	$140
1860 DeSoto, NT - $1 Bank of Desoto (Red) (B)	$400
1860 DeSoto, NT - $2 $3 $5 Bank of Desoto (Red) (B)	$550
1860 DeSoto, NT - $1, $2, $3, $5 Corn Exchange Bank (B)	$200
1933 Douglas County - $10 Douglas County Employee's Committee (D)	$400
1856 Florence, NT - $1 $2 $3 $5 $10 The Bank of Florence (B)	$140
1933 Fremont - 5¢, 25¢, $1 Retail Merchants Association (D)	$150
1933 Grand Island - $1 S N Wolbach Sons (D)	$100
1933 Hastings - Var.$ Hastings Clearing House (D)	$125
1933 Holdrege - 5¢ Chamber of Commerce (D)	$150
1933 Lexington - $1 City of Lexington (D)	$100
1878 Lincoln - $1 $2 The City of Lincoln	$260
1890s Lincoln - $1 $5 $10 College Currency, Business Dept., (C)	$100
1900c Lincoln - $1 $5 $10 Lincoln Business College Currency,. (C)	$75
1907 Lincoln - $1 $2 $5 $10 City Nat'l Bank of Lincoln (D)	$250
1907 Lincoln - $1 $2 $5 $10 Farmer's and Merchant's Bank (D)	$250
1907 Lincoln - $1 $2 $5 $10 $20 First NB of Lincoln (D)	$250

DENOMINATION	PRICE
1907 Lincoln - $10 Nat'l Bank of Commerce (D)	$400
1902 Madison - (var.) Madison County Warrant (W)	$40
1858 Nebraska City, NT - $1, $2, $5, $10 Platte Valley Bank (B)	$2350
1870 Nelson - $5 Nelson's College Currency First International Bank (B)	$135
1933 Nelson - 25¢ Moratoriun Shin Plaster (D)	$50
1933 Norfolk - $1 City of Norfolk (D)	$135
1933 Norfolk - $1 Norfolk Cereal & Flour Mills (D)	$140
1880s Omaha - 233 Iler & Co. American Life Bitters. Indians (A)	$345
1880c Omaha - Iler & Company American Life Bitters (A)	$200
18-- Omaha City - $2, $5 Omaha & Chicago Bank (proof $600) reg issue (B)	$2000
1880c Omaha - $3 F. Johnson Dry Goods. (M)	$375
1857 Omaha, NT - $3 $5 $10 Brownville Bank & Land Co. (B)	$300
1857 Omaha, NT - $1 $3 $5 City of Omaha (B)	$175
1858 Omaha City, NT - $25 Territorial Warrant. Female Riding Deer (G)	$50
1861 Omaha City, NT - (var.) Territorial Warrant	$70
1856 Omaha, NT - $1, $2, $5, $10 Bank of Nebraska (B)	$250
1856 Omaha, NT - $1, $2, $3, $5, $10, $20 Western Exchange Fire & Marine (B)	$90
1856 Omaha City - $10 $20 Western Exchange Fire & Marine Insurance Co. (B)	$550
1857 Omaha, NT - $3, $5, $10 Brownville Bank & Land Co. (B)	$300
1857 Omaha, NT - $1, $3, $5 City of Omaha (B)	$155
1857 Omaha, NT - $1, $2 Nebraska Land & Banking (B)	$2250
1857 Omaha, NT - $1, $2, $5, $10 Omaha Bank & Land Co. (B)	$140
1857c Omaha, NT - $1, $5, $10 Western Exchange and Land Co. (B)	$2300
1933 Omaha - 5¢, 25¢, 50¢, $1, $5 Married Men's Council of Omaha (D)	$130
1885 Omaha - 10c Rathbun's Business College (C)	$225
1890's Omaha - $10 Johnson & Flodman, "The legal Tender Store" Dry Goods. (M)	$345
1907 Omaha - $1000 $5000 $10,000 Omaha Clearing House (D)	$500
1907 Omaha - $1 $5 First Nat'l Bank of Omaha (D)	$325
1907 Omaha - $2 Merchants Nat'l Bank of Omaha (D)	$440
1907 Omaha - $1 $2 $5 $10 Nat'l Bank of Commerce, Omaha (D)	$200
1907 Omaha - $2 $5 $10 $20 Nebraska Nat'l Bank of Omaha (D)	$475
1907 Omaha - $1 $5 Omaha Nat'l Bank, Omaha (D)	$375
19-- ND Omaha - 10,000 Omaha Athletic Club, probably club money for events.	$80
1933 Omaha - 5¢, 25¢, 50¢, $1, ¢5 Married Men's Council of Omaha	$130
1933 Roseland - 10¢, 25¢, 50¢, $1 Snyder's Shop (D)	$60
1907 South Omaha - $1 $2 $5 $10 South Omaha Nat'l Bank of South Omaha	$260
1907 South Omaha - $1 $5 $10 $20 Union Stock Yards Nat'l Bank	$250
1869 Superior - $3 Padden, Ebert & Padden. Hardware & Cutlery (A)	$200
1857 Tekama, NT - $1, $2, $5 Bank of Tekama (B)	$170
1908 Wausa - $5 $10 Commercial Bank (D)	$50
1900c York - 50¢ York College of Commerce (C)	$225
1933 York County - 5¢ York County Scrip (D)	$180

NEVADA

1872c $50 Manhattan Silver Mining Co.

DENOMINATION	PRICE
1917c Aurora - $20 (CSA) Esmeralda Hotel Ad Note. (A)	$700
1872c Austin - $1 $5 $10 $20 Manhattan Silver Mining Co. (M)	$130
1872c Austin - $1, $3, $5, $10, $20, $50, $100 Manhattan Silver Mining Co. (M)	$1610
1872c Austin - $3 $50 $100 Manhattan Silver Mining Co. (M)	$375
1870–80c Bristol - 25c Store of J. N. Curtis. (M)	$5500
1870–81 Carson City - Var$, State Controller's Warrant Legislature Fund. (W)	$70
1877 Carson - $20 Carson City Savings Bank, Cert of Deposit (CD)	$70
1886 Carson City - Var $ State Controller's Warrant General Fund. (W)	$90
1900c Carson City - Var $ State Controller's Warrant Orphans Home Fund. (W)	$85
1881 Carson City - $500 (var) Carson City Savings Bank (B)	$125
1886 Carson City - Var $ State Controller's Warrant (W)	$80
1876 Carson City - $500 (var.) Carson City Savings Bank (B)	$125
1913–28 Carson City - $1000 Slippery Gulch Currency (A)	$650
18-- Comsolidated Mines - 5 Exploitation Mercantile Co. (M)	$650
19-- ND Elko - Dodson & Dodson Chiropracters, Cardboard (M)	$50
1925 Ely - $500, $1000, $2000, $4000 First Nat'l Bank of Ely (CD)	$1000
187- Eureka - $2, $3 $5 $10 Butter Cup Silver Mining Co. (M)	$5500
18-- ND Eureka - Wm. Joannes advertising note on Confederate $500. (S)	$950
1915 Eureka - $5 Lincoln Hotel Cafe punch card (M)	$150
1915 Eureka - $10 $30 Var$ Eureka County Warrant (G)	$15
1880–90s Fay - 10c, 25c, 50c Shawmut and Nevada Mining & Milling Co. (M)	$4300
1861–64 Goldhill, NT - (var.) Wells Fargo & Co., Nevada Territory CD (B)	$245
1907c Goldfield - 10c, 25c, $1 Consolidated Mines Co. (M)	$1050
1881 Gold Hill - $120 Town of Gold Hill warrant (W)	$85
1930–50 Lovelock - 12 1/2c Davin's Rendevous (G)	$60
1930–50 Lovelock - 12 1/2c Davin's Rendevous (CS)	$80
1918c Luning - Luning Hotel advertising note (A)	$900
1906 Palisade - One Trip "Scrip" "Issued by Eureka, Hmltn & Ely Stage Line" (M)	$750
1914 Pioche - Var$ Bank of Pioche - Certificate of Deposit (CD)	$125
1908 Rawhide - 25¢, 50¢ The Northern (Saloon) (M)	$130
1890s Reno - $5 $10 The Reno Savings Bank. Dollars in Gold.	$7,500
1907 Reno - $1 Reno Clearing House (D)	$2000
1907 Rhyolite - $1, $5, $10, $20 Rhyolite Clearing House (D)	$6500
1950 South Tahoe - South Tahoe Casino. Good for $2 (M)	$22

DENOMINATION	PRICE
1870 Storey - Var$ County of Storey Warrant (G/W)	$80
1886 Storey - Var$ County of Storey Warrant (G/W)	$45
18-- ND -5c Southern Nevada Mercantile Co. (M)	$1200
1900 Tonopah - Var$ Midway Milling Co. warrant (W)	$40
1862 Virginia City, NT - $39 White & Murphy Gold & Silver Mining (W)	$265
1870 Virginia - (var.) Storey, County of (plum color) (W)	$150
1877 Virginia - $5 $10 $20 Society of Pacific Coast Pioneers (M)	$450
1878 Virginia - $3 C. P. Babcock. Advertiser signed on back. (M)	$1200
1878c Virginia - $3 M. Friedmann advertiser (A)	$1300
1886 Virginia - County of Storey Warrant (W)	$40
1880s Virginia - $5 H. S. Beck. Furniture and household decorations. (A)	$550
1918–19 Winnemucca - Var$ Humboldt County warrant	$12
19-- ND State of Nevada - 100 grams of silver, Houston Duo-Monetary System.	$35

NEW MEXICO

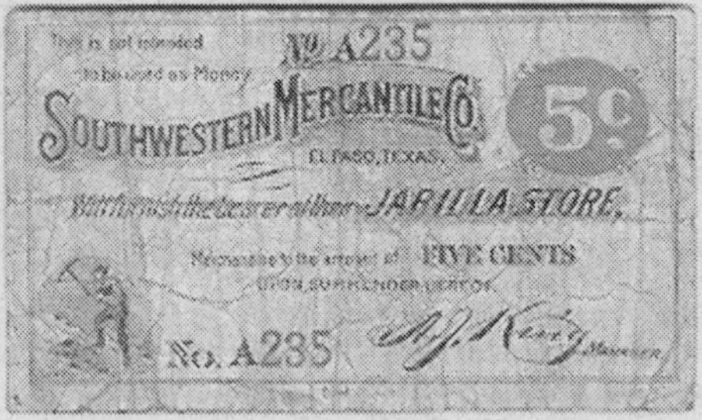

1900c 5¢ Southwestern Mercantile. Jarilla, NM Territory

DENOMINATION	PRICE
1864 Albuquerque - $600 James Murphy Holygraph in Spanish (M)	$420
1890 ND El Capitan, NMT - 5¢ El Capitan Store Blue/Yellow (M)	$2250
1909 Cimarron - $5 Continental Tie & Lumber. February 1, 1909. (M)	$1275
1933 ND 1933 Gallup - 5¢, 10¢, 25¢, 50¢, $1, $5, $10 Gallup American Coal Co. (M,D)	$600
1899c Havre - $5 Southwestern Mercantile. (M)	$725
1900c Jarilla, NMT - 5¢ Southwestern Mercantile. Jarilla became Orogrande in 1905 (M)	$2500
1862–64 Las Cruces, NMT - J.L. May "Good For Two Drinks" Ptd on cloth. (M)	$5750
1895 Las Cruces, NMT - $5 Bounty for Mountain Lion (W)	$180
1907 Las Vegas - $1 $5 $10 $20 Las Vegas Clearing House Assn. (D)	$1750
1898 Lincoln County, NMT - Blue/Stag Territory of New Mexico warrant (W)	$200
1904 Lincoln County, NMT - Territory of New Mexico warrant (W)	$180
1890s North Capitan - 5¢ Southwestern Mercantile Company of New Mexico (M)	$2250
1914 Obar - $5 New Mexico Land & Immigration Co. (M)	$230
1860c Pinos Altos, NMT - $3 Buckhorn Furnace Store (M)	$4200
1904 Raton - 50¢ Blossburg Mercantile Company. 10¢, 25¢. (M)	$1250
1863 Santa Fe, Nuevo Mejico - 12 1/2¢. Spiegelberg Hermanos (M)	$12,500

DENOMINATION	PRICE
1863 Sante Fe, Nuevo Mejico. - 50c Spiegelberg Hermanos. All red/Small eagle. (M)	$8000
1863 Sante Fe - 12 1/2c A. & L. Zeckendorf. Possibly Unique (M)	$12,000
1863 Sante Fe - $58 Var$ Territorial Treasurer's warrant. (M)	$300
1869 Sante Fe - $125 Territory of New Mexico Treasurer's warrant.	$350
1925 Sante Fe - 1/4c Fidel Bros - Nat'l Cert Corp Green (M)	$160
1925 Sante Fe - 1 Fidel Bros - Nat'l Cert Corp Brown (M)	$135
1899 Santa Rita - 25c Gilchrist & Dawson, Inc., Santa Rita, N.M.T. (M)	$1000
1959 Tatum - 5c Lovington National Bank. Green or Black on wood (A)	$25

NORTH DAKOTA

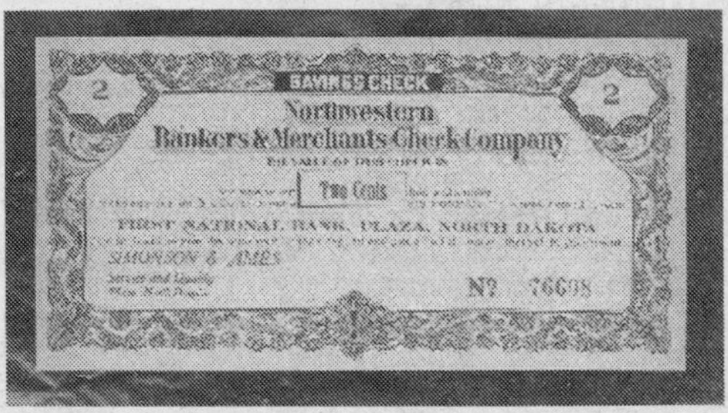

DENOMINATION	PRICE
1893c Fargo - $5, $10, $50, $100, $200, $500 Fargo Business College (Bliss) (B)	$175
1907 Fargo - $5 $10 $100 Fargo Clearing House Assoc. (D)	$750
1933 State - $1, $5 (Two issues of each) State of North Dakota (D)	$195
1910c ND Plaza - 1/2¢ 1¢ 2¢ 4¢ First Nat'l Bank of Plaza, NW Bankers & Merchants (B)	$35

OKLAHOMA STATE, INDIAN TERRITORY, BAD LANDS

1894 Eufala—Foley and Tully, Indian Territory

DENOMINATION	PRICE
1862 Baptist Mission, Choctaw Nation - 25c C. N. William A. Musgrove.	$5000
1897 Blue County - vars $ Blue County Warrant	$140
1862 Boggy Depot, Choctaw Nation I.T. - 75c Franke & Eastburn.	$7000
1900c Buck, Indian Territory - 10¢ 25c, $1 McAlester Coal Mining Co.	$700
1903 Canadian County - 50c Okla. Terr. Treasurer's District School Warrant	$135
1850 Cherokee Nation - $75 Exec. Dep't. Signed Chief John Ross. (G)	$4500
1864 Choctaw City - Vars.$ Choctaw Nation Auditor's Warrant	$2600
1863 Choctaw Nation - $1 Choctaw Treasury Warrant	$1400
1864 Choctaw Nation - 25c 50c $1 B.H.Epperson, pay ain TX. (M)	$8,500
1862 Choctaw City - $1 Nat'l Treas. Choctaw Nation, Armstrong Acad. (M)	$5000
1892 Choctaw Railway Line - 25c $1 Grady Trading Co., (M)	$600
1933 Enid - $1 Enid Retail Merchants Assoc.	$140
1894 Eufala - 25c Foley & Tully. (M)	$500
1898 Eufaula, IT. - $2 C. H. Tully, $2 on Demand in Merchandise. (M)	$285
1898 Eufala, IT - $5 Tully Mercantile Co. (M)	$450
1903 Eufala - 10c 50c $1 Tully Mercantile Co.	$500
1862 Fort Gibson, C.N. - 25c, 50c F.H. Nash.	$4000
1862 Ft McCulloch, C.N. - $1 $3 Major Wm. Quesenbury, (G)	$25,000
1893 Grady - 25c $1 Grady Trading Co. Choctaw Coal & Railway (M)	$535
1902–08 Guthrie - $1, $2 Guthrie Savings Bank	$85
1909 Hailey - 5c, 10c, 25c, 50c Hailey Coal & Mining Co. (M)	$100
1900–08 Haileyville, IT - 5c, 10c, 25c, 50c, $1 Hailey-Ola Coal Co. (M)	$80
1890c Heliswa, I. T. - 15c C.C. Bruner & Son, Heliswa Store, Seminole Nation	$1840
1900 Hillabee, IT - 10c Porter Bros' General Merchant. 10c in Goods. (M)	$525
1890c Kingfisher City - $1 $2 $5 Treasurer of the Village of Kingfisher City.	$1500
1898 Krebs, IT - $1 Osage Trade Company, One Dollar in Merchandise. (M)	$225
1888 Lehigh, IT - 10c A.N. Garland Co. Train vignette/red reverse (M)	$1500
1933 Luther - $1, $5, $10 Morgan and Hayes	$140
1895–07 Lutie, IT - 5c, 10c, 25c, 50c, $1, Hailey Coal Co.	$175
1895–07 McAlester, IT - 5c, 10c, 25c, 50c, $1, $2 JJ McAlester Trade Note	$50
1890s Midway, IT - $2 $5 Midway Store (M)	$1,400
1895 Muskogee Nation - $3 Court House, Stag. "Court Scrip" at end. (G)	$950
1869c North Fork, Creek Nation - 25c, 50c Robt. Sanger	$35,000
1933 Okla. City - $1, $5, $10 Cash Relief Trust (D)	$150
1933 Okla. City - 5c, 10c, 25c, 50c, $1 Self Help Exchange	$90
1933 Okla. City - $1 The Shirtsleeve Exchange	$60
1933 Okla. srarewide - $1 Oklahoma Independents Thrift Currency (D)	$150
1896 Okmulgee - $1, $2, $5, $10, Parkinson Store due bill for merchandise	$225
1933 Okmulgee - $1 City of Okmulgee Trade Script (D)	$35
1896 Osage - $1 Osage Trading Company (M)	$225
1894–96 Perry, IT - 50c, $1, $5 Treasurer of "P" County (W)	$125
1924 Ponca City - $1, $5 $10, $20 Miller 101 Ranch	$80
1933 Ponca City - $1, $5, $10, Kay County Clearing House	$95
1933 Ponca City - $1, $5 Ponca City News	$100
1933 Sapulpa - 25c, 50c, $1, $5, $10 Sapulpa Chamber of Commerce	$80
1903 Sasakwa, I. T. - 50c, $1.50, $2.50, Jno. F. Brown & Sons. Seminole	$2600
189- South McAlester - 25c Indian Trading Co. issued remainder.	$350
1862 Tahlequah - 50c, $1 Cherokee Nation	$8500

1933 Wellston - $1, $5 Morgan & Hayes	$175
1890s Wewoka, IT - 5c $1 $5 Wewoka Trading Company, (M)	$1700

OREGON

1897 1/10 Toledo Labor Exchange. Pay in hours

DENOMINATION	PRICE
1933 Albany - 25¢ 50¢, $1 $5 Albany Scrip Assoc. City of Albany (D)	$110
1933 Albany - $1 Thrift Currency, merchant scrip (D)	$195
1933 Albany - 10¢ Sternberg Saddlery/Albany Tanning Co. Scallop Leather (D)	$200
1933 Albany - 25¢, $1 Sternberg Saddlery/Albany Tanning Co. Rectangle Leather (D)	$235
1933 Albany - 50¢ Valley Bottling Co. (D)	$160
1948 Albany - 5c Albany Centennial Wood (A)	$18
1933 Astoria - $1 Astoria Budget Newspaper scrip. Blue (D)	$175
1933 Astoria - 10¢ Guardsman's Scrip; Oregon Nat'l Guard. Pink (D)	$80
1934 Astoria - 10¢ Guardsman's Scrip; Oregon Nat'l Guard (D)	$95
1890c Baker - $1 $2 $5 $19 $20 $50 $100 $500 Business College (C)	$300
1986 Baker - $3 State of Eastern Oregon Yellow/Brown (A)	$15
1959 Bend - $1 Bend Buck printed on Deerskin (A)	$15
1915c ND Canyon City - $10 Whiskey Gulch Gang (A)	$40
1933c Cascade Locks - Five Dam Bucks - Merrill's BBQ (D)	$250
1907 Clatskanie - $1, $2, $5 Columbia County Clearing House (D)	$400
1933 Clatskanie - 50¢, $2, $5 Merchant's "Windmill" Scrip (D)	$180
1897 Corvallis - 1/2 Labor Exchange (W)	$750
1933 Enterprise - 50¢, $1 Chamber of Commerce, Series A, Buckskin Currency (D)	$180
1933 Enterprise - 50¢, $1 C of C, Series B, Buckskin Currency (Deer Hide) (D)	$500
1933 Enterprise - 25¢ C of C, Series C (paper) (D)	$100
1933 Enterprise - 50¢, $1 C of C, Series D Black, Buckskin Currency (Deer Hide) (D)	$165
1907 Eugene - $1, $2, $5, $10 Eugene Clearing House (D)	$500
1933 Eugene - 50¢ Townsend Recovery Certificate (D)	$700
1850–66 Ft. Dalles - 1 2 3 5 10 20 Loaves of Bread signed Post Treas. Steel (S)	$850
1933 Grant's Pass - 25¢, 50¢, $1 The Oregon Caveman, Inc. (D)	$175
1933 Heppner - 5¢, 25¢, 50¢, $1, $5 Heppner Sheepskin Scrip on paper (D)	$10
1933 Heppner - 25¢ ,50¢, $1, $5 Heppner Sheepskin Scrip on Leather (D)	$125
1959 Hermiston - 100th Anniversary of Oregon, Green on Yellow (M)	$25
1933 Hillsboro - 25¢, 50¢, $1, $5, $10 Washington County Scrip (D)	$10
1959 Independence - 100th Anniversary of Oregon on Leather (M)	$18
1933 Klamath Falls - 25¢ Capt. O.C. Applegate/American Legion Wood/round (D)	$18
1896 La Grande - 1/10 hour Labor Exchange, Branch 122 (W)	$400

DENOMINATION	PRICE
1933 LaGrande - 5¢, 20¢ LaGrande Emergency Wage (D)	$125
1940 Lake County - 5¢ Lake County Centennial, silver cardboard (M)	$25
1959 Lake County - $1 Lake County Buck printed on Cowhide (M)	$14
Lincoln Cnty - 25¢ 50¢ $1 $5 $10 Lincoln County School Scrip- (D)	$175
1997 Marshfield - $1/4 Marshfield Labor Exchange (W)	$600
1918 Marshfield - $5, $10, $20 Homeguard WW1 Scrip (M)	$185
1910c Marshfield - $1 Marshfield Fuel & Supply Co. (M)	$100
1933 Medford - 10¢, 50¢, $1, $5 Association Labor Agreement (D)	$245
1933 Medford - $1 Colonial Bakery (D)	$375
1933 Medford $1 Medford Chamber of Commerce (D)	$285
1933 Medford - $1 The Toggery	$400
1933 Multnomah - 25¢, 50¢, $1, $5 Mulnomah County Scrip (D)	$12
1859 Myrtle Creek - State Centennial (G)	$15
1860 Napolean - (var) Treasurer of Josephine County (W)	$250
1858 New Clackamas, OT - New Clackamas Banking House, Territorial (B)	$2200
1933 Newport - Newport Relief Committee Script (D)	$23
1933 North Bend - 50¢, $1, $2 1/2, $5, $10 City of North Bend (1st series wood) (D)	$40
1933 North Bend - 25¢, 50¢, $1, $5, $10 City of North Bend. (2nd series wood) (D)	$25
1959 North Bend - 25¢, 50¢ City of North Bend, Oregon Centennial (wood) (M)	$15
1925 Oakridge - $20 End of Steel (continental railroad) Green Goes 201 form (M)	$45
1925 Oakridge - $20 End of Steel Celebration, Green, Buffaloes (M)	$50
1847 Oregon City, OT - $5.00 Circulating Order Bond for 6% Int.	$4200
1848 Oregon City OT - American Soc. for Encouraging Settlement of OR Terr. (M)	$5,500
1855 Oregon City, OT - $10 John B. Preston, Surveyor General. Due Bill	$750
1881 Oswego - 5c Oswego Iron Companys (M)	$4750
1882 Oswego - $3 Oswego Iron & Steel Companys (M)	$4750
1907c Parkdale - $5 Mount Hood Lodge (M)	$350
1873 ND Pendleton - 25¢ Boston Store (M)	$900
1890s Pendleton - $500 Pendleton Business College MAV-350 overprint (C)	$210
1933 Pendleton - 25¢, 50¢, $1 City of Pendleton (D)	$90
1933 Pendleton - $5 City of Pendleton (D)	$225
1915 Pendleton - $10 Pendleton Round-up (negotiable) (A)	$80
1920–39 Pendleton - $10 Pendleton Round-up (negotiable). (A)	$25
1950s Pendleton - $10 Pendleton Round-up (A)	$80
1933 Pilot Rock - 25¢, 50¢, $1 Pilot Rock Wheat Scrip (D)	$100
1866 Portland - $1, $2, $5, $10, $20, $50, $100, $500 Portland Business College (M)	$185
1873 Portland - $20 A.F. Smith Pianos and Organs. Tiffany Scrip (M)	$1000
1880c Portland - $1, $2, $5, $10, $20, $50, $100, $500 Portland Business College (M)	$100
1881c Portland - $1 Portland Business College. Ship left, man ctr. (C) R7	$650
1882 Portland - $1 Portland Business College (M)	$250
1887 Portland - $5 Eastman Printing, Engraving, Photography (A)	$450
1888c Portland - $1 $10 $20 $50 Portland Business College. scroll ctr(C)	$185
1900c Portland - $1 $2 $5 $10 $20 $50 $100 $500 Port Bus College. lamp (C)	$100
1905c Portland - $1 Portland Business College Fancy/ornate R7 (C)	$250
1907 Portland - $1, $5 Portland Clearing House. Large/Plain (D)	$325
1907 Portland - $1, $2, $5, $10, $20 Portland Clearing House. Lion (D)	$235

DENOMINATION	PRICE
1933 Portland - $1, $5, $10, $20 Portland Clearing House. Eagle (D)	$18
1933 Portland - $2 Pacific Savings Bank (D)	$450
19-- ND Portland - 50¢ Unemployed Citizens League Montavilla Local (D)	$250
1933 Portland - $1 Western Industrial Pioneers, Inc. (D)	$200
18-- ND (1870–1910) Portland - Oregon Coal & Navigation Co. Due Bill (M)	$100
1926–34 ND (1926–34) Portland - $1 Anne Louise Millinery, Hollywood Theatre Bldg. (M)	$165
1959 Prineville - $1 Crook County Centennial Buck printed on deerskin	$12
1933 Reedsport - 25¢, $1 Reedsport Emergency Scrip (D)	$100
1933 Reedsport - $2.50 Reedsport Emergency Scrip (not issued) (D)	$250
1936 Roseburg - 25c Roseburg Golf and Country Club (M)	$25
1937 Roseburg - 75c Bridgeway Golf Course (M)	$30
1933 St.Helens - $1, $2, $5 St. Helen's Chamber of Commerce (D)	$95
1933 St.Helens - 50¢, $1, $2, $5 Sentinel-Mist Publishing (D)	$300
1880c Salem - #3 Adolph Mayer, Dry Goods, Fancy Goods. Advertiser	$550
1896 Salem - 1/2, 1, 2 Labor Exchange (W)	$500
1880c Salem - $1, $2 Capital Business College (M)	$295
1900 Salem - Var$ Treasurer of Marion County Warrant (W)	$27
1913 Salem - 5 Kopecks Salem Bing Cherry Festival (M)	$375
1922 Salem - 25 Kopecks Salem Bing Cherry Festival (M)	$375
1925 Salem - $100 American Legion Armistice Day. Blu/Yel, (W)	$80
1932–33 Salem - 5c Capitol Press. Good for 5c (D)	$25
1933 Salem - 25¢, 50¢ Local Exchange/Premium Currency (D)	$90
1933 Sherman County - 25¢ Sherman County Scrip Association (D)	$600
1933 Silverton - $1 Appeal Tribune issued on Coolidge-McClaine Bank (D)	$750
1933 Silverton - 25¢, 50¢, $1 Silverton American Legion Scrip (D)	$30
1897 Toledo - 1/10 Labor Exchange (CS)	$750
1933 Union County - 5¢, 25¢ ,50¢, $1 Union County Emergency Wage (D)	$125
1933 Union County - 5¢, 10¢, 25¢, 50¢, $1, $5 Labor Exchange Certificate (D)	$135
1985 Wallowa - 50¢ $2 Wallowa County centennial scrip printed on buckskin. (A)	$18
1933 Woodburn - 5¢ Woodburn Clearing House (D)	$800

SOUTH DAKOTA

1932 $1 The City of Elk Point, SD

DENOMINATION	PRICE
1880s–90s Watertown DT - $5 Chalmers Bonded Investment Co., (A)	$9500
1948 Bonesteel - 5c Gregory County Jubilee. Wood flat (A)	$15
1888 Deadwood, DT - I.H. Chase 1888 Baseball Adv. Note (A)	$7200
1895c A Deadwood - (var.) State of South Dakota, Lawrence County (W)	$70
1899 Deadwood - $5 or 1 Sh. Carbonate Flume Co. Uncancelled (M)	$55
1932 Elk Point - $1 The City of Elk Point (D)	$110
1900c Flandreau - Var$ Flandreau State Bank. Cert of Deposit (CD)	$30
1933 Huron - (var) Huron College Warrant (D)	$600
1933 Madison - $1 The City of Madison (D)	$600
1933 Marion - $1 The City of Marion (D)	$600
1910 Newell - 10c Greene Clothing Company/NW State Bank Stork (A)	$750
1948 Rapid City - $5 KOTA Radio, c/s Bean Bag Market (M)	$40
1948 Rapid City - $10 KOTA Radio, c/s Rapid City Clothing (M)	$35
1895 Tyndall - $1 County of Bon Homme warrant (W)	$125

TEXAS

DENOMINATION	PRICE
186– Anderson - $3 Treasurer of Grimes County	$565
1863 Austin - 25c Chief Justice of Travis County	$395
1839 Austin - $1 $5 $10 $20 $50 REPUBLIC OF TEXAS. CutCanc.	$195
1839 Austin - $1 $5 $10 $20 $50 REPUBLIC OF TEXAS. Not Cancelled.	$400
1841 Austin - $25 $50 City of Austin, For Men of Texian Navy	$130
1862 Austin - $1 $2.50 $3 $5 $10 $20 $50 $100 Treasury Warrant State	$40
1878 Austin - $4 Var$ City of Austin, City Warrant	$130
1863 Beaumont - $1 Treasurer of Jefferson County. Beaumont	$700
1862 Bend - $10 County of Fort Bend	$450
1933 Borger - 25c Borger Clearing House	$230
1933 Borger - $2 Borger Daily Herald	$225
1862 Brazos - $2 Treasurer of Brazo County	$325
1862 Brenham - $5 Brenham, Payable in CSA notes.	$225
1862 Brenham - 50c $1 $2 $3 $5 Washington County Scrip	$120
1862 Caldwell - 50c Burleson County Scrip	$295
18-- Columbia $1 Commercial & Agricultural Bank of Texas	$360
18-- Columbia $2, $3 Comm'l & Agricultural Bank of Texas (B)	$2400
1863 Corpus Christi - 25c Nueces County Court note	$190
1908 Ft. Bend - Var.$ Treas. of Fort Bend County	$20
1862 Goliad - 25c Goliad County, Goliad Supply Warrant	$700
1862 Hill Cnty - 25c $2.50 Treasurer of Hill County	$330

DENOMINATION	PRICE
1837 Houston - $100 $500 Consolidated Funds, Houston	$90
1837 Houston - $1 $3 $5 $10 $20 $50 THE GOVERNMENT OF TEXAS	$195
1837 Houston - $100 THE TREASURER OF THE REPUBLIC OF TEXAS	$90
1838 Houston - $1 $3 $5 $10 $20 $50 $100 GOVERNMENT OF TEXAS	$180
1863–4 Houston - $1 W.H. Eliot "Redeemable in CSA notes" (M)	$350
1865 Jefferson - 5c 10c C.D. Cosner	$300
1933 Kristenstad - $1 $2.50 $5 $10 $50 $100 John Kristensen	$30
1862 Lamar - $2, Treasurer of Lamar County	$525
1863 Madisonville - $1 Madison County, Jan. 1, 1863	$350
1862 Marion - 10c County Court of Marion County	$200
1862 Matagorda - 50c $2 The County of Matagorda,	$450
1862 Nacogdoches - $5 Treasurer of Nacogdoches County	$690
18- Nacogdoches - $2 $3 $5, Kelsey Douglas	$315
1862 New Braunfels - 10c City of New Braunfels Oct. 29, 1862	$1100
1863 Newton Cnty - $1 Treasurer of Newton County	$900
1931 San Antonio - $1 First National Bank of San Antonio, Junior Thrift	$130
1933 San Antonio - $1 San Antonio Panic Scrip	$450
1863 Springfield - 25c $1 Treasurer of Limestone County	$300
1865 Titus - $5 County of Titus	$150
1890c Tyler, Texas - $1000 College National Bank (C)	$135
1938 Waco, $5 $10 Mt. Carmel Trade Currency	$18
1862 Walker - $1.50 Walker County Warrant	$85
1844 Wash. on Brazos - Var.$ TREASURER OF THE REPUBLIC OF TEX., Texian Print,	$100
186- Wharton Cnty - $2 Treasurer of Wharton County	$200
1862 - $2 $5 R. W. Rodgers, Train/Ship, Green Rev. AU	$70

UTAH

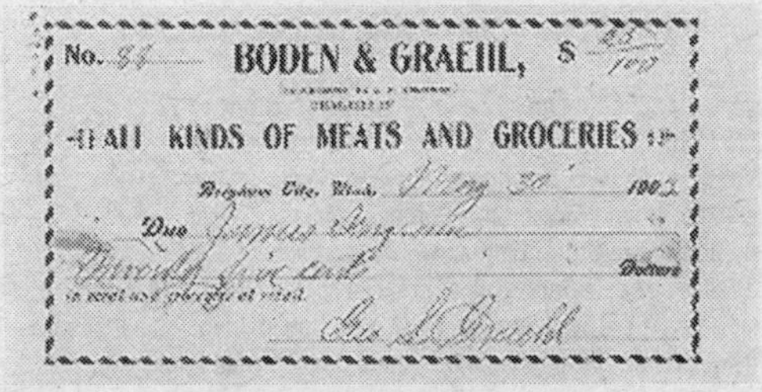

1903 25¢ Boden & Grahl, Meats and Groceries, Brigham City

DENOMINATION	PRICE
1878 Bingham Canyon - $10. Issued by Frisco Anne Mine. (M)	$3500
1876c Brigham City - 10¢ Brigham City Co-Operative (M)	$1400
1903 Brigham City - 25¢ Boden & Grahl, Meats and Groceries (M)	$750
1890s Fairview - 10¢, 50¢ Fairview Co-Op. Mercantile Co. (G)	$1750
1890s Fairview - 10¢, 25¢ Swen & Lars Neilson. Store (M)	$1100
1868 Fort Bridger, UT - $1 to $10 Utah Territory; W.A. Carter Post Trader (S)	$1000

DENOMINATION	PRICE
1890's Goshen - 15¢ Ercanbrack & Sons (M)	$5500
1877 Grantsville - 5c Grantsville Co-Operative Store. (G)	$2500
1880c Koosharem - $? J.B. Sorenson Co. Unissued, amt blank (M)	$380
1890s Lehi - 5¢, 15¢ Peoples Co-Op Institution (W)	$5750
1875 Logan - 25¢, 50c. Logan Branch, Z.C.M.I. (CS)	$7500
1880s. Logan. - 5c, 25c United Order Manufacturing & Building Co. (CS)	$7475
1890s Logan - 10¢ Cache Valley Mercantile Co. (M)	$1700
1890s Logan - 5¢ ,10¢, 50¢ Equitable Co-Op. Association, Limited (G)	$4900
1890s Logan - 5¢, 10¢, 25¢, $1 Fourth Ward Co-Op (G)	$750
1890s Logan - 5¢ Fifth Ward Co-Op (G)	$650
1890s Logan - 10¢, 25¢, $1, $2 Goodwin Brothers (M)	$5000
1890s Logan - 10¢, 25¢, 50¢, $1 Logan Branch Z.C.M.I. (G)	$565
1890s Logan - 10¢, 25¢ Logan Meat Market (M)	$4550
1890s Logan - 5¢ Logan Meat Market Co. (M)	$4600
1890s Logan - 5¢, 15¢ Second Ward Store (G)	$4600
1895–97 Logan - 5¢ Cache Stake Tithing Store House (G)	$7000
1901 Logan - 5¢, 25¢ - Logan Store House (G)	$2250
1890s Magna - Louis Falvo & Son's (M)	$3750
1890s Manti City - 5¢ Sanpete Tithing Store House (G)	$5000
1890s Mount Pleasant - 5c 10c Sanpete Co-Op. (G)	$6000
1890s Murray - 10¢ Workingmen's Store (M)	$4750
1933 Mutual - 2¢ 5¢ 10¢ 25¢ Mutual Store (M)	$165
1907 Ogden - $1, $2, $5, $10 Ogden Clearing House (D)	$375
1907 Ogden - $1 $2 $5 $10 $20 First Nat'l Bank of Ogden (D)	$225
1900c ND Park City - 10¢ The Cozy (M)	$70
1890s Payson - 5¢ Payson Co-Operative Store (M)	$4500
18-- Pleasant Grove - 5¢ Pleasant Grove, Utah Store (G)	$5000
1878 Provo - 10c 50c Sup't Provo Co-operative Mercantile Inst., charge Provo woolen (G)	$2750
1890s Provo - $75 Provo Tithing Office/Deseret Dramatic Association. 3" x 1 1/2" G)	$2000
1890s Provo - 10¢, 25¢ Co-Operative Institution West Branch (G)	$800
1890s Provo - 25¢, $5 Sup't Provo Co-Operative Institution (G)	$3800
1890s Provo - 25¢, $5 W.H. Freshwater "in merchandise at retail" (G)	$3800
1893 Provo - 10c Provo Woolen Mills Company (M)	$3800
1899 Provo - 15c Provo Store. Woman w/sword balancing scale. Red (M)	$1250
1864 Rush Valley - Tooele Cnty. 200' of ore. Rush Valley Mining Dist. (M)	$600
1890s Scipio - 5¢, 10¢, 15¢, 25¢, 50¢, $1, $2, $5 Co-Op. Mercantile Institution (G)	$400
1908 Richfield - $1, $2, $5, $10 Gold Mountain Consolidated Mining Co. (D)	$260
1933 Roosevelt City - $1 Roosevelt City Scrip (D)	$150
1901 St. George - 5¢, 10¢ St. George StoreHouse (G)	$4200
1849 Salt Lake, UT - 50¢, $1, $2, $3 Valley Notes w/ "B Young" sig. (M)	$2750
1849 Salt lake, UT - 25¢ Valley Note unsigned remainder. (G)	$395
1849 SLC, UT - $1 2 3 5 10 Reissued Kirtland Safety Society Bank. (G)	$14,000
1856 Salt Lake, UT - $1, $2, $3 The Drover's Bank (B)	$1450
1858 Salt Lake, UT - $1, $2, $3, $5 Deseret Currency Association (M)	$11,000
1858–61 Salt Lake, UT - $3 Utah Territory Mercantile Currency (M)	RARE
1858–61 SLC, UT - Mercantile Currency, Great SLC copper plate.	$24,000

DENOMINATION	PRICE
1858 Salt Lake, UT - $10, $50 California & Salt Lake Mail Line (M)	$14,000
1862 Salt Lake, UT - $625 Due Bill, United States to Gov. of Utah Terr. (G)	$165
1863 Salt Lake City, UT - 50¢, $3 Walker Brothers (Bankers) (M)	$6000
1865 Salt Lake City, UT - $50 Holladay & Halsey (Bankers) (M)	$6500
1867 Salt Lake, UT - (var.) First Nat'l Bank of Utah (B)	$3800
1866 Salt Lake, UT - 25¢, 50¢, $1, $2 Great Salt Lake City Corporation (B)	$1200
1868 Salt Lake, UT - 5¢, $1, $5, $10, $50 Deseret University Bank (B)	$4100
1869 Salt Lake City. $1 James Townsend/SLC Theatre. Holygraphic (W)	$400
1870 Salt Lake, UT - 25¢, 50¢, $1, $2, $5, $10 Zion's Co-Operative Mercantile Institution (M)	$2750
1870 Salt Lake, UT - $1, $2, $5 Series A Zion's Co-Operative Mercantile Institution (M)	$3750
1870s Salt Lake, UT - $1 Salt Lake City, Utah Territory "workmen" (M)	$2550
1874 Salt Lake, UT - $1, $2, $3, $5 $10 WB Welles, Salt Lake City Nat'l Bank (B)	$3000
1890s ND Salt Lake - $10 Mill Creek Commercial Bank (B)	$2500
1890s Salt Lake City - 5¢ Deseret Meat Market (M)	$2200
1890–95 Salt Lake, UT - Elk Liquor Co. Advertiser (A)	$435
1887–96 Salt Lake, UT - 5¢, 10¢, 25¢, 50¢ - General Tithing Store House (G)	$375
1896–1897 Salt Lake - 5¢, 10¢ ,25¢, 50¢ State - General Tithing Store House (G)	$225
18-- ND Salt Lake - 5¢, 10¢, 25¢ Bishop's Office Coupon. Brn/blk Gen'l Store Hse (G)	$450
1896–97 Salt Lake - 5¢, 10¢, 25¢, 50¢, $1, $10 Bishop's General Store House (G)	$200
1898–1906 Salt Lake - 5¢, 10¢, 25¢, 50¢ Bishop's General Store House (G)	$90
1890s ND Salt lake City - 25¢, $5, $10 Beaver Wool Manufacturing & Milling Co. (M)	$1700
1890c ND Salt Lake, UT - $1000 LDS Business College (C)	$1275
1893 Salt Lake City - 5¢ Gen'l Tithing Store House. "For Meat" overprinted "Produce" (M)	$5000
1900c Salt Lake - 10¢ United Order of Tailors (M)	$750
1907 Salt Lake - $1 Deseret Nat'l Bank (Cashiers Checks) (D)	$450
1907 Salt Lake - $1 McCormick Bank (D)	$450
1907 Salt Lake - $1 Utah-Idaho Sugar Co. (D)	$550
1907 Salt Lake - $100 Salt Lake City Clearing House (D)	$385
1933 Salt Lake - $1 Church of Jesus Christ of Latter-Day Saints (D)	$1250
1933 Salt Lake - 5¢ ,10¢, 25¢, 50¢, $1 Natural Development Association (D)	$275
1933 Salt Lake - $1 Trade Stimulus Certificate (D)	$175
1936 Salt Lake - $1 United National Prosperity - ESSAY (D)	$475
1937 Salt Lake - $1 Pension Prosperity (D)	$200
1890s Spanish Fork - 25¢ Spanish Fork Co-Op. (M)	$5000
1890s Spanish Fork - 10¢ Young Men's Co-Op. Institution (M)	$5000
1903 Tooele City - Var$ Treasurer of the 43rd Quorum (G)	$65

WASHINGTON

1933 25¢ Everett, WA Sockeye Trade Note

DENOMINATION	PRICE
1906 Aberdeen - $5 Palace Restaurant Meal Card (M)	$50
1933 Aberdeen - 25¢ Old Ironsides/Samuel Benn Wood/round (D)	$16
1933 Almira - 5¢ Almira Grand Coulee Dam Scrip (D)	RARE
1907 Anacortes - $1 Bank of Commerce (D)	$775
1910c Avon - 5c 25c Small 3 x 1 1/2" Cardboard Chit (M)	$18
1893 Bellingham - $1 Fair Department Store (M)	$400
1907 Bellingham - $1, $2, $5, $10, $20 Bellingham Clearing House (D)	$150
1933 Bellingham - $1, $5, $10, $20 Bellingham Clearing House (D)	$175
1933 Bellingham - 5¢ Henry Roeder Round/wood (D)	$40
1933 Blaine - 5¢, 10¢, 25¢, 50¢, $1 Blaine Relief Assoc. (D)	$24
1933 Blaine - 5c 10c 25c 50c $1 Blaine Relief Assoc. (no # or initials) (D)	$12
1933 Bremerton - 25¢ Old Ironsides/American Legion Wood/round (D)	$15
1933 Brewster - $1 Townsend Test Fund - 1st Nat'l Bank (D)	$650
1933c Bridgeport - $5 $10 Columbia Trading Co. Pay at FNB Brewster (D)	$375
1895 Buckley - 1/20 Labor Exchange #61 Green. (CS)	$650
1933 Camas - $10 American Legion - 50th Anniv. of Camas (D)	$600
1933 Centralia - 1c, 5c SW Washington Pioneer. Wood, (D)	$70
1933 Centralia - 25¢, 50¢, $1, $5 Centralia Daily Chronicle (D) (4 known)	$450
1935 Centralia - Emergency Tax Token (Orange cardboard) (US)	$30
1933 Chelan - 10¢, 25¢, 50¢, $1 Townsend Test Fund - Miners & Merchants Bank (D)	$500
1933 Callam County - $1 Angeles Co-Operative Creamery (D)	$170
1907 Chehalis County - $1 Associated Banks of Chehalis County (D)	$600
1907c Chehalis - 5c The Olympia, popular early watering hole. Cardboard (M)	$25
1937 Chelan - 50c Townsend Test Fund - provide $200@ month pensions. (M)	$500
1933 Clallam County - 1c 25c Bloedel-Donovan (D)	$12
1911–19 Coupeville - Var. Denoms. County of Island Warrants (W)	RARE
1932–3 Cowlitz County - 5c 15c 25c $1 Liberty Service Token (D)	$150
1932–3 Cowlitz County (Port Angeles) - 5¢ (other denoms may exist) Liberty Service Token (D)	$250
1934 Cowlitz County - 1c Co-Operative Exchange (D)	$100
1933 Deer Park - $1, $2, $5 Deer Park Lumber Co. (D)	$350
1907 Ellensburg - $1 Associated Banks of Ellensburg (D)	$425
1910c Ephrata - 25c The Ephrata Pool Hall. (M) Cardboard	$15
1933 Everett - 25¢ Sockeye (Salmon shaped). Convention Committee (D)	$600
1933 Everett - $1 City of Everett Trade Extension Warrant (D)	$400
1991 Fairhaven - Var. Denoms. Fairhaven Street Warrants.	RARE
1933 Friday Harbor - 25¢, 50¢, $1 Haxkett-Larson American Legion Post (D)	$50
1933 Grand Coulee - 25¢ Grand Coulee Dam Quarter (concrete) (D)	$40

DENOMINATION	PRICE
1933 Grays Harbor - $1, $5, $10, $20 Grays Harbor Associated Banks (D)	$140
1910c Harrington - The Magnet. Cardboard 1x2" Scrip (M)	$15
1912 Hoquiam - 10c Rychard Bros & Cox, Stork System (M)	$450
1933 Hoquiam - $1 Olde Ironsides (Round wood) (D)	$135
1912 Hoquiam - 1¢, 2¢ ,3¢, 4¢, 5¢, 10¢, 25¢, 50¢ Stork System Savings 1912 (D)	$50
1933 Hoquiam - 1¢, 2¢, 3¢, 4¢, 5¢, 10¢ Stork System Savings @ 1917 (D)	$16
1939 Hoquiam - 25¢ Hoquiam Jubilee Assoc. 3" round wood (A)	$18
1933 Ilwaco - 5¢, 25¢, 50¢, $1 Ilwaco Salmon Currency (D)	$125
1933 Issaquah - 25¢ Farmer's Trade Note (D) (6 known)	RARE
1933 Kalama - Port of Kalama Scrip (D)	$130
1933 Kelso - $3, $10, $15 County Dairymen's Assocation (D)	$200
1913 Kennewick - 10 Bones Columbia River Valley Grape Festival (A)	$85
1897 LaCenter - 5/100, 1/4, 1, 2, 10 Labor Exchange #259. (G)	$650
1933 Linden - $1 City of Linden (D)	$500
1933 Longview - 25¢ Longview Chamber of Commerce (D)	$17
1935 Longview - Retail Merchants Emergency Tax Token (Green)	$19
1949 Longview - 5c Silver Jubilee of Longview (G)	$15
1896 Marysville - 1/4 1 Labor Exchange #62 by Cole/Fisher Lumber (CS)	$750
1933 Montesano - 5¢, 10¢ United Producer's Money (D)	$150
1933 Mt. Rainier - $10 Mt. Ranier Clearing House (D)	$500
1893 Mount Vernon - $1 Mount Vernon Red Shingle Scrip. None known	
1893 New Whatcom - 5c, 15c, 25c, 50¢, $1, $5 Cissna Dept. Store. (M)	$800
1894 New Whatcom - 50¢ U.S. Postal note April 24, 1894 (M)	$1150
1933 Okanogan - $1 Okanogan Commercial Club "WineSap" (D)	$170
1888 Okanogan County - $40 Okanogan County Territorial Warrant (W)	$325
1898 Olympia - $5, $10 Commissioners Scrip Treas. State of Washington. (W)	$750
1907 Olympia - $1 Associated Banks of Olympia (D)	$250
1933 Olympia - 25¢, $1 $2 $5 Community Service Bureau (D)	$50
1933 Olympia - 25¢ Olympia Oyster Money, Chamber of Commerce (D)	$350
1933 Omak - $1, $5, $10 Bile-Coleman Lumber Co. (D)	$175
1933 Pasco - 50¢, $1 Pasco Relief Scrip (D)	$225
1935 Pasco-Kennewick - Emergency Tax Token (Red) (US)	$30
1933 Peshastin - 25¢, 50¢, $1 Peshastin Ponderosa Scrip (D)	$185
1887 Port Angeles, WT - 5c, 10c, 25c, 50c, $1 Puget Sound Co-Op Colony (D)	$2200
1893 Port Angeles - 50c G.M. Lauridsen. Yellow tint, diagonal title. (D)	$1500
1894 Port Angeles - (var.) City of Port Angeles - City Council (D)	$600
1933c Port Ludlow - 5c 10c 25c Puget Mill Co. Scrip (M)	$25
1933 Port Townsend - $1, $5, $10 First American Bank (D)	$40
1910c Pullman - City Club, Small cardboard Chit (M)	$14
1910c Pullman - Smoke House, Small cardboard Chit (M)	$14
1933 Raymond - 25¢, 50¢, $1, $5 Raymond Oyster Money (D)	$85
1933 Rock Island - 25¢ Rock Island Dam Scrip (D)	$130
1907 Seattle - $1000 The Seattle Clearing House Assoc. (D)	$1380
1907 Seattle - $1, $2, $5, $10, $20 Seattle Clearing House Assoc. (D)	$175
1907 Seattle - $500 $1000 $5000 $10000 Seattle Clearing House Assoc. (B)	RARE
1931 Seattle - 1 vote Citizens of the City of Seattle (A)	$50
1932 Seattle - 10¢ Theatre Scrip for Unemployed (D)	$135
1933 Seattle - $1, $5, $10, $20 Seattle Clearing House Assoc. (D)	$150

DENOMINATION	PRICE
1933 Seattle - 25¢ $1 Community Service Bureau (D)	$80
1935 Seattle - 1/5 mil Five Points Cafes Tax Chit cardboard (M)	$20
1935 Seattle - 1/5 mil Neuperts Grocery Tax Chit cardboard (M)	$27
1915c ND 1915c Sequim - $1 Chas. Fenwick Rifles (A)	$37
1907 Skagit County - $1, $5 Skagit County Clearing House (D)	$450
1933 Skagit County - $1 Skagit Community Scrip (D)	$230
1907 Snohomish - $1, $2, $5, $10, $20 Snohomish County Associated Bank (D)	$350
1933 South Bend - 25¢, 50¢, $1, $5, $10 Willapa Harbor Currency (wood) (D)	$100
1933 South Bend - 25¢, 50¢, $1, $5, $10 Willapa Harbor Currency (paper) (D)	$130
1894 Spokane - 2¢ U.S. Postal note May 14, 1894. (US)	$750
1907 Spokane $1, $2, $5, $10, $20 Clearing House Association (D)	$150
1910c Spokane - 25¢ Imperial Pool Room. Red Cardboard 1 x 2" (M)	$18
1929 Spokane - Exchange Lumber Co. Description of new 1929 notes (A)	$50
1933 Spokane - 50¢, $1, $5 Baird-Naundorf Lumber Co. (D)	$130
1933 Spokane - $1 Commercial Creamery (D)	$150
1933 Spokane - 25¢ ,50¢, $1 Davenport Hotel (D)	$130
1933 Spokane - 25¢, 50¢, $1, $5 Dessert Hotel (D)	$130
1933 Spokane - $2, $5 Federated Exchange Cert. McClintock-Turnkey Co. (D)	$95
1933 Spokane - $1 John W. Graham Co. (D)	$225
1933 Spokane - $1, $5 Long Lake Lumber Co. (D)	$80
1933 Spokane - 50¢, $1, $5 Spokesman-Review Newspaper (D)	$175
1933 Spokane - $1 Tull & Gibbs (D)	$300
1935 Spokane - City of Spokane Emergency Tax Scrip cardboard (G)	$18
1939 Spokane - 5¢ Columbia Cavalcade Golden Jubilee (A)	$18
1910c Sprague - 25c Ludtke & Whiteside cardboard Chit	$28
1880c Tacoma, W.T. - $5 W.H. Fife Advertising Note (A)	$1800
1880c Tacoma, WT - $3 George J. Turrell Shoe Dealer, Wash. Territory (A)	$1500
1907 Tacoma - $1, $2, $5, $10, $20 Tacoma Clearing House Assoc. (D)	$165
1907 Tacoma - $500 $1000 $5000 Tacoma Clearing House Assoc. (B)	$1200
1933 Tacoma - 25¢, $1, $2, $5, $10 Community Service Bureau (D)	$50
1933 Tacoma - 5¢, 10¢, 25¢, 50¢ Natural Development Assoc. Centi/Vallars (D)	$450
1933 Tacoma - 1 U, 5 Units, New Commonwealth (D)	$130
1931–32 Tenino- 25¢, $1, $5, $10 (Paper) Chamber of Commerce (D)	$130
1932–33 Tenino - 25¢, 50¢, $1 (Wood) Chamber of Commerce (D)	$100
1932 Tenino - 25¢, 50¢ (Wood) Chamber of Commerce Double Denomination (D)	$9000
1933c Tenino - 5¢ Jiffy Lunch, small/wood (D)	$125
1933c Tenino - 5¢ D.M. Major, small/wood (D)	$130
1933c Tenino - 5¢ Tenino Chamber of Commerce, small/wood (D)	$90
1933c Tenino - 1¢ 2¢ 3¢ Thurston County Independent, small/wood with postal stamp (D)	$4000
1933–35 Tenino A series of 1/5¢ wooden sales tax "chits" approximately 1" square were issued by several firms and are sought after. They include: Campbell & Campbell, Drug Store, Jack Horner, Jiffy Lunch, L.A. McLain, Mecca Cafes, Paramount Service Station, Penny's Garage, Tenino Cash Market, Thurston County Independent, E.E. Walker, and White Front Garage. Most are valued in the range of	$40
1939 Tenino - 25¢ Lions Club, Lion Money (A)	$65
1971 Tenino - 25c 50c $1 Tenino Centennial on Wood (A)	$8

DENOMINATION	PRICE
1933 Toppenish - $10 The Traders Bank (D)	$800
1933 Toppenish - $1 Toppenish Commercial Club "Toppenish Wampum" (D)	$750
1933 Waitsburg - $1 Waitsburg Civic Relief Committee (D)	$350
1883 Walla Walla, WT - 50¢ U.S. Postal note, Sept. 3, 1883. (US)	$11,000
1894 Walla Walla - 1¢ U.S. Postal note June 28, 1894. (US)	$775
1910c Walla Walla - 5c 10c The Maze. Blue cardboard 2x1" (M)	$15
1936 Walla Walla - 10c Whitman Centennial numbered. (G)	$10
1937 Walla Walla - 10c Southeastern Washington Fair cow. (M)	$38
1933 Wapato - 25¢ Community Service Bureau (D)	$100
1933 Wenatchee - $1 Wenatchee Chamber of Commerce - Apple Jack (D)	$225
1933 Wenatchee - 25¢,50¢, $1 Wenatchee Daily World Publishing Co. (D)	$22
1933 Woodland - 5¢, 10¢, 25¢, 50¢ City of Woodland - Welfare Scrip (D)	$125
1933 Yakima - 10c City Creamery (M)	$100

WYOMING

1870 $8 Post Trader, Fort Bridger, Wyoming Territory

DENOMINATION	PRICE
1908 Cambria - $1 Cambria Trading Company. Blue print. Miner on front (M)	$200
1897 Cambria - $5 Kirkpatrick Brothers & Collins. Gray print. Miner	$300
1867 Cheyenne, WT - $3000 Morton E Post Banking House Wyoming Terr.	$500
1869c ND Cheyenne, WT - Wyoming Territory - Gray & Pearse Advertising Note	$4200
1869c ND Cheyenne, WT - 50¢ Central House, C.W. Tappan (A)	$2250
1931 Cheyenne - $1 Cheyenne Frontier Night Show (blue)	$395
1907 Cheyenne - $1, $5, $10 Cheyenne Clearing House (D)	$450
1907 Cheyenne - $1 $5 $10 First Nat'l Bank of Cheyenne (D)	$500
1907 Cheyenne - $1 $5 $10 Stock Grower's NB of Cheyenne (D)	$550
1907 Cheyenne - $1 $5 $10 Citizen's Nat'l Bank of Cheyenne (D)	$550
1910 Cheyenne - 1¢ 2¢ 3¢ 4¢ 5¢ 10¢ A E Roedel Druggist, Citizen's Nat'l bank, (M)	$300
1910 Cheyenne - 1¢ 2¢ 3¢ 4¢ 5¢ 10¢ The Bon Company, Citizen's Nat'l Bank, Stork (M)	$350
1910 Cheyenne - 1¢ 2¢ 3¢ 4¢ 5¢ 10¢ Cheyenne Creamery Co. Stock Grower's NB (M)	$325
1933 Cheyenne - $50 City of Cheyenne - The Scrip Commission (D)	$275
1933–34 Cheyenne - $1 Cheyenne Frontier Days (D)	$275
1933 Cheyenne - Natural Development Assoc. Centi/Vallars SENC (D)	RARE
1964 Cheyenne - $1 Cheyenne Autumn Trail Dedication "Cheyenne Wampum" (W)	$30
1877 Evanston, WT - (var.) Territory of Wyoming, County of Uinta warrant (W)	$125
1870 Ft. Bridger. WT - $1 to $8 Sutler note; WA Carter Post Trader, Wyo. Territory (S)	$4500
1882 Laramie City, WT - $10 A.M. Watkins. "Hats, Caps, Boots, Shoes, NOTIONS, ETC." (A)	$3800

DENOMINATION	PRICE
1912 Laramie - 3¢ 25¢ A E Roedel Druggist, Citizen's Nat'l Bank, Stork (1910 Copyright) (D)	$425
1912 Laramie - 50¢ Gem City Grocery, First State Bank, Stork (1910 Copyright) (D)	$325
1933 Laramie - 50¢ City of Laramie Scrip - Scrip Commission (D)	$350
1912 Laramie - 10c Woodford Clothing. First State Bank, Stork	$450
1912 Laramie - 10c Laramie Drug Store, First State Bank, Stork	$350
1933 Laramie - 50c County of Albany (G)	$600
1933–34 Riverton - 5¢, 10¢, 25¢, 50¢, $1 Riverton Lion's Club. Paper (D)	$200
1933–34 Riverton - 50¢ Riverton Lion's Club. Paper (D)	$200
1933 Riverton - 50¢ Riverton Lions Club. Scrip printed on buckskin (D)	$185

Glossary: Adv.=Advertising; c(following date)=circa; CD=Certificate of Deposit; CS=Communal Scrip, ND=No Printed Date; Var $=Various amounts, Ctf=Counterfeit, G=Government, U.S., State. Local or Communal

MISC WARRANTS, BILLS of EXCHANGE, BOUNTIES, FORMS

CALIFORNIA

DENOMINATION	PRICE
1859 Hensley & Merrill, Sacramento, Ca Engraved Bill of Exchange, Fine.	$120
1851 RF Hastings & Co. Bankers, Sacramento, Ca Bill of Exchange, Fine.	$120
1855 D. O. Mills & Co, Sacramento, Ca, Second Bill of Exchange. Fine	$575
1852 Page, Bacon & Co, Sacramento Ca, Vignetted 2nd Exch, F-VF.	$300
1852 Burgoyne & Co., San Fran, Cal, Bank Check Fine with cancels.	$165
1851 Burgoyne & Co., San Francisco, Ca, Bill of Exchange, Fine.	$325
1851 Drexel, Sather & Church, San Fran, Cal Duplicate Bill of Exch. Whaling VF.	$2185
1856 Drexel, Sather & Church, San Fran, Cal. Second Bill of Exchange. Bldg Fine.	$400
1859 Nathan Mayer de Rothschild & Co, San Fran, Second Bill of Exchange. F	$2300
1858 Auditor's Office Warrant, Santa Clara County, California. County Treasurer	$320
1869 Alexander Cohen, San Fran, First Bill of Exchange. $106.00 Dog/steamer Fine.	$320
1863 Hentsch & Berton. Second Bill of Exchange. sailing vignette. Fine	$375
1869 Hickox & Spear. Original Bill of Exchange. By Lecount & Mansour. VG	$350
1861 Tallant & Wilde. Second Bill of Exchange. $125.00. July 10, 1861. Fine;	$300
1867 Knox & Beans, San Jose. Second Bill of Exchange. $300.00. Sailor Fine.	$400
1880s Pacific Bank, San Fran, Cal. Cert of Deposit Form. VF by A. Gast & Co.	$175
1859 Pacific Loan & Security Bank, San Fran, Cal. Cert of Deposit. VF	$550
1853 Cal Water Co Bearer Draft. Tuolumne Hydraulic Assoc, Sonora. Fine;	$275
1853 Republican Water Company, Algiers, Ca. Bearer Draft $15.00. Mar	$300
1858 Langton's Pioneer Express. Package receipt for transit gold dust	$1400
1869 Hentsch & Berton, San Fran, Cal, Bank Checks. (#) Fine.	$1,100
18-- Miner's Exchange & Savings Bank, San Fran First Bill of Exchange. Fine.	$950
18-- First Bill of Exch. by Britton & Rey, San Fr. Vignette of Banking House, F	$900
18-- S. Molitor & Co, Assayers, San Fr, Cal. Three Cents Red Postal Envelope with Marysvill Freeman & Co red advertising banner Fine	$550

HAWAII

1907 Honolulu—$100 First of Exch on Bishop & Co. (B)	$750

MONTANA

1862 Wright & Co. NY. Sight Draft - Two sailors taking Columbia out to sea	$700
1867 L.H. Hershfield, Banking House, Helena,, Mont Terr. miner/dog.	$220
1869 First NB of Helena, Montana Terr. Orig Bill of Exch. Fine.	$1,900
1853 American Express Co. Wells, Butterfield & Co., NY Sight Draft. Fine.	$1,800
1863 Territorial Warrant, $8 "bounty for killing one bear" Helena, Montana Terr.	$500

NEBRASKA

1863 Office of Territorial Auditor, Omaha, Territory of Nebraska. Pay Warrant	$750

TEXAS

1974 Joseph Metcalf & Co. Original Bill of Exchange VF	$235

SPECIAL REPORT: UNCUT SHEETS

As very few notes exist in the form of full uncut sheets, this is a limited area for the collector. Also, the prices are high, well out of range for most hobbyists.

Uncut sheets available on the market are of Small Size Notes exclusively. In most instances it is not known precisely how they reached public hands. Some were undoubtedly presented as souvenir gifts to Treasury Department officials. In any event, uncut sheets have never been illegal to own, since the notes they comprise are precisely the same as those released into general circulation.

The sheets differ in the number of notes, from a low of six in National Currency sheets to a high of eighteen for some sheets of United States (Legal Tender) Notes and Silver Certificates. Others have twelve notes. These differences are due entirely to the printing method being used at their time of manufacture. Any given note was always printed in sheets of the same size, with the same number of specimens per sheet. If you have an uncut sheet with twelve notes, it means that all notes from the series were printed twelve to a sheet.

The condition standards for uncut sheets are the same as those for single notes. Obviously, an uncut sheet did not circulate as money, but some specimens became worn or damaged as a result of careless storage, accident, or other causes. These impaired sheets do turn up in the market, but there is not much demand for them. Almost every buyer of uncut sheets wants Uncirculated condition. Quite often an uncut sheet will be framed when you buy it. This should be considered a plus, as the frame has probably kept the sheet in immaculate condition. Just to be entirely safe, however, it is wise to examine the reverse side of the sheet for possible staining or other problems.

The following prices were current for uncut sheets in Uncirculated grade at publication time. Gem Uncirculated sheets in absolutely pristine condition command higher prices than those shown.

SILVER CERTIFICATES

DENOMINATION	SERIES	NO. OF NOTES PER SHEET	CURRENT PRICE RANGE IN UNC. CONDITION
$1	1928	12	2000.00–4000.00
$1	1934	12	3000.00–4000.00
$5	1934	12	2000.00–3000.00
$10	1934	12	3000.00–5500.00
$1	1935	12	1200.00–1800.00
$5	1953	18	1500.00–2000.00
$10	1953	18	RARE

UNITED STATES NOTES (LEGAL TENDER NOTES)

DENOMINATION	SERIES	NO. OF NOTES PER SHEET	CURRENT PRICE RANGE IN UNC. CONDITION
$1	1928	12	RARE
$2	1928	12	RARE
$5	1928	12	2000.00–3000.00
$2	1953	18	1000.00–2000.00
$5	1953	18	1800.00–3200.00

NATIONAL CURRENCY

DENOMINATION	SERIES	NO. OF NOTES PER SHEET	CURRENT PRICE RANGE IN UNC. CONDITION
$5	1929	6	2000.00–4000.00
$10	1929	6	2000.00–3000.00
$20	1929	6	1000.00–3000.00
$50	1929	6	RARE
$100	1929	6	RARE
EMERGENCY NOTES:			
Hawaii $1	1935A		RARE
No. Africa $1	1935A		RARE

MULES (MIXED PLATE NUMBERS)

All U.S. currency has plate numbers on the face and back. These plate numbers are in the lower right corner somewhat close to the fine scroll design. They refer to the number of the engraved plate used to print the sheet of notes. Each plate can be used for about 100,000 impressions. It is then destroyed and a new plate with the next number in sequence is put into use.

During the term of Treasury officials Julian and Morgenthau, the plate numbers were changed from almost a microscopic to a larger size, far easier to read. Due to this improvement the series designation then in use was an advance on United States Notes, Silver Certificates, and Federal Reserve Notes. The signatures remained Julian-Morgenthau. National Currency and Gold Certificates were not affected, as these were discontinued earlier.

During the changeover period in printing, plates were sometimes mixed up, producing a note with a large number on one side and a small number on the other side. Notes of this variety are called "mules," or "mule notes." This is from a term applied to coins struck with the obverse or reverse die of one year and the opposite side from a die of another year.

Many collectors are eager to add one or more of these mule notes to their collection. Some of the most common mule notes are:

$2 UNITED STATES NOTES
1928-C, 1928-D

$5 UNITED STATES NOTES
1928-B, 1928-C, 1928-D, 1928-E

$1 SILVER CERTIFICATES
1935, 1935-A

$5 SILVER CERTIFICATES
1934, 1934-A, 1934-B, 1934-C

$10 SILVER CERTIFICATES
1934, 1934A

Mules were also issued in the Federal Reserve Note Series. However, these are not as popular with collectors as the United States Notes and Silver Certificates because of the higher denominations and the twelve districts involved.

The schedule below shows some of the most common mule notes and their values in new condition. The combination of the prefix and suffix letters of the serial numbers on notes is known as "Blocks." For instance: A—A Block, B—A Block.

			UNC.
$2 UNITED STATES NOTE	1928-D	B—A	625.00
		C—A	250.00
		*—A	250.00
$5 UNITED STATES NOTE	1928-B	E—A	250.00
		*—A	650.00
	1928-C	E—A	250.00
		*—A	250.00
$1 SILVER CERTIFICATE	1935	N—A	
		Thru	250.00
		P—A	
	1935-A	M—A	
		Thru	220.00
		V—A	
		C—B	220.00
$5 SILVER CERTIFICATE	1934-A	D—A	
		Thru	220.00
		G—A	
		*—A	210.00
$10 SILVER CERTIFICATE	1934	A—A	200.00
		*—A	200.00
	1934-A	A—A	335.00

Front **SIZES DIFFERENT** **Back**

INTRODUCTION TO UNITED STATES FRACTIONAL CURRENCY

Events following the outbreak of the Civil War resulted in a shortage of circulating coinage. Trade was hampered as many merchants, especially in large cities, were unable to make change and only customers presenting the exact amount for a purchase could buy—but they were generally as short on coins as the shop proprietors. Various attempts were made to solve this problem by issuing credit slips (which most customers didn't care for), tokens (which they also didn't care for), and using postage stamps as money. Finally, in 1862, the government stepped in, recognizing that the economy was being seriously hurt, and issued a series of small paper notes as equivalents of coinage denominations. They carried designs adapted from the current postage stamps of the day and were known as Postage Currency or Postal Currency. The more popular title is now Fractional Currency. There were five separate issues of Fractional Currency, three of which occurred during the Civil War and two thereafter, the final one as late as 1874. That a need existed for coin substitutes as late as the 1870s demonstrates the drain placed upon coinage during the war and the long period of recovery. A total of six denominations were issued, from 3¢ to 50¢, comprising 23 designs and more than 100 varieties. Because of its small size and lack of visual impact, Fractional Currency was long shunned by collectors. In recent years it has enjoyed an unprecedented surge of popularity, which, if continued, promises to drive prices beyond present levels. All told, more than $360,000,000 worth of Fractional Currency was circulated. It would be extremely plentiful today but for the fact that most notes were redeemed, leaving only about $2,000,000 outstanding. This is what collectors have to work with, and a good deal of these are badly preserved.

FIRST ISSUE—Postage Currency August 21st, 1862
5-10-25-50

SECOND ISSUE—Fractional Currency October 10th, 1863
5-10-25-50

THIRD ISSUE—Fractional Currency December 5th, 1864
3-5-10-15-25-50

FOURTH ISSUE—Fractional Currency July 14th, 1869
10-15-25-50

FIFTH ISSUE—Fractional Currency February 26th, 1874
10-25-50

THE FRACTIONAL CURRENCY SHIELD

Fractional currency shields were sold by the Treasury Department in 1866. Specimen notes printed only on one side were used. Very Good–condition shields are valued at $2500 to $5000. Choice condition shields in contemporary frames can sell for $6000. Shields with pink, green, or other backgrounds are more valuable.

FRACTIONAL CURRENCY NOTES

The following notes may be collected by issue or by denomination. We list them here by denomination for convenience. Also, since most of these notes were hastily cut from large sheets, the margin size can vary. Specimens are narrow margined while proofs have wide margins. Prices listed are for Nice "well centered" Uncirculated notes.

THREE-CENT NOTES

THIRD ISSUE
Face Design: Portrait of President Washington.

SPECIMEN	FACE	REVERSE
Light Port.	175.00	150.00
Dark Port.	100.00	100.00
PROOF		
Light Port	625.00	350.00
Dark Port	350.00	350.00

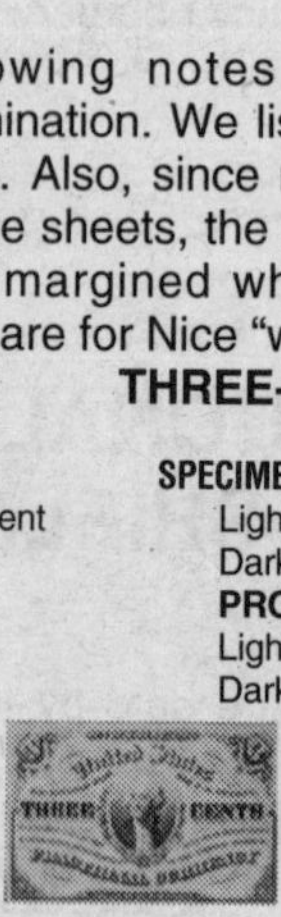
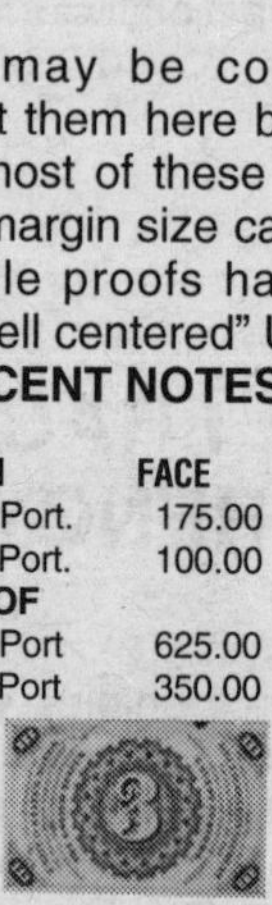

Back Design: Large "3" green.

REGULAR ISSUES	A.B.P.	GOOD	V.FINE	UNC.
☐ With Light Portrait	14.00	25.00	40.00	275.00
☐ With Dark Portrait	14.00	25.00	50.00	305.00

FIVE-CENT NOTES

FIRST ISSUE				
SPECIMEN	FACE	150.00	REVERSE	75.00
PROOF	FACE	400.00	REVERSE	300.00

Face Design: Portrait of President Jefferson, brown.

Back Design: "5" black.

REGULAR ISSUES	A.B.P.	GOOD	V.FINE	UNC.
☐ Perforated edges, monogram ABNCO on back	10.00	18.00	35.00	475.00
☐ Perforated edges, without monogram on back	10.00	15.00	60.00	690.00
☐ Straight edges, monogram ABNCO on back	10.00	20.00	35.00	280.00
☐ Straight edges, without monogram on back	10.00	20.00	35.00	335.00

FIVE-CENT NOTES

SECOND ISSUE	**SPECIMEN**	**FACE**	100.00	**REVERSE**	65.00
	PROOF	**FACE**	275.00	**REVERSE**	250.00

Face Design: Portrait of President Washington.

Back Design: Shield and brown, "5"s.

REGULAR ISSUES	A.B.P.	GOOD	V.FINE	UNC.
☐Value only in bronze on back	8.00	12.00	30.00	360.00
☐Surcharges 18-63 on back	8.00	12.00	30.00	360.00
☐Surcharges S-18-63 on back	11.00	18.00	30.00	390.00
☐Surcharges R-1-18-63 on back, fiber paper	10.00	18.00	65.00	695.00

FIVE-CENT NOTES

THIRD ISSUE	**SPECIMEN**	**FACE**	100.00	**REVERSE**	65.00
	PROOF	**FACE**	260.00	**REVERSE**	220.00

Face Design: Portrait of Spencer M. Clark.

Back Design: Green or red.

REGULAR ISSUES	A.B.P.	GOOD	V.FINE	UNC.
☐Without letter "A" on face, red back	8.00	12.00	35.00	525.00
☐With letter "A" on face, red back	8.00	12.00	35.00	525.00
☐Without letter "A" on face, green back	6.00	10.00	30.00	260.00
☐With letter "A" on face, green back	6.00	10.00	30.00	220.00

This note was authorized to have the portraits of the explorers Lewis and Clark on the face. Mr. Spencer M. Clark, who was then head of the Bureau of Currency, flagrantly placed his own portrait on this note. This caused Congress to pass legislation forbidding the likeness of any living person on U.S. currency.

TEN-CENT NOTES

FIRST ISSUE	**SPECIMEN**	**FACE**	125.00	**REVERSE**	100.00
	PROOF	**FACE**	425.00	**REVERSE**	335.00

Face Design: Portrait of President Washington.

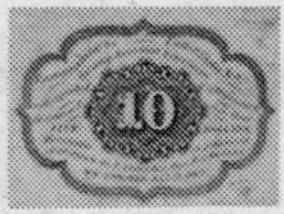

Back Design: "10," black.

REGULAR ISSUES	A.B.P.	GOOD	V.FINE	UNC.
☐Perforated edges, monogram ABNCO on back	8.00	10.00	42.00	472.00
☐Perforated edges, without monogram on back	8.00	10.00	42.00	478.00
☐Plain edges, monogram ABNCO on back	6.00	12.00	30.00	395.00
☐Plain edges, without monogram on back	7.00	12.00	48.00	1110.00

TEN-CENT NOTES

SECOND ISSUE					
	SPECIMEN	FACE	125.00	REVERSE	100.00
	PROOF	FACE	325.00	REVERSE	300.00

Face Design: Portrait of President Washington.

Back Design: "10," green.

REGULAR ISSUE	A.B.P.	GOOD	V.FINE	UNC.
☐Value only surcharge on back	4.00	10.00	38.00	270.00
☐Surcharge 18-63 on back	4.00	10.00	38.00	270.00
☐Surcharge S-18-63 on back	5.00	8.00	32.00	270.00
☐Surcharge I-18-63 on back	9.00	20.00	55.00	450.00
☐Surcharge 0-63 on back	140.00	400.00	1110.00	2600.00
☐Surcharge T-1-18-63 on back, fiber paper	12.00	25.00	140.00	912.00

TEN-CENT NOTES

THIRD ISSUE					
	SPECIMEN	FACE	110.00	REVERSE	150.00
	PROOF	FACE	300.00	REVERSE	260.00

Face Design: Portrait of President Washington.

Back Design: "10," green or red.

REGULAR ISSUES	A.B.P.	GOOD	V.FINE	UNC.
☐Printed signatures Colby-Spinner, green back	6.00	10.00	52.00	205.00
☐As above, figure "1" near left margin on face	6.00	10.00	52.00	205.00
☐Printed signatures Colby-Spinner, red back	7.00	10.00	38.00	415.00
☐As above, figure "1" near left margin, red back	7.00	14.00	47.00	450.00
☐Autographed signatures Colby-Spinner, red back	11.00	16.00	136.00	720.00
☐Autographed signatures Jeffries-Spinner, red back	11.00	16.00	136.00	672.00

TEN-CENT NOTES

FOURTH ISSUE **SPECIMEN** **FACE** 335.00 **REVERSE** RARE
PROOF **FACE** 335.00 **REVERSE** RARE

Face Design: Bust of Liberty.

Back Design: Green with TEN and "10."

REGULAR ISSUES	A.B.P.	GOOD	V.FINE	UNC.
☐Large red seal, watermarked paper	7.00	12.00	38.00	158.00
☐Large red seal, pink fibers in paper	7.00	12.00	38.00	158.00
☐Large seal, pink fibers in paper, right end blue	7.00	12.00	38.00	158.00
☐Large brown seal	16.00	30.00	100.0	200.00
☐Small red seal, pink fibers, right end blue	7.00	12.00	42.00	196.00

TEN-CENT NOTES

FIFTH ISSUE **PROOF** **FACE** RARE **REVERSE** $400.00

Face Design: William Meredith.

Back Design: Green.

REGULAR ISSUES	A.B.P.	GOOD	V.FINE	UNC.
☐Green seal, long narrow key	6.00	10.00	22.00	170.00
☐Red seal, long narrow key	6.00	10.00	22.00	100.00
☐Red seal, short stubby key	6.00	10.00	22.00	100.00

FIFTEEN-CENT NOTES

FACES AND BACKS PRINTED SEPARATELY

THIRD ISSUE ALL ARE SPECIMENS AND UNISSUED.

Face Design: Sherman and President Grant.

Back Design: Green or red.

	SPECIMEN UNC.	PROOF UNC.
☐With printed signatures Colby-Spinner	300.00	750.00
☐With autographed signatures Colby-Spinner	2200.00	RARE
☐With autographed signatures Jeffries-Spinner	300.00	725.00
☐With autographed signatures Allison-Spinner	300.00	725.00
☐Green back	180.00	335.00
☐Red back	175.00	335.00

FIFTEEN-CENT NOTES

FOURTH ISSUE	PROOF	FACE	RARE	REVERSE	500.00

Face Design: Bust of Columbia.

Back Design: Green with "15"s.

REGULAR ISSUES	A.B.P.	GOOD	V.FINE	UNC.
☐Large seal, watermarked paper	20.00	35.00	82.00	425.00
☐Large seal, pink fibers in paper	20.00	35.00	82.00	425.00
☐Large seal, pink fibers in paper, right end blue	20.00	35.00	82.00	425.00
☐Large brown seal	26.00	46.00	185.00	RARE
☐Smaller red seal, pink fibers, right end blue	20.00	35.00	82.00	425.00

TWENTY-FIVE-CENT NOTES

FIRST ISSUE	SPECIMEN	FACE	110.00	REVERSE	110.00
	PROOF	FACE	300.00	REVERSE	225.00

Face Design: Five 5¢ Jefferson Stamps.

Back Design: Black, large "25."

REGULAR ISSUES	A.B.P.	GOOD	V.FINE	UNC.
☐Perforated edges, monogram ABNCO on back	9.00	12.00	37.00	548.00
☐Perforated edges, without monogram on back	8.00	14.00	65.00	690.00
☐Straight edges, monogram ABNCO on back	8.00	10.00	28.00	280.00
☐Straight edges, without monogram on back	9.00	15.00	75.00	690.00

TWENTY-FIVE-CENT NOTES

SECOND ISSUE	SPECIMEN	FACE	110.00	REVERSE	110.00
	PROOF	FACE	275.00	REVERSE	225.00

Time and climatic condition have changed the purple color on the back of this note into many variations.

Face Design: Portrait of President Washington.

Back Design: Purple with "25."

REGULAR ISSUES	A.B.P.	GOOD	V.FINE	UNC.
☐Value only surcharge on back	8.00	12.00	35.00	290.00
☐Surcharge 18-63 on back	8.00	14.00	35.00	382.00
☐Surcharge A-18-63 on back	8.00	12.00	35.00	382.00
☐Surcharge 1-18-63 on back	20.00	40.00	218.00	710.00
☐Surcharge 2-18-63 on back	8.00	12.00	35.00	382.00
☐Surcharge S-18-63 on back	9.00	16.00	35.00	382.00
☐Surcharge T-1-18-63 on back, fiber paper	11.00	25.00	108.00	510.00
☐Surcharge T-2-18-63 on back, fiber paper	11.00	25.00	108.00	510.00

TWENTY-FIVE-CENT NOTES

THIRD ISSUE					
	SPECIMEN	FACE	165.00	REVERSE	100.00
	PROOF	FACE	325.00	REVERSE	200.00

All notes have printed signatures of Colby-Spinner.

Face Design: Portrait of Fessenden.

Back Design: Green or red with "25"

	A.B.P.	GOOD	V.FINE	UNC.
☐Face—bust of Fessenden between solid bronze surcharges, fiber paper, back—green, surcharge M-2-6-5 in corners	125.00	225.00	910.00	4200.00
☐As above, with letter "A" in lower left corner of face	150.00	300.00	1372.00	RARE
☐Face—Fessenden, open scroll bronze surcharges, fiber paper, back—green, surcharges M-2-6-5 in corners	12.00	20.00	136.00	658.00
☐As above with letter "A" in lower left corner of face	10.00	19.00	180.00	690.00
☐Face—Fessenden, open scroll surcharges, plain paper, back—green, value surcharges only	8.00	15.00	52.00	218.00
☐As before, letter "A" in lower left corner of face, back—green, plain paper	10.00	18.00	52.00	218.00
☐Face—Fessenden, red back, value surcharge only	12.00	25.00	80.00	330.00
☐As above, letter "A" in lower left corner of face	12.00	20.00	80.00	330.00

TWENTY-FIVE-CENT NOTES

FOURTH ISSUE SPECIMENS AND PROOFS RARE

Face Design: Portrait of President Washington and Treasury Seal.

Back Design: Green.

REGULAR ISSUES	A.B.P.	GOOD	V.FINE	UNC.
☐Large seal, plain watermarked paper	6.00	10.00	26.00	175.00
☐Large seal, pink silk fiber in paper	6.00	10.00	26.00	175.00
☐Large seal, pink fibers in paper, right end blue	6.00	8.50	25.00	150.00
☐Large brown seal, right end blue	35.00	70.00	325.00	1200.00
☐Smaller red seal, right end blue	6.00	10.00	25.00	150.00

TWENTY-FIVE-CENT NOTES

FIFTH ISSUE SPECIMENS AND PROOFS RARE

Face Design: Portrait of Walker and red seal.

Back Design: Black.

REGULAR ISSUES	A.B.P.	GOOD	V.FINE	UNC.
☐With long narrow key in Treasury Seal.	6.00	10.00	21.00	130.00
☐With short stubby key in Treasury Seal	6.00	10.00	21.00	130.00

FIFTY-CENT NOTES

FIRST ISSUE	SPECIMEN	FACE	150.00	REVERSE	125.00
	PROOF	FACE	600.00	REVERSE	425.00

Face Design: Five 10¢ Washington stamps.

Back Design: Green.

REGULAR ISSUES	A.B.P.	GOOD	V.FINE	UNC.
☐Perforated edges, monogram ABNCO on back	15.00	15.00	120.00	790.00
☐Perforated edges, without monogram on back	13.00	20.00	82.00	790.00
☐Straight edges, monogram ABNCO on back	8.00	10.00	53.00	510.00
☐Straight edges, without monogram	11.00	20.00	108.00	510.00

FIFTY-CENT NOTES

SECOND ISSUE	SPECIMEN	FACE	140.00	REVERSE	150.00
	PROOF	FACE	350.00	REVERSE	270.00

Face Design: Portrait of President Washington.

Back Design: Red.

REGULAR ISSUES	A.B.P.	GOOD	V.FINE	UNC.
☐Surcharge 18-63 on back	8.00	15.00	42.00	400.00
☐Surcharge A-18-63 on back	8.00	15.00	22.00	400.00
☐Surcharge O-1-18-63, fiber paper	9.00	25.00	105.00	650.00
☐Surcharge R-2-18-63, fiber paper	12.00	18.00	55.00	550.00
☐Surcharge T-1-18-63, fiber paper	7.00	15.00	55.00	510.00

FIFTY-CENT NOTES

THIRD ISSUE	SPECIMENS	FACE	175.00	REVERSE	175.00
	PROOFS	FACE	330.00	REVERSE	280.00

Face Design: Justice with sword, shield, scales.

Back Design: Green or red.

The following notes have printed signatures of Colby-Spinner and have *green backs.*

REGULAR ISSUES	A.B.P.	GOOD	V.FINE	UNC.
☐Value surcharge and S-2-6-4 on back, fiber paper			16500.00	RARE
☐Value surcharge and A-2-6-5 on back, fiber paper	16.00	30.00	130.00	1540.00
☐As above with "1" and letter "A" on face, A-2-6-5 on back	55.00	85.00	825.00	3850.00
☐As above with "1" only on face, A-2-6-5 on back	14.00	32.00	108.00	910.00
☐As above with letter "A" only on face, A-2-6-5 on back	14.00	36.00	108.00	910.00
☐A-2-6-5 on back, *narrowly spaced,* plain paper	10.00	12.00	118.00	760.00

	A.B.P.	GOOD	V.FINE	UNC.
☐As above, numeral "1" and letter "A" on face	10.00	20.00	85.00	690.00
☐As above, numeral "1" only on face	10.00	12.00	70.00	690.00
☐As above, letter "A" only on face	10.00	18.00	130.00	575.00
☐A-2-6-5 on back, *widely spaced,* plain paper	10.00	18.00	130.00	600.00
☐As above, numeral "1" and letter "A" on face	20.00	45.00	380.00	1650.00
☐As above, numeral "1" only on face	9.00	12.00	92.00	795.00
☐As above, letter "A" only on face	9.00	12.00	92.00	795.00
☐Without position letters or back surcharges	9.00	12.00	92.00	575.00
☐As above with numeral "1" and letter "A" on face	15.00	25.00	162.00	1650.00
☐As above with numeral "1" only on face	7.00	12.00	85.00	690.00
☐As above with letter "A" only on face	7.00	12.50	85.00	690.00

The following notes have printed signatures of Colby-Spinner and *red backs.*

	A.B.P.	GOOD	V.FINE	UNC.
☐Value surcharge and S-2-6-4 on back, fiber	150.00	180.00	2200.00	RARE
☐As above, numeral "1" and letter "A"	150.00	350.00	3200.00	RARE
☐As above, numeral "1" only on face	125.00	200.00	1320.00	RARE
☐As above, letter "A" only on face	135.00	225.00	1320.00	RARE
☐Value surcharge and A-2-6-5 on back, plain	10.00	20.00	108.00	875.00
☐As above, numeral "1" and letter "A"	47.00	77.00	550.00	2420.00
☐As above, numeral "1" only on face	10.00	20.00	165.00	795.00
☐As above, letter "A" only on face	10.00	20.00	165.00	795.00
☐No surcharge on back, plain paper	10.00	20.00	125.00	795.00
☐As above, numeral "1" and letter "A" on face	25.00	50.00	290.00	2420.00
☐As above, numeral "1" only on face	13.00	24.00	195.00	1100.00
☐As above, letter "A" only on face	13.00	30.00	195.00	850.00

The following notes have autographed signatures of Colby-Spinner and *red backs.*

	A.B.P.	GOOD	V.FINE	UNC.
☐Value surcharge and S-2-6-4 on back, fiber	37.00	100.00	380.00	1760.00
☐Value surcharge and A-2-6-5 on back, fiber	35.00	75.00	220.00	1650.00
☐Value surcharge only on back, plain paper	16.00	30.00	128.00	1320.00

FIFTY-CENT NOTES

THIRD ISSUE	SPECIMEN	FACE	165.00	REVERSE	140.00
	PROOF	FACE	400.00	REVERSE	325.00

Face Design: Bust of Spinner with surcharges.
Back Design: Green or red.

The following notes have printed signatures of Colby-Spinner, and *green backs.*

REGULAR ISSUES	A.B.P.	GOOD	V.FINE	UNC.
☐Value surcharge and A-2-6-5 on back	9.00	27.00	130.00	415.00
☐As above, numeral "1" and letter "A" on face	22.00	41.00	250.00	825.00
☐As above, numeral "1" only on face	9.00	20.00	825.00	465.00
☐As above, letter "A" only on face	9.00	18.00	110.00	550.00
☐Value surcharge only on back	9.00	12.00	85.00	510.00
☐As above, numeral "1" and letter "A" on face	12.00	28.00	85.00	510.00
☐As above, numeral "1" only on face	9.00	15.00	85.00	510.00
☐As above, letter "A" only on face	9.00	15.00	85.00	510.00
TYPE II BACK DESIGN				
☐No back surcharge	9.00	18.00	65.00	440.00
☐Numeral "1" and letter "A" on face	20.00	37.00	105.00	605.00
☐Numeral "1" only on face	9.00	17.00	65.00	465.00
☐Letter "A" only on face	9.00	22.00	80.00	605.00

The following notes have a portrait of Spinner, printed signatures of Colby-Spinner, *red backs*, and are Type I.

REGULAR ISSUES	A.B.P.	GOOD	V.FINE	UNC.
☐Value surcharge and A-2-6-5 on back	10.00	50.00	65.00	465.00
☐As above with numeral "1" and letter "A"	20.00	50.00	155.00	1100.00
☐As above with numeral "1" only on face	10.00	17.00	82.00	550.00
☐As above with letter "A" only on face	10.00	25.00	140.00	550.00

The following notes have autographed signatures, *red backs,* and are Type I.

	A.B.P.	GOOD	V.FINE	UNC.
☐Autographed signatures COLBY-SPINNER, back surcharged value and A-2-6-5	25.00	50.00	155.00	650.00
☐Autographed signatures ALLISON-SPINNER, back surcharged value and A-2-6-5	25.00	40.00	155.00	690.00
☐Autographed signatures ALLISON-NEW, back surcharged value and A-2-6-5	400.00	675.00	2200.00	RARE

FIFTY-CENT NOTES

FOURTH ISSUE SPECIMENS AND PROOFS RARE

Face Design: Bust of Lincoln.

Back Design: Green.

	A.B.P.	GOOD	V.FINE	UNC.
☐Plain paper	20.00	30.00	65.00	730.00
☐Paper with pink fibers	20.00	30.00	85.00	630.00

FIFTY-CENT NOTES

FOURTH ISSUE SPECIMENS AND PROOFS RARE

Face Design: Bust of Stanton.

Back Design: Green with "50."

	A.B.P.	GOOD	V.FINE	UNC.
☐Red seal and signatures ALLISON-SPINNER, paper with pink fibers, blue ends	12.00	20.00	70.00	410.00

FIFTY-CENT NOTES

FOURTH ISSUE SPECIMENS AND PROOFS RARE

Face Design: Bust of Samuel Dexter.

Back Design: Green with "50."

	A.B.P.	GOOD	V.FINE	UNC.
☐Green seal, pink fibers, blue ends	8.00	12.00	42.00	445.00

FIFTY-CENT NOTES

FIFTH ISSUE SPECIMENS AND PROOFS RARE

Face Design: Bust of Crawford.

Back Design: Green with "50."

	A.B.P.	GOOD	V.FINE	UNC.
☐Signatures ALLISON-NEW, paper with pink fibers, blue ends	6.00	10.00	42.00	130.00

FIFTY-CENT NOTES

FIFTH ISSUE SPECIMENS AND PROOFS RARE

Face Design: Bust of Seward.

Back Design: Red & Brown with "$50–4%"

A.B.P.	GOOD	V.FINE	UNC.
75.00	100.00	1218.00	2065.00

ERROR OR FREAK NOTES

Notes have been misprinted from time to time since the earliest days of currency. The frequency of misprintings and other abnormalities has increased in recent years due to heavier production and high-speed machinery. This has provided a major sub-hobby for note collectors. Freaks and errors have become very popular, their appeal and prices showing upward movement each year.

On the following pages we have pictured and described most of the more familiar and collectible Error Notes. Pricing is approximate only because many notes bearing the same general type of error differ in severity of error from one specimen to another. As a general rule, the less glaring or obvious errors carry a smaller premium value. Very valuable Error Notes include double denominations, or bills having the face of one denomination and reverse side of another.

Error and Freak Notes do turn up in everyday change. Specimens are located either in that fashion or from bank packs. As far as circulated specimens are concerned, some Error Notes have passed through so many hands before being noticed that the condition is not up to collector standards. This, of course, results in a very low premium valuation.

Values given below are for the specimens pictured and described. Different premiums may be attached to other specimens with similar errors, or notes showing the same errors but of different denominations.

MISMATCHED SERIAL NUMBERS

On ordinary notes, the serial number in the lower left of the obverse matches that in the upper right. When it fails to, even by the difference of a single digit, this is known as a "mismatched serial number." It occurs as the result of a cylinder or cylinders in the high-speed numbering machine becoming jammed. If more than one digit is mismatched, the value will be greater.

	V. FINE	UNC.
□$1 Federal Reserve Note, Series 1969, signatures Elston-Kennedy	215.00	485.00

	V. FINE	UNC.
□$1 Silver Certificate, Series 1957B, signatures Granahan-Dillon	150.00	457.00

	V. FINE	UNC.
□$1 Federal Reserve Note, Series 1977A, signatures Morton-Miller	170.00	375.00

INVERTED THIRD PRINT

The inverted third print is also known as "inverted overprint." The Treasury Seal, District Seal, Serial Numbers, and District Number are inverted on the obverse side of the note, or printed upside-down, caused by the sheet of notes (having already received the primary design on front and back) being fed upside-down into the press for this so-called "third print." (The back design is the "first print," the front is the "second print," and these various additions comprise the "third print." It is not possible to print these third print items at the same time as the obverse design, since they are not standard on every bill. At one time the signatures were included in the third print, but these are now engraved directly into the plate and are part of the second print.)

Though very spectacular, inverted third print errors are not particularly scarce and are especially plentiful in 1974 and 1976 series notes.

	V. FINE	UNC.
□$5 Federal Reserve Note, Series 1974, signatures Neff-Simon	182.00	320.00

	V. FINE	UNC.
□$2 Federal Reserve Note, Series 1976, signatures Neff-Simon	482.00	710.00

	V. FINE	UNC.
□$1 Federal Reserve Note, Series 1974, signatures Neff-Simon	280.00	555.00

	V. FINE	UNC.
□$50 Federal Reserve Note, Series 1977, signatures Morton-Blumenthal	565.00	775.00

	V. FINE	UNC.
□$20 Federal Reserve Note, Series 1974, signatures Neff-Simon	380.00	775.00

	V. FINE	UNC.
□$10 Federal Reserve Note, Series 1974, signatures Neff-Simon	265.00	545.00

COMPLETE OFFSET TRANSFER

Offset transfers are not, as is often believed, caused by still-wet printed sheets coming into contact under pressure. Though very slight offsetting can occur in that manner, it would not create notes as spectacular as those pictured here, in which the offset impression is almost as strong as the primary printing. These happen as a result of the printing press being started an instant or so before the paper is fed in. Instead of contacting the paper, the inked plate makes its impression upon the machine bed. When the paper is then fed through, it picks up this "ghost" impression from the bed, in addition to the primary impression it is supposed to receive. Each successive sheet going through the press will acquire the impression until all ink is totally removed from the machine bed. But, naturally, the first sheet will show the transfer strongest, and the others will be weaker and weaker. Obviously, the market value of such notes depends largely on the strength of the offset impression. The heavier and more noticeable it is, the more valuable the note will be—all other things being equal.

	V. FINE	UNC.
□$5 Federal Reserve Note, Series 1977, signatures Morton-Blumenthal, offset of reverse side of face		
Dark	195.00	450.00
Light	182.00	355.00

	V. FINE	UNC.
□$1 Federal Reserve note, Series 1974, signatures Neff-Simon, offset of reverse side of face.		
Dark	210.00	567.00
Light	160.00	235.00

PARTIAL OFFSET TRANSFER

The most logical explanation for this error is that a sheet of paper fed into the press incorrectly became mangled or torn, and part of the inked plate contacted the printing press bed. Therefore, wet ink was left on those portions of the press bed not covered by paper. When the next sheet was fed through, it received the correct impression, plus it acquired a partial offset transfer by contacting this wet area of the press bed. Just as with offset transfers, the first sheet going through the press following an accident of this kind will receive the strongest transfer, and it will become gradually less noticeable on succeeding sheets.

	V. FINE	UNC.
□$1 Federal Reserve Note, Series 1969D, signatures Banuelos-Schultz, offset of a portion of reverse side on face		
Dark	83.00	193.00
Light	83.00	193.00

PRINTED FOLD

Notes showing printed folds occur as the result of folds in the paper before printing, which probably happen most often when the sheet is being fed into the press. If the sheet is folded in such a manner that a portion of the reverse side is facing upward, as shown here, it will receive a part of the impression intended for its obverse. Naturally the positioning of these misplaced portions of printing is very random, depending on the nature and size of the fold.

	V. FINE	UNC.
□$20 Federal Reserve Note, Series 1977, signatures Morton-Blumenthal, Federal Reserve District seal and District number printed on reverse	160.00	420.00

THIRD PRINT ON REVERSE

The cause of this error is obvious, the sheet having been fed through the press on the wrong side (back instead of front) for the third impression or "third print." In the so-called third print, the note receives the Treasury and Federal Reserve District seals, district numbers, and serial numbers.

	V. FINE	UNC.
□$1 Federal Reserve Note, third print on reverse	171.00	460.00

BOARD BREAKS

The terminology of this error is misleading. It suggests that the fernlike unprinted areas were caused by a broken printing plate. Actually they must have resulted from something—probably linty matter—sticking to the printing ink. The assumption reached by the public, when it encounters such a note, is that the blank streaks were caused by the paper being folded in printing. This, however, is not possible, as that would yield an error of a much different kind (*see* Printed Fold).

It should be pointed out that board breaks are easily created by counterfeiters by erasing portions of the printed surface, and that the collector ought to examine such specimens closely.

	V. FINE	UNC.
□$20 Federal Reserve Note, board breaks on reverse	132.00	395.00

MISSING SECOND PRINT

The "second print" is the front face, or obverse of the note—the "first print" being the reverse or back. A note with a missing second print has not received the primary impression on its obverse, though the back is normal and the front carries the standard third print matter (Treasury Seal, serial numbers, etc.). These errors, while they probably occur frequently, are so easily spotted by B.E.P. checkers that such notes are very scarce on the market.

	V. FINE	UNC.
□$10 Federal Reserve Note, missing second print	375.00	845.00

PRINTED FOLD

This note was folded nearly in half before receiving the third print, which fell across the waste margin on the reverse side. Had the note not been folded, this waste margin would have been removed in the cutting process. This note, when unfolded, is grotesque in shape.

	V. FINE	UNC.
□$1 Federal Reserve Note, printed fold with Federal Reserve District seal, district numbers, and serial numbers on reverse. (Naturally, this note lacks the "third print" matter, such as the Treasury Seal, that was supposed to appear on the righthand side of the obverse.)	395.00	870.00

	V. FINE	UNC.
□$5 Federal Reserve Note. Printed fold with entire Federal Reserve District seal, portion of another Federal Reserve District seal, and portion of two different serial numbers on the reverse. It may be hard to imagine how a freak of this nature occurs. This note was folded diagonally along a line bisecting the Lincoln Memorial building slightly to the right of center. The lefthand portion of the reverse side was thereby drawn down across the lefthand side of the obverse, extending well below the bottom of the note. It reached far enough down to catch the district seal intended for the note beneath it, as well as a bit of the serial number. This is why the two serial numbers are different; they were supposed to go on two different notes. Obviously, when something this dramatic happens in printing, not only one error note is created but several—at least—at the same time. Not all necessarily reach circulation, however.	785.00	1910.00

THIRD PRINT BLACK INK MISSING OR LIGHT

Though the machinery used is ultramodern, U.S. currency notes are printed by the same basic technique used when printing was first invented more than 500 years ago. Ink is spread on the metal plates and these are pressed on the sheets as they go through the press. Because the inking is manually fed (as is the paper), an even flow is usually achieved. When an under-inked note is found, it is generally merely "light," giving a faded appearance. But sometimes the plate will be very improperly inked, due to mechanical misfunction or some other cause, resulting in whole areas being unprinted or so lightly printed that they cannot be seen without close inspection. These are not especially valuable notes but counterfeit specimens are frequently made.

	V. FINE	UNC.
□$1 Federal Reserve Note, Series 1977, signatures of Morton-Blumenthal. Federal Reserve District seal and District numbers missing from lefthand side, remainder of "third print" material light but distinct. If the lefthand serial number was strong, there might be suspicion of this being a counterfeit.	128.00	485.00

THIRD PRINT GREEN INK MISSING OR LIGHT

In this case, the green, rather than the black, ink was applied too lightly to the printing plate.

	V. FINE	UNC.
□$5 Federal Reserve Note, Series 1977, signatures of Morton-Blumenthal	88.00	345.00

NOTE FOLDED DURING OVERPRINT

This note was folded as it was being overprinted and failed to receive the District seal and District numbers at the left side of its obverse. This kind of error, like all involving missing portions of printing, has been extensively counterfeited.

	V. FINE	UNC.
□$2 Federal Reserve Note, Series 1976, signatures of Neff-Simon	130.00	375.00

FAULTY ALIGNMENT

Notes of this kind were formerly called "miscut," and sometimes still are. "Faulty alignment" is a more inclusive term which encompasses not only bad cutting but accidents in printing. If the sheet shifts around in the press, it will not receive the printed impressions exactly where they should be. Even if the cutting is normal, the resulting note will be misaligned; the cutting machine cannot correct botched printing. It is very easy to determine where the fault lies. If one side of the note has its design higher than the opposite side, this is a printing error. If the misalignment occurs equally on both sides, the problem was in cutting. Since the two sides are not printed in the same operation, it would be a one-in-a-million chance for them to become equally misaligned.

The value of such notes depends upon the degree of misalignment. Collectors are especially fond of specimens showing a portion—even if very slight, as with the one pictured, of an adjoining note.

	V. FINE	UNC.
□$5 Federal Reserve Note, bottom left of reverse shaved (or "bled"), corresponding portion of adjoining note just visible at top. This ranks as a "dramatic" specimen.		
Slight	105.00	293.00
Dramatic	125.00	386.00

INSUFFICIENT PRESSURE

Under-inking of the printing plate is not the only cause of weak or partially missing impressions. If the press is not operating correctly and the inked plate meets the sheet with insufficient pressure, the result is similar to under-inking. This probably happens as a result of a sheet going through just as the press is being turned off for the day, or at other intervals. Supposedly all action ceases at the instant of turnoff, but considering the rapidity of this operation, it is likely that a random sheet could pass through and be insufficiently impressed. The note pictured here received normal "third print," as is generally the case with notes whose first or second print is made with insufficient pressure.

	V. FINE	UNC.
□$20 Federal Reserve Note, Series 1977, signatures of Morton-Blumenthal	182.00	303.00

PRINTED FOLD

This note, along with a large portion of the adjoining note, became folded after the second print. When it passed through the press to receive the third print or overprints (seals, serial numbers, etc.), these naturally failed to appear on the folded area.

	V. FINE	UNC.
□$1 Federal Reserve Note, printed fold with overprints partially missing		
Small	144.00	340.00
Large	226.00	575.00

DOUBLE IMPRESSION

Double impressions have traditionally been traced to the sheet of notes passing through the press twice, which would be the logical explanation. However, in considering the method by which currency is printed, it would seem more likely that double impression notes have not made two trips through the press. They probably result from the automatic paper feed jamming. The sheet just printed fails to be ejected, and the printing plate falls upon it a second time instead of on a fresh sheet. This does not merely create a strong impression, but a twin, or a ghost, impression, since the sheet is not positioned exactly the same way for the second strike. Though the paper feed may not be operating properly, there will still be some slight movement—enough to prevent the second impression from falling directly atop the first.

	V. FINE	UNC.
□$1 Federal Reserve Note, Series 1977A, signatures of Morton-Miller, double "second print" impression		
Partial	400.00	738.00
Complete	635.00	1600.00

DOUBLE IMPRESSION OF OVERPRINTS ("DOUBLE THIRD PRINT")

This note is normal as far as the primary obverse and reverse printings are concerned. It received twin impressions of the overprints or "third print." This was not caused by jamming of the paper feed as discussed above. Naturally, the serial numbers are different, as the automatic numbering machine turns with every rise and fall of the press.

	V. FINE	UNC.
□$20 Federal Reserve Note, Series 1950, signatures of Priest-Humphrey, double impression of overprints.		
Partial	365.00	840.00
Complete	600.00	1360.00

THIRD PRINT (OR OVERPRINTS) SHIFTED

Whenever the overprints (serial number, seals, etc.) are out of position, vertically or horizontally, this is known as "third print shifted" or "overprints shifted." In the example pictured, shifting is extreme. This is a premium value specimen which would command the higher of the two sums quoted. Normally, the overprinting on a "shifted" note fails to touch the portrait, or touches it only slightly. The cause of this kind of error is a sheet feeding incorrectly into the press for the overprinting operation. As striking and desirable as these notes are to collectors, they often go unnoticed by the public.

	V. FINE	UNC.
□$100 Federal Reserve Note, Series 1969C, signatures of Banuelos-Schultz, third print shifted.		
Slight	280.00	680.00
Dramatic	260.00	590.00

INK SMEARS

Ink smearing is one of the more common abnormalities of currency notes. Generally it can be attributed to malfunction of the automatic inking device which inks the printing plate. When performing properly, ink is applied at a steady, controlled pace to the printing plate. A very minor disorder in the machine can dispense enough extra ink to yield very spectacular "smeared notes," such as the one illustrated. The value of ink smear notes depends upon the area and intensity of the smear. They are quite easily faked, so the buyer should be cautious.

	V. FINE	UNC.
☐$1 Federal Reserve Note, ink smear		
Small	38.00	180.00
Large	130.00	215.00

PRINTING FOLD

This note was crumpled along the right side prior to the third printing or application of overprints. Hence the "third print" matter on the lefthand side is normal, but portions of

the overprint on the right appear on the note's reverse side.

	V. FINE	UNC.
☐$20 Federal Reserve Note, Series 1977, signatures Morton-Blumenthal.	255.00	420.00

BLANK CREASE

It occasionally happens that a note becomes creased prior to the reverse or obverse printing in such a way that a small fold is created. During the printing procedure this fold hides a portion of the note's surface, which fails to receive the impression. These notes are actually double errors—the cutting machine cuts them without knowledge of the fold, and when the fold is opened out the bill is then of larger than normal size. Since "crease errors" are difficult to spot in the Bureau of Engraving and Printing's checking, they find their way into circulation in rather sizable numbers. It is difficult to place standard values on them because the price depends on the exact nature of the specimen. The wider the crease, the more valuable the note will be. Premium values are attached to notes with multiple creases that cause the blank unprinted area to fall across the portrait.

	V. FINE	UNC.
☐Blank crease note, any denomination. Value stated is collector premium over and above face value. (If note has additional value because of series, signatures, etc., this too must be added.)		
Single crease	54.00	160.00
Multiple crease	63.00	171.00

MIXED DENOMINATION

The two notes pictured are normal in themselves, and if they were not owned together as a set, no premium value would be attached to them. The error (which may be dubious to term as such) lies with their serial numbers. The $5 Note has a serial number one digit higher than the $1, suggesting that it was fed into the printing machine intended to print overprints (or "third prints") on $1 bills. Even when this does happen (probably infrequently), it is very difficult to obtain "matching" notes of the kind illustrated, in which the serial numbers are only a single digit apart. Even if you had a $5 Note and $1 Note (or other combination of denominations) from sheets that were fed one after the other, the odds on getting one-digit-apart serial numbers are extremely small.

The value is given for an Uncirculated set only, as there would be no possibility of finding such matched notes except in a bank pack. Once released into circulation, they may never again be mated.

	UNC.
☐Mixed denomination pair from bank pack, $5 Federal Reserve Note within pack of $1 Federal Reserve Notes	RARE

BLANK REVERSE

U.S. currency has its reverse printed before the obverse—in other words, back before front. The only logical explanation for blank reverse notes is that blank paper found its way into the batch of sheets on which reverses had already been printed. They were then fed—without detection—into the press for application of the obverse. They continued to escape notice during printing of the overprints, and miraculously got into circulation.

	V. FINE	UNC.
☐$100 Federal Reserve Note, blank reverse	640.00	1640.00

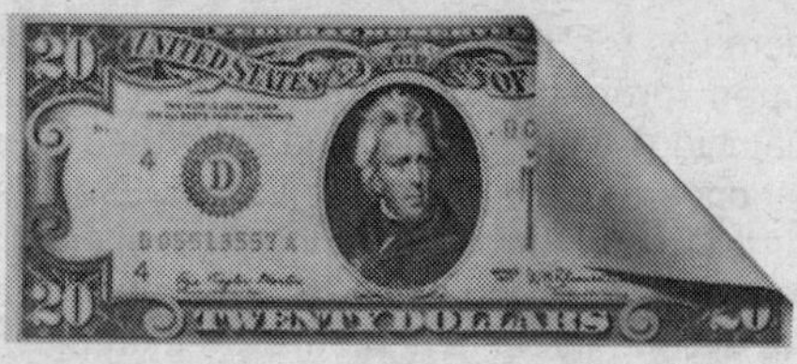

	V. FINE	UNC.
□$20 Federal Reserve Note, Series 1977, signatures of Morton-Blumenthal Blank reverse	315.00	675.00

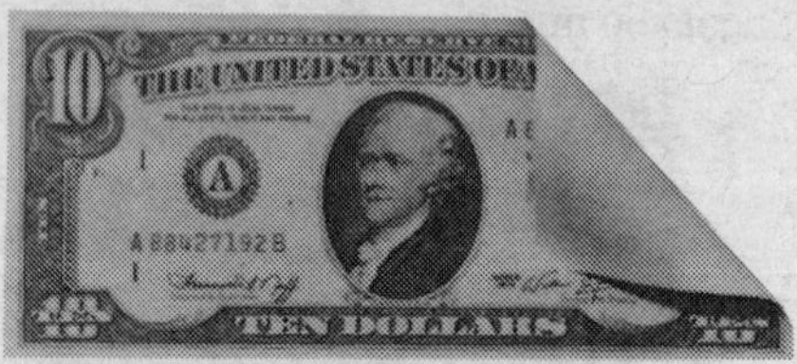

	V. FINE	UNC.
□$10 Federal Reserve Note, Series 1974, signatures of Neff-Simon Blank reverse	345.00	700.00

	V. FINE	UNC.
□$1 Federal Reserve Note, Series 1977, signatures of Morton-Blumenthal Blank reverse	300.00	635.00

DOUBLE DENOMINATION COUNTERFEIT

This is a counterfeit or faked error. We include it to show the kind of work done by counterfeiters, and how such items can be made to resemble genuine errors. This happens to be a counterfeit of an error note that cannot exist in its genuine state. Thus, there can be no hesitancy in proclaiming it a fake. Anyone who is even slightly familiar with the way currency is printed should instantly recognize this item as a fraud.

Nevertheless, fakers succeed in selling (often at high prices) specimens of this kind, probably because some collectors want the impossible for their albums. Genuine double or twin denomination notes have the obverse of one denomination and the reverse of a different denomination. They do not consist of two obverses or two reverses, such as the one pictured. The note illustrated carries four serial numbers. For it to be genuine, it would have had to pass through the "third print" (overprinting) process twice. Obviously it was made by gluing a $1 and $5 Note together. Much more deceptive paste-ups are created with the notes correctly paired so that the obverse of one and reverse of the other shows. Beware!

INVERTED OBVERSE

U.S. currency is printed reverse first. Therefore, when the back and front do not face in the same vertical direction (as they should), the note is known as an "inverted obverse." The term "inverted reverse" is never used. This, of course, results from the sheet being fed through upside-down for the obverse or second print. Though these specimens are scarce in Uncirculated condition, they often pass through many hands in circulation before being spotted. The uninformed public is not even aware that a note with faces in opposite directions is an error and has premium value.

	V. FINE	UNC.
□$2 Federal Reserve Note, Series 1976, signatures of Neff-Simon, inverted obverse	525.00	1300.00

MISSING THIRD PRINT

This error is also known as "missing overprint." It consists of a note released into circulation without having gone through the "third print" operation.

	V. FINE	UNC.
□$1 Federal Reserve Note, Series 1977, signatures Morton-Blumenthal, missing third print	235.00	590.00

FOREIGN MATTER ON OBVERSE

Sometimes foreign matter, usually paper scraps of one kind or another, gets between the printing plate and the sheet. This naturally results in the area covered being blank on the note. Because of the extreme pressure exerted in printing, the foreign matter is occasionally "glued" to the note and travels with it into circulation. If the appendage is paper, it will normally be found to be of the same stock from which the note is made—apparently a shred from one of the sheet margins that worked its way into a batch of sheets awaiting printing. The value of such notes varies greatly, depending on the size of the foreign matter and its placement. It's rare to find notes in which foreign matter became attached before the first or second print. Nearly always, they found their way to the note after the second print and before the third.

	V. FINE	UNC.
□$1 Federal Reserve Note, Series 1974, signatures Neff-Simon, foreign matter on obverse	150.00	375.00

	V. FINE	UNC.
□$1 Silver Certificate, Series 1935E, signatures of Priest-Humphrey. Foreign matter on obverse. More valuable than the preceding because of the note's age and the foreign matter being larger.	390.00	845.00

MISSING PORTION OF REVERSE DESIGN (DUE TO ADHERENCE OF SCRAP PAPER)

In this instance, the foreign matter got in the way of the first print, or reverse printing. It prevented the covered area from being printed, but it later became dislodged and is no longer present. What appears on the illustration to be a strip of paper on the note is really the blank unprinted area once covered by the strip. Obviously a note that merely had a random strip of paper attached, over a normally printed design, would have no collector interest.

	V. FINE	UNC.
☐$1 Federal Reserve Note, missing portion of reverse design due to adherence of scrap paper	160.00	365.00

OVERPRINT PARTIALLY MISSING

The overprint or third print on this note is normal on the righthand side and missing entirely on the left. This was caused by the note being folded (more or less in half, vertically) immediately before overprinting. Had the lefthand side been folded over the face, this would have interfered with the overprints on the righthand side. Instead, this specimen was folded over the reverse side, or downward, with the result that the missing portion of overprint did not strike the note at all—it simply hit the printing press bed. The reverse side of this note is normal.

	V. FINE	UNC.
☐$1 Federal Reserve Note, Series 1963A, overprint partially missing	390.00	485.00

THIRD PRINT OFFSET ON REVERSE

This note is normal on the obverse but carries an "offset" of the third print or overprints on its reverse. It would appear that the overprints are showing through to the reverse, as if the note were printed on very thin paper. Actually, this "mirror image" is caused by a malfunction in the printing or paper-feeding machinery. The inked plate for printing the overprints contacted the machine bed without a sheet of paper being in place. Therefore, as the next sheet came through it received the normal overprint on its face and picked up the offset impression on its reverse from the machine bed. Each successive sheet going through the press also received an offset, but it naturally became fainter and fainter as the ink was absorbed. The value of a note of this kind depends on the intensity of the impression.

	V. FINE	UNC.
□$5 Federal Reserve Note, offset impression of overprints on reverse	210.00	485.00

CONFEDERATE MONEY

The Civil War Centennial of 1961–65 has generally been credited with sparking an interest in the collecting and study of Confederate or C.S.A. Notes. This, however, is not totally borne out by facts, as C.S.A. currency had advanced steadily in value since the 1940s. It rides a crest of popularity today surpassing the early 1960s. This is due in part to the exhaustive research carried out since that time and numerous books and articles published. Even today, some C.S.A. Notes would still appear to be undervalued based on their availability vs. regular U.S. issues.

History. It became apparent upon the outbreak of the Civil War that both sides would experience extreme coinage shortages, and each took to the printing of notes that could be exchanged in lieu of bullion or "real money" (which always meant coined money until the 1860s). The South suffered more serious difficulties than the North, as it did not have as many skilled printers or engravers at its command. Also, with the war being fought on its territory rather than the North's, there was an ever-present danger of sabotage to plants printing money or engaging in related activities. The Confederacy tried by all available means to satisfy the currency demand and succeeded in distributing quite a large quantity of notes. Its shortage was taken up by notes issued by private banks, individual states, counties, railroads, and private merchants. Merchant tokens, to take the place of rapidly disappearing small change, poured forth in abundance during this period. All told, the Confederate Congress authorized the printing of about one and a half billion dollars' worth of paper currency. It is impossible to determine the total actually produced, but it would appear that this figure was far surpassed. At the war's conclusion, these notes were worthless, as the C.S.A. no longer existed and the federal government refused to redeem them. Many were discarded as scrap, but a surprising number were held faithfully by their owners who believed "the South will rise again." The South did indeed rise, industrially and economically, and those old C.S.A. Notes rose, too. They still aren't spendable, but many are worth sums in excess of face value as collectors' pieces. Until about 1900, however, practically no value was placed on Confederate currency—even by collectors.

Designs. Some surprising designs will be observed, including mythological gods and goddesses that seem to relate very little to the Southern artistic or cultural climate of the 1860s. Many scholarly efforts have been made to explain away the use of such motifs, but the simple fact is that they appeared not so much by choice as by necessity. Southern printers, not having the facilities of their Northern counterparts, were compelled to make do with whatever engravings or "stock cuts" were already on hand, as inappropriate as they might have proved. However, a number of original designs were created reflecting unmistakably regional themes and at times picturing heroes or leaders of the Confederacy. Slaves at labor, used as a symbol of the South's economic strength and its supposed advantage over the North, where labor was hired, was a frequent motif. Sailors were also depicted, as well as railroad trains and anything else that appeared symbolic of Southern industry. Probably the most notable single design, not intended to carry the satirical overtones it now possesses, is "General Francis Marion's Sweet Potato Breakfast" on the $10 1861 issue note.

In general, the C.S.A. Notes are not so badly designed a group as might be anticipated in light of conditions. The designing was, in fact, several leagues improved over the printing, which often left much to be desired. George Washington is depicted—not for being the first U.S. President but as a native son of Virginia. Jefferson Davis, President of the C.S.A., is among the more common portraits. He became even more disliked in the North than he otherwise might have been because of his picture turning up on currency. But after the war he took a moderate stand

and erased the old ill feelings; he even had words of praise for Lincoln. Other individuals whose portraits (not necessarily very faithful) will be encountered are:

- John C. Calhoun, U.S. Senator who led the battle for slavery and Southern Rights (later called "states rights")
- Alexander H. Stephen, Davis' Vice-President of the C.S.A.
- Judah P. Benjamin, holder of various official titles in the Southern government
- C.G. Memminger, Secretary of the Treasury and Secretary of War
- Lucy Pickens, wife of South Carolina's governor and the only woman (aside from mythological types) shown on C.S.A. currency
- John E. Ward
- R.M.T. Hunter

Printers. The study of printers of C.S.A. Notes is complex, made no less so by the fact that some contractors produced only plates, others did only printing (from plates procured elsewhere), and some did both. The principal Southern printer was the lithography firm of Hoyer & Ludwig of Richmond, Virginia. Also located in Richmond were Keatinge & Ball, which did commendable, if not exactly inspired, work, and B. Duncan, who also worked in Columbia, South Carolina. Another firm involved in quite a bit of note printing was J.T. Paterson of Columbia. The so-called "Southern Bank Note Company" was a fictitious name used to disguise the origin of notes prepared in the North. Some early notes were marked "National Bank Note Co., New York," but it was subsequently decided to remove correct identification from the notes of this printer, undoubtedly on the latter's request (fearing prosecution for aiding the enemy).

Cancellations. Two varieties of cancels are commonly found on C.S.A. Notes. First is the Cut Cancel (CC), in which a knife or similar instrument has been used to make piercings in a design or pattern. Unless roughly executed, such cuts do not materially reduce a specimen's value. In the case of some notes, examples without cancellation are almost impossible to find. The COC, or Cut-Out Cancel, is more objectionable because, instead of merely leaving slits, a portion of the paper was removed. The reduction of value for a Cut-Out Cancel averages around 25 percent. These are considered "space fillers" if the issue is fairly common, but a rare note with a COC may be very desirable. Pen Cancellations (PC) are far less frequently encountered. These show the word "Canceled" written out by hand across the note's face, in ink. Unless the ink is heavy or blotchy, a Pen Cancel will not have too much bearing on value. As the note is not physically injured, it would seem to be the least offensive of the three varieties. Whenever a note is being sold, presence of a cancel, of whatever type, should be plainly spelled out. Some collectors are not interested in canceled specimens. In time, as the scarce issues become even scarcer, they will probably have to be accepted as a fact of life.

Signatures. The first six notes issued, the four from Montgomery and T5 & 6 from Richmond, were hand-signed by the Register and Treasurer themselves. Thereafter, because the Treasury Secretary felt hand signatures helped prevent counterfeiting, and because of the quantities of notes spewing forth, clerks were hired to sign "for Register" and "for Treasurer." There were about 200 different people who signed for each Treasury official, making for thousands of signature combinations. Mostly the clerks were women, many the wives or daughters of soldiers who had been killed in action. Since the notes were signed in Richmond through April of 1864 (when all operations were removed to Columbia, South Carolina), most of the signers were from there. Some moved to Columbia, and others were hired there.

It is most interesting to many people to find that they had relatives who signed Confederate money, and many people search for such notes. A complete listing of all the names from the Confederate Records appears in Colonel Criswell's extensive book, *Confederate and Southern States Currency*.

Condition Grades. While condition standards are basically the same for Confederate currency as other notes of their age, some allowance must be made for paper quality and deficiencies in printing and cutting. These matters have nothing to do with the preservation or wear and can be observed just as frequently in Uncirculated specimens as in those in average condition. Without a source of good paper, printers were obliged to use whatever was most easily and quickly obtainable. Often the paper was thin, or stiff, or contained networks of minute wrinkles which interfered with printing. Cutting was generally not done by machine, as in the North, but by hand with a pair of scissors—workers actually took the sheets and cut apart notes individually. When paper-cutting devices were employed, they were apparently not of the best quality. In any case, regular edges on C.S.A. Notes are uncommon, and their absence does not constitute grounds for classifying an otherwise perfect specimen in a condition grade below Uncirculated. When the occasional gem is located—a well-printed, well-preserved note on good paper, decently cut—its value is sure to be higher than those listed. The collector is not advised to confine himself to such specimens, as his activities would become seriously limited.

Uncirculated—UNC. An Uncirculated note shows no evidence of handling and is as close to "new condition" as possible. An Uncirculated specimen may, however, have pinholes or a finger smudge, which should be mentioned in a sales offering. If these are readily noticeable, the note deserves to be classified as "Almost Uncirculated." Crispness is hardly a criterion of uncirculation as this quality is expected in notes graded as low as Very Fine.

Almost Uncirculated—A.U. Similar to the above grade, but not quite as good as an Uncirculated specimen. The note bears no indication of having actually circulated but has minor flaws resulting from accident or mishandling, such as individuals' counting crinkles.

Extremely Fine—X.F. An X.F. note is on the borderline between Uncirculated and Circulated. It has not been heavily handled but may reveal several imperfections: a pinhole, finger smudge, counting crinkles, or a light wallet fold. The fold is not so heavy as to be termed a crease.

Very Fine—V.F. Has been in circulation but is not worn or seriously creased. It must still be clean and crisp, without stains or tears. Fine to Very Fine condition is considered the equivalent of "Average Circulated" but not "Average" condition (which is another term for poor).

Fine—F. A note that has been in circulation and shows it, but has no physical injuries or just slight ones.

Very Good—V.G. A well-circulated note bearing evidence of numerous foldings. It may possibly have creased corners and wrinkles as well as light staining, smudging, or pinholes, but major defects (such as a missing corner) would place it into an even lower category.

Good—G. Good notes have been heavily circulated, worn, possibly stained or scribbled on edges, could be frayed or "dog-eared." There may be holes larger than pin punctures, but not on the central portion of design. This is the lowest grade of condition acceptable to a collector, and only when nothing better is available. Unless very rare, such specimens are considered space-fillers only.

Average Buying Prices—A.B.P. The Average Buying Prices given here are the approximate sums paid by retail dealers for specimens in Good condition. As selling prices vary, so do buying prices, and in fact they usually vary more. A dealer who is overstocked on a certain note is sure to offer less than one who has no specimens on hand. The dealer's location, size of operation, and other circumstances will also influence the buying price. We present these figures merely as approximate guides to what sellers should expect.

Type Numbers. Each Confederate Note pictured has a "Type" number as well as a "regular" Criswell catalog number. The Criswell numbers are listed in the beginning of each of the price listings, and the Type numbers appear immediately following in parentheses. These numbers are used for identification and are cross-referenced in Grover Criswell's publications.

FOR MORE INFORMATION

Considered to have been the foremost authority on Confederate currency, the late Col. Grover Criswell has a variety of books available. His last release, *Confederate and Southern States Currency* ($75), covers all the currency issued by the Confederate States Central Government, the Southern States, the Indian Territories, the Florida Republic and Territory, and the Republic and Independent Government of Texas. This edition also gives interesting discovery information that you are sure to enjoy. There are also current market values listed, as well as rarities. This is the best reference available for the serious collector, libraries, and the casual reader.

CONFEDERATE STATES OF AMERICA—
1861 ISSUE, MONTGOMERY, ALABAMA
$1,000,000 authorized by "Act of March 9th."
Written dates "1861."
"NATIONAL BANK NOTE CO., NY"

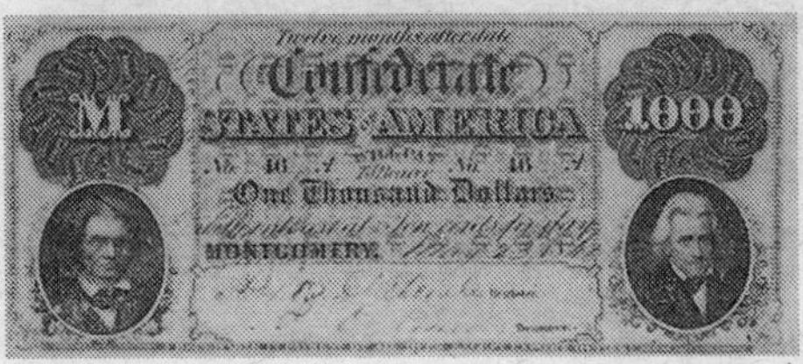

TYPE 1

Face Design: Green and black, bears "Interest Ten Cents Per Day," 607 issued. John C. Calhoun left, Andrew Jackson right.

CRISWELL	NOTE	A.B.P.	GOOD	UNC.
☐1	$1000	—	—	RARE

"NATIONAL BANK NOTE CO., NY"

TYPE 2

Face Design: Green and black, bears "Interest Five Cents Per Day," 607 issued. Cattle crossing a brook.

CRISWELL	NOTE	A.B.P.	GOOD	UNC.
☐2	$500	—	—	RARE

CONFEDERATE STATES OF AMERICA—
1861 ISSUE
"NATIONAL BANK NOTE CO., NY"

TYPE 3

Face Design: Green and black, bears "Interest One Cent Per Day." Railway train, Minerva left.

CRISWELL	NOTE	A.B.P.	GOOD	UNC.
□3	$100	4500.00	—	RARE

"NATIONAL BANK NOTE CO., NY"

TYPE 4

Face Design: Green and black, bears "Interest Half A Cent Per Day." Negroes hoeing cotton.

CRISWELL	NOTE	A.B.P.	GOOD	UNC.
□4	$50	4000.00	—	RARE

CONFEDERATE STATES OF AMERICA—1861 ISSUE
"AMERICAN BANK NOTE CO., NY"
(Though ostensibly by the "SOUTHERN BANK NOTE CO.")

TYPE 5

Face Design: Green and black, red fibre paper, bears "Interest One Cent Per Day." Railway train, Justice left and Minerva right.

CRISWELL	NOTE	A.B.P.	GOOD	UNC.
□5	$100	550.00	925.00	4125.00

TYPE 6

Face Design: Green and black, red fibre paper, bears "Interest Half A Cent Per Day." Pallas and Ceres seated on bale of cotton, Washington at right.

CRISWELL	NOTE	A.B.P.	GOOD	UNC.
□6	$50	400.00	900.00	4125.00

CONFEDERATE STATES OF AMERICA—1861 ISSUE
$20,000,000 authorized by "Act of May 16th, 1861"
(All lithographic date "July 25th, 1861")
"HOYER & LUDWIG, RICHMOND, VA"

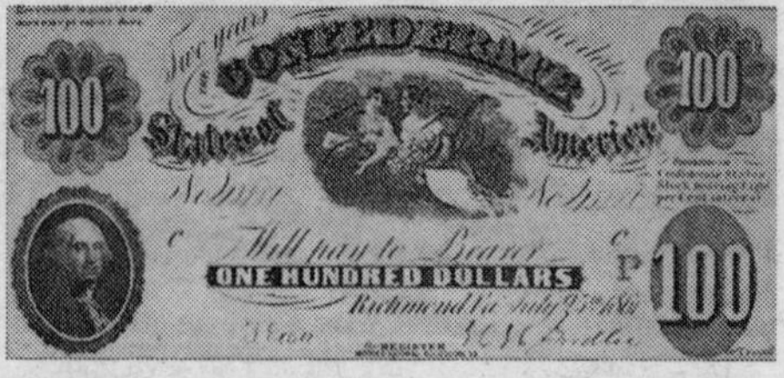

TYPE 7

Face Design: Ceres and Proserpina flying, Washington left.

CRISWELL	NOTE	A.B.P.	GOOD	UNC.
□7-13	$100	500.00	800.00	3800.00

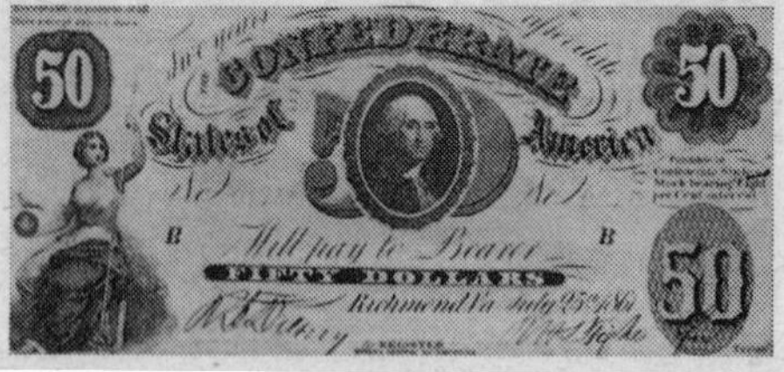

TYPE 8

Face Design: Washington, Tellus left.

CRISWELL	NOTE	A.B.P.	GOOD	UNC.
□14-22	$50	200.00	350.00	4850.00

CONFEDERATE STATES OF AMERICA—1861 ISSUE

TYPE XXI

Face Design: Exists in a variety of colors.

CRISWELL	NOTE	A.B.P.	GOOD	UNC.
☐XXI	$20	200.00	350.00	575.00

The above type notes were bogus. For years it was thought they were a regular Confederate issue, and evidence exists that they were circulated as such. No collection of Confederate Notes is complete without one. There is no evidence as to who the printer was, but the authors have reason to believe he was located somewhere in Ohio. It is not a product of S.C. Upham, of Philadelphia, the well-known counterfeiter of Confederate Notes.

TYPE 9

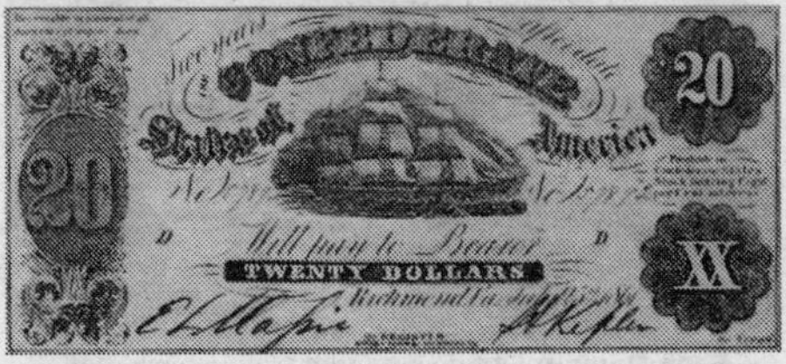

Face Design: Large sailing vessel, "20" at left.

CRISWELL	NOTE	A.B.P.	GOOD	UNC.
☐23-33	$20	250.00	375.00	575.00

CONFEDERATE STATES OF AMERICA—1861 ISSUE

TYPE 10

Face Design: Liberty seated by eagle, with shield and flag.

There are at least forty-two minor varieties of this note, including a supposed ten or eleven stars on shield. Usually the stars are so indistinct that a note may show from six to fifteen stars. The other differences are minute changes in the size of the "10" in the upper corners. We list only the major type.

CRISWELL	NOTE	A.B.P.	GOOD	UNC.
□34-41	$10	100.00	195.00	4450.00

TYPE 11

Face Design: Liberty seated by eagle, sailor left.

CRISWELL	NOTE	A.B.P.	GOOD	UNC.
□42-45	$5	600.00	900.00	RARE

CONFEDERATE STATES OF AMERICA—1861 ISSUE

(Written date "July 25th, 1861")

"J. MANOUVRIER, NEW ORLEANS"

TYPE 12

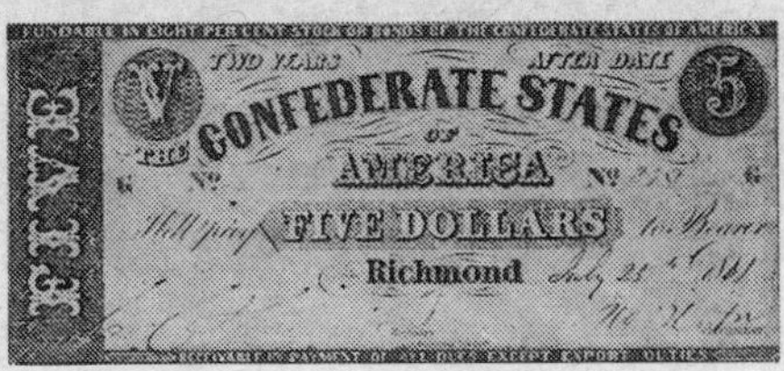

Face Design: CONFEDERATE STATES OF AMERICA in blue on blue reverse.

CRISWELL	NOTE	A.B.P.	GOOD	UNC.
□46-49	$5	1000.00	1630.00	RARE

$100,000,000 authorized by "Act of Aug. 19th, 1861."

$50,000,000 authorized by "Act of Dec. 24th, 1861."

"HOYER & LUDWIG, RICHMOND, VA"

TYPE 13

(Lithographic date "September 2nd, 2d, & s, 1861")

Face Design: Negroes loading cotton, sailor left.

CRISWELL	NOTE	A.B.P.	GOOD	UNC.
□50-58	$100	150.00	210.00	3895.00

CONFEDERATE STATES OF AMERICA—1861 ISSUE

TYPE 14

Face Design: Moneta seated by treasure chests, sailor left.

CRISWELL	NOTE	A.B.P.	GOOD	UNC.
□59-78	$50	80.00	128.00	535.00

"SOUTHERN BANK NOTE CO., NEW ORLEANS"

TYPE 15

Face Design: Black and red on red fibre paper. Railway train, Justice right, Hope with anchor left.

CRISWELL	NOTE	A.B.P.	GOOD	UNC.
□79	$50	1000.00	1620.00	RARE

CONFEDERATE STATES OF AMERICA—1861 ISSUE
"KEATINGE & BALL, RICHMOND, VA"

TYPE 16

Face Design: Black and green, red fibre paper. Portrait of Jefferson Davis.

CRISWELL	NOTE	A.B.P.	GOOD	UNC.
□80-98	$50	175.00	282.00	1985.00

"HOYER & LUDWIG, RICHMOND, VA"

TYPE 17

Face Design: Black with green ornamentation, plain paper. Ceres seated between Commerce and Navigation, Liberty left.

CRISWELL	NOTE	A.B.P.	GOOD	UNC.
□99-100	$20	375.00	525.00	3465.00

CONFEDERATE STATES OF AMERICA—1861 ISSUE
"HOYER & LUDWIG, RICHMOND, VA"

TYPE 18

Face Design: Large sailing vessel, sailor at capstan left.

CRISWELL	NOTE	A.B.P.	GOOD	UNC.
□101-136	$20	60.00	104.00	272.00

"SOUTHERN BANK NOTE CO., NEW ORLEANS"

TYPE 19

Face Design: Black and red on red fibre paper. Navigator seated by charts, Minerva left, blacksmith right.

CRISWELL	NOTE	A.B.P.	GOOD	UNC.
□137	$20	1200.00	1620.00	RARE

CONFEDERATE STATES OF AMERICA—1861 ISSUE

"B. DUNCAN, COLUMBIA, SC"

TYPE 20

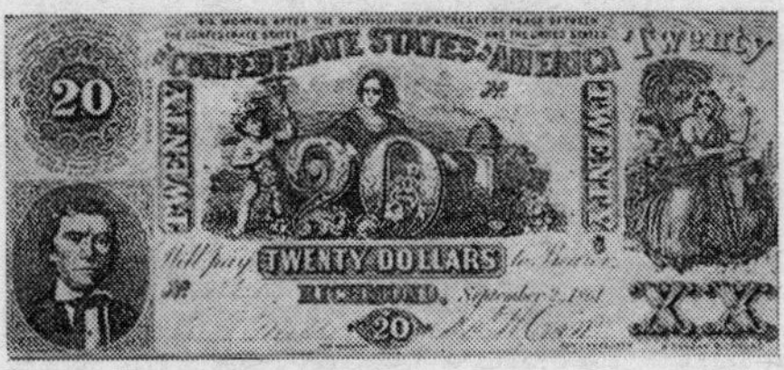

Face Design: Industry seated between cupid and beehive, bust of A. H. Stephens left.

CRISWELL	NOTE	A.B.P.	GOOD	UNC.
□139-140	$20	75.00	128.00	538.00

"B. DUNCAN, RICHMOND, VA"

CRISWELL	NOTE	A.B.P.	GOOD	UNC.
□141-143	$20	50.00	128.00	432.00

"KEATINGE & BALL, COLUMBIA, SC"

TYPE 21

Face Design: Portrait of Alexander H. Stephens.

YELLOW-GREEN ORNAMENTATION

CRISWELL	NOTE	A.B.P.	GOOD	UNC.
□144	$20	175.00	264.00	2320.00

DARK-GREEN ORNAMENTATION

CRISWELL	NOTE	A.B.P.	GOOD	UNC.
□145-149	$20	120.00	346.00	2915.00

CONFEDERATE STATES OF AMERICA—1861 ISSUE
"SOUTHERN BANK NOTE CO., NEW ORLEANS"

TYPE 22

Face Design: Black and red, red fibre paper. Group of Indians, Thetis left, maiden with "X" at right.

CRISWELL	NOTE	A.B.P.	GOOD	UNC.
□150-152	$10	350.00	525.00	2920.00

"LEGGETT, KEATINGE & BALL, RICHMOND, VA"

TYPE 23

Face Design: Black and orange/red. Wagon load of cotton, harvesting sugar cane right. John E. Ward left.

CRISWELL	NOTE	A.B.P.	GOOD	UNC.
□153-155	$10	675.00	890.00	4915.00

CONFEDERATE STATES OF AMERICA—1861 ISSUE
"LEGGETT, KEATINGE & BALL, RICHMOND, VA"

TYPE 24

Face Design: Black and orange/red. R.M.T. Hunter left, vignette of child right.

CRISWELL	NOTE	A.B.P.	GOOD	UNC.
□156-160	$10	175.00	332.00	1625.00

"KEATINGE & BALL, RICHMOND, VA"

CRISWELL	NOTE	A.B.P.	GOOD	UNC.
□161-167	$10	85.00	225.00	1400.00

"KEATINGE & BALL, RICHMOND, VA"

TYPE 25

Face Design: Hope with anchor, R.M.T. Hunter left, C. G. Memminger right.

CRISWELL	NOTE	A.B.P.	GOOD	UNC.
□168-171	$10	75.00	178.00	957.00

CONFEDERATE STATES OF AMERICA—1861 ISSUE
"KEATINGE & BALL, RICHMOND, VA"

TYPE 26

Face Design: Hope with anchor, R.M.T. Hunter left, C.G. Memminger right.

Face Design: *Solid red "X" and "X" overprint.

CRISWELL	NOTE	A.B.P.	GOOD	UNC.
□173-184	$10	100.00	169.00	1242.00

*There are three types of red "X" and "X" overprints. That section of the note on which the overprints appear is illustrated in double size.

Face Design: *Coarse lace "X" and "X" red overprint.

CRISWELL	NOTE	A.B.P.	GOOD	UNC.
□189-210	$10	100.00	172.00	910.00

CONFEDERATE STATES OF AMERICA—1861 ISSUE

Face Design: Fine lace "X" and "X" red overprint.*

CRISWELL	NOTE	A.B.P.	GOOD	UNC.
□211–214	$10	100.00	171.00	910.00

TYPE 27

Face Design: Liberty seated by shield and eagle.

CRISWELL	NOTE	A.B.P.	GOOD	UNC.
□221-229	$10	6000.00	8150.00	

CONFEDERATE STATES OF AMERICA—1861 ISSUE
"HOYER & LUDWIG, RICHMOND, VA"

TYPE 28

Face Design: Ceres and Commerce with an urn.

CRISWELL	NOTE	A.B.P.	GOOD	UNC.
□230-234	$10	275.00	510.00	1097.00

"J. T. PATERSON, COLUMBIA, SC"

CRISWELL	NOTE	A.B.P.	GOOD	UNC.
□235-236	$10	165.00	236.00	1097.00

"B. DUNCAN, RICHMOND, VA"

TYPE 29

Face Design: Negro picking cotton.

CRISWELL	NOTE	A.B.P.	GOOD	UNC.
□237	$10	300.00	538.00	2325.00

CONFEDERATE STATES OF AMERICA—1861 ISSUE

"B. DUNCAN, COLUMBIA, SC"

TYPE 30

Face Design: Gen. Francis Marion's "Sweet Potato Dinner." R. M. T. Hunter left, Minerva right.

CRISWELL	NOTE	A.B.P.	GOOD	UNC.
□238	$10	125.00	218.00	742.00

NO ENGRAVER'S NAME

CRISWELL	NOTE	A.B.P.	GOOD	UNC.
□239-241	$10	75.00	237.00	643.00

"SOUTHERN BANK NOTE CO., NEW ORLEANS"

TYPE 31

Face Design: Black and red on red fibre paper. Minerva left; Agriculture, Commerce, Industry, Justice, and Liberty seated at center; statue of Washington right.

CRISWELL	NOTE	A.B.P.	GOOD	UNC.
□243-245	$5	300.00	535.00	2718.00

CONFEDERATE STATES OF AMERICA—1861 ISSUE
"LEGGETT, KEATINGE & BALL, RICHMOND, VA"

TYPE 32

Face Design: Black and orange/red. Machinist with hammer, boy in oval left.

CRISWELL	NOTE	A.B.P.	GOOD	UNC.
□246-249	$5	600.00	792.00	4275.00

"LEGGETT, KEATINGE & BALL, RICHMOND, VA"

TYPE 33

Face Design: Black and white note with blue-green ornamentation. C.G. Memminger, Minerva right.

CRISWELL	NOTE	A.B.P.	GOOD	UNC.
□250-256	$5	275.00	422.00	1725.00

CONFEDERATE STATES OF AMERICA—1861 ISSUE
"KEATINGE & BALL, RICHMOND, VA"

TYPE 34

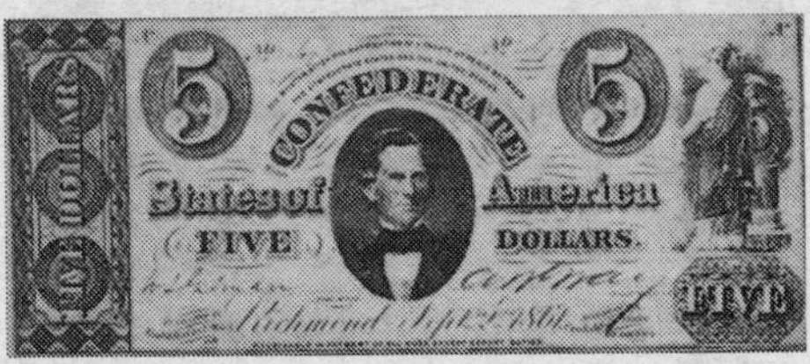

Face Design: C.G. Memminger, Minerva right.

CRISWELL	NOTE	A.B.P.	GOOD	UNC.
□262-270	$5	85.00	212.00	1318.00

"HOYER & LUDWIG, RICHMOND, VA"

TYPE 35

Face Design: Loading cotton left, Indian princess right.

CRISWELL	NOTE	A.B.P.	GOOD	UNC.
□271	$5	4000.00	—	—

CONFEDERATE STATES OF AMERICA—1861 ISSUE
"HOYER & LUDWIG, RICHMOND, VA"

TYPE 36

Face Design: Ceres seated on bale of cotton, sailor left.

CRISWELL	NOTE	A.B.P.	GOOD	UNC.
□272	$5	125.00	238.00	692.00

"J. T. PATERSON & CO., COLUMBIA, SC"

CRISWELL	NOTE	A.B.P.	GOOD	UNC.
□274	$5	120.00	215.00	392.00
□276-282	$5	120.00	215.00	392.00

CONFEDERATE STATES OF AMERICA—1861 ISSUE
"B. DUNCAN, RICHMOND, VA"

TYPE 37

Face Design: Sailor seated beside bales of cotton, C.G. Memminger left, Justice and Ceres right.

CRISWELL	NOTE	A.B.P.	GOOD	UNC.
□284	$5	100.00	186.00	1092.00

"B. DUNCAN, COLUMBIA, SC"

CRISWELL	NOTE	A.B.P.	GOOD	UNC.
□285	$5	70.00	179.00	1092.00

"B. DUNCAN, COLUMBIA, SC"

TYPE 38

Face Design: Personification of South striking down Union, J.P. Benjamin left. Dated "September 2, 1861" through an error. No Confederate Note less than $5 was authorized in 1861.

CRISWELL	NOTE	A.B.P.	GOOD	UNC.
□286	$2	425.00	756.00	1092.00

CONFEDERATE STATES OF AMERICA—1862 ISSUE
$165,000,000 Authorized by "Act of April 17th."
"HOYER & LUDWIG, RICHMOND, VA."

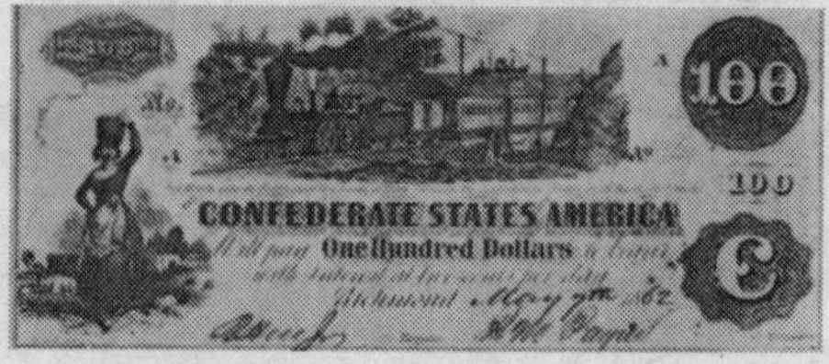

TYPE 39

Face Design: Railway train, straight steam from locomotive, milkmaid left. Bears "Interest at Two Cents Per Day."

CRISWELL	NOTE	A.B.P.	GOOD	UNC.
□287-289	$100	80.00	164.00	372.00
Dated May 5 to May 9, 1862				
J.T. PATERSON, COLUMBIA, S.C. (At Lower Left)				
□290-293	$100	80.00	132.00	238.00
VARIOUS WRITTEN DATES, MAY THROUGH OCTOBER, 1862				
J.T. PATERSON, COLUMBIA, S.C. (At Lower Right)				
□294-296	$100	70.00	105.00	268.00
VARIOUS WRITTEN DATES, MAY THROUGH OCTOBER, 1862				

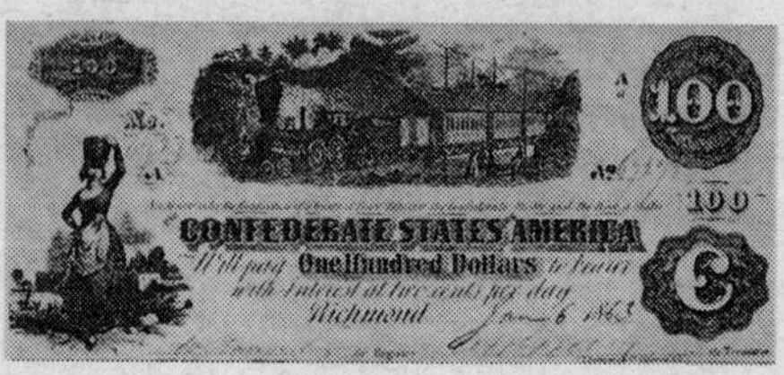

TYPE 40

"J.T. PATERSON, COLUMBIA, S.C."

Face Design: Railway train, diffused steam from locomotive, milkmaid left. Bears "Interest at Two Cents Per Day."

CRISWELL	NOTE	A.B.P.	GOOD	UNC.
□298-309	$100	100.00	164.00	372.00
VARIOUS WRITTEN DATES, MAY THROUGH OCTOBER, 1862				

CONFEDERATE STATES OF AMERICA—1862 ISSUE
"KEATINGE & BALL, COLUMBIA, S.C."

On the following notes there are two types of ornamental scrolls in the upper right corners.

TYPE 41

Face Design: "Hundred" overprint in orange/red. Bears "Interest at Two Cents Per Day." Negroes hoeing cotton, J.C. Calhoun left, Columbia right.

CRISWELL	NOTE	A.B.P.	GOOD	UNC.
□310-314	$100	120.00	266.00	485.00
Dated "August 26th, 1862" (Date all written, scroll No. 1.)				
□315-324	$100	80.00	158.00	390.00
Written dates, AUG. to DEC. "1862." ("186" of date is engraved.)				
□325-331	$100	80.00	158.00	390.00
Dated January 1 to January 8, 1863.				

CONFEDERATE STATES OF AMERICA—1862 ISSUE
$5,000,000 authorized by "Act of April 18th, 1862"
$5,000,000 authorized by "Act of September 23rd, 1862"
"B. DUNCAN, COLUMBIA, S.C."

TYPE 42

Face Design: Personification of South striking down Union, J.P. Benjamin left.

CRISWELL	NOTE	A.B.P.	GOOD	UNC.
□334-337	$2	80.00	128.00	568.00

TYPE 43

Face Design: "2" and "Two" in green overprint. Personification of South striking down Union, J.P. Benjamin left.

CRISWELL	NOTE	A.B.P.	GOOD	UNC.
□338	$2	75.00	158.00	1890.00

CONFEDERATE STATES OF AMERICA—1862 ISSUE

TYPE 44

Face Design: Steamship at sea. Lucy Holcombe Pickens right. Liberty left.

CRISWELL	NOTE	A.B.P.	GOOD	UNC.
□339-341	$1	65.00	129.00	415.00

TYPE 45

Face Design: "1" and "One" green overprint. Steamship at sea. Lucy Holcombe Pickens right. Liberty left.

CRISWELL	NOTE	A.B.P.	GOOD	UNC.
□342-342A	$1	150.00	266.00	2600.00

CONFEDERATE STATES OF AMERICA—1862 ISSUE

"HOYER & LUDWIG, RICHMOND, VA."

This is a Sept. 2, 1861 note, dated through error "September 2, 1862." No engraver's name appears, but it is a product of Hoyer & Ludwig, Richmond, VA.

TYPE 46

Face Design: Ceres reclining on cotton bales. R.M.T. Hunter at right.

CRISWELL	**NOTE**	**A.B.P.**	**GOOD**	**UNC.**
□343-344	$10	125.00	172.00	815.00

(Essay Note, Printed Signatures.)

"KEATINGE & BALL, COLUMBUS, S.C."

TYPE 47

Face Design: Liberty seated on bale of cotton. R.M.T. Hunter right.

CRISWELL	**NOTE**	**A.B.P.**	**GOOD**	**UNC.**
□345	$20		EXTREMELY RARE	

CONFEDERATE STATES OF AMERICA—1862 ISSUE

(Essay Note, Printed Signatures.)

"KEATINGE & BALL, COLUMBUS, S.C."

TYPE
48

Face Design: Ceres holding sheaf of wheat. R.M.T. Hunter right.

CRISWELL	NOTE	A.B.P.	GOOD	UNC.
□346	$10	EXTREMELY RARE		

CONFEDERATE STATES OF AMERICA—1862 ISSUE

$90,000,000 authorized by "Act of Oct. 13th, 1862"

"KEATINGE & BALL, COLUMBIA S.C."

TYPE
49

Face Design: Fancy green reverse. Lucy Holcombe Pickens. George W. Randolph right.

CRISWELL	NOTE	A.B.P.	GOOD	UNC.
□347-349	$100	225.00	478.00	1615.00

CONFEDERATE STATES OF AMERICA—1862 ISSUE
"KEATINGE & BALL, RICHMOND, VA." (THIRD SERIES)

TYPE 50

Face Design: Black and green. Ornate green reverse. Jefferson Davis.

CRISWELL	NOTE	A.B.P.	GOOD	UNC.
□350-356	$50	165.00	268.00	2115.00

"KEATINGE & BALL, COLUMBIA, S.C." (THIRD SERIES)

CRISWELL	NOTE	A.B.P.	GOOD	UNC.
□357-362	$50	200.00	316.00	1115.00

CONFEDERATE STATES OF AMERICA—1862 ISSUE
"KEATINGE & BALL, COLUMBIA, S.C."

TYPE 51

Face Design: Fancy blue reverse. State Capitol at Nashville, Tennessee. A.H. Stephens.

CRISWELL	NOTE	A.B.P.	GOOD	UNC.
□363-368	$20	175.00	282.00	1115.00

CONFEDERATE STATES OF AMERICA—1862 ISSUE

TYPE
52

Face Design: Fancy blue reverse. State Capitol at Columbia S.C., R.M.T. Hunter. Printed on pink paper.

"B. DUNCAN."

CRISWELL	NOTE	A.B.P.	GOOD	UNC.
□369-375IB	$10	60.00	106.00	458.00

"EVANS & COGSWELL"

CRISWELL	NOTE	A.B.P.	GOOD	UNC.
□376-378	$10	60.00	129.00	365.00

TYPE
53

Face Design: Fancy blue reverse. State Capitol at Richmond, VA., C.G. Memminger. Printed on pink paper.

There are many varieties of printers names on notes of this issue, though all have the same engraver's names. In general, the only valuable ones are those with two "Printers" names.

CRISWELL	NOTE	A.B.P.	GOOD	UNC.
□379-390	$5	80.00	158.00	276.00

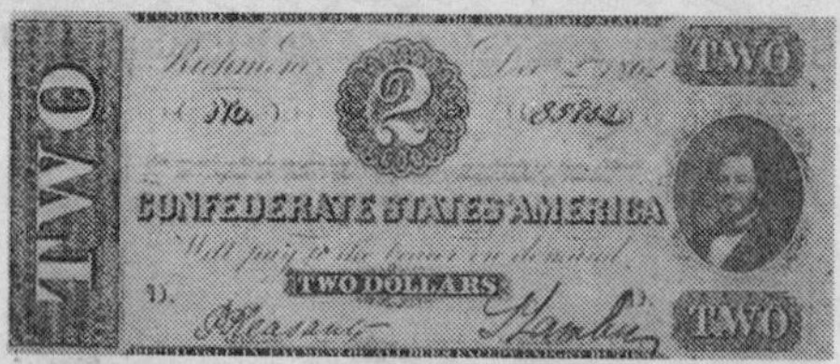

TYPE 54

Face Design: Judah P. Benjamin. Printed on pink paper.

CRISWELL	NOTE	A.B.P.	GOOD	UNC.
□391-396	$2	80.00	168.00	500:00

TYPE 55

Face Design: Clement C. Clay. Printed on pink paper.

CRISWELL	NOTE	A.B.P.	GOOD	UNC.
□397-401	$1	150.00	248.00	615.00

CONFEDERATE STATES OF AMERICA—1863

$50,000,000 authorized monthly, from April 1863 to January 1864, "By Act of March 23rd, 1863."

All notes of this year dated April 6th, 1863, but a red overprinted date appears on all the $5, $10, $20, $50, and $100 denominations showing the year and month of issue.

"KEATINGE & BALL, COLUMBIA, S.C."

TYPE 56

Face Design: Green reverse. Lucy H. Pickens. Two soldiers left. George W. Randolph right.

CRISWELL	NOTE	A.B.P.	GOOD	UNC.
□402-404	$100	200.00	294.00	550.00

"KEATINGE & BALL, RICHMOND, VA."

TYPE 57

Face Design: Green and black, ornate green reverse, Jefferson Davis.

CRISWELL	NOTE	A.B.P.	GOOD	UNC.
☐406-417	$50	185.00	272.00	555.00

CONFEDERATE STATES OF AMERICA—1863

TYPE 58

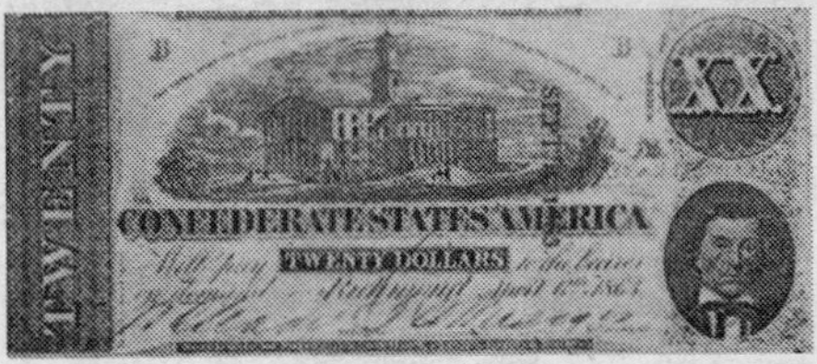

Face Design: Fancy blue reverse. State Capitol at Nashville, TN., A.H. Stephens.

CRISWELL	NOTE	A.B.P.	GOOD	UNC.
☐418-428	$20	100.00	188.00	410.00

TYPE 59

Face Design: Blue back. State Capitol at Columbia, S.C., R.M.T. Hunter.

CRISWELL	NOTE	A.B.P.	GOOD	UNC.
□429-447	$10	80.00	160.00	355.00

Engravers' names on lower margin.

TYPE 60

Face Design: Fancy blue reverse. State Capitol at Richmond, VA. C.G. Memminger.

CRISWELL	NOTE	A.B.P.	GOOD	UNC.
□448-469	$5	60.00	108.00	320.00

Pink Paper.

TYPE 61

Face Design: Judah P. Benjamin.

CRISWELL	NOTE	A.B.P.	GOOD	UNC.
□470-473	$2	70.00	149.00	420.00

TYPE 62

Face Design: Clement C. Clay. Pink Paper.

CRISWELL	NOTE	A.B.P.	GOOD	UNC.
□474-484	$1	75.00	158.00	445.00

"ARCHER & DALY. RICHMOND, VA."

TYPE 63

Face Design: Bust of Jefferson Davis. Pink Paper.

CRISWELL	NOTE	A.B.P.	GOOD	UNC.
□485-488	50 Cents	40.00	82.00	172.00

CONFEDERATE STATES OF AMERICA—1864

$200,000,000 was authorized by "Act of February 17th, 1864." All notes of this year are dated "Feb. 17th, 1864."

The actual amount issued was probably ten times the figure given above and the amount printed even greater. Thus there are many minor varieties of each type including color variations, flourishes, and more signature combinations than any other year. The authors list only the **important** types. The most common Confederate Notes appear in this year.

"KEATINGE & BALL, COLUMBIA, S.C."

TYPE 64

Face Design: Reddish horizontal line background. Equestrian statue of Washington and Confederate flag at left. Gen. T.J. "Stonewall" Jackson right.

CRISWELL	NOTE	A.B.P.	GOOD	UNC.
□489-489A	$500	300.00	525.00	1525.00

"A CONFEDERATE COUNTERFEIT."

Same as $100 Note illustrated on the next page, but 1/4 inch narrower, and 1/4 inch shorter. This note only exists in Serial Letter "D."

CRISWELL	NOTE	A.B.P.	GOOD	UNC.
□ 492	$100	85.00	150.00	375.00

Although a counterfeit, this note was listed in Bradbeer as a genuine, and evidence exists proving that it was accepted as such in the Confederacy. It is an excellent copy, in some ways better engraved than the genuine, but is easily distinguishable by its small size. The authors list it herein with the regular issues because few collectors desire to be without one. It is by far the most popular Confederate counterfeit.

TYPE 65

Face Design: Reddish network background. Intricate blue reverse with "Hundred" in large letters. Lucy Pickens. Two soldiers left. George W. Randolph right.

CRISWELL	NOTE	A.B.P.	GOOD	UNC.
□490-494	$100	120.00	214.00	432.00

TYPE 66

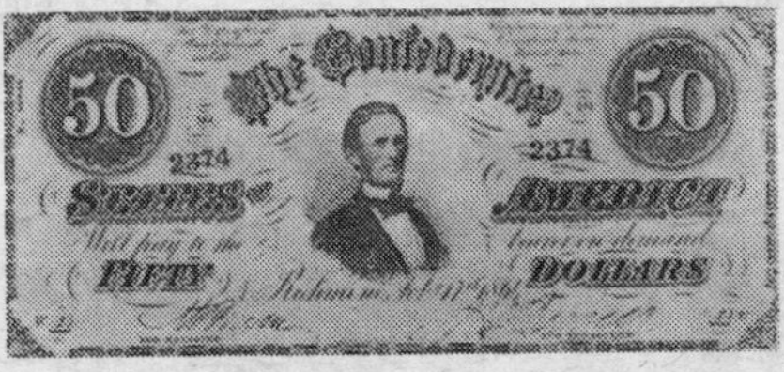

Face Design: Reddish network background. Intricate blue reverse with "Fifty" in large letters. Jefferson Davis.

CRISWELL	NOTE	A.B.P.	GOOD	UNC.
□495-503	$50	75.00	157.00	345.00

TYPE 67

Face Design: Reddish network background. Intricate blue reverse with "Twenty" in large letters. State Capitol at Nashville, TN. A.H. Stephens right.

CRISWELL	NOTE	A.B.P.	GOOD	UNC.
□504-539	$20	75.00	132.00	198.00

"KEATINGE & BALL, COLUMBIA, S.C."
("PTD. BY EVANS & COGSWELL" On left end)

TYPE 68

Face Design: Reddish network background. Intricate blue reverse with "Ten" in large letters. Horses pulling cannon. R.M.T. Hunter at right.

CRISWELL	NOTE	A.B.P.	GOOD	UNC.
□540-553	$10	35.00	62.00	142.00

"KEATINGE & BALL, COLUMBIA, S.C."

TYPE 69

Face Design: Reddish network background. Intricate blue reverse with "Five" in large letters. State Capitol at Richmond, VA. C.G. Memminger at right.

CRISWELL	NOTE	A.B.P.	GOOD	UNC.
□558-565	$5	30.00	68.00	148.00

TYPE
70

Face Design: Reddish network background. Judah P. Benjamin.

CRISWELL	NOTE	A.B.P.	GOOD	UNC.
□566-571	$2	80.00	162.00	365.00

TYPE
71

Face Design: Reddish network background. Clement C. Clay.

CRISWELL	NOTE	A.B.P.	GOOD	UNC.
□572-577	$1	80.00	162.00	365.00

"ENGRAVED BY ARCHER & HALPIN, RICHMOND, VA."

TYPE
72

Face Design: Bust of Jefferson Davis. Pink Paper.

CRISWELL	NOTE	A.B.P.	GOOD	UNC.
□578-579	50 Cents	45.00	85.00	149.00

The Blackbooks!

978-0-375-72320-9
$8.99 (Canada: $9.99)

978-0-375-72323-0
$7.99 (Canada: $8.99)

978-0-375-72317-9
$8.99 (Canada: $9.99)

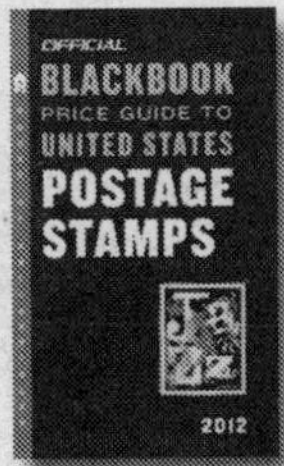

978-0-375-72326-1
$8.99 (Canada: $9.99)

The leading authorities on U.S. coins, U.S. paper money, U.S. postage stamps, and world coins!

All national bestsellers, these dynamic books are the *proven* annual guides for collectors in these fields!

- **Coins**—Every U.S. coin evaluated . . . features the American Numismatic Association Official Grading System
- **Paper Money**—Every government-issued note covered
- **World Coins**—Features the most popular and collectible foreign coins from forty-eight countries around the world
- **Postage Stamps**—Brings the current value of each U.S. postage stamp along with its illustration on every page

BUY IT ● USE IT ● BECOME AN EXPERT™

Available from House of Collectibles in bookstores everywhere!

Turn Your Pennies into Profits!

Discover in **One-Minute Coin Expert** how to find valuable coins in your pocket change. This top-grade book contains invaluable information, including:

- how to handle and store your coins
- the best coins for starting a collection
- buying and selling tips
- how to grade coins
- top-twelve coin picks for future price appreciation

978-0-375-72040-6 / $14.95 (Canada $21.00)

BUY IT ● USE IT ● BECOME AN EXPERT™

Available from House of Collectibles in bookstores everywhere!

HOUSE OF COLLECTIBLES SERIES

Title	ISBN	Price	Author
The Official® Price Guides to			
Antique Jewelry, 7th ed.	9780609809136	$27.95	Kaplan
Collecting Books, 6th ed.	9780375722936	$21.95	Tedford/Goudey
Collector Knives, 15th ed.	9780375722806	$21.95	Price
Disney Collectibles, 2nd ed.	9780375722622	$29.95	Hake
Dolls	9780375720369	$20.00	Van Patten
Glassware, 4th ed.	9780375721823	$24.95	Pickvet
Hislop's International Fine Art, 2nd ed.	9780375722141	$24.95	Hislop
Mickey Mouse Collectibles	9780375723070	$12.95	Hake
Overstreet Comic Book Companion, 11th ed.	9780375723087	$12.99	Overstreet
Overstreet Comic Book Grading Guide, 3rd ed.	9780375721069	$24.95	Overstreet
Overstreet Comic Books, 39th ed.	9780375723117	$29.95	Overstreet
Overstreet Indian Arrowheads, 11th ed.	9780375723124	$31.99	Overstreet
Pop Culture Memorabilia	9780375722820	$34.95	Hake
Star Wars Memorabilia	9780375720758	$17.95	Beckett
The Official® Guides to			
Coin Collector's Survival Manual, 7th ed.	9780375723391	$22.99	Travers
One-Minute Coin Expert, 6th ed.	9780375720406	$14.95	Travers
Scott Travers' Top 88 Coins to Buy and Sell	9780375722219	$13.95	Travers
The Official® Beckett Sports Cards Price Guides			
Baseball Cards 2010, 30th ed.	9780375723360	$8.99	Beckett
Basketball Cards 2011, 20th ed.	9780375723377	$8.99	Beckett
Football Cards 2011, 30th ed.	9780375723384	$8.99	Beckett

AMERICAN
NUMISMATIC
ASSOCIATION

Membership has its perks.

Have **12** issues of *The Numismatist* magazine — packed with feature stories, hobby news, collecting tips and ANA updates — delivered to your doorstep.

Learn from the **experts** and join a 32,000-member community.

Borrow books from the largest numismatic lending library in the world.

Get **consumer awareness** information.

Receive **discounts** on numismatic books and supplies, collection insurance, car rentals and depository services.

Submit your coins directly to ANA-endorsed **grading** and **conservation** services.

JOIN TODAY!

DISCOVER THE WORLD OF MONEY AND HOW MEMBERSHIP WORKS FOR YOU.

800.514.2646
membership@money.org | www.money.org

BBP08